PRAISE FOR BIOINFORMATICS IN THE POST-GENOMIC ERA

"Augen is to be congratulated on producing an indispensable book. He not only lays out and explains the essential tools in bioinformatics, but also validates the critical role that computational biology will play in the future of medical research. This is a fabulous achievement—there is something here for novice and expert alike."

—*Kevin Davies, Editor-in-Chief, Bio IT World*

"This is a monumental effort. Jeff Augen has created an erudite, yet amazingly accessible overview of the intersection between biology, biomedicine, and high-performance computing."

—*Andrea Califano, Director, Genome Center Bioinformatics, Columbia University*

"Augen's book provides a thorough review of bioinformatics that presages the coming era of information-based medicine. Unlike other books that focus only upon the mathematical and algorithms of bioinformatics, Augen's book provides the reader with a broad introduction to the algorithmic, application, and database fundamentals of bioinformatics in the context of their genomic, proteomic, and biochemical heritage—better enabling the practicing bioinformaticians to apply the right tool to the right problem."

—*John Reynders, VP of Informatics, Celera Genomics*

"Jeff Augen has a unique perspective on the fusion of biology and information sciences that will revolutionalize medicine over the next decade. In this book, he has provided an accessible and comprehensive description of the current state of knowledge in genomics and proteomics that is essential for anyone wishing to understand this information technology transformation of the life sciences. He deals carefully with many of the subtle but critical issues that are often ignored or overlooked."

—*W.R. Pulleyblank, Director, Deep Computing Institute, IBM Research*

"Because of its unusually broad scope, Jeff Augen's new book has the capacity to deliver value to a wide variety of audiences. As a longtime investor in biotechnology and healthcare, I find the discussions surrounding the future of medicine and information technology particularly interesting and useful."

—*G. Steven Burrill, Chief Executive Officer, Burrill and Company*

"Augen takes you on a complete guided tour of computational biology, combining historical perspectives with discussions of the leading-edge technologies being employed today. This book would be useful for anyone in the field. It provides an entire overview to scientists new to computational biology, while giving experts detailed information about new developments in the field."

—*Salvatore Salamone, Senior IT Editor, Bio-IT World and Health-IT World*

"There are books about bioinformatics with a focus on information technology and books on molecular biology with a focus on bioscience, but I am not aware of any book that provides a summary of fundamentals of both bioscience and information science with a technical bridge between the two disciplines. This book is unique in covering theoretical and practical aspects of bioinformatics. Everyone from biologists and geneticists to computer scientists and engineers will benefit from Augen's book."

—*O.K. Baek, Chief Architect, Biomedical Informatics and Information-based Medicine, IBM*

Bioinformatics in the Post-Genomic Era

Genome, Transcriptome, Proteome, and Information-Based Medicine

Jeff Augen

♦♦ Addison-Wesley

Boston · San Francisco · New York · Toronto · Montreal

London · Munich · Paris · Madrid

Capetown · Sydney · Tokyo · Singapore · Mexico City

The publisher offers discounts on this book when ordered in quantity for bulk purchases and special sales. For more information, please contact:

U.S. Corporate and Government Sales
(800) 382-3419
corpsales@pearsontechgroup.com

For sales outside of the U.S., please contact:

International Sales
(317) 581-3793
international@pearsontechgroup.com

Visit Addison-Wesley on the Web: www.awprofessional.com

Library of Congress Cataloging-in-Publication Data
A CIP catalog record for this book can be obtained from the Library of Congress

ISBN 0-321-17386-4
LOC 2004106573
This product is printed digitally on demand.

To Lisa, whose soft voice in the back of my mind has kept me going for longer than I can remember

Acknowledgments

I would like to thank the team that helped pull the book together. First and foremost must be Jessica Goldstein, whose sound advice has dramatically improved the flow and readability of the text. That said, Audrey Doyle, who carefully read each and every word, provided a critical eye that an author can never have for his own work. Likewise, the technical team—O. K. Baek, Chris Dwan, and Aaron Mackey—were instrumental in expanding various sections and making them more accessible to various audiences. The field of computational biology is certainly a moving target, and our goal has been to produce the best work possible at the time of this writing. I hope that we have accomplished that goal to the satisfaction of our readers.

Contents

3 GENE STRUCTURE

4 COMPUTATIONAL TECHNIQUES FOR SEQUENCE ANALYSIS

5 TRANSCRIPTION

6 OVERVIEW OF THE PROTEOME AND THE PROTEIN TRANSLATION PROCESS

About the Author

Jeff Augen has a 20-year history in information technology and computational biology. Most recently, as President and CEO of TurboWorx Inc., a technical computing software company, Jeff has been focused on the design of parallel computing solutions for the biotech industry. Formerly, as one of the founding executives of IBM's Life Sciences business, Jeff was responsible for the company's entry into several new areas of the life sciences computing market including, most notably, information-based medicine. He is a frequent speaker at industry events, a member of several editorial boards, and an author of many recent review articles and editorials, in addition to a chapter on computational biology for *Anti-Cancer Drug Development*, Lippincott 2003.

Augen's academic background includes graduate and undergraduate degrees in Biochemistry and Molecular Biology from the University of Texas and Rice University, respectively. His thesis research involved the development of algorithms for predicting protein tertiary structure.

Preface

Computational biology is an unusual science, not because it lies at the intersection of two distinctly different disciplines, but because its development is strongly dependent on simultaneous technical advances in both areas—information technology and molecular biology. Moreover, molecular biology at its core has always been an information science built on an ever-growing list of code words, sequences, patterns, three-dimensional structures, and the general flow of information from gene to protein to complete organism.

Today we take it for granted that biological information is carried in gene sequences, which are ultimately transcribed into messages that form the template for protein synthesis. However, 50 years ago, when James Watson and Francis Crick published their landmark paper describing the three-dimensional structure of DNA, none of these concepts were obvious. The DNA code words had yet to be deciphered, there was no hint of a messenger molecule, and the mechanisms that underlie protein synthesis were still a mystery. During the ensuing years, some of the most ingenious scientific experiments of our time were used to solve these problems. The system that emerged is remarkably straightforward at the level of an overview, yet enormously complex and flexible. One might expect such a system to embody many levels of subtlety because it must be capable of storing enough information, in a very small space, to code for a living creature.

Recent advances in information technology coupled with new chemical and physical techniques have allowed researchers to capitalize on this understanding of molecular biology. The result has been a new generation of tools for studying gene and protein sequences, macromolecular structures, and the interactions that comprise metabolic systems. These tools, both computational and physical, are the subject of this book.

APPROACH AND ORGANIZATION

Throughout the book I attempt to present an equal mix of biology and computer science. The goal has been to create a framework for thinking about molecular biology as an information science. In this sense the current work is unique. Its design parallels the flow of biological information from gene to message to protein and finally to metabolic system. I've also chosen to extend this theme by including a section on the emerging field of information-based medicine. Because it builds on topics presented throughout the book, such as database infrastructure design and transcriptional profiling, this chapter is presented near the end. However, some have commented that they skipped to this section first, and I have tried to make the information as accessible as possible to the first-time reader. Moreover, the book is intended as an in-depth introduction to many areas of computational biology, and you are encouraged to pursue specific subject areas in greater depth through the scientific literature.

I tried to focus on a number of topics that have enormous biological impact but have been almost universally overlooked elsewhere. Most significant among these is the discussion about minor messages—those expressed in vanishingly small quantities within a cell. It has recently come to light that the majority of intracellular mRNA species are present in very small copy counts and that, despite their scarcity, these messages can have important implications for health and disease. That said, the strengths and weaknesses of various transcriptional profiling techniques emerges as an important topic because some are specifically designed to provide accurate copy counts at very low levels. As a result, I have included a lengthy section on technologies for transcriptional profiling with the goal of presenting a balanced view of the strengths and weaknesses of each. I have also included a section on neural networks and pattern-discovery algorithms as an adjunct to the more common statistical techniques used to analyze such data.

AUDIENCE

When developing the content, I attempted to create a reference with broad appeal. In that regard, the discussions of gene and protein structure, transcription, and translation are perfectly reasonable standalone tutorials on those topics. The introductory sections on gene and protein sequence databases, basic bioinformatic tools, and transcription profiling share the same design characteristic; they should be accessible to anyone with a basic knowledge of biological processes. Generally speaking, the book was designed for undergraduate and graduate students entering the field of bioinformatics or professionals with a need to understand bioinformatics and a desire to frame that understanding in a biological context. Conversely, the chapter on information-based medicine is designed to be helpful to doctors and other clinical professionals who are in the process of developing next-generation computer infrastructure for delivering medical care. This portion of the book is also likely to appeal to pharmaceutical and insurance company executives whose organizations are core components of the healthcare delivery system. I hope that the content will prove helpful to those who already have strong backgrounds in biology and computation and are seeking a reference with a broad base of coverage across the field. For those readers, I have included information about many new developments, such as high-throughput whole genome sequencing, systems biology, and presymptomatic disease prediction. These topics are relatively new and usually covered only in the scientific literature.

1

Introduction

OVERVIEW

Today, 50 years after the elucidation of the structure of DNA, high-performance computing, data management, and the Internet are making possible the large-scale industrialization of many aspects of biomedical research. The basic steps of identifying, purifying, and cloning a gene, followed by purification and characterization of the proteins coded for by that gene, have been automated and streamlined to a degree that no one could have predicted just ten years ago. Superimposed on this trend has been a rapid evolution in the design of large-scale computing infrastructure for bioinformatics. Coupled with explosive growth in the quantity of available bioinformatic data, these improvements are driving a migration from *in vivo* (observations of real life) to *in vitro* (test tube experimentation) to *in silico* (experimentation by computer simulation).

Central to this theme is an emerging understanding of the complex relationship between genotype and phenotype. A genotype is inherited as a code; a phenotype is the physical manifestation of that code. Between the two lie an enormous number of probabilistic events. In principle, a complete understanding of the code and the rules for its expression, coupled with information about the environment, should be enough to allow the prediction of phenotype. However, the tremendous number of variables involved makes such predictions nearly impossible given today's technology.

This book discusses the relationship between genotype and phenotype with a focused view of the flow and management of biological information. Its organization parallels that flow—gene to transcript to protein to metabolic system. It is the emerging understanding of this information flow and the migration to *in silico* research that promises the greatest advance of our time: the launch of molecular-based medicine and the first true understanding of the molecular basis of health and disease.

The theme of information flow from gene to complete organism rests on a foundation composed of a very small number of key concepts. These concepts are referred to throughout the book and form the core of many important discussions. They are illustrated in the sections that follow.

COMPUTATIONALLY INTENSE PROBLEMS: A CENTRAL THEME IN MODERN BIOLOGY

The ability to solve computationally intense problems has become a core competency and a driver of many industries and academic pursuits. Although the trend is not new, the complexity and size of the information infrastructure required to solve such problems has increased dramatically over the past few years. The result has been a noticeable increase in the rate of development of new algorithms and technologies that address technical computing problems in new and ingenious ways. For instance, today's aerospace industry is built on a computer infrastructure that facilitates the complete *in silico* design of jet aircraft, the automotive industry lives on a diet of algorithms for computational fluid mechanics and thermodynamics, and the petroleum industry relies on computer-assisted geophysical exploration to discover oil.

Each of these industries has evolved to take advantage of the rapid advances in information technology that continue to shift the balance from physical to *in silico* experimentation.

An important computational milestone was reached in 1995, when the new Boeing 777 aircraft was designed entirely *in silico* by 238 cross-functional engineering teams collaborating across 2,200 workstations using the computer-aided three-dimensional interactive application (CATIA) system. The system worked so well that the first assembled flight vehicle was only 0.03mm out of alignment and perfectly safe for carrying passengers [1].

During the past few years, biology and medicine have taken their rightful place on the list of industries that depend on high-performance technical computing. As a result, two new fields have emerged—computational biology and its derivative, information-based medicine. Computational biology is a superset of traditional bioinformatics because it includes new technical initiatives such as *in silico* molecular modeling, protein structure prediction, and biological systems modeling. Information-based medicine is a system of medical care that supplements traditional evidence-based diagnoses with new insights gleaned through computerized data acquisition, management, and analysis. Throughout this book, it will become clear that information-based medicine depends heavily on computational biology. This new and emerging era of medicine depends strongly on a broad array of new technologies such as high-throughput DNA sequencing, gene-expression profiling, detection and quantification of trace amounts of specific proteins, and new algorithms for pattern matching in large heterogeneous datasets. The successful deployment of most of these technologies depends on the availability of very high-performance computing infrastructure. Most recently the focus has been clusters of commodity-priced machines.

Computational biology is built on a new class of technical problem and associated algorithms that are still evolving. Over the past few years, it has become clear that most biological problems that can be described mathematically can also be divided into a large number of small self-contained computations. This characteristic of biological problems makes them amenable to solution in a cluster of computers rather than on a single large machine. The high-performance computing community typically refers to such problems as being "embarrassingly parallel," and designers of bioinformatic algorithms have been quick to take advantage of these attributes by building parallel infrastructure (most often Linux-based clusters composed of large numbers of relatively small machines). Such clusters have now become a dominant force in bioinformatics and, despite its recent emergence, computational biology has become a principal driver of one of the most important trends in information technology: the migration from traditional large multiprocessing servers to clusters of commodity-priced machines.

Bioinformatic problems generally fall into one of two broad technical categories: floating point or integer. Algorithms that ultimately count something (e.g., number of correct alignments in a sequence comparison) are considered to be integer in nature. Conversely, complex calculations that involve statistical analysis or operations of higher mathematics are considered to be floating point in nature. Such problems tend to execute faster on systems with more powerful floating-point processors, whereas their integer-intensive counterparts tend to execute fastest on machines with the highest possible clock speed. Floating-point bioinformatic problems typically involve complex algorithms borrowed from physical chemistry or quantum mechanics. In recent years, molecular modeling and metabolic systems simulation have become central to the drug discovery process. Such applications tend to be floating-point-intensive. Many of the newest applications that form the basis of information-based medicine, such as image processing, visualization of 3D graphics, and natural language processing (NLP), are also floating-point-intensive. Conversely, integer-based bioinformatic problems typically depend on algorithms that compare characters in sequences or search databases for matching phrases and terms. Much of contemporary molecular biology, including genome sequencing, is built on the solutions to such problems. The algorithms used to align gene sequences and search for patterns are important examples of integer-intensive bioinformatic problems. One of the most significant applications in this class is the assembly algorithm that was used to construct the human genome from millions of sequence fragments. The new technique, known as whole genome shotgun sequencing, is enormously compute-intensive. Not surprisingly, the complete assembly of the three-billion-base human genome represents one of the most complex logic problems ever solved.

Bioinformatic problems, both floating point and integer, are often well suited to solution in parallel computing environments because the operations they depend on are atomic in nature. Protein folding is an excellent example; the problem may be broken into thousands of individual calculations, each representing the attractive force between two atoms in the protein. These pairwise force calculations are each assigned to a different node in the cluster. A typical folding calculation consists of an enormous number of time steps—typically on the order of 10^{15}. During each time step, the forces acting between each pair of atoms in the molecule are calculated and a new transitional structure is generated. The process is iteratively repeated on every node for every time step, and the atomic nature of the calculations ensures that the problem will scale linearly as compute nodes are added to the cluster. This property of linear scalability distinguishes clustered computing environments from large symmetrical multiprocessing machines. Unfortunately, even today's largest clusters are too small to solve thousands of pairwise force calculations for thousands of trillions of time steps. Additionally, communication latencies can prevent such problems from scaling linearly across very large numbers of nodes. The solution has been to restrict the problem to only the most relevant portion of the molecule.

Sequence-homology and pattern-discovery problems also lend themselves to solution in clustered computing environments. In many cases, a large number of sequences need to be matched against a single genome or the contents of a sequence database. There are two distinct approaches for dividing the problem among a large number of machines. The first involves using each node to compare a single test sequence against the entire database; the second involves dividing the target sequence (sometimes an entire genome) across the cluster, using each node to compare all test sequences with a small fragment of the sequence, and managing overlap at the boundary of each node. Although fundamentally more complex, the second solution is well suited to situations where a small number of search sequences are compared to a large target.

BUILDING THE PUBLIC INFRASTRUCTURE

This book refers to data gathered during the past 25 years by the collective community of molecular biologists. This information is warehoused in a public infrastructure maintained by the scientific community and available to anyone with an Internet connection. Virtually all work performed in the life sciences community depends in some way on the availability of this ever-growing body of knowledge. Because of its importance, we have chosen to spend some time describing the infrastructure and have included sample records from some of the databases. Not surprisingly, the size of these databases has grown exponentially over the past two decades. The history of its evolution is significant because today's medical community is embarking on a similar program designed to build a public infrastructure to support medical informatics.

Early bioinformatic efforts, which focused on the construction of databases containing protein and DNA sequences, depended more on advances in the chemistry of protein and nucleotide sequencing than on advances in computer science. Regardless of the focus, biology and information science became entangled in a symbiotic relationship that has provided tremendous benefits to both disciplines. During the early part of the 1980s, while the first protein and nucleotide sequence databases were being built, physical biochemists began writing the first computer programs for Fourier transform analysis of x-ray crystallographic data, enzyme and chemical kinetics, various types of spectroscopy, statistical analysis of protein structure, and ligand binding experiments. Molecular biology, however, was still a new science in the process of maturing from its early focus on bacterial genetics into a mainstream medical discipline based on a broad understanding of eukaryotic chromosomes—most notably those of the human genome. In the mid-1980s, it would have been impossible to predict that the one-gene-one-protein model would collapse during the human genome sequencing project and that the level of complexity would skyrocket as researchers unraveled the complex control mechanisms that form the foundations of gene expression. In those days, genes and proteins were sequenced one at a time using tedious processes that limited the amount of data generated and microarrays capable of simultaneously measuring expression levels for hundreds of thousands of genes were 15 years in the future. A small group of scientists began to envision the industrialization of molecular biology and, as DNA sequencing techniques improved, leaders in the field began to articulate a plan for sequencing the entire human genome. These thoughts spawned the public infrastructure that now contains dozens of protein and DNA sequence and structure databases. The wide availability of computer horsepower also spawned the development of algorithms for pattern discovery and sequence-homology testing. These algorithms became the foundation for today's science of bioinformatics—computational biology was becoming a recognized discipline that would soon be worthy of its own advanced degree programs.

These trends continued through the late 1980s with the emergence of the National Center for Biotechnology Information (NCBI), a division of the National Library of Medicine (NLM) at the National Institutes of Health (NIH), and other international centers for the management of biological data, such as the European Bioinformatics Institute (EBI). Then, in October 1992, NCBI assumed responsibility for the GenBank DNA sequence database. GenBank, the first publicly available nucleotide sequence database, remains the most comprehensive source of gene sequence information to this day. During its first year in operation, the database grew by approximately 1.7 bases per hour. Rapid advances in nucleotide sequencing technology coupled with improvements in the algorithms used to analyze alignments drove this number to more than 850,000 bases per hour by the end of the decade. During the same timeframe, similar advances in protein sequencing technology enabled the development and rapid expansion of a number of protein sequence and structure resources, including the Protein Information Resource (PIR), Swiss-PROT, Protein Research Foundation (PRF), and Protein Data Bank (PDB). Since then, the public infrastructure for aggregating, managing, and disseminating biological data has grown to include hundreds of such databases which, coupled with proprietary sources, has become the foundation for modern-day, computer-driven, rational drug design.

THE HUMAN GENOME'S SEVERAL LAYERS OF COMPLEXITY

A recurring theme visible throughout this book is the incredible density of information contained within the human genome. We have come to take for granted the shocking fact that all the information needed to code for an entire person can easily fit within the nucleus of a single cell. That thought is not lost within the pages of this book, and we will spend a considerable amount of time discussing the information-processing mechanisms that enable such density of information to be achieved.

Over the past several years, our understanding of gene expression has evolved to reveal a multistep process that embodies an order of magnitude increase in complexity at each step, starting with transcription and ending with the metabolic pathways that define a functioning organism. Without this stepwise increase in complexity, it would be impossible for the human genome, which contains approximately 25,000 genes, to code for more than a million proteins. Nature, in an incredible display of efficiency, has created a system that requires only ten times as much information to code for a person as for an *E. coli* bacterium [2].

The following mechanisms achieve tremendous diversity from the relatively small number of coding regions that make up the human genome:

- Each coding region contains six distinct reading frames—three in each direction.
- A single messenger RNA molecule, through alternative splicing, can code for dozens of different messages called splice variants. Each variant codes for a different protein.
- Individual proteins are post-translationally modified. These modifications can include the removal of amino acids as well as the addition of chemical side chains—sugars, acetyl groups, carboxyl groups, methyl groups, and many others. Protein function is highly dependent on these modifications and, in some cases, improperly processed proteins are completely dysfunctional.
- Protein function is context sensitive in the sense that identical proteins can have completely different roles in different parts of an organism.
- Protein-protein interactions are the final determinant of phenotype. Hundreds of millions of such interactions form the metabolic basis of life.

Figure 1-1 contains a diagrammatic representation of this stepwise buildup of complexity.

Without molecular-level mechanisms for adding diversity at each step in the gene-expression process, the human genome would need to be considerably larger and more complex. However, because a genome organized in this fashion would contain separate coding regions for each protein, bioinformatics would become a much less complex science. Protein sequences would be determined directly from the gene sequence; the lack

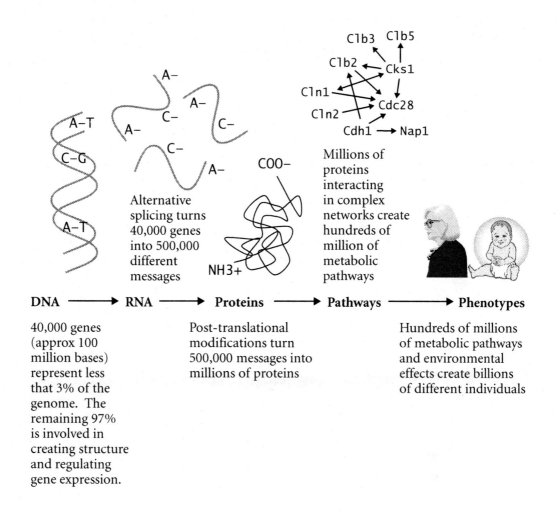

Figure 1-1 Human diversity is achieved through a stepwise progression that adds complexity at each step in the gene-expression process.

of splice sites within coding regions would ensure that start and stop signals for a given protein would always appear in the same reading frame; only one DNA strand would contain code, the complementary strand would again be referred to as the nonsense strand as it was 20 years ago; lack of splicing at the mRNA level would ensure a direct correlation between gene-expression studies and the base genome sequence; and a point mutation in the base DNA sequence could affect only a single protein. Unfortunately, the human genome is not constructed in this way; fortunately, bioinformatics has evolved to include complex statistical analysis techniques and pattern-matching algorithms for solving these problems.

TOWARD PERSONALIZED MEDICINE

Our previous discussions have made many references to the flow of biological information from genome to complete organism. In its complete form, that information and associated computational tools form the basis of a discussion that can be meaningful only at the level of an entire organism. For our purposes, that organism is a human being, and our discussion will be framed in the context of personalized medicine.

We have chosen to place this section near the end of the book because it builds on all the concepts presented in earlier sections; personalized medicine is a sophisticated application of computational biology and basic bioinformatics. The modern drug discovery process is undeniably central to this discussion. The process, often visualized as a discovery "pipeline," begins with basic research and ends with disease-specific pharmaceuticals. Like biology and medicine, drug discovery has also become an information science. The impact of this trend has been tremendous. For example, using traditional drug development techniques it took nearly 40 years to capitalize on a basic understanding of the cholesterol biosynthesis pathway to develop statin drugs—those that inhibit the enzyme HMG-CoA Reductase, the rate-limiting step in cholesterol biosynthesis [3, 4]. Conversely, a molecular-level understanding of the role of the HER-2 receptor in breast cancer led to the development of the chemotherapeutic agent Herceptin within only three years [5]. The developers of Herceptin enjoyed the advantages of *in silico* molecular modeling, high-throughput screening, and access to databases containing genomic and proteomic information. Biochemistry and pharmacology have advanced considerably since the launch of statin drugs, and today's computational biologists enjoy the advantages of a new generation of applications for studying molecular dynamics, predicting protein tertiary structure, and identifying genes that are coregulated in various disease states and individuals. As these tools mature, larger portions of the drug discovery process will make their way from the lab bench to the computer. We are already witnessing the beginning of this trend as evidenced by the emphasis being placed by large pharmaceutical companies on the power of their information technology platforms. These platforms have become key differentiators and true sources of value creation in the drug discovery business.

ILLNESSES ARE POLYGENIC

Systems that are capable of supporting personalized medicine must be built on an infrastructure consisting of many different clinical and research databases. The aggregation of large quantities of such content has fostered a variety of important statistical studies. One important realization that has emerged from these studies is that virtually all diseases are complex in the sense that they are polygenic.

Building on this thought, it is important to note that the past several years have witnessed the collapse of two overly simplistic views of biology: the one-gene-one-protein model of molecular genetics and the one-protein-one-disease model of medicine. For most of the twentieth century, biochemical research was focused on the delineation of complex metabolic pathways. Much of this early work was concerned with identifying individual proteins, their functions, and the roles they play in metabolism. A natural consequence of such work was to uncover the relationships between metabolic defects—missing or aberrant proteins—and disease. These discoveries were the genesis of a monogenic view of many diseases. For example, diabetes was traditionally viewed as an insulin deficiency, and cardiovascular disease was thought of as being caused by improper regulation of cholesterol biosynthesis. Although these assertions are true at a basic level, most diseases are, in reality, complex polygenic disorders that can be fully understood only at a systems level. Diabetes is now thought of as a very complex disorder with a variety of environmental and genetic components. The standard nomenclature that divides the disease into two major classes—type I and type II—is now known to mask a more complex variety of genetically distinct subtypes. Not surprisingly, changes in the expression levels of many of these genes have far reaching impacts that are difficult to predict. For example, a well-documented but subtle relationship exists between type II diabetes and certain mood disorders; depression and many of its associated symptoms constitute a major risk factor for the development of the disease [6].

Likewise, as molecular-level data became available, cardiovascular disease evolved from a simple problem of arterial obstruction to a metabolic disease and finally to part of an inflammatory process.

Variations in base gene sequence represent only a small part of the story. Within the context of molecular medicine, four basic sets of parameters make each of us what we are

- Basic genetic sequence at the DNA level
- Environmental effects (including exposure to radiation and mutagens) on gene expression
- Stochastic and nonstochastic probabilistic functions that affect gene expression
- Viral infections that alter the genomes of individual cells

Each of these parameters plays an important role in gene expression. An individual's genome sequence contains important information about polymorphisms that are the root cause of many diseases as well as basic information that can be used to predict many physical characteristics. Over time, exposure to various elements in the environment has profound effects on gene expression. The expression levels of most genes are controlled by molecular-level feedback mechanisms, and these are often affected by the environment. Stochastic processes are sequences of probabilistic events that cause the expression levels of specific genes to vary between predictable values. Finally, viral infections can alter the genomes of individual cells by inserting new sequences into the chromosomal material. Such changes accumulate throughout an individual's life, and the effects associated with them are only vaguely understood.

In the past, lack of detailed information about each of these parameters has caused the medical community to rely exclusively on phenotypic descriptions of illnesses. The process of defining diseases by their phenotypes is giving way to a more precise set of molecular-level definitions. For example, psychiatric disorders such as schizophrenia and depression are no longer thought of as simple diseases but as broad phenotypes displayed by patients with many different gene-expression profiles, genome sequences, and medical histories. An accurate view requires an understanding of large numbers of proteins, protein interactions, and many metabolic pathways [7]. Responding to this complexity, researchers have turned to mRNA expression profiling, where the goal is to correlate the complex patterns of gene expression and medical history with treatment outcomes. The technique involves profiling the up and down regulation of specific genes using microarray technology and analyzing the resulting data to help identify potential protein targets for drug therapy. Information technology is a crucial component at many stages of the process, beginning with target identification where a single microarray can produce hundreds of thousands of individual spots, each containing information about the expression of a single nucleotide sequence. Software products are often used to reorganize the information according to certain criteria such as cell function—protein synthesis, carbohydrate metabolism, energy production, etc. When clusters of coregulated genes are identified, heterogeneous database access tools are often used to search the public database infrastructure for the most current and accurate relevant information. Automating this process and linking the databases is a daunting challenge. After the data are retrieved, they are often compared with internal proprietary sources inside the corporate firewall. Additionally, large-scale database searches utilizing pattern-matching algorithms are used to find expression profile matches in databases containing millions of such patterns. The task is similar to that of scanning a database containing millions of fingerprint records for patterns similar to a specific reference fingerprint. In the vast majority of situations, where thousands of genes are involved, it is necessary, for a given set of expressed genes, to correlate specific up and down regulation patterns with treatment outcomes and phenotypic changes. Establishing the relevant correlations requires analyzing complex datasets using knowledge-management tools and searching data sources with different schemas and data structures.

The challenge of properly classifying illnesses is further complicated by the fact that virtually all diseases affect only a particular subpopulation of cells. To address this problem, medical research databases must be populated with cell-specific gene-expression data for specific diseases. Additionally, cell specificity is a complex affair because it is not always possible to predict all the different populations of cells that might be affected by a specific illness, and changes in gene-expression patterns across different populations of cells are likely to be relevant in almost any disease state. When this sort of exhaustive data is available for specific diseases across a large population, it will likely be possible to improve patient stratification. One possible result will be the rejuvenation of previously abandoned lead compounds that failed clinical trial or appeared to lack specificity for the target patient population. Large-scale microarray data analysis has also revealed new relationships between disease categories that were previously considered to be unrelated.

Pre-1930: History and physical examination

1930-1950: Simple diagnostic tools

Limited biochemical insight
No bio or medical informatics

1950-2000: Advanced diagnostics including sophisticated chemical tests.

Beginning of medical informatics

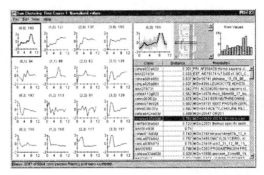

Rapid advances in biochemical technology

Elucidation of basic metabolic pathways

Compute power doubles every 18 months

Launch of bioinformatics

2000-: Era of computational biology and information-based medicine. Molecular-level understanding of disease supported by advanced computing infrastructure and new tools for data analysis.

Figure 1-2 The history of medicine from simple diagnostic tools to advanced computing infrastructure and computational biology.

For example, at the genetic level some types of chronic inflammation share gene-expression profiles with certain malignancies. This discovery has led to the testing of cyclooxygenase (cox-2) inhibitors as possible treatments for lung and colon cancer. (Cox-2 inhibitors can interfere with angiogenesis and, therefore, block the vascularization process for many tumors.) The transformation of medicine from an empirical science, limited by the knowledge and personal experience of individual physicians, to a precise discipline built on databases and algorithms is depicted in Figure 1-2.

Recent gene-expression experiments have revealed that many proteins involved in specific disease states are expressed as "minor messages," mRNA transcripts that appear only in vanishingly small quantities within the cell. This discovery has added an additional level of complexity because such messages exercise their control at the single-copy-count level where accurate measurement is extremely difficult. It is becoming clear that single-digit changes in the number of such molecules can signal the onset of disease. The presence of large numbers of low-copy-count messages dictates that measurement ranges be accurately extended far below traditional levels. Table 1-1 presents a relative count of the number of distinct mRNA species in each copy-count category for a typical human monocyte. The data reveal that the vast majority of transcripts, more than 75%, are present in fewer than 100 copies, and that half are present in fewer than 10 copies. Because a typical human cell contains approximately one million mRNA transcripts at any point in time, these small copy-count species can be thought of as existing in the part-per-million range.

Table 1-1 Total Number of mRNA Species Grouped into Size Classes

Total Number of mRNA Transcripts in Each Class	Number of Different mRNA Species in Each Class
> 10,000	6
1,000–9,999	133
100–999	1,418
10–99	10,642
5–9	24,890

Source: Lynx Therapeutics, Hayward California

NEW SCIENCE, NEW INFRASTRUCTURE

Most of the discussion to this point has been concerned with computationally intense data-analysis techniques and their application to new areas—most notably information-based medicine. These new advances are strongly dependent on the power available in contemporary computing platforms. Fortunately, the platforms are rapidly evolving to meet this challenge. The trend is remarkable because it is unusual for advances in one science to become the engine of growth for another. However, that is exactly what is happening in the worlds of medicine and drug discovery, where improvements in information technology are becoming both a growth engine and a core value.

Several forces and technical trends have become evident: Expression array technology is becoming a commodity; high-throughput gene sequencing technologies are becoming available at reasonable cost; diagnostic imaging (CAT, MRI, PET, x-ray, and various ultrasound techniques) are generating large volumes of digital data; new algorithms for pattern discovery and large-scale data mining are facilitating statistical analysis across large patient populations; clusters of commodity-priced computers are replacing super-computers at a fraction of the cost; and low-latency network connectivity has fostered the launch of a new information architecture known as a "computer grid."

Computer grids allow geographically dispersed systems to be linked into a single entity that appears to users as one system. Grids are often described as falling into one of two different categories: compute grids and data grids. Compute grids allow the parallelization of processor-intensive applications and provide a level of compute performance that cannot be achieved on individual systems. Compute grids are already impacting such diverse fields as protein folding and image processing.

Data grids provide similar functionality by linking geographically dispersed databases into a single view that can be queried from a single system. Among the most complex of these challenges is the linking of geographically dispersed heterogeneous systems with dissimilar datasets. These datasets often have different structures and internal references creating "schema" mismatches, an area of intense research within the IT community.

One of the focus areas for personalized medicine involves the analysis of imaging data from various sources mentioned earlier—CAT, x-ray, PET, MRI, and diagnostic ultrasound. Someday, in the not-too-distant future, doctors will compare medical images of their patients to millions of other images, and fast pattern-matching algorithms capable of spotting similar images will be used in conjunction with other clinical and genomic information to identify close matches. Information contained in the medical records of these matching patients will be used to select the best treatment strategies. The process will also involve comparing base DNA sequence information and ongoing gene-expression profiles for large numbers of patients—both healthy and ill. The collection of gene-expression profiles will occupy an enormous amount of storage space and, because data will be collected across many time points, algorithms for comparing mRNA expression profiles in a time-dependent fashion will form a core component of the clinical tool set. During the next few years, high-throughput sequencing techniques, supported by a new generation of fragment-assembly algorithms, are likely to make the collection of complete genome sequences a standard component of routine medical care. As previously mentioned, the computational challenges associated with sequencing are significant. For instance, fragment assembly for the human genome project required constant operation of two maximally configured supercomputers for more than one year.

The computer infrastructure required to support widely available clinical genome sequencing will be significantly larger than today's hospital information systems, and each will be local to an individual medical institution. Results from sequencing operations are likely to be shared in a data grid along with the images and gene-expression profiles mentioned earlier. After a patient is classified as belonging to a particular group composed of metabolically similar individuals, an ongoing record of the treatment results, expression profiles, and other relevant data will be added to the ever-growing pool of information.

Several technical challenges must be overcome to make this vision a reality. Huge amounts of data must be collected and shared across a large dispersed infrastructure— most likely a computer grid, tools for analyzing and comparing the data must be made available to researchers and clinicians, new database schemas must be designed and deployed, and the medical community must come to agreement on a new set of standards for the representation of clinical medical records. These technical challenges form the core of an infrastructure development effort that is proceeding at major medical centers and government installations all over the world today.

These enhancements to the clinical infrastructure are beginning to drive the development of a new generation of applications that improve the human/computer interface.

Included are systems for natural language processing, automated workflow management, and the generation of ontology-based semantic queries against disparate data sources. The last example is particularly significant for this discussion because biology and medicine are technical disciplines described using a variety of objects and concepts. An ontology is an explicit specification of such a conceptualization. As discussed in Chapter 2, precise ontologies are rapidly becoming the basis for database query systems across all life science disciplines.

Perhaps the most urgent item on this list is the need to generate queries across heterogeneous databases. In response to this need, researchers have begun to create a new generation of tools capable of translating the standard SQL queries generated by most desktop tools into the language of each underlying data source and joining the results into a consolidated response. Various vendors have created tools to facilitate this process—most are based on "wrapping" individual data sources with code that provides a standard interface to a single query tool. Systems that use such virtualizations of data are routinely referred to as being "federated." Alternative approaches involve the construction of large "data warehouses" containing restructured and consolidated information from the various heterogeneous sources. Each approach has strengths and weaknesses, but together they can form the basis of a complete information-management platform for bioinformatics.

THE PROACTIVE FUTURE OF INFORMATION-BASED MEDICINE

Predictive power is the ultimate test of any science. With this view in mind, we have decided to close our discussion of personalized medicine on the subject of predictability. The area is characterized by two major dimensions. The first involves predicting clinical outcomes for illnesses that have already been diagnosed. The second, sometimes referred to as presymptomatic testing, is the focus of the present discussion. As one might expect, presymptomatic testing involves proactively predicting the onset of disease before any physical symptoms become apparent. The databases and computational tools that comprise the infrastructure for information-based medicine coupled with a new generation of ultrasensitive chemical techniques for identifying trace amounts of circulating proteins and minor messages within cells are all part of the arsenal of tools required for this new and emerging discipline. The presymptomatic testing process depends on the development of disease-specific databases populated with cell-specific metabolic and gene-expression data, clinical and demographic information, and extensive statistical information regarding the onset of disease in treated and untreated individuals. Figure 1-3 depicts the logistics of presymptomatic testing.

The logistics of presymptomatic testing for disease include complex queries against disease-specific databases; new algorithms for pattern recognition and data mining; and algorithms for joining clinical, demographic, and gene-expression data in a single query. Solutions will ultimately be deployed at thousands of sites.

Presymptomatic testing for disease is destined to become a core component of the healthcare system because it has the potential to reduce downstream medical costs.

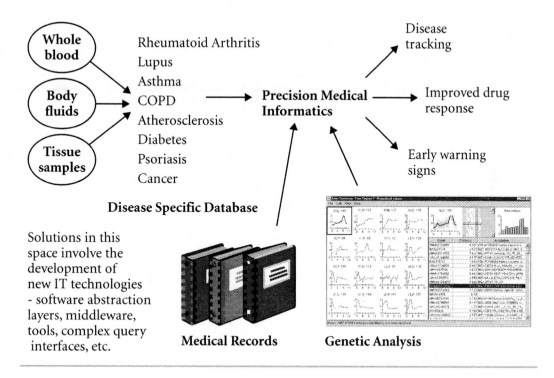

Figure 1-3 The logistics of presymptomatic testing.

However, because the testing occurs at an early stage, before the onset of symptoms, it is necessary to accurately measure very small amounts of biologically active substances— proteins and nucleotides. Such measurements require a more sophisticated set of chemical tools and techniques for mathematical analysis than those commonly used for medical diagnostics or gene-expression profiling. One of the greatest challenges is extending the range of measurement. Gene-expression studies must scale from copy counts in the single-digit range to tens of thousands, and circulating protein levels must be measurable from milligrams to nanograms. These measurement ranges have mathematical implications as well. For example, the statistical analysis that underlies gene-expression profiling depends on a variety of algorithms for clustering together coregulated messages. Most of the current crop of statistical algorithms are designed to function in the high-copy-count range where microarrays are the measurement technology of choice. Counting individual copies of expressed genes requires both new chemistry and new statistical methods. Furthermore, these experiments are time-dependent in a very sensitive way, and new mathematical methods are being developed to analyze the large number of datasets that must be generated to cover a meaningful number of time points. Presymptomatic testing is likely to become one of the most influential forces in modern computational biology. Advanced molecular diagnostics, time-dependent gene-expression studies, and new techniques for detecting trace amounts of metabolites are central to the newest biological science—systems biology. The systems approach is central to information-based medicine. Over the next few years, standardization efforts will allow the technology to become a true source of value creation for the clinical physician.

ENDNOTES

1. Norris, G., and Wagner, M. *Boeing 777: The Technological Marvel (Jetliner History)*. Motorbooks International, 2001.

2. The reference is to the number of coding regions rather than the number of total bases. The human genome contains nearly 1,000 times as many bases (3.2 billion versus 4.6 million) but fewer than 10 times as many coding regions as the *E. coli* genome. The structure of the human genome is covered in detail in a later section.

3. Corsini A., Bellosta S., Baetta R., Fumagalli R., Paoletti R., Bernini F. 1999. New insights into the pharmacodynamic and pharmacokinetic properties of statins. *Pharmacology & Therapeutics* 84: 413–428.

4. Corsini A., Maggi F. M., Catapano A. L. 1995. Pharmacology of competitive inhibitors of HMG-CoA reductase. *Pharmacology Research* 31: 9–27.

5. Slamon D. J., Godolphin W., Jones L. A., et al. 1989. Studies of the HER-2/neuproto-oncogene in human breast and ovarian cancer. *Science.* 244: 707–712.

6. Dominique L. M., Betan E., Larsen H., Phillips L. S. 2003. Relationship of depression to diabetes types 1 and 2: epidemiology, biology, and treatment. *Biological Psychiatry* 54 (3): 317–329.

7. Kitano H. 2002. Systems biology: a brief overview. *Science* 295: 1662–1664.

2

Introduction to Bioinformatics

INTRODUCTION

This chapter introduces the field of bioinformatics and its most basic algorithms. The discussion begins with a review of the structure of the databases that house information about genes and proteins; this discussion is also intended to provide an historical context by reviewing the events that launched today's public database infrastructure. It would be inappropriate to do otherwise because the designs and record structures of those early databases have persisted through the years. These designs, commonly referred to as database schemas, are the forces that shape the algorithms and programs that comprise the science of bioinformatics.

Modern drug discovery and medical informatics depend strongly on the ability to link these databases into a coherent structure and to build query systems that facilitate its navigation. We review several approaches to linking and querying these systems and include detailed examples that illustrate the complexities associated with optimizing and executing a query plan across heterogeneous data sources. Three basic approaches are surveyed: terminology servers containing ontology engines that translate queries; indexed and linked systems; and federated databases that provide a virtual view spanning several data repositories. Each of these approaches has distinct strengths and weaknesses that relate flexibility to ease of use.

Our progression continues with a review of attempts to construct a standard language for communicating biological information. Much of this discussion focuses on the many XML vocabularies emerging in the space. We begin this discussion with a review of the structure and standard features common to all XML variants and continue with a more detailed analysis of features specific to certain vocabularies.

This chapter closes with a review of the basic algorithms for comparing and searching sequences. Because the logic that underlies these techniques tends to be invariant, we have chosen representative examples that convey the concepts rather than focus on the fine differences between the algorithms. Sequence comparison logic lies at the core of this discussion, and we present various scoring methodologies that you can use to optimize sequence alignments. Central to this issue is the concept of local versus global alignment, and our discussion is framed in this context. In addition, this chapter includes an alignment example using the Needleman-Wunsch algorithm with detailed illustrations of each step in the scoring process. We could have replaced Needleman-Wunsch with any of a number of other algorithms; although specific scoring rules and logic would change, the essential concepts we are illustrating would not. You are encouraged to use this information as a springboard to make such comparisons when selecting algorithms for your own research.

THE EMERGENCE OF BIOINFORMATICS

Most of twentieth-century biochemistry involved the development of new physical techniques—protein sequencing, x-ray crystallography, various forms of spectroscopy, DNA/RNA sequencing, and gene cloning, to name just a few. These pioneering efforts, and the discoveries they enabled, became the foundation for the next era of biochemical discovery. This new era began during the early 1980s when several technical achievements came together to enable the launch of modern bioinformatics. Wide availability of the following technologies was critical to the emergence of this new science:

- Large-scale storage systems
- Personal computers
- A new generation of symmetrical multiprocessing (SMP) UNIX-based midrange computers
- Automated nucleotide sequencing

- New sequencing strategies such as "shotgun" sequencing with computerized fragment alignment
- Ultrasensitive protein purification and sequencing techniques
- Telecommunication networks that span, and connect, large organizations

The remainder of this section discusses the role that each technology has played in the emergence of bioinformatics.

IMPROVEMENTS IN IT AND CHEMISTRY

Relational databases became the platform upon which the public infrastructure for storing biological information evolved. Relational databases typically embody complex table structures containing large numbers of intertable links organized around an indexing strategy. (It is important to note that although many large publicly available data sources are built on well-structured relational systems, a huge amount of information continues to reside in more basic systems designed around unlinked "flat files" or two-dimensional tables. Although tremendously useful, such systems are not as extensible because a large effort is required to logically link pieces of information between the tables.)

These data-management technologies would have been useless to the academic community without a powerful but cost-effective hardware platform. Fortunately, this same era saw the launch of a new generation of powerful midrange systems based on the UNIX operating system. These computers had enough capacity to host large multiuser relational databases, but they cost far less than traditional mainframe systems. Development of a public infrastructure for bioinformatics relied heavily on the combined efforts of the academic community. Without high-speed modems (eventually broadband Internet connections) and telecommunications infrastructure, end users at academic institutions would have been unable to download data and submit queries to the small but growing databases of protein and DNA sequences and three-dimensional protein structure.

Whereas information technology improvements provided the computing platform for the early bioinformatics revolution, advances in chemistry and biochemistry provided the data. During this timeframe, rapid advances in the identification and purification of trace amounts (quantities in the nanomolar range) of protein, coupled with new techniques for rapid nucleotide sequencing, laid the groundwork for the human genome project and today's efforts to unravel the entire human "proteome"— the fully enumerated set of all proteins contained in all cells of the organism. Nucleotide sequencing in the early 1980s relied on bench-top electrophoresis of relatively large samples and ingenious chemical-staining techniques. These new sequencing strategies, which were important enough to eventually merit a Nobel Prize for Walter Gilbert and Frederick Sanger, form the basis of today's automated technologies. In 1985, a hard-working graduate student could sequence a couple of hundred nucleotides per day; today's industrialized sequencing platforms can manage approximately one million bases per day per sequencing machine. Today, large "farms" of such machines continually feed data to personal computers housing relational databases. These databases are, in turn, linked to large supercomputers running assembly algorithms that identify and align fragments from the sequencing operations to produce a final complete sequence.

It is no accident that the emergence of bioinformatics occurred at the same time, and at the same pace, as the emergence of the personal computer. Today the desktop is home to machines that can execute more than two billion instructions per second, store hundreds of billions of bytes of information, display structures with more resolution than the human eye can resolve, and communicate across the Internet at speeds that facilitate real-time collaboration among researchers. As a result, the personal computer has become the engine that drives modern biomedical research. By 1985, almost every laboratory instrument shipped with a personal computer, which became the standard data-collection and analysis device for most researchers. Consequently, large numbers of graduate students wrote millions of lines of computer code, and most of these programs became available as part of the public infrastructure for bioinformatics.

A SHIFTING FOCUS

Superimposed on these trends and technical accomplishments was a migration in focus from prokaryotic to eukaryotic genetics. Although it seems logical that the focus should move up the evolutionary chain over time, there was also a practical reason related to the difficulties associated with gene cloning in bacteria. Early gene-cloning experiments involved splicing known DNA sequences into bacterial chromosomes along with antibiotic-resistant genes, selecting for modified organisms using growth media infused with the antibiotic, and ramping up production of the surviving bacteria. (The cells that survived antibiotic treatment necessarily contained the cloned gene.) This process enabled the cloning of very important gene sequences, such as insulin, and even fostered the growth of a gene-cloning industry.

However, most proteins are post-translationally modified and the enzymes responsible for the modifications are not present in prokaryotes. These modifications—glycosylation, acetylation, methylation, carboxylation, etc.—are important to the folding process. Because nonmodified proteins are not normally functional, the only way to produce functional proteins was to use cloning systems based on higher organisms such as yeast [1, 2, 3, 4]. The need to work directly in eukaryotic systems simultaneously accelerated the process and advanced the science, shifting the focus of the medical community toward eukaryotic genetics.

THE PUBLIC DATABASE INFRASTRUCTURE

As eukaryotic genetics became a mainstream science, scientists began storing DNA sequence information (along with protein sequence information) in large, publicly shared databases. As DNA sequencing techniques improved, leaders in the field began to articulate a plan for sequencing the entire human genome. These thoughts spawned the public infrastructure that now contains dozens of protein and DNA sequence and structure databases. The wide availability of computer horsepower also spawned the development of algorithms for pattern discovery and sequence-homology testing. These algorithms became the foundation for today's science of bioinformatics—a critical component of today's drug discovery process. These trends continued through the late 1980s with the emergence of the National Center for Biotechnology Information (NCBI) and other international centers for the management of biological data such as the European Bioinformatics Institute (EBI). Such centers were instrumental in the launch of computational biology and continue to play a key role in the biomedical community.

THE NATIONAL CENTER FOR BIOTECHNOLOGY INFORMATION

The NCBI, established in 1988, is a division of the National Library of Medicine(NLM) at the National Institutes of Health (NIH). NLM was chosen for its experience in creating and maintaining biomedical databases; and because it is part of the NIH, it could establish an intramural research program in computational molecular biology. The collective research components of the NIH currently make up the largest biomedical research facility in the world.

NCBI assumed responsibility for the GenBank DNA sequence database in October 1992. The NCBI staff, trained in molecular biology, builds the database from sequences submitted by individual laboratories and by data exchange with the other two members of the International Nucleotide Sequence Databases Collaboration, the European Molecular Biology Laboratory (EMBL) and the DNA Database of Japan (DDBJ). The three organizations exchange data on a daily basis. Arrangements with the U.S. Patent and Trademark Office enable the incorporation of patent sequence data into these data sources. In addition to GenBank, NCBI supports and distributes a variety of databases for the medical and scientific communities. These include the Online Mendelian Inheritance in Man (OMIM), the Molecular Modeling Database (MMDB) of three-dimensional protein structures, the Unique Human Gene Sequence Collection (UniGene), a Gene Map of the Human Genome, the Taxonomy Browser, and the Cancer Genome Anatomy Project (CGAP), in collaboration with the National Cancer Institute.

THE EUROPEAN BIOINFORMATICS INSTITUTE

Another center for genomic information and biological research, the EMBL was established in 1974. In 1980, the EMBL Data Library was founded—the first central repository of nucleotide sequence data in the world, and the precursor to EMBL's EBI outstation, which officially opened in Hinxton, UK, in 1997. The EBI has been highly successful as a center for research and services in bioinformatics. The institute manages databases of biological information, including nucleic acid and protein sequences as well as molecular structures [5]. One of the most significant data sources maintained by EBI is the Swiss-PROT protein information database. (Swiss-PROT was established in

1986 and is collaboratively maintained by the Swiss Institute of Bioinformatics and the EBI). Despite its origins as a simple sequence database, Swiss-PROT has grown to include a broad spectrum of information about proteins in the form of annotations. This ancillary data includes, but is not limited to, the following:

- Physiological function
- Post-translational modifications (e.g. glycosylation, phosphorylation, acetylation, GPI-anchor, etc)
- Domains and sites (for example, calcium-binding regions, ATP-binding sites, and zinc fingers)
- Three-dimensional structure and similarities to other proteins
- Diseases associated with deficiencies in the protein
- Sequence conflicts, variants, etc.

THE PROTEIN DATA BANK

Likewise, the Protein Data Bank (PDB)—operated by Rutgers University, The State University of New Jersey; the San Diego Supercomputer Center at the University of California, San Diego; and the National Institute of Standards and Technology—provides information about protein three-dimensional structure. The PDB is supported by funds from the National Science Foundation, the Department of Energy, and two units of the National Institutes of Health: the National Institute of General Medical Sciences and the National Library of Medicine. The database has experienced enormous growth paralleling the expansion of new technologies for structure determination. Figure 2-1 depicts this growth.

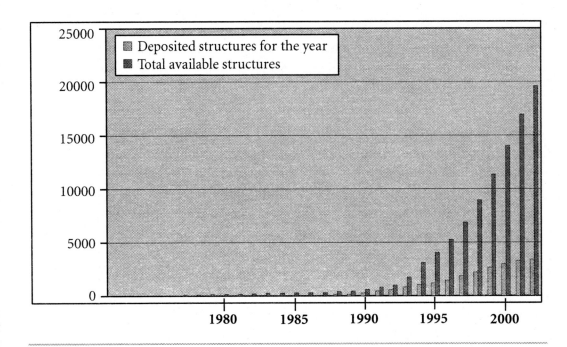

Figure 2-1 Growth in the number of structures contained in the Protein Data Bank.
Source: Protein Data Bank [6]

BUILDING DATABASE INFRASTRUCTURE FOR BIOINFORMATICS

The creation of consistent data formats is one of the most difficult challenges in modern bioinformatics. Because information is contained in many disparate databases, differences in data representation or format make it extremely difficult to use a single query tool to search more than a single data source. Moreover, overlap between various coding systems—those used to represent chemical structures, amino acids, and nucleotide sequences—automatically generates a certain level of ambiguity. For example, protein sequence databases contain much more than simple amino acid sequences, and there are many options for representing such data. At the most basic level, individual residues can be represented using one- or three-letter codes with or without demarcation between the letters. Wildcard characters are often used to represent residues that are variable or unconfirmed. Likewise, additional indicators can be added to represent attachment sites for sugar chains or other post-translational modifications. Finally, other indicators might be used to mark an amino acid that is removed during translation. Even if every protein sequence database in the world were structured under a consistent set of parameters, underlying technical differences in the databases would drive developers to make differing decisions about data types, field lengths, and other underlying data structures. For example, one database might dedicate a record to each amino acid, and individual fields within each record might contain information about that particular part of the sequencing operation as well as other annotations about that portion of the protein. Another approach might involve a single record for each protein with the complete sequence represented in a single "long text" field and other information about the protein in subsequent fields. Databases that don't support long text fields might divide the complete sequence into shorter sections, perhaps one field per 100 residues with additional fields for annotations. In actual practice, most designers of sequence databases have chosen the latter. Sequences are divided into numbered fragments with appropriate annotations and other relevant information. Remote users who want to download the data often develop programs that scan for the numeral 1 to locate the beginning of a sequence. The data is then downloaded as simple text with line feeds separating portions of the sequence. Figure 2-2 illustrates this approach. The upper part of the figure contains a single record composed of annotations and a sequence broken into numbered fragments. The lower part of the figure contains two records linked through an index—the first record contains information about the sequence and the second contains a single long text stream. One advantage of this approach is that it allows researchers to manage sequence information separately without removing annotations and other related information. Statistical analyses that consume large amounts of sequence information but don't require access to annotations can sometimes benefit from such a structure.

When dealing with nucleotide sequence data, it is also possible to reduce the amount of storage space required by using less than a single byte (8 bits) of data to store each piece of information. DNA sequence searches must contain codes for the four bases: adenine, guanine, cytosine, and thymine. (RNA databases substitute uracil for thiamine.) Four letters can be represented by two binary bits. NCBI BLAST (Basic Local Alignment and Search Tool), a commonly used sequence-alignment tool, takes advantage of this fact by representing nucleotides with fewer than one byte. Conversely,

Record ID: 28549248

Organism: Mus musculus Eukaryota; Metazoa; Chordata; Craniata; Vertebrata; Euteleostomi; Mammalia; Eutheria; Rodentia; Sciurognathi; Muridae; Murinae; Mus.

Definition: Regulatory factor X, 4 (influences HLA class II expression)

Protein 1..727 product =regulatory factor X, 4 (influences HLAclass II expression)

Region 37..118 region_name = RFX DNA-binding domain. RFX is a regulatory factor which binds to the X box of MHC class II genes and is essential for their expression. The DNA-binding domain of RFX is the central domain of the protein and binds ssDNA as either a monomer or homodimer"/note= "RFX_DNA_binding

```
  1 mcrkayeswierclnesenkrysshtslgnvsndeneekennraskphstpatlqwleen
 61 yeiaegvciprsalymhyldfcekndtqpvnaasfgkiirqqfpqlttrrlgtrgqskyh
121 yygiavkessqyydvmyskkgaawvsetgkrevtkqtvaysprsklgtllpdfpnvkdln
181 lpaslpeekvstfimmyrthcqrildtviranfdevqsfllhfwqgmpphmlpvlgsstv
241 vnivgvcdsilykaisgvlmptvlqalpdsltqvirkfakqldewlkvalhdlpenlrni
301 kfelsrrfsqilrrqtslnhlcqasrtvihsaditfqmledwrnvdlssitkqtlytmed
361 srdehrrliiqlyqefdhlleeqspiesyiewldtmvdrcvvkvaakrqgslkkvaqqfl
421 lmwscfgtrvirdmtlhsapsfgsfhlihlmfddyvlylleslhcqeranelmramkgeg
481 staeaqeeiilteatpptpspgpsfspaksatsvevpppsspvsnpspeytglstagamq
541 sytwsltytvttaagspaensqqlpcmrsthmpsssvthripvyshreehgytgsynygs
601 ygnqhphplqnqypalphdtaisgplhyspyhrssaqypfnsptsrmepclmsstprlhp
661 tpvtprwpevptanacytspsvhstrygnssdmytplttrrnseyehmqhfpgfayinge
721 astgwak
```

Annotation Table

Record ID: 28549248

Organism: Mus musculus Eukaryota; Metazoa; Chordata; Craniata; Vertebrata; Euteleostomi; Mammalia; Eutheria; Rodentia; Sciurognathi; Muridae; Murinae; Mus.

Definition: Regulatory factor X, 4 (influences HLA class II expression)

Protein 1..727 product =regulatory factor X, 4 (influences HLAclass I expression)

Region 37..118 region_name = RFX DNA-binding domain. RFX is a regulatory factor which binds to the X box of MHC class II genes and is essential for their expression. The DNA-binding domain of RFX is the central domain of the protein and binc ssDNA as either a monomer or homodimer"/note= "RFX_DNA_binding

Relational Link

Sequence Table

Record ID: 28549248

```
mcrkayeswierclnesenkrysshtslgnvsndeneekennraskphstpatlqwleen
yeiaegvciprsalymhyldfcekndtqpvnaasfgkiirqqfpqlttrrlgtrgqskyh
yygiavkessqyydvmyskkgaawvsetgkrevtkqtvaysprsklgtllpdfpnvkdln
lpaslpeekvstfimmyrthcqrildtviranfdevqsfllhfwqgmpphmlpvlgsstv
vnivgvcdsilykaisgvlmptvlqalpdsltqvirkfakqldewlkvalhdlpenlrni
kfelsrrfsqilrrqtslnhlcqasrtvihsaditfqmledwrnvdlssitkqtlytmed
srdehrrliiqlyqefdhlleeqspiesyiewldtmvdrcvvkvaakrqgslkkvaqqfl
lmwscfgtrvirdmtlhsapsfgsfhlihlmfddyvlylleslhcqeranelmramkgeg
staeaqeeiilteatpptpspgpsfspaksatsvevpppsspvsnpspeytglstagamq
sytwsltytvttaagspaensqqlpcmrsthmpsssvthripvyshreehgytgsynygs
ygnqhphplqnqypalphdtaisgplhyspyhrssaqypfnsptsrmepclmsstprlhp
tpvtprwpevptanacytspsvhstrygnssdmytplttrrnseyehmqhfpgfayinge
astgwak
```

Figure 2-2 Two possible record structures for a protein sequence database.

additional symbols used to represent variable or unconfirmed residues number more than four and require additional bits for storage. The NCBI BLAST storage conventions are represented in Tables 2-1 and 2-2.

Although the majority of biological data is stored in traditional relational database format, many of the newer systems expose an XML (eXtensible Markup Language) interface. XML is particularly interesting because a variety of XML vocabularies are available for the life sciences, and many significant data sources are designed to export data in XML format. However, XML databases tend to be very large, so designers typically use a different underlying technology and transform their data into an XML

Table 2-1 Structure Encoding for NCBI BLAST 2.0 Sequence Files

Nucleotide	Encoded As
A	0 (binary 00)
C	1 (binary 01)
G	2 (binary 10)
T / U	3 (binary 11)

Source: National Center for Biotechnology Information

format for export to other systems. Many of today's relational systems are compatible with XML and allow the construction of relational databases with XML-formatted data that can be searched with traditional query tools.

The query interface for a particular database is also an important concern for developers and users. Whereas differences in underlying database structure are not always

Table 2-2 Encoding of Additional Information at the End of Each NCBI BLAST 2.0 Sequence File (4 Bits per Symbol)

Nucleotide	Encoded As	Nucleotide	Encoded As
-	0 (binary 0000)	T	8 (binary 1000)
A	1 (binary 0001)	W (A / T)	9 (binary 1001)
C	2 (binary 0010)	Y (A / G)	10 (binary 1010)
M (A / C)	3 (binary 0011)	H (A / T / C)	11 (binary 1011)
G	4 (binary 0100)	K (G / T)	12 (binary 1100)
R (C / T)	5 (binary 0101)	D (A / T / G)	13 (binary 1101)
S (C / G)	6 (binary 0110)	B (T / G / C)	14 (binary 1110)
V (A / G / C)	7 (binary 0111)	N (A / T / G / C)	15 (binary 1111)

Source: National Center for Biotechnology Information

apparent to a researcher generating a query, different interfaces are. Some data sources can be queried using Structured Query Language (SQL), a standard of the American National Standards Institute (ANSI), whereas others display proprietary interfaces. The Entrez query language used by NCBI is an excellent example of a custom system. Underneath Entrez is a traditional relational database, and many programmers would prefer to access the system using standard SQL. The designers chose to create a simplified query language that serves the needs of the majority of users even though that language has limitations. Such tradeoffs are common in the world of public databases, where simplicity and ease of use is often more desirable than power and flexibility. Query interfaces and alternative database structures such as XML are covered in more detail later in this chapter.

At a deeper level, it is often desirable to construct a single query that spans more than one database using "external joins." Joining fields from different databases that have different data types is particularly difficult and is discussed in more detail in the section "Heterogeneous Database Infrastructure for Bioinformatics" later in this chapter.

UNDERSTANDING THE STRUCTURE OF A TYPICAL NUCLEOTIDE SEQUENCE DATABASE

The ability to build "warehouses" containing biological data from recognized and trusted sources, and to create bioinformatic infrastructure composed of multiple heterogeneous databases, is a key theme in the life sciences domain. We return to the issues surrounding query systems that span heterogeneous databases in a later section. However, before returning to this topic it is important to understand the structure of a typical nucleotide sequence database at the individual record level. Although nucleotide database structures may vary, the concepts are fundamentally the same. For consistency, we use GenBank as our example.

Structure of the GenBank Sequence Database

As mentioned earlier, sequence databases contain a variety of information spanning a much broader scope than sequence data alone. The complete database infrastructure is typically composed of sequence data, annotations, search algorithms, links to other data sources, and a variety of programs for statistical analysis and data submission.

The GenBank sequence database, mentioned earlier, is an excellent example. In 1990, GenBank contained approximately 39,000 sequences composed of 49 million base pairs of DNA. As of the writing of this book, those numbers have grown to over 18 million sequences and 18 billion bases from more than 105,000 different organisms.

Such growth must be comprehended in the original database architecture for the design to be extensible [7]. The fact that GenBank's basic structure has remained constant since 1982 is a reflection of the excellent job done by the original architects. Each entry includes a concise description of the sequence, the scientific name and taxonomy of the source organism, bibliographic references, and a table of features that identifies coding regions and other sites of biological significance (e.g., transcription units, repeat regions, mutation sites). The feature table also includes amino acid translations across coding regions.

In addition to data, the complete GenBank system includes a variety of search algorithms and programs that support the submission of new data to the site. A researcher can log in to the NCBI Web site and search GenBank for specific sequences using several programs available on the site. One of the most popular programs in the public domain is BLAST. Many versions of this useful tool have been created over the years, and NCBI provides some of the most popular on their Web site for use in searching GenBank. These include, but are not limited to, BLASTn (nucleotide sequence searching), BLASTp (protein sequence searching), and BLASTx (translated sequence searching).

The site also provides tools for creating queries against many other NCBI databases. These queries can span more than a single data source. One of the most popular tools, Entrez, is a retrieval system for searching a large number of NCBI-linked databases. It provides access to the following:

- PubMed (biomedical literature)
- GenBank (nucleotide sequence database)
- Protein sequence database
- Structure (three-dimensional macromolecular structures)
- Genome (complete genome assemblies)

- PopSet (population study datasets)
- OMIM (Online Mendelian Inheritance in Man)
- Taxonomy (organisms in GenBank)
- Books (online books)
- ProbeSet (gene-expression and microarray datasets)
- 3D Domains (domains from Entrez structure)
- UniSTS (markers and mapping data)
- SNP (single nucleotide polymorphisms)
- CDD (conserved domains)
- Journals (journals in Entrez)
- UniGene (gene-oriented clusters of transcript sequences)
- PMC (full-text digital archive of life sciences journal literature)

Precomputed similarity searches are also available for most database records, producing a list of related sequences, structure neighbors, and related articles. Finally, the site also includes a separate collection of reference sequences known as RefSeq. Although separate from GenBank, the RefSeq database contains cross-references to corresponding GenBank records. The RefSeq collection aims to provide a comprehensive, integrated, nonredundant set of sequences, including genomic (DNA), transcript (RNA), and protein products, for major research organisms. RefSeq standard sequences often serve as the basis for various medical, functional, and diversity studies by providing a stable reference for gene identification and characterization, mutation analysis, expression studies, polymorphism discovery, and other comparative analyses. As a result, RefSeq data are often used as a "reagent" for the functional annotation of new genome sequencing projects.

Although large, the GenBank database is relatively portable, and many academic and private sites have licensed the data for research purposes. The Pittsburgh Supercomputing Center, for example, hosts GenBank along with a variety of search algorithms that are distinct from those offered on the NCBI Web site. These include FSHIFT, which is used to compare a protein query sequence with a translated DNA library sequence; MAXSEGS, an optimal local-sequence alignment program that will find the n-best alignments between two nucleic acid sequences or two protein sequences; and NWGAP, a global-sequence alignment program. In addition to these search algorithms, the center provides a variety of statistical analysis programs for studying nucleic acid and protein sequences, programs for performing multiple-sequence alignments, RNA-folding algorithms, and a variety of graphical front ends for viewing data.

The GenBank database is composed of 17 major divisions:

- PRI (primate sequences)
- ROD (rodent sequences)
- MAM (other mammalian sequences)
- VRT (other vertebrate sequences)
- INV (invertebrate sequences)
- PLN (plant, fungal, and algal sequences)
- BCT (bacterial sequences)
- VRL (viral sequences)
- PHG (bacteriophage sequences)
- SYN (synthetic sequences)
- UNA (unannotated sequences)
- EST (expressed sequence tags)
- PAT (patent sequences)
- STS (sequence-tagged sites)
- GSS (genome survey sequences)
- HTG (high-throughput genomic sequences)
- HTC (unfinished high-throughput cDNA sequencing)

There is no maximum limit on the size of a sequence that can be submitted to GenBank. In principle, it is possible to submit an entire genome if the sequence represents a contiguous piece of DNA. However, GenBank imposes a limit of 350K for individual records [8]. That limit was agreed upon by the international collaborating sequence databases to facilitate handling of sequence data by various software programs.

The components of a complete GenBank record are displayed in Figure 2-3 along with descriptions of each of the individual fields.

U49845. Saccharomyces cer...[gi:1293613]

```
LOCUS           SCU49845              5028 bp     DNA        linear    PLN 21-JUN-1999
DEFINITION      Saccharomyces cerevisiae TCP1-beta gene, partial cds; and Axl2p
                (AXL2) and Rev7p (REV7) genes, complete cds.
ACCESSION       U49845
VERSION         U49845.1  GI:1293613
KEYWORDS        .
SOURCE          Saccharomyces cerevisiae (baker's yeast)
  ORGANISM      Saccharomyces cerevisiae
                Eukaryota; Fungi; Ascomycota; Saccharomycotina; Saccharomycetes;
                Saccharomycetales; Saccharomycetaceae; Saccharomyces.
REFERENCE       1  (bases 1 to 5028)
  AUTHORS       Torpey,L.E., Gibbs,P.E., Nelson,J. and Lawrence,C.W.
  TITLE         Cloning and sequence of REV7, a gene whose function is required
                for DNA damage-induced mutagenesis in Saccharomyces cerevisiae
  JOURNAL       Yeast 10 (11), 1503-1509 (1994)
  MEDLINE       95176709
  PUBMED        7871890
REFERENCE       2  (bases 1 to 5028)
  AUTHORS       Roemer,T., Madden,K., Chang,J. and Snyder,M.
  TITLE         Selection of axial growth sites in yeast requires Axl2p, a novel
                plasma membrane glycoprotein
  JOURNAL       Genes Dev. 10 (7), 777-793 (1996)
  MEDLINE       96194260
  PUBMED        8846915
REFERENCE       3  (bases 1 to 5028)
  AUTHORS       Roemer,T.
  TITLE         Direct Submission
  JOURNAL       Submitted (22-FEB-1996) Terry Roemer, Biology, Yale University,
                New Haven, CT, USA
```

Figure 2-3 GenBank record for the Saccharomyces cerevisiae TCP1-beta gene. (The sequence has been abbreviated to save space.)
(Source: http://www.ncbi.nim.nih.gov/entrez/viewer.fcgi?cmd=Retrieve&db=nucleotide&list_uids=1293613&dopt=GenBank&term=tcp1-beta&qty=1)

```
FEATURES            Location/Qualifiers
    source          1..5028
                    /organism='Saccharomyces cerevisiae'
                    /mol_type='genomic DNA'
                    /db_xref='taxon:4932'
                    /chromosome='IX'
                    /map='9'
    CDS             <1..206
                    /codon_start=3
                    /product='TCP1-beta'
                    /protein_id='AAA98665.1'
                    /db_xref='GI:1293614'
                    /translation='SSIYNGISTSGLDLNNGTIADMRQLGIVESYKLKRAVVSSASEA
                    AEVLLRVDNIIRARPRTANRQHM'
    gene            687..3158
                    /gene='AXL2'
    CDS             687..3158
                    /gene='AXL2'
                    /note='plasma membrane glycoprotein'
                    /codon_start=1
                    /product='Axl2p'
                    /protein_id='AAA98666.1'
                    /db_xref='GI:1293615'
                    /translation='MTQLQISLLLTATISLLHLVVATPYEAYPIGKQYPPVARVNESF
                    TFQISNDTYKSSVDKTAQITYNCFDLPSWLSFDSSSRTFSGEPSSDLLSDANTTLYFN
                    VILEGTDSADSTSLNNTYQFVVTNRPSISLSSDFNLLALLKNYGYTNGKNALKLDPNE
                    VFNVTFDRSMFTNEESIVSYYGRSQLYNAPLPNWLFFDSGELKFTGTAPVINSAIAPE
                    TSYSFVIIATDIEGFSAVEVEFELVIGAHQLTTSIQNSLIINVTDTGNVSYDLPLNYV
                    YLDDDPISSDKLGSINLLDAPDWVALDNATISGSVPDELLGKNSNPANFSVSIYDTYG
                    DVIYFNFEVVSTTDLFAISSLPNINATRGEWFSYYFLPSQFTDYVNTNVSLEFTNSSQ
                    DHDWVKFQSSNLTLAGEVPKNFDKLSLGLKANQGSQSQELYFNIIGMDSKITHSNHSA
                    NATSTRSSHHSTSTSSYTSSTYTAKISSTSAAATSSAPAALPAANKTSSHNKKAVAIA
                    CGVAIPLGVILVALICFLIFWRRRRENPDDENLPHAISGPDLNNPANKPNQENATPLN
                    NPFDDDASSYDDTSIARRLAALNTLKLDNHSATESDISSVDEKRDSLSGMNTYNDQFQ
                    SQSKEELLAKPPVQPPESPFFDPQNRSSSVYMDSEPAVNKSWRYTGNLSPVSDIVRDS
                    YGSQKTVDTEKLFDLEAPEKEKRTSRDVTMSSLDPWNSNISPSPVRKSVTPSPYNVTK
                    HRNRHLQNIQDSQSGKNGITPTTMSTSSSDDFVPVKDGENFCWVHSMEPDRRPSKKRL
                    VDFSNKSNVNVGQVKDIHGRIPEML'
```

Figure 2-3 (continued)

```
        gene            complement(3300..4037)
                        /gene='REV7'
        CDS             complement(3300..4037)
                        /gene='REV7'
                        /codon_start=1
                        /product='Rev7p'
                        /protein_id='AAA98667.1'
                        /db_xref='GI:1293616'
                        /translation='MNRWVEKWLRVYLKCYINLILFYRNVYPPQSFDYTTYQSFNLPQ
            FVPINRHPALIDYIEELILDVLSKLTHVYRFSICIINKKNDLCIEKYVLDFSELQHVD
            KDDQIITETEVFDEFRSSLNSLIMHLEKLPKVNDDTITFEAVINAIELELGHKLDRNR
            RVDSLEEKAEIERDSNWVKCQEDENLPDNNGFQPPKIKLTSLVGSDVGPLIIHQFSEK
            LISGDDKILNGVYSQYEEGESIFGSLF'
ORIGIN
         1 gatcctccat atacaacggt atctccacct caggtttaga tctcaacaac ggaaccattg
        61 ccgacatgag acagttaggt atcgtcgaga gttacaagct aaaacgagca gtagtcagct
    .
    .
    .

      4981 tgccatgact cagattctaa ttttaagcta ttcaatttct ctttgatc
```

Figure 2-3 (continued)

The Locus Field

| LOCUS | SCU49845 | 5028 bp | DNA | PLN | 21-JUN-1999 |

   The Locus field contains several different data elements, including locus name, sequence length, molecule type, GenBank division, and modification date. The locus name was originally designed to help group entries with similar sequences: The first three characters usually designated the organism; the fourth and fifth characters were used to show other group designations, such as gene product; for segmented entries, the last character was one of a series of sequential integers. However, the ten characters in the locus name are no longer sufficient to represent the amount of information origi-nally intended to be contained in the locus name. The only rule now applied in assign-ing a locus name is that it must be unique. For example, for GenBank records that have six-character accessions (e.g., U12345), the locus name is usually the first letter of the genus and species names, followed by the accession number. For eight-character charac-ter accessions (e.g., AF123456), the locus name is just the accession number.

The Locus field for the record shown in Figure 2-3 contains the following information:

- Locus name is SCU49845.
- Sequence length is 5028 base pairs.
- Molecule type is DNA.
- GenBank division is PLN (plant, fungal, and algal sequences).
- Last modification date is June 21, 1999.

The Definition Field

DEFINITION Saccharomyces cerevisiae TCP1-beta gene, partial cds, and Axl2p (AXL2) and Rev7p (REV7) genes, complete cds.

The Definition field provides a brief description of the record, including information such as source organism, gene name/protein name, or some description of the sequence's function (if the sequence is noncoding). If the sequence has a coding region (CDS), the description may be followed by a completeness qualifier, such as "complete cds."

Although nucleotide definitions follow a structured format, GenBank does not use a controlled vocabulary—authors determine the content of their records with the result that a search for a specific term might not retrieve the desired records. Such problems are not uncommon and necessitate that researchers use multiple terms that authors might have used in their records, such as synonyms, full spellings, and abbreviations. Additionally, some search programs such as Entrez have a "related records" (or "neighbors") function that allows the search to be broadened to retrieve records with similar sequences, regardless of the descriptive terms used by the original submitters.

The Accession Number

ACCESSION   U49845

The accession number is a formal database record number. GenBank records typically have six-character accessions (e.g., U12345); the locus name is usually the first letter of the genus and species names, followed by the accession number.

Unlike locus names, accession numbers are not directly related to information contained in the record, so they are very stable. If the accession number is known, it is a better search target than the locus name because accessions are stable and locus names can change.

The Version Number

VERSION   U49845.1 **GI:** 1293613

The version number is a nucleotide sequence identification number that represents a single, specific sequence in the GenBank database. This identification number uses the "accession. version" format implemented by GenBank/EMBL/DDBJ in February 1999. Any change to the sequence data will trigger an increase to the version number (e.g., U12345.1 → U12345.2); the accession portion will remain unchanged. The accession.version system of sequence identifiers parallels the GI (GenInfo Identifier) number system in the sense that any update to a sequence triggers both the creation of a new GI number and an increase to the version number. Additionally, a Sequence Revision History tool is available to track GI numbers, version numbers, and update dates for GenBank records. A separate GI number is also assigned to each protein translation within a nucleotide sequence record. Any update to a translated protein sequence triggers the creation of a new GI for that protein (as discussed in more detail in the section "The Features Field" later in this chapter).

The Keywords Field

```
KEYWORDS    .
```

Keywords describe the sequence. If no keywords are included in the entry, the field contains only a period. The Keywords field is present in sequence records primarily for historical reasons and is not based on a controlled vocabulary. Keywords are generally present in older records. They are generally not included in newer records unless (1) they are not redundant with any feature, qualifier, or other information present in the record; or (2) the submitter specifically asks for them to be added and (1) is true; or (3) the sequence needs to be tagged as an EST (expression tag sequence), STS (sequence-tagged site), GSS (genome survey sequences), or HTG (high-throughput genomic sequences).

The Source Field

```
SOURCE    baker's yeast.
```

This field is composed of free-format information, including an abbreviated form of the organism name, sometimes followed by a molecule type.

The Organism Field

```
ORGANISM    Saccharomyces cerevisiae Eukaryota; Fungi; Ascomycota; Hemi-
            ascomycetes; Saccharomycetales; Saccharomycetaceae; Saccha-
            romyces.
```

43

This field provides the formal scientific name for the source organism (genus and species, where appropriate) and its lineage, based on the phylogenetic classification scheme used in the NCBI Taxonomy Database. If the complete lineage of an organism is very long, an abbreviated lineage will be shown in the GenBank record, and the complete lineage will be available in the Taxonomy Database.

The Reference Field

REFERENCE   1 (bases 1 to 5028)

"References" refer to publications by the authors of the sequence that discuss the data reported in the record. References are automatically sorted within the record based on date of publication, showing the oldest references first.

The Authors Field

AUTHORS   Torpey L.E., Gibbs P.E., Nelson J. and Lawrence C.W.

"Authors" is the list of authors in the order in which they appear in the cited article.

The Title Field

TITLE   Cloning and sequence of REV7, a gene whose function is required for DNA damage-induced mutagenesis in Saccharomyces cerevisiae

"Title" refers to the original published work or tentative title of an unpublished work. Sometimes the words "Direct Submission" appear rather than an article title. This is usually true for the last citation in the Reference field because it tends to contain information about the submitter of the sequence, rather than a literature citation. The last citation is therefore called the "submitter block."

The Journal Field

JOURNAL   Yeast 10 (11), 1503-1509 (1994)

Journal refers to the MEDLINE abbreviation of the journal name.

The Medline Field

MEDLINE	95176709
REFERENCE	2 (bases 1 to 5028)
AUTHORS	Roemer,T., Madden,K., Chang,J. and Snyder,M.
TITLE	Selection of axial growth sites in yeast requires Axl2p, a novel plasma membrane glycoprotein
JOURNAL	Genes Dev. 10 (7), 777-793 (1996)
MEDLINE	96194260
REFERENCE	3 (bases 1 to 5028)
AUTHORS	Roemer,T.
TITLE	Direct Submission
JOURNAL	Submitted (22-FEB-1996) Terry Roemer, Biology, Yale University, New Haven, CT, USA

"Medline" refers to the Medline unique identifier (UID). References that include Medline UIDs contain links from the sequence record to the corresponding Medline record. Conversely, Medline records that contain accession numbers in the SI (Secondary Source Identifier) field contain links back to GenBank sequence records.

The Direct Submission Field

The Direct Submission field provides contact information for the submitter, such as institute/department and postal address. This is always the last citation in the References field. Some older records do not contain the Direct Submission reference. However, it is required in all new records. The Authors subfield contains the submitter name(s), Title contains the words *Direct Submission*, and Journal contains the address.

The date in the Journal subfield is the date on which the author prepared the submission. In many cases, it is also the date on which the sequence was received by the Gen-Bank staff, but it is not the date of first public release.

The Features Field

```
FEATURES          Location/Qualifiers


     source    1..5028
               /organism="Saccharomyces cerevisiae"
               /db_xref="taxon:4932"
               /chromosome="IX"
               /map="9"
     CDS       <1..206
               /codon_start=3
               /product="TCP1-beta"
               /protein_id="AAA98665.1"
               /db_xref="GI:1293614"
               /translation="SSIYNGISTSGLDLNNGTIADMR
                   QLGIVESYKLKRAVVSSASEAAE
                   VLLRVDNIIRARPRTANRQHM"
```

gene   687..3158

/gene="AXL2"

CDS   687..3158

/gene="AXL2"

/note="plasma membrane glycoprotein"

/codon_start=1

/product="Axl2p"

/protein_id="AAA98666.1"

/db_xref="GI:1293615"

/translation="MTQLQISLLLTATISLLHLVVATPYEAYPIGKQYPPVAR
VNESFTFQISNDTYKSSVDKTAQITYNCFDLPSWLSFDSSSRTFSGEP
SSDLLSDANTTLYFNVILEGTDSADSTSLNNTYQFVVTNRPSISLSSD
FNLLALLKNYGYTNGKNALKLDPNEVFNVTFDRSMFTNEESIVSYY
GRSQLYNAPLPNWLFFDSGELKFTGTAPVINSAIAPETSYSFVIIATDI
EGFSAVEVEFELVIGAHQLTTSIQNSLIINVTDTGNVSYDLPLNYVYL
DDDPISSDKLGSINLLDAPDWVALDNATISGSVPDELLGKNSNPAN
FSVSIYDTYGDVIYFNFEVVSTTDLFAISSLPNINARGEWFSYYFLPS
QFTDYVNTNVSLEFTNSSQDHDWVKFQSSNLTLAGEVPKNFDKLS
LGLKANQGSQSQELYFNIIGMDSKITHSNHSANATSTRSSHHSTST
SSYTSSTYTAKISSTSAAATSSAPAALPAANKTSSHNKKAVAIACGVAI
PLGVILVALICFLIFWRRRRENPDDENLPHAISGPDLNNPANKPNQ
ENATPLNNPFDDDASSYDDTSIARRLAALNTLKLDNHSATESDISS
VDEKRDSLSGMNTYNDQFQSQSKEELLAKPPVQPPESPFFDPQNR
SSSVYMDSEPAVNKSWRYTGNLSPVSDIVRDSYGSQKTVDTEKLFD
LEAPEKEKRTSRDVTMSSLDPWNSNISPSPVRKSVTPSPYNVTKRN
RHLQNIQDSQSGKNGITPTTMSTSSSDDFVPVKDGENFCWVHSM
EPDRRPSKKRLVDFSNKSNVNVGQVKDIHGRIPEML"

gene   complement (3300..4037)

/gene="REV7"

CDS   complement (3300..4037)

/gene="REV7"

/codon_start=1

/product="Rev7p"

/protein_id="AAA98667.1"

/db_xref="GI:1293616"

/translation="MNRWVEKWLRVYLKCYINLILFYRNVYPPQSFDYT
TYQSFNLPQFVPINRHPALIDYIEELILDVLSKLTHVYRFSICIINKKN
DLCIEKYVLDFSELQHVDKDDQIITETEVFDEFRSSLNSLIMHLEKL
PKVNDDTITFEAVINAIELELGHKLDRNRRVDSLEEKAEIERDSNW
VKCQEDENLPDNNGFQPPKIKLTSLVGSDVGPLIIHQFSEKISGDDK
ILNGVYSQYEEGESIFGSLF"

The Features field contains information about genes and gene products, as well as regions of biological significance reported in the sequence. These regions include portions of the sequence that code for proteins and RNA molecules, as well as a number of other biological parameters such as post-translational modification sites. The location of each feature is provided as well and can be a single base, a contiguous span of bases, or a joining of sequence spans. If a feature is located on the complementary strand, the word *complement* appears before the base span. If the less than symbol (<) precedes a base span, the sequence is partial on the 5'end (e.g., CDS <1..206). If the greater than symbol (>) follows a base span, the sequence is partial on the 3' end (e.g., CDS 435..915>). Table 2-3 includes examples of sequence designations.

Table 2-3 Examples of GenBank "Gene" Feature Descriptions

Description	Example Designation	Comments
Complete	687..3158	Feature extends from base 687 through base 3158.
Partial on the 5' end of the molecule	< 1..206	The feature extends from base 1 through base 206 in the sequence, and is partial on the 5' end of the molecule.
Partial on the 3' end of the molecule	4821..5028 >	The feature extends from base 4821 through base 5028, and is partial on the 3' end of the molecule.
Feature located on the complementary DNA strand	Complement (3300..4037)	The feature extends from base 3300 through base 4037, but is actually on the complementary DNA strand—it must be read in the opposite direction on the reverse complement sequence. (For an example, see the third CDS feature in the sample record shown above). In this case, the amino acid translation is generated by taking the reverse complement of bases 3300 to 4037 and reading that reverse complement sequence in its 5' to 3' direction.)

The sample record shown earlier includes only a small number of features. Here is a description of each:

- Source is a mandatory feature in each record. It summarizes the length of the sequence, scientific name of the source organism, and Taxon ID number. The source can also include other information such as map location, strain, clone, tissue type, etc., if provided by the submitter.

- Taxon is a stable unique identification number related to the taxonomy of the source organism. A taxonomy ID number is assigned to represent each species, genus, and family combination in the NCBI Taxonomy Database. The Taxon identifier is closely related to the Organism field.

- CDS refers to coding sequence; a region of nucleotides that corresponds to the sequence of amino acids in a protein (location includes start and stop codons). The CDS feature includes an amino acid translation. Authors can specify the nature of the CDS by using the qualifier /evidence=experimental or /evidence = not experimental. Submitters are also encouraged to annotate the mRNA feature, which includes the 5' untranslated region (5'UTR), coding sequences (CDS, exon), and 3' untranslated region (3'UTR).

- Protein ID refers to a protein sequence identification number in the accession.version format that was implemented by GenBank/EMBL/DDBJ in February 1999. Protein IDs consist of three letters followed by five digits, a dot, and a version number. Updates to the sequence data trigger an increase in the version number (the accession portion will remain stable (e.g., AAA98665.1 will change to AAA98665.2). Likewise, because the GI system of sequence identifiers runs parallel to the accession.version system, updates to the protein sequence will also trigger a new GI number; the suffix of the protein ID will be incremented by one.

- Translation refers to the amino acid translation from the DNA sequence—the nucleotide coding sequence (CDS). In many cases, the translations are conceptual. Authors can indicate whether the CDS is based on experimental or nonexperimental evidence.

The Base Count Field

BASE COUNT   1510 a   1074 c   835 g   1609 t

"Base count" refers to the number of A, C, G, and T bases in the sequence.

The Origin Field

ORIGIN   Unreported

The Origin field may be left blank, may appear as "Unreported," or may give a local pointer to the sequence start, usually involving an experimentally determined restriction cleavage site or the genetic locus (if available). This information is present only in older records.

The sequence data begin on the line immediately below "ORIGIN." Users of the database can view or save just the sequence data or display the record using the conventions of the commonly used FASTA sequence homology program. A portion of the sequence from the record we have been reviewing (accession number U49845) is shown here.

```
  1 gatcctccat atacaacggt atctccacct caggtttaga tctcaacaacggaaccattg

 61 ccgacatgag acagttaggt atcgtcgaga gttacaagct aaaacgagca gtagtcagct

121 ctgcatctga agccgctgaa gttctactaa gggtggataa catcatccgt caagaccaa

181 gaaccgccaa tagacaacat atgtaacata tttaggatat acctcgaaaataataaaccg

                                   ·

                                   ·

                                   ·

4801 gatctcaagt tattggagtc ttcagccaat tgctttgtat cagacaattg actctctaac

4861 ttctccactt cactgtcgag ttgctcgttt ttagcggaca aagatttaat ctcgttttct

4921 ttttcagtgt tagattgctc taattctttg agctgttctc tcagctcctc atattttct

4981 tgccatgact cagattctaa ttttaagcta ttcaatttct ctttgatc
```

The volume and complexity of this record is an example of the sort of structure that one encounters in the many bioinformatic, medical, and chemical databases. We will return briefly to a discussion of database formats in Chapter 8 when we review protein structure databases. The nature of the information they contain makes structure databases exceptionally complex. Moreover, the query tools used to search such databases must contain facilities that enable researchers to define three-dimensional constructs using simple language that can be embedded in a query.

HETEROGENEOUS DATABASE INFRASTRUCTURE FOR BIOINFORMATICS

Despite the scope and complexity of databases such as GenBank, bioinformatics still requires access to large numbers of individual data sources that differ with regard to naming conventions and data structures. Even if we gained consensus around these simple parameters, databases are often designed around specific query interfaces, many of which are proprietary and can be searched only using vendor-specific applications.

Vendor-specific databases typically have a set of application programming interfaces (APIs) that are made available to subscribers. With a detailed knowledge of these APIs, programmers can often modify existing search applications to work with a proprietary system. Alternatively, a skilled programmer with knowledge of the APIs can create a software translator—often referred to as a wrapper—that can interpret queries issued in standard formats, such as SQL, into instructions that the underlying database can understand. When several different proprietary databases are "wrapped" to expose a common query interface that can be accessed from a single program, these databases are said to belong to a "federated" system. The alternative to a federated system is a single "data warehouse" designed to contain the combined information from the various data sources in a single consolidated structure. Data warehousing is not feasible if the individual databases are very large, updated on a regular basis, or not available to be copied for legal reasons. The two architectures, federated database and data warehouse, are depicted in Figures 2-4 and 2-5.

Regardless of the method used to combine heterogeneous databases—federated or data warehouse—the problem of differing data structures and naming conventions is persistent and must be solved before a common query environment can be constructed. This problem is commonly referred to as a "schema" mismatch. A schema defines the database environment and contains information about table structures, data types, users

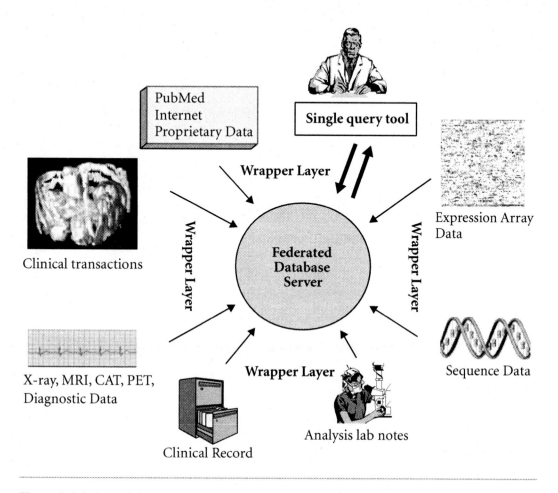

Figure 2-4 Federated database.

and permissions, and relational links between tables. Collectively, a large number of schemas make up the system catalog that describes the entire database environment.

Schema mismatches are a very important problem for architects designing database environments for bioinformatics because these mismatches often occur at many different levels. For example, two databases might differ with regard to the data types used to represent a nucleotide sequence. One database might use a string of one-byte-long ASCII characters, whereas the other might use two-byte integers. A search program

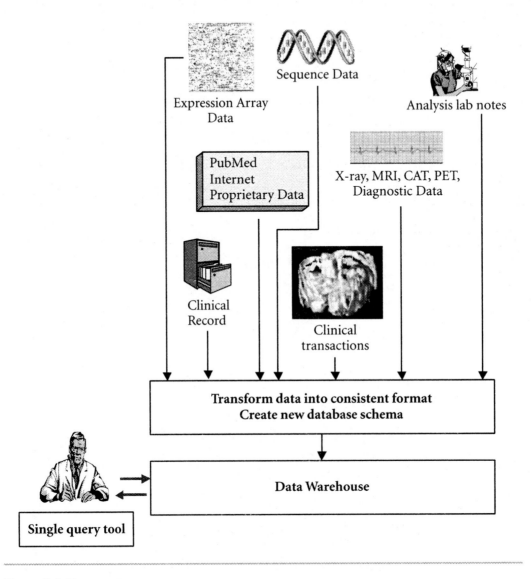

Figure 2-5 Data warehouse.

designed to translate search strings into integers would not be able to search the first database, and a query tool that generated ASCII characters would not be able to search the second.

Alternatively, the two databases might agree at the data type level but the field names might differ (e.g., one database might have a field named Sequence and the other might contain the same information in a field called DNASeq). Such problems are relatively easy to solve at the programming level, but limit the flexibility of the system because users can only search databases that have been comprehended in the original program design.

Program maintenance is an ongoing concern because problems always arise when structural changes are made to one of the databases—a common occurrence in federated systems, where individual databases are the property of different organizations.

Even in situations where all the databases in a federated system are built on parallel schemas, individual data elements might be derived from different vocabularies (e.g., Acetaminophen in one database and Tylenol in another). For example, a recent search of NCBI's PubMed database turned up 7,868 journal articles for Tylenol and 9,095 articles for Acetaminophen. Worse still, a search for the term *leukemia* gives dramatically different results than a search for *leukaemia*. Although recent years have seen a movement within the life sciences community to create common vocabularies for representing biological data, query mismatches such as those discussed here are still prevalent, are extremely difficult to solve, and require the construction of shared data dictionaries with programs that perform automatic translation. Table 2-4 summarizes the issues associated with schema and query term mismatches.

Table 2-4 Various Issues Related to Schema and Query Term Mismatches

Mismatch Type	Description	Example
Data type	Byte structure of individual data elements	Integer versus character formatting for members of a sequence
Field name	Naming conventions for data categories	Column names such as "Sequence" and "DNASeq"
Vocabulary	Descriptive terms for data items	Same substance referred to as "Acetaminophen" in one database and "Tylenol" in another

The mismatches illustrated in Table 2-4 are typically solved at the level of the search application. Data type mismatches can be solved by supplementing the query program with additional code that is sensitive to the structure of the source being queried and can make appropriate data conversions prior to issuing the query. Likewise, vocabulary mismatches are often solved by supplementing query programs with search algorithms that are designed to scan a lookup table for appropriate translations. The field name problem can be solved either at the database side with a "wrapper" that uses a lookup table to translate into the underlying structure of the target database, or on the query side with a context-sensitive search application designed to scan a lookup table for field name equivalences prior to transmitting the query to the data source. Each of these options is complex but workable.

Searching Heterogeneous Databases

If a federated database system is in place, the next step is to build a set of tools that can be used to construct queries that cross multiple data sources. Heterogeneous databases are a challenge, even in the absence of schema mismatches, when the underlying databases cannot understand the same query language. The goal is to construct a virtual data repository that can respond to an arbitrarily complex query where the data needed to respond is distributed across the data sources and none of the sources, by itself, is capable of responding.

The most straightforward solution to this problem involves front ending each database with a wrapper designed to make appropriate translations. These translations are much more complex than simple conversions from one term, field name, or data type to another because they involve syntactical and semantic conversions. In each case, the wrapper must translate the query into a set of commands that the underlying database understands.

The problem is tantamount to stating a complex question in English to a group of individuals who speak three different languages (other than English), each of whom is able to solve a portion of the problem. The most straightforward solution involves breaking the problem up into pieces and presenting each piece to the appropriate individual through a translator. Each person will then solve his or her piece of the problem and communicate the answer back, through the translator, in English. The final step involves comparing and assembling the individual answers into a complete picture. Although this solution might seem straightforward with regard to logistics, it is actually very complex for a number of reasons: The person posing the original question might not have precise knowledge of the capabilities of the individuals answering; portions of the question might not translate properly into certain languages; and dividing up the question might destroy some of the original context, making some of the translations impossible.

Each of these issues has real meaning in the bioinformatics/database world. For example, the original SQL query might require floating-point arithmetic, and one of the data sources might be limited to integer calculations. In such a case, the wrapper design must embody "function compensation" so that the data source can respond despite its deficiency.

Heterogeneous databases present a second challenge, this one related to variable response time. Each query must be decomposed and the components submitted to various databases for processing. The length of time required to process each piece depends on many factors, such as the size and complexity of the database, the number of matches likely to be found, and the performance of the hardware the database resides on.

An important part of the search involves selecting an appropriate query plan that optimizes the order of external joins between the data sources to reduce the total time required for the search. For example, in a search that crosses three data sources, it might be more efficient to search the first and third, join the results to find overlapping records (a logical AND) and use these to scan for matches in the second database. Conversely, if database 3 is excessively large and slow, it might make more sense to limit the size of searches against this data set by first joining results from databases 1 and 2, and using these to construct a query against database 3. An optimized query plan can be orders of magnitude faster than one that proceeds in a random order.

Three different query plans are represented in Figures 2-6, 2-7, and 2-8. In all three cases, the task being executed can be represented by this phrase: Identify all compounds that have been tested against the serotonin family of receptors and have IC50 values in the nanomolar range. The goal is to optimize the search by reducing the time required for external joins between heterogeneous data sources.

The first plan, depicted in Figure 2-6, proceeds as follows:

1. Search Protein database for "serotonin-like" proteins. (Store results in a temporary table.)
2. Retrieve a structure from the Compound database.
3. Check the Assay database for the IC50 value of this compound.
4. If the IC50 for this compound $< 10^{-8}$, then scan the temporary "serotonin-like" protein table for records containing an ID that matches the "screen name" from the assay—return this result to the user.
5. Retrieve the next structure from the Compound database and restart the process.

This scenario exhibits poor performance if there are many compounds because every structure must be retrieved and subsequently used in a search against the Assay database.

The second plan, depicted in Figure 2-7, proceeds as follows:

1. Search the Protein database for "serotonin-like" proteins (store results in a temporary table).
2. Retrieve an assay result from the Assay database.
3. If the IC50 value of this assay is $< 10^{-8}$, then search the Compound database for the structure tested.
4. If the IC50 for this compound $< 10^{-8}$, then scan the temporary "serotonin-like" protein table for records containing an ID that matches the screen name from the assay—return this result to the user.
5. Retrieve the next assay result from the Assay database and restart the process.

This plan is extremely efficient because it reduces the number of compound searches by only retrieving assays with low IC50 values. The "temp. table" limits the scope of join 2.

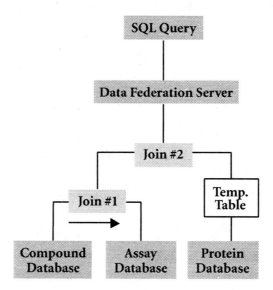

Query Description: Identify all compounds that have been tested against the serotonin family of receptors and have IC50 values in the nanomolar range.

1. Search Protein database for "serotonin - like" proteins (store results in a temporary table)

2. Retreive a structure from the Compound database

3. Check the Assay database for the IC50 value of this compound

4. If the IC50 for this compound < 10-8 then scan the temporary "serotonin - like" protein table for records containing an "id" that matches the "screen name" from the assay – return this to the user

5. Retrieve the next structure from the Compound Database and restart the process

Poor performance if there are many compounds since every structure is retreived and generates a search against the assay database

Figure 2-6 Sample query plan 1. (See text for details.)

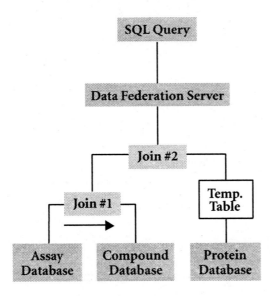

Query Description: Identify all compounds that have been tested against the serotonin family of receptors and have IC50 values in the nanomolar range.

1. Search Protein database for "serotonin-like" proteins (store results in a temporary table)

2. Retreive an assay result from the Assay database

3. If the IC50 value of the assay is < 10-8 the search the Compound database for the structure tested

4. If the IC50 for this compound < 10-8 then scan the temporary "serotonin - like" protein table for records containing an ID that matches the screen name from the assay – return this result to the user

5. Retreive the next assay result from the Assay database and restart the process

Very efficient—only retreives assays with low IC50 values reducing the number of compound searches. Temp. table limits the scope of Join #2.

Figure 2-7 Sample query plan 2. (See text for details.)

The third plan, depicted in Figure 2-8, proceeds as follows:

1. Build a temporary table of all assay results with IC50 values $<10^{-8}$.
2. Retrieve a "serotonin-like" protein record and check the temporary assay table for a record that links to this protein.
3. If a match is found, search the Compound database for records containing an ID that matches the screen name from the assay—return this result to the user.
4. Retrieve the next "serotonin-like" protein, match against the table of low IC50 values, and restart the process.

This plan is only efficient when the number of "serotonin-like" proteins is small because the search strategy involves comparing every successful join 1 against every compound.

The overall architecture of a heterogeneous system is relatively simple. The design typically depends on the presence of a query server that contains information about the databases that comprise the federated system. The IBM DiscoveryLink server is one example of such a server. Desktop applications connect to DiscoveryLink through a variety of standard interfaces, such as Open Database Connect (ODBC) or Java Database Connect (JDBC), and submit their queries in standard SQL format. Information required to respond to the queries is housed in the federated databases previously identified to the DiscoveryLink server through a process known as "registration." The registration process identifies wrappers to the system and matches each to specific data sources. Detailed information about the physical capabilities of each underlying database is stored in the DiscoveryLink server catalog at the time of registration; this information is ultimately used to design an optimized query plan.

Upon receiving a query, the DiscoveryLink server checks its catalog for specific information about the individual data sources and uses this information to create query fragments. A cost-based optimizer is used to determine the length of processing time that will be required for each data source to respond to each query fragment. These calculations can be extended to comprehend network bandwidth and system load issues. Based on these calculations, DiscoveryLink creates an optimized query plan and submits the fragments for processing. Part of the execution process involves rewriting queries to

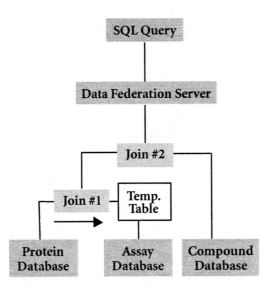

Query Description: Identify all compounds that have been tested against the serotonin family of receptors and have IC50 values in the nanomolar range.

1. Build a temporary table of all assay results with IC50 values < 10-8

2. Retreive a "serotonin-like" protein record and check the temporry assay table for a record that links to this protein

3. If a match is found then search the Compound database for records containing an ID that matches the screen name from the assay – return this result to the user

4. Retreive the next "serotonin-like" protein, match against the table of low IC50 values, and restart the process

Efficient if the number of "serotonin-like" proteins is small. However, this plan compares every successful Join #1 against every compound

Figure 2-8 Sample query plan 3. (See text for details.)

compensate for missing functionality that would not allow an individual data source to respond to a portion of the SQL query. It is common for complex queries to include questions that none of the data sources can respond to or that cannot be responded to as phrased in standard SQL format. Function compensation and query rewrite are important search technologies that permit incorporation of a broad spectrum of databases into a federated system without regard to vocabulary or schema-related limitations.

After the query plan has been created, the fragments are translated for submission to the various federated databases through appropriate wrappers that are dynamically loaded by the DiscoveryLink server. DiscoveryLink coordinates execution of the chosen plan, requesting data from the wrappers as the plan dictates. As results are returned, they are stored in a local table prior to execution of the final joins. After all joins are completed and a final answer to the query is assembled, the results are passed back to the requesting desktop application for viewing by the user [9, 10]. The diagram in Figure 2-9 shows this flow of information through DiscoveryLink.

The DiscoveryLink architecture is common to many heterogeneous systems, including TSIMMIS, DISCO, Pegasus, DION, and Hermes [11, 12, 13, 14, 15]. Each of these systems relies on a central query server to assemble and parse the fragments and a set of wrappers to translate queries into executable commands. Despite excellent technology, most of these systems suffer from logistical problems related to keeping wrappers up to date for each of the underlying databases. This problem can be daunting because even the smallest change to one of the data sources can completely invalidate a wrapper.

One solution has been to develop schema-independent wrappers that embody information about the processing and data-handling capabilities of the data sources but are not specific for individual database designs. However, even schema-independent wrappers must be maintained by skilled programmers with specific knowledge of the individual data sources. It is clear that wrapper developers must have domain-specific knowledge about the way the database is typically used in addition to very advanced programming skills. One solution is to team domain experts with database programmers. Such teamwork is characteristic of the convergence of molecular biology and information science.

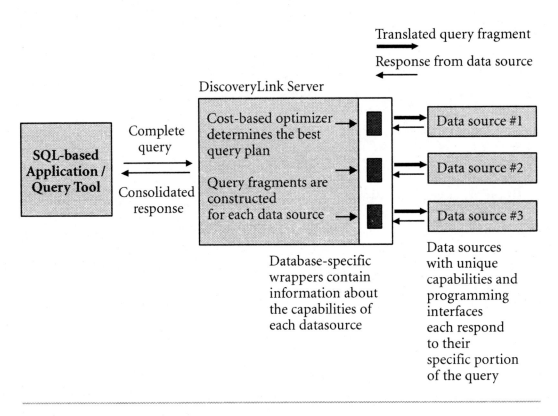

Figure 2-9 Flow of information through a DiscoveryLink federated database system.

Managed Ontologies and Custom-Tailored Database Infrastructure

The concept of an ontology is important to any discipline that depends on data mining or knowledge management, especially in the context of heterogeneous databases. Generally speaking, an ontology is a formal specification that includes descriptions of objects and concepts and the relationships that connect them. In the simplest sense, an ontology is a descriptive vocabulary; in the more complex sense, it is a framework that lends formal definition to a conversation about an area of study. As computational biology matures, ontologies are becoming core components of the database infrastructure that supports drug discovery and medical informatics.

As discussed earlier, one of the largest obstacles to searching heterogeneous databases is the existence of alternative names for genes, proteins, disease conditions, and other biological parameters. For example, a gene that codes for an enzyme might be named according to its mutant phenotype by a geneticist and by its enzymatic function by a biochemist. Likewise, research groups working with different organisms will often give the same molecule a different name. Formal naming conventions are unlikely to be adapted, and they often prove counterproductive to the research community that depends so heavily on syntactical conventions that are specific to individual fields. As a result, information about biologically active molecules is often difficult to retrieve because representations vary, even within a single database.

These discrepancies cause users to select multiple identifiers and synonyms, including gene and protein accession numbers and protein and locus symbols. This strategy, often referred to as expansion by synonyms, is imprecise and often causes problems because the synonyms are usually less specific than the original query. However, well-structured queries that are expanded with carefully selected terms have been shown to be very effective at improving search results.

Another approach involves broadening the query to include less-precise terminology and filtering the output with additional qualifiers to remove extraneous information. Examples of query expansion and successive filtering are included in Figure 2-10.

Figure 2-10 begins with a search for papers describing treatments for leukemia using activated natural killer T-cells. The initial question is simplified into a set of basic query terms that are subsequently expanded into a more comprehensive list. For example, the initial question mentions treatments for leukemia, the list of basic search terms includes immunotherapy, and the expanded set includes immunotherapy and alloimmunotherapy. Fully expanded searches are used to retrieve references and further refine the search.

Yet another approach to solving the heterogeneous search problem in a system of databases that contains mismatches of vocabulary involves the creation of a new middleware layer for managing ontologies. The new layer contains a terminology database that interprets queries and translates them into search terms consistent with each of the underlying sources. This approach does not exclude the development of wrappers and federated databases because the new layer can sit on top of a federated system. In such a hybrid system, the terminology server can issue queries to individual data sources as well as to a federated system, where queries are further decomposed at the level of database wrappers. Figure 2-11 shows a diagram of such a system.

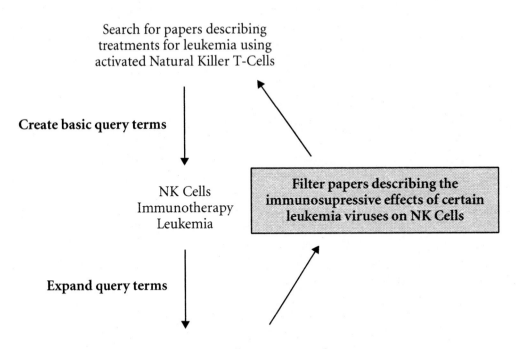

Search for papers describing
treatments for leukemia using
activated Natural Killer T-Cells

Create basic query terms

NK Cells
Immunotherapy
Leukemia

**Filter papers describing the
immunosupressive effects of certain
leukemia viruses on NK Cells**

Expand query terms

NK Cells, Natural Killer Cells, NK T-Cells, NK T-Lymphocytes
Immunotherapy, Immunetherapy, Alloimmunetherapy
Leukemia, Leukaemia, Leukemic, Lymphoproleferative Disease

Figure 2-10 Query expansion and successive filtering are an effective solution to the heterogeneous search problem.

A real-world example of a hybrid system, TAMBIS (Transparent Access to Multiple Bioinformatics Information Sources), was recently developed at the University of Manchester in the United Kingdom [16]. The TAMBIS architecture includes a terminology server based on an extensive source-independent global ontology of molecular biology and bioinformatics represented in a descriptive logic. The ontology and underlying descriptive logic is used by an interface component that provides linguistic services to transform queries into consistent language that can be used to search all databases in the system.

More recently, ontology-based designs have evolved from static dictionaries into dynamic systems that can be extended with new terms and concepts without modifica-

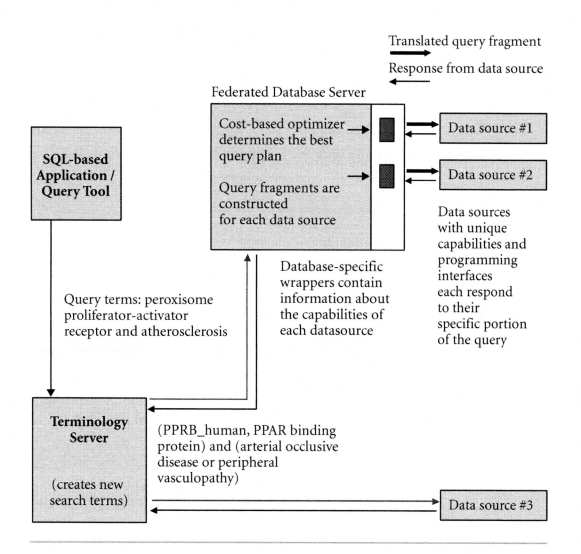

Figure 2-11 Complex heterogeneous system, including a terminology server based on a life sciences.

tions to the underlying database. The CELL platform from InCellico, Inc. is an excellent example. CELL embodies just two concepts: entities and relationships. Entities can be any concept (e.g., gene, protein, literature reference, pathway) that a researcher deems to be important. Unlike TAMBIS, which uses a predefined dictionary of ontologies, CELL allows entities to represent concepts not already included in the database. An entity represents a single concept or individual of that type.

Redundant database entries from multiple sources are automatically merged into single entities that contain alternative identifiers. Relationships contain information about the links between entities and support the capture of knowledge from different sources. Together entities and relationships form an ontology-based network that captures the concepts and terminology of computational biology. For example, the predicted C. elegans protein YKD3_CAEEL or Q03561 from Swiss-PROT is also represented in PIR as S28280, and in WormPep as B0464.3 or CE00017. In the CELL system, these database entries are collapsed into a single entity extended with individual identifiers as aliases. A researcher can search for all the relationships linked to the entity by querying with any of its aliases. In this way, CELL automatically expands queries with synonyms [17].

CELL also includes additional information about entities and relationships in the form of confidence levels. These confidence levels are based on inferences and correlations commonly employed in biotechnology and are designed to better enable application of these relationships as a more exact and analytical science. This additional knowledge can be harnessed by reasoning engines to create more valid and accurate virtual experiments, and sometimes leads to the discovery of new relationships that are subsequently built in to the system. Although complex to design and build, such systems add tremendous value by enabling researchers to search heterogeneous databases without specific knowledge about schemas and vocabularies. At the time of this writing, the CELL ontology system embodies more than 60 million entities and 200 million relationships. Figure 2-12 shows, in block diagram form, a typical ontology-based query system with a terminology server and several underlying heterogeneous databases.

INDEXED AND LINK-BASED SYSTEMS

Wrapper-based query systems and ontology-driven terminology servers represent two very important solutions to the heterogeneous database problem. However, each of these is extremely complex to build—often beyond the capabilities of many information technology departments. Link-based systems offer a valuable alternative that, although limited in flexibility, is often broad enough in scope for the specific application. Additionally, because none of the systems mentioned is mutually exclusive, it is perfectly

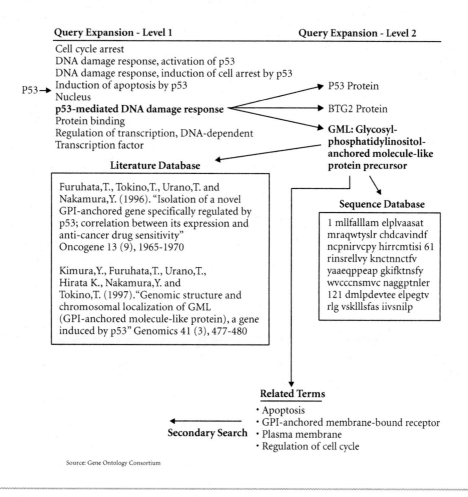

Figure 2-12 A discovery framework based on a terminology server and ontology engine.

reasonable to build a hybrid database platform with some databases directly linked, some federated through wrapper architectures, and some shared through a terminology engine using an underlying ontology. A complete hybrid system that embodies all three alternatives is depicted in Figure 2-13.

In such a system, all three methodologies—linked table systems, federated database servers, and terminology servers—are used simultaneously to join heterogeneous data sources. The user interacts with these systems through an abstraction layer designed to

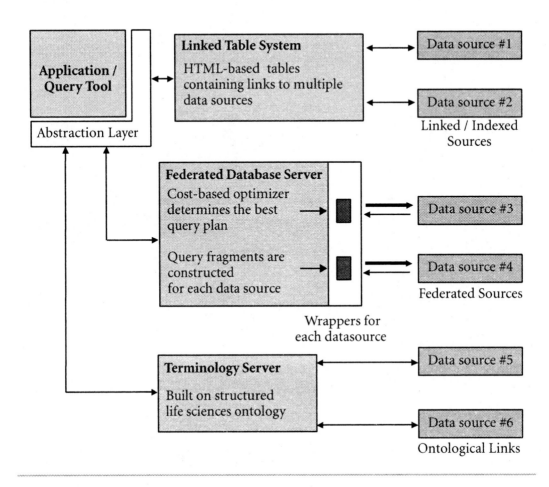

Figure 2-13 Hybrid structure for a heterogeneous database system.

provide a single system image. Because the underlying application interacts only with the abstraction layer, its design does not need to comprehend the complexities of the entire system.

Link-based systems bring together information and knowledge from many sources in the form of curated linked documents such as HTML-based Web pages. Such systems are designed to be navigated through a menu-driven process that involves selecting and following links to collect information. They are relatively simple to use but have limited search and data-mining capabilities because they completely lack flexibility.

Indexed systems that also contain linked documents are much more complex and functional than systems containing links alone. The most popular such system is the Sequence Retrieval system (SRS), which is designed to work with dozens of public and private data sources. Information about searchable fields in supported databases is collapsed into representative metadata, which is stored in simple flat files. SRS builds indices to these flat files, which it uses to find information in the heterogeneous databases it supports. Links between records are also indexed, permitting searches to traverse data sources.

From a user perspective, SRS contains two types of links: hyperlinks and query links. Hyperlinks connect entries that are displayed in typical hypertext format. These links are hard coded into the system and are useful for examining entries that are directly referenced by other entries. Alternatively, query links enable users to construct searches using known relationships between databases. A query link search causes SRS to check its indices for possible matches between entries in different databases. SRS contains a sophisticated interface that provides users with many options for searching supported databases and identifying links. In addition, users can further filter search results by joining them to additional searches and keeping only the overlap. Systems such as SRS enable users to build an iterative process that involves joining results to a secondary search, using the combined results to identify new links, and following those links to new data. The system is limited only by the size and complexity of the underlying metadata layer that stores information about the heterogeneous database infrastructure [18].

XML DATABASES AND XML VOCABULARIES FOR LIFE SCIENCES

The World Wide Web is built on a collection of Web pages that are displayed using a browser. Through the collaborative efforts of various operating system and application software vendors, as well as the general IT community and the World Wide Web Consortium (W3C), a set of standards has been created that allows a browser to display information. This standard is commonly referred to as Hypertext Markup Language (HTML). HTML, like all markup languages, contains instructions that are designed to be interpreted by the display program without being visible to the user. These instructions, also called markup tags, tell the Web browser how to display the page. HTML documents are text files made up of "elements" that are defined using tags. Tags are surrounded by angle brackets<> <> and normally come in pairs. The first tag in the pair is called the start tag; the second tag is referred to as the end tag. Elements are defined and bounded by start and end tags. The simple code in Listing 2-1 illustrates the concepts of HTML tags and elements:

Listing 2-1
HTML Code Fragment

```
<html>
<head>
<title>Title of page</title>
</head>
<body>
This is an example of an HTML element. <b>This text is bold</b>
</body>
</html>
```

The first tag in the document is <html>, which indicates the start of an HTML document. Likewise, the last tag, also </html>, indicates the document end. The text between the <head> tag and the </head> tag is called "header" information. Header information does not display in the browser window. The text between the <title> and </title>tags is the title of the document; this text displays in the browser's caption line. The text between the <body> and </body> tags is displayed by the browser. The HTML specification includes extensive formatting information—the text between the <b> and </b> tags, for instance, will display in a bold font. In each case the text between the tags—e.g., This text is bold—represents "elements" that are defined by the tags.

HTML is an excellent language for describing the way a document should look. However, it was never meant to be a data-interchange standard. The existence of a standard set of rules for representing documents only served to highlight the need for a second set of rules that could be used to describe, store, retrieve, and exchange data. In 1998, the W3C consortium responded to this challenge by approving a new standard called XML. XML is a subset of the Standard Generalized Markup Language (SGML) defined in ISO standard 8879:1986. One common misconception is that markup languages were invented to support the Internet. In actuality, markup languages were the foundation that fostered the growth of the World Wide Web. SGML predates the Web by approximately 20 years and has its roots in a 1969 research project led by Charles Goldfarb of IBM. The goal of this project was to create an integrated information system for law offices. Understanding the need for a standard set of rules to describe documents, the researchers created the Generalized Markup Language (GML). GML supported text editing, formatting, and document information retrieval. The first working draft of an SGML standard, published by ANSI in 1980, was built on these original concepts. The standard evolved through six working drafts and in 1983 SGML became an industry standard (GCA 101-1983). The United States Internal Revenue Service and Department of Defense were early adopters of the new standard. A draft ISO standard was published in October 1985 and adopted by the Publications Office of the European Union. Another year of review and comment resulted in the final version (ISO 8879:1986). As a framework, SGML was the perfect platform on which to develop the XML standard. XML is not a replacement for HTML; each was designed with a different goal in mind. The two specifications complement each other—HTML was designed to enable the display of data, and XML was designed to describe data. More precisely, XML is a cross-platform, software- and hardware-independent tool for transmitting information.

XML, like HTML, depends on tags to demarcate elements. Unlike HTML, however, XML does not predefine the tags; authors must define their own tags and document structure. XML should be thought of as a framework with a set of rules that enable authors and database developers to define the structure of their documents. This is a very important distinction that has paved the way to the creation of a variety of new XML vocabularies, many of which are specific to bioinformatics.

Two mechanisms exist within XML for defining tags. The first method, document type definition (DTD), has been historically popular because of its simplicity. By using DTDs to define the role of each element of text, users of XML can check that each component of a document occurs in a valid place within the interchanged data stream. For example, an XML DTD might allow a program to verify that users do not accidentally enter a third-level heading without first having entered a second-level heading, something that cannot be checked by HTML. Such functionality is crucial to the data-cleansing process that supports the construction of most bioinformatic infrastructure. However, DTDs lack some of the flexibility of a newer construct called an XML schema. Schemas, the descendants of DTDs, have very important characteristics that make them preferable for most projects. Most significant is their ability to define data types. This characteristic makes Schemas superior for working with databases, especially when data transformation is required. The extra flexibility that schemas bring to element definition also enables developers to enhance the process of validating an XML document for correctness. Although a complete review of XML DTDs and schemas is beyond the scope of this book, it is important to understand that XML is continuing to evolve in a direction that facilitates the construction of document-based relational databases, and that this direction will have significant impact on the life sciences and bioinformatics.

The code in Listing 2-2 is meant to illustrate the richness of XML as compared to HTML. In an HTML document, the name Jane Doe might be represented as follows:

<B>Jane Doe</B>

This notation tells an HTML-based browser or other display software to display the name using a bold (<B>) font. However, HTML encoding does not recognize Jane Doe as a person's name, and a search of HTML-encoded pages will not distinguish this particular Doe from doe, a female deer, and DOE, the Department of Energy.

The XML-encoded version would contain much more detailed information about specific elements. A reasonable DTD would define tags for the elements person, last name, and first name. A representative code sample is included in Listing 2-2.

Listing 2-2
Representative XML-Based Description of a Name

```
<Person>
  <LastName>Doe</LastName>
  <FirstName>Jane</FirstName>
</Person>
```

Although the HTML version is perfectly adequate for display purposes, it cannot capture the semantics of the content (i.e., the fact that Jane Doe is a person's name consisting of two parts—a last name and a first name).

BSML AS A DATA INTERCHANGE STANDARD FOR BIOINFORMATICS

Bioinformatic Sequence Markup Language (BSML), an XML vocabulary, was developed with funding from the National Human Genome Research Institute (NHGRI) to provide a public standard for encoding bioinformatic content that addressed the problems associated with transmitting, storing, and retrieving biological sequence information. A publicly run consortium manages the work, and results are maintained in the public domain. Moreover, because BSML is an XML application, any software that can read XML can read BSML, and any software that can render XML in a generic way can render BSML. (An XML-aware HTML browser is fully capable of displaying BSML as text.) This new XML vocabulary was initially developed as a response to the need for a standard set of rules that defines biological sequence representation, which has increased in proportion to the number of international sequence databases, and the sophistication of computational methods for sequence analysis. The primary objective behind the creation of BSML was the creation of a data representation model that would enable graphical rendering of biologically meaningful objects links between these objects and the underlying data (i.e., links between the behavior of display objects and the sequences and annotations that they represent). Although it is possible to use BSML strictly for data encoding, the addition of visualization capabilities parallels the evolution of infrastructure for storage, analysis, and linking of biological data across computer networks. These trends position BSML as an excellent platform for dealing with the critical issues of post-genomic computational biology.

BSML is a comprehensive data model for managing sequences and their annotations. Unlike other data representation standards, it can be used to describe sequence-related phenomena at all levels, from the biomolecular level to the level of the complete organism and phenotype, and thus it provides an excellent medium for genomics research. Because BSML encodes the semantics of the data it represents, it facilitates both human and machine interaction with sequences and annotations. These attributes are very important when building automated systems of analysis in which, for example, robots and synthesis machines may be instructed to create molecules with specific properties.

BSML has been evolving rapidly since 1997, and the public data specification for the XML data type definition (the BSML DTD) was publicly released in 2001 as version 2.2. It was created primarily to solve the biosequence data-management problem and support the semantics of sequence annotation. In summary, the version 2.2 specification explicitly supports the following features:

- Comprehensive description of biological sequences, their properties, and functions
- A method to manage biological sequence data and to capture semantics of sequence-related biology
- Support for human or machine interface through an enhanced attributes model
- Support for physical characteristics of represented sequences (overhang, modifications)
- Restriction enzyme target sites
- Digest products (bands)
- Edited DNA molecules (5' and 3' overhangs and phosphorylation state)
- Locations of multi-element feature motifs
- Classified feature types (CLASS attribute)
- Pairwise and multiple alignments
- Linking model for relating one feature to any linkable resource (database, URL, etc.)
- Linking model between objects within a BSML document
- Linking model between BSML documents
- Multiple (unlinked) sequences in one document

The BSML standard has evolved substantially since the original version. Version 3.1, current at the time this writing, provides all the benefits of version 2.2 plus additional support for the following:

- New elements for the resource description to associate people, organizations, and software systems directly with sequence annotation
- New research section to describe queries, searches, analyses, and experiments as sources of evidence for claims about sequence annotation
- New genome element to describe genomes (organism, chromosomes, extra-chromosomal, cytoband, etc.) more completely and to associate sequence regions with positions on a genome
- New section on isoforms to associate sequences and their annotations with SNPs, mutations, and other polymorphism content (multiple alleles)

- Direct representation of NCBI BLAST, Clustal, and Primer 3 formats to handle results of these analyses and to associate these with sequence annotation
- Clearer data model for associating sequence regions with clones and chromosomes, complete with version identification for builds
- An improved linking description that includes a cross-reference element that defines the nature of a relationship (e.g., homologous mouse protein)

As mentioned earlier, sequences may be described at various levels: complete genome, chromosome, regulatory region, gene, transcript, gene product, etc. Because each level may define a different type of biological object, BSML can capture the semantics of almost any type of biological data construct. However, like any XML vocabulary, BSML is meant to be used in conjunction with appropriate software that enables interactive access to the full range of information that can be encoded. The BSML sample code in Listing 2-3 illustrates a well-structured approach to representing biological sequence data and annotations.

Listing 2-3
Representative BSML-Encoded Description of a Sequence

```
<?xml version="1.0"?>
<?format DECIMAL="." ?>
<!DOCTYPE Bsml PUBLIC "-//TurboWorx, Inc. BSML DTD//EN"
"http://www.TurboWorx.com/dtd/bsml3_1.dtd">
<Bsml>
 <Definitions>
  <Sequences>
   <Sequence id="jaugen.20030212165300" title="Jaugen_PCR_Primer"
    local-acckey="Primer_0034" locus="Jaugen_PCR_Primer" molecule="dna"
    representation="raw" topology="linear" length="18">
    <Seq-data>
     ACTGAGATCGCTCGAGATATATGCGCTAGA
    </Seq-data>
   </Sequence>
  </Sequences>
 </Definitions>
</Bsml>
```

Between the <Bsml> and </Bsml> tags, the document is divided into three sections, each of which is optional:

- **Definitions**—Encoding of genomes and sequences, data tables, sets, and networks
- **Research**—Encoding of queries, searches, analyses, and experiments
- **Display**—Encoding of display widgets that represent graphical representations of biological objects (e.g., styles, pages)

BSML has become a popular format for data distribution throughout the life sciences community. For example, the publicly available EMBL/GenBank/DDBJ data are kept at the EBI in an Oracle relational database from which flat files are created for the purpose of distribution. Because flat files have severe limitations, the data is ultimately distributed in XML format—more precisely BSML [19].

However, as we have seen, XML documents tend to be sparsely populated with much descriptive information. Rather than follow a rigid set of design criteria, each document defines its own structure through the selective use of predefined tags. Unfortunately, this design trades efficient use of space for flexibility. Due to the inefficient use of space, the cost of storing large amounts of XML data is often prohibitive. Furthermore, the lack of a rigidly defined structure makes it difficult to build efficient search engines that function in XML format.

The optimized solution involves storing data in relational format using well-defined schemas that specify the placement, length, and data type for each field, and transforming the information into BSML format for transfer between systems. After data is retrieved in BSML format, the receiving system can extract the data for storage in a custom-designed relational format or display any portion of the data using a BSML-enabled viewer. Alternatively, a search engine that retrieves limited amounts of information in BSML format can be used to construct an XML-style database in situations where size and search speed are not limiting factors and the direct storage of individual documents is a major design criterion. Finally, many other XML vocabularies have been designed to support specific life sciences applications such as microarray analysis (Microarray Markup Language, MAML) and (Microarray / Gene Expression Markup Language, MAGE XML), biopolymer research (Biopolymer Markup Language, BIOML), sequence analysis using BLAST (BLAST XML), and haplotype mapping

(HapMap XML). Although each provides a unique set of capabilities, they are all based on XML and can be processed by any XML-capable software as long as the appropriate DTD (or schema) is made available.

Before leaving our discussion of bioinformatic databases, it is important to mention the importance of building systems for propagating corrections across a large number of related sources. Most information in biological databases is annotated via similarity to other entries in the same or other databases. If a piece of information is found to have been the result of a laboratory or other error, it is imperative that the information derived from that erroneous datum be found and corrected. Even today, such mistakes are not always corrected. The result is a "transitive catastrophe" of poisoned data that can persist for some time.

TRADITIONAL BIOINFORMATIC TOOLS AND ALGORITHMS

The scope of modern computational biology has expanded to include such diverse areas as structure prediction, diagnostic image processing, pattern discovery, and molecular systems modeling. Each of these areas has benefited from a variety of technical improvements and each has played a special role in the migration from physical to *in silico* biology. Table 2-5 delineates some of the key areas and identifies critical enabling technologies for each.

Throughout this book we will examine these technical areas in the context of specific biological processes. For example, our review of the transcription process includes a discussion of the technologies and algorithms surrounding microarrays, algorithms for the identification of coding regions is prominently featured in a section on structure of the genome, and our description of the proteome includes a description of the algorithms used for protein tertiary structure prediction. However, the relevance of sequence comparison technologies to virtually every area of computational biology, coupled with their historical significance, makes them an appropriate topic for early discussion. In addition, much of the preceding database discussion focused on sequence databases, many of which are directly associated with these technologies.

Table 2-5 Key Technologies Supporting Computational Biology

Research Area	Representative *In Silico* Tasks	Enabling Information Technologies
Molecular modeling	Target to lead compound binding simulations Protein structure determination by NMR and x-ray crystallography Protein / DNA/ RNA structure prediction Creation of structure databases (protein and nucleotide)	-Fourier transform -Quantum mechanics Atomic force simulations Distance geometry Data-mining algorithms for structure identification
Image processing	Image enhancement and diagnostic review of x-ray, CAT, MRI, PET, ultrasound Rendering of biological molecules	Pattern-discovery and other algorithms for image enhancement and analysis
Sequence analysis	Sequence homology experiments for studying the evolution of organisms Forensics Identification of coding regions Genome assembly Experiments correlating sequence and structure (protein and nucleotide)	Integer-intensive calculations (machines with very large memory and high processor-to-memory bus bandwidth) Hidden Markov model calculations Large parallel computing environments characterized by large clusters
Microarray data analysis	Identification of coregulated genes in support of systems modeling and drug response analysis Gene sequencing Transcription profiling	Statistical algorithms for gene clustering Neural network and other artificial intelligence techniques for pattern identification

SEQUENCE COMPARISON

During the 1980s, new automated sequencing technologies coupled with advances in protein and DNA purification allowed researchers to begin generating large amounts of sequence data. Early collaborative efforts between sequencing groups and relational database experts soon became the driving force that launched the public database infrastructure. Academic research groups were quick to develop algorithms that enabled them to match new sequences against these data sources; many were widely accepted by the bioscience community.

Despite the fact that a relatively small number of proteins had been sequenced along with their coding regions, researchers were quick to learn that DNA sequences in higher organisms are fundamentally different from the bacterial gene sequences they were accustomed to working with. Whereas bacterial genes are built from an uninterrupted stretch of nucleotides, gene-coding sequences of higher organisms contain coding regions (exons) that are interrupted by long noncoding sequences (introns). These introns are ultimately spliced out in the final mRNA transcript. The complete process involves additional splicing steps at the level of the primary mRNA transcript by a complex of RNA processing enzymes. As a result, each coding region can code for many different mRNA transcripts, which ultimately are translated into different proteins.

Alternative splicing of primary messages is the primary driver of complexity in the human genome because it makes the protein synthesis process much more versatile by allowing different proteins to be produced from the same gene. The fact that it is not unusual for a single gene to code for dozens of different proteins makes the process of matching a protein sequence to a gene sequence relatively difficult. Furthermore, the genetic code is degenerate, meaning that more than one code can be used to represent a single amino acid. The combination of degeneracy, alternative splicing, and the intron-exon structure of coding regions makes it impossible to automatically translate DNA sequences into proteins and vice versa.

In response to this challenge, researchers have created a class of algorithms designed to find the best fit between a test DNA sequence and potential transcription products in the case where the protein sequence is already known. One of the most popular, PRO-CRUSTES, is based on a spliced-alignment algorithm that explores all possible exon assemblies and finds the multi-exon structure with the best fit to a related protein. Developed and maintained by the Computational Biology Department at the University of Southern California, PROCRUSTES is designed to handle situations where the query DNA sequence contains either partial or multiple genes [20]. (Readers can access and use the PROCRUSTES Web server at http://www-hto.usc.edu/software/procrustes/wwwserv.html.)

Programs such as PROCRUSTES are part of a broader class of statistical methods for identifying coding regions in genomic DNA sequences. The evolution of such programs has given rise to another interesting approach that employs neural networks that have been trained to recognize characteristic sequences of known exons, intron-exon boundaries, and transcription start sites in a particular organism. Such networks, once trained, are often capable of discerning complex and subtle relationships between sequence elements that are not otherwise detectable [21, 22]. We return to the transcription process in Chapter 5 with a more detailed discussion of various approaches to feature identification.

Despite steady and rapid improvement in computer-based sequence analysis, one simple charting technique continues to prove its value: the two-dimensional dot-matrix comparison. This straightforward method facilitates the visual comparison of two sequences written across the axes of a two-dimensional grid. Each two-dimensional coordinate in the grid corresponds to a position in each of the sequences. A dot is placed on the grid to mark overlapping positions between the sequences. A pattern of diagonal lines emerge in regions of the grid where the sequences overlap, with the longest lines corresponding to the best alignments. The visual nature of the grid facilitates identification of regions that are locally similar, even when the complete sequences do not align well; many researchers achieve an additional level of simplification by filtering regions that contain a threshold number of exact matches. Figure 2-14 shows a dot-matrix plot for two sequences containing several homologous regions.

The dot-matrix method can be used to compare any sequence information regardless of the length of the two sequences or type of sequence data. Its insensitivity to gaps and inconsistencies makes it particularly valuable for identifying coding regions contained within complex sets of intron-exon boundaries. Furthermore, back-translated protein sequences can be compared against genomic data despite the degeneracy of the genetic code because matching sequences will emerge as broken lines where at least two of three nucleotides can be expected to match in each amino acid triplet [23]. (The third letter in the code is often referred to as a "wobble" base and varies for most amino acids. In

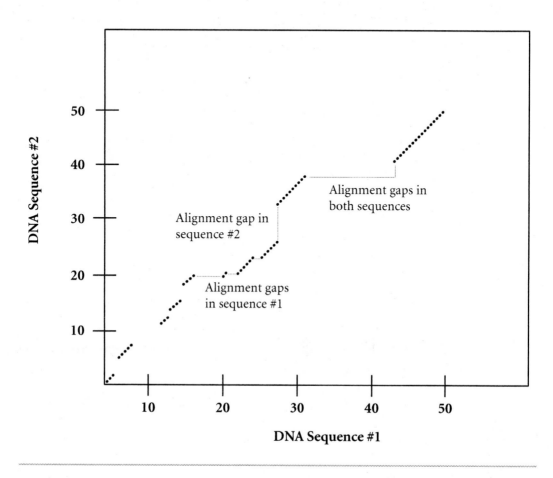

Figure 2-14 Dot-matrix plot for two DNA sequences containing several short homologous regions.

addition, the codes for three amino acids—arginine, leucine, and serine—vary in other positions.) Longer gaps in the line pattern may represent intervening sequences destined to be spliced out of the final transcript. One example is the wobble-aware block alignment algorithm (WABA) developed by James Kent and Alan Zahler [24]. The same group has also produced a set of tools for exploring RNA splicing and gene structure in the Nematode (C. elegans). Such tools are significant to our discussion because they emphasize the role of transcriptional splicing—a topic covered in great detail in Chapter 5.

After a suspect match is identified, further analysis of the individual nucleotides often reveals the presence of known splice sites and noncoding regions that do not contain amino acid triplets. Figure 2-15 displays such a comparison. The x-axis represents a back-translated protein sequence. The third base of each amino acid triplet is represented by the letter *x* because of degeneracy in the code. (The genetic code is discussed in more detail in the next chapter.) The y-axis represents a DNA sequence obtained through direct sequencing. Like most genomic sequence data, it contains both coding and noncoding regions. A pattern emerges despite gaps at the wobble bases and relatively long noncoding regions. Further analysis of the intervening gaps is required to rationalize the proposed match.

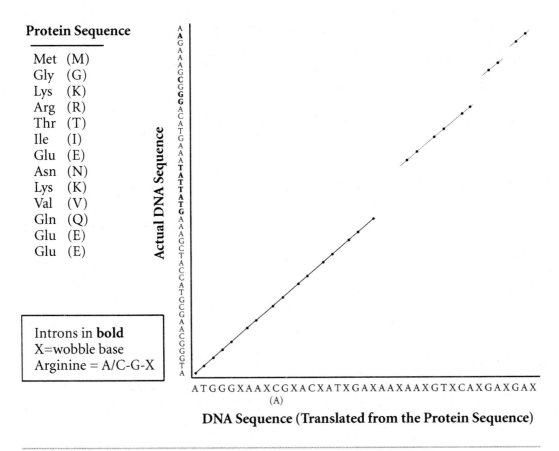

Protein Sequence
_____

Met (M)
Gly (G)
Lys (K)
Arg (R)
Thr (T)
Ile (I)
Glu (E)
Asn (N)
Lys (K)
Val (V)
Gln (Q)
Glu (E)
Glu (E)

Introns in **bold**
X=wobble base
Arginine = A/C-G-X

A T G G G X A A X C G X A C X A T X G A X A A X A A X G T X C A X G A X G A X
(A)

DNA Sequence (Translated from the Protein Sequence)

Figure 2-15 Dot-matrix comparison of genomic DNA and a back-translated protein sequence.

In principle, the dot-matrix method forms the basis of all sequence matching programs regardless of algorithmic complexity. As you'll see in the next section, all of today's sequence-matching programs are built on some variation of this theme, with various methods for managing gaps and misalignments. A simple version, illustrated in Figure 2-16, contains a matrix that awards a score of +5 for a match, −4 for a mismatch, and −3 for a gap.

It is very important to note that although researchers have created dozens of algorithms for comparing sequences, none is inherently superior to the others. Each has strengths and weaknesses and was designed to solve a particular class of problem. We will discuss various approaches to sequence comparison in the next section, with an emphasis on differentiating characteristics.

A NOTE ON SEQUENCE ABERRATIONS

Understanding and predicting the genetic-level structure of specific coding regions, even at the single base level, is critical to the drug discovery process because specific differences at the DNA sequence level are responsible for aberrations in protein structure that become the basis for new therapeutics and diagnostics. Such differences are especially significant when the elucidation of a metabolic pathway reveals a key role for a specific protein, and the coding region for that protein is discovered to contain mutations that are linked to a specific aberrant phenotype. These mutations often take the form of a single nucleotide polymorphism (SNP), which maintains the reading frame but causes replacement of a single critical DNA base. Other anomalies such as frame shift mutations are more complex and usually lead to a nonfunctioning protein or no protein at all. Furthermore, because most coding regions contain splice variants, a given mutation is likely to affect more than one protein. The volume of literature relating tumor biology and cancer to specific genetic changes has increased exponentially during the past several years, paralleling similar increases in bioinformatic sophistication. The elucidation of various molecular mechanisms of oncogenesis has led to an understanding of the role that tumor suppressors, oncogenes, and DNA repair genes play in the development of various cancers. Many of these alterations can occur sporadically; conversely, some are inherited. The presence of specific genetic alterations is often used to diagnose a tumor that otherwise would be difficult to verify. Genetic mutations can also can be prognostic indicators and guide the treatment plan of the physician [25].

Sophisticated Approaches to Sequence Comparison

A variety of programs have been created to assist researchers with similarity searches. All of these programs have as their basis some type of scoring algorithm for comparing the fit between sequences. As mentioned earlier, the scoring algorithm is always coded in a form that can be represented in some variation of a two-dimensional matrix with a sequence represented on each axis. Various algorithms operate against the matrix, often using it iteratively by returning for additional passes. After all matrix operations are complete, the best alignment can be visualized by tracing a sequence of scores through the array. Despite many complex variations, the basic process remains unchanged across the entire family of algorithms.

Global Alignment vs. Local Alignment

Some programs are designed to find the best "global" alignment by attempting to match as much of the sequence as possible. Conversely, "local" alignment programs provide greater weight to regions with the highest density of matches; these sequences ultimately form the core of the final alignment. Local-alignment tools are excellent for finding the longest possible exact matches, whereas global-alignments tools are excellent for identifying sequences with statistically close relationships even though they may have subtle differences that hide their similarities. Local alignments are important because they represent conserved regions in related proteins. One advantage to local-alignment problems is that the underlying statistics are better understood than those of global alignments. The simplest case, local alignment without gaps, is trivial because it involves nothing more than adjusting the relative positions of two sequences until the longest region of continuous matches is found. This solution is tantamount to reading the longest run directly from a dot-matrix plot. Figure 2-17 illustrates the basic difference between global- and local-alignment strategies.

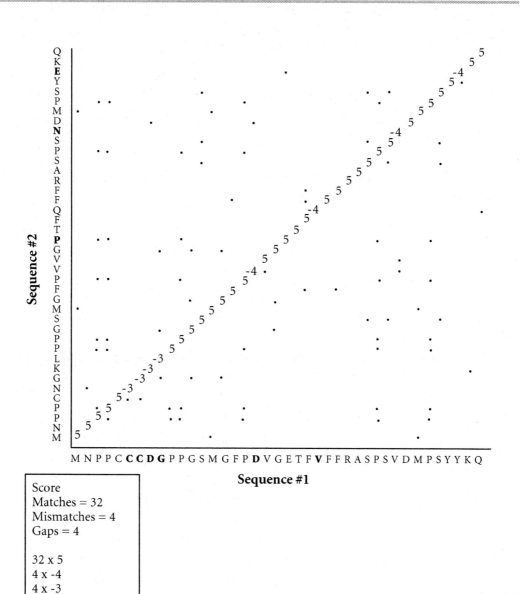

Figure 2-16 Representative comparison matrix for two sequences, including penalties for gaps and misalignments.

Global alignment—highest possible match count

Local alignment—most consecutive matches

Figure 2-17 Global versus local alignment strategies.

Local-Alignment Tools

BLAST, mentioned earlier, is one of the most popular local-alignment tools. Like other local-alignment algorithms, BLAST is able to detect relationships among sequences that share only isolated regions of similarity. The heuristics of traditional BLAST are relatively straightforward. The algorithm first finds "seed" sequences—short homologous segments shared by the query and database sequences. These seeds are then extended in both directions, without including gaps, until the highest scoring sequence is identified.

Like most publicly available bioinformatic algorithms, BLAST is designed to work equally well with protein or DNA sequences. However, it is always better to compare protein translations than their associated DNA sequences. The reason for this bias is complex and related to the statistics that relate chance mutations in individual bases with amino acid substitutions in the final protein. Furthermore, because DNA sequences involve triplets, gaps must be adjusted to accurately fall on reading frame boundaries. Conversely, when noncoding regions are being studied, the option to use protein sequences goes away. Finally, there is one very common case where the statistics of sequence comparison break down: comparisons between coding regions that, for biological reasons, do not contain a broad distribution of different amino acids. Not surprisingly, some statistical studies have shown that as many as one fourth of all residues in protein sequences occur within regions with highly biased amino acid composition. Attempts to align such regions will often generate very high scores despite the fact that the results relate more to the distribution of amino acids in these regions than to their specific order. Consequently, low-complexity alignments have little biological significance and the correspondence between residues that gives rise to unusually high-alignment scores is not statistically significant. Generally speaking, global-alignment approaches are more susceptible to this problem than their local counterparts because they depend less on contiguous matches than on high-alignment counts across an entire sequence. One solution is to set a minimum threshold for the number of contiguous matches that must be present to increment the score.

It is also important for designers of sequence matching algorithms to understand the mechanisms that allow high-alignment scores to be achieved by random chance. Historically, randomly generated sequences have been used to model this process. For proteins, the simplest approach involves constructing sequences using specific known probabilities for the appearance of each residue. The algorithm must then be constructed so that the expected score for aligning a random pair of amino acids is negative. Ignoring this problem results in the creation of algorithms that assign higher scores to longer sequences independent of whether they are biologically related. Unfortunately, the statistical basis of the problem varies from one protein family to another (e.g., membrane proteins have long hydrophobic segments; soluble proteins tend to be more hydrophilic).

Sequence gaps are also a major consideration for alignment experiments. Consider the two sequence comparisons illustrated in Figure 2-18.

The first alignment, which receives the higher of the two scores, depends on two gaps—one in each sequence—for its solution. The second alignment, which fails to match up the glutamic acid residues (E), does not require the creation of any gaps. Which alignment is correct? The answer is not straightforward, but it is important to study the question in the context of sequence evolution. It is well documented that the evolutionary process regularly inserts or deletes amino acids from proteins and that many of these changes do not adversely affect the structures that convey function to these proteins. That being the case, many protein sequences containing parallel structures that create similar functionality can be properly aligned with each other only if

K	L	E	_	**S**		**K**	L	E	S
|		|		|		|			|
K	_	E	H	**S**		**K**	E	H	S

Alignment Score = 3   Alignment Score = 2

The gapped solution produces a higher score than the perfectly aligned solution

Figure 2-18 Two possible alignments for a sequence pair. The gapped solution produces a higher score than the perfectly aligned sequence.

gaps are ignored. Therefore, in most cases, the sequence on the left would represent the best alignment.

Much of the theory behind sequence-alignment algorithms was developed by a small group of pioneering scientists who conducted most of their research in the absence of large databases and fast computers. Despite these limitations, they created work of enduring value that persists in the algorithms and programs of today. One of the great pioneers of this era was Margaret Dayhoff, who published an important reference called the *Atlas of Protein Sequence and Structure.*

This unique book published in the late 1970s contained every protein sequence known at the time, along with associated structural information. The book represented a turning point in the history of biochemistry because it became the foundation for the public database infrastructure [26]. Dayhoff made the important observation that each amino acid in a protein has a predictable likelihood of being replaced in a given time-frame by the evolutionary process. The probability of each of these changes was estimated using sequences that were determined to be at least 85% similar and belonged to a family of related proteins. For each amino acid, the frequency of replacement was determined by adding up the changes at each evolutionary step. A matrix was constructed that contained probabilities for all possible substitutions. The data was then normalized into values that represented the probability that 1 amino acid in 100 would undergo substitution. The resulting values are referred to as percent accepted mutation values (PAM-1). Additional probability matrices for proteins that had undergone

X independent mutations were then derived by multiplying PAM-1 values by themselves X times. The result is a set of matrices—PAM-160, PAM-250, etc. [27, 28].

PAM matrices are normally transformed into "log odds" matrices, which are populated with numbers representing the frequency of change divided by the probability of each amino acid pair aligning by pure chance. (The probability of chance alignment is calculated from the average frequency of occurrence for each amino acid in proteins.) The chance that an alignment between two different amino acids will occur by chance is directly proportional to the probability of each of the amino acids appearing in a protein sequence. Alignments between rare amino acids are considered to be more significant. The complete PAM-250 matrix, in log odds form, is displayed in Table 2-6. Each value was calculated by dividing the frequency of change for an amino acid pair by the probability of a chance alignment. The data come from related proteins that are separated by one step in the evolutionary tree.

The BLOSUM (BLOcks SUbstitution Matrix), first devised by Steve Henikoff in the early 1990s, represents a statistical alternative to PAM [29]. The developmental goal of BLOSUM was to apply a more precise measure of the differences between two proteins—specifically, distantly related proteins. This bias tends to improve the usefulness of BLOSUM for searches involving sequences that contain relatively sparse regions of close evolutionary relatedness. BLOSUM and PAM differ in two very significant Matrix, first devised by Steve Henikoff ways:

- The PAM method assumes that mutations occur at a constant frequency—the same rate that is observed in the short term for any given amino acid. Conversely, BLOSUM matrices are derived by observing all amino acid changes in an aligned region from a related family of proteins, regardless of the level of similarity between the two sequences. Because the proteins are biochemically related, it is expected that they share a common ancestry; closer versus more distant relationships are ignored in the analysis.
- PAM matrices are based on scoring all amino acid positions, whereas BLOSUM matrices are based on conserved positions that occur in blocks representing the most similar regions of related sequences. A detailed comparison of PAM and BLOSUM is beyond the scope of this text, but you can find several excellent sources in the literature or on the Internet.

Table 2-6 PAM-250 Matrix in "Log Odds" Form (Ratios expressed as base 10 logarithms)

	C	S	T	P	A	G	N	D	E	Q	H	R	K	M	I	L	V	F	Y	W
C	12																			
S	0	2																		
T	-2	1	3																	
P	-3	1	0	6																
A	-2	1	1	1	2															
G	-3	1	0	-1	1	5														
N	-4	1	0	-1	0	0	2													
D	-5	0	0	-1	0	1	2	4												
E	-5	0	0	-1	0	0	1	3	4											
Q	-5	-1	-1	0	0	-1	1	2	2	4										
H	-3	-1	-1	0	-1	-2	2	1	1	3	6									
R	-4	0	-1	0	-2	-3	0	-1	-1	1	2	8								
K	-5	0	0	-1	-1	-2	1	0	0	1	0	3	5							
M	-5	-2	-1	-2	-1	-3	-2	-3	-2	-1	-2	0	0	6						
I	-2	-1	0	-2	-1	-3	-2	-2	-2	-2	-2	-2	-2	2	5					
L	-8	-3	-2	-3	-2	-4	-3	-4	-3	-2	-2	-3	-3	4	2	8				
V	-2	-1	0	-1	0	-1	-2	-2	-2	-2	-2	-2	-2	2	4	2	4			
F	-4	-3	-3	-5	-4	-5	-4	-6	-5	-5	-2	-4	-5	0	1	2	-1	9		
Y	0	-3	-3	-5	-3	-5	-2	-4	-4	-4	0	-4	-4	-2	-1	-1	-2	7	10	
W	-8	-2	-5	-6	-6	-7	-4	-7	-7	-5	-3	2	-3	-4	-5	-2	-6	0	0	17
	C	**S**	**T**	**P**	**A**	**G**	**N**	**D**	**E**	**Q**	**H**	**R**	**K**	**M**	**I**	**L**	**V**	**F**	**Y**	**W**

Global-Alignment Tools

Global-alignment algorithms tend to be more complex than local algorithms because they accomplish a more imprecise task—finding the best alignment for a complete end-to-end sequence. Unlike local-alignment algorithms, which can operate in environments where gaps are not permitted, global programs always use gaps in their analysis. The statistical rules that govern global comparisons are enormously complex and, at the time of this writing, incompletely understood. Yet, despite their complexity, global-alignment algorithms are built on the exact same two-dimensional matrix structure as all basic sequence comparisons. At the core of every global-alignment process is an iterative set of scoring operations designed to discover the very best alignment between two sequences. Part of the discovery process necessarily involves uncovering gaps that improve the match. In some sense, the process of identifying a best global fit for two sequences is very similar to many of the newer local-alignment methods that allow the use of gaps because gaps allow expansion of the original seeds beyond regions of mismatch. Differences between gapped local alignments and global alignments are mostly related to scoring rules used throughout the iterative process.

The Needleman-Wunsch algorithm represents a powerful systematic method for identifying the optimal global alignment of two sequences. The following example is adapted from the original paper, which, despite being published more than 30 years ago, maintains its relevance as a reference for the theory behind global comparisons [30].

Table 2-7 encodes the sequences to be compared in a simple two-dimensional matrix. The amino-terminal (N-terminal) end of the protein is at the upper left and the carboxyl-terminal (C-terminal) is at the lower right.

Beginning at the C-terminal ends of the molecules and moving toward the upper left, each cell receives a value equal to its own plus the maximum sum of all downstream values (cells directly below and to the right are excluded). As the process advances, the number in each cell will be the largest number of pair matches that can be found if that cell is used as the origin for an alignment.

Table 2-8 contains the first round, which, except for the PxP alignment, is necessarily composed of all zeros because there are no downstream residues.

The next round, shown in Table 2-9, contains the first nontrivial values. The DxD match is incremented to 2, and all other cells upstream of the PxP match receive a value

Table 2-7 Simple Two-Dimensional Matrix Used to Launch a Needleman-Wunsch Comparison of Two Protein Sequences

	A	D	C	N	S	R	Q	C	L	C	R	P	M
A	1												
S					1								
C			1					1		1			
S					1								
N				1									
R						1					1		
C			1					1		1			
K													
C			1					1		1			
R						1					1		
D		1											
P												1	

of 1. The DxD match receives a 2 because there is a possibility that the sequences could be aligned at residues D and P, as indicated in Figure 2-19. The other residues receive scores of 1 because they may be included in an alignment that contains a downstream match at the C-terminal proline (P). This particular alignment contains a large gap and produces a score of only 2.

The third round, displayed in Table 2-10, assigns incremental values to three RxR matches because each is potentially associated with a C-terminal (downstream) RxP alignment. Note that the arginine (R) near the lower left of the chart inherits a value of 2 from the potential downstream D . . . P alignment identified in Figure 2-19. As one might expect, alignment scores tend to increase toward the upper-left (N-terminal) end

Table 2-8 First Round of the Needleman-Wunsch Algorithm Example

	A	D	C	N	S	R	Q	C	L	C	R	P	M
A	1												0
S					1								0
C			1					1		1			0
S					1								0
N				1									0
R						1					1		0
C			1					1		1			0
K													0
C			1					1		1			0
R						1					1		0
D		1											0
P	0	0	0	0	0	0	0	0	0	0	0	1	0

of the proteins because more residues have the potential to become involved in alignments.

In the next iteration, five cells emerge as potential alignment start sites. Each of these receives a score of 3—the initial value of each cell plus the maximum sum of the downstream values in the original matrix. Table 2-11 displays the array after completion of four scoring rounds.

We have been filling in the array through successive iterations for illustrative purposes only. In principle there is no reason why the scores cannot all be calculated in a single pass. It is very important to remember that the score for an individual cell is the sum of the initial value of that cell plus the maximum value that can be obtained by aligning downstream cells. This process of selecting the best alignment by maximizing

Table 2-9 Second Round of the Needleman-Wunsch Algorithm Example (Note the possible alignment at residues D...P indicated by the score of 2)

	A	D	C	N	S	R	Q	C	L	C	R	P	M
A	1											0	0
S					1							0	0
C			1					1		1		0	0
S					1							0	0
N				1								0	0
R						1					1	0	0
C			1					1		1		0	0
K												0	0
C			1					1		1		0	0
R						1					1	0	0
D	1	2	1	1	1	1	1	1	1	1	1	0	0
P	0	0	0	0	0	0	0	0	0	0	0	1	0

the sum of the downstream scores involves creating gaps that allow the sequences to fit together. After the process is complete, it will be possible to read through the matrix, beginning at the upper-left corner, and trace the path with the highest score. This path represents the best global alignment for the two sequences. Table 2-12 displays the completed matrix.

Careful observation of Table 2-12 reveals two optimal paths or global alignments. These paths are traced through the array from upper left to lower right by selecting the highest-scoring cells that also represent alignments between the sequences (cells that achieved a score of 1 in the first array). In the example, we start with the AxA match at the upper left (row 1, column 1) and proceed through the CxC alignment in row 3,

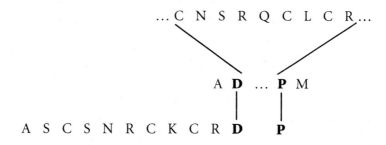

Figure 2-19 Possible alignment with a large gap represented in the Needleman-Wunsch example (Table 2-9).

Table 2-10 Third Round of the Needleman-Wunsch Example
(Each of the RxR matches now receives a value of 2 because they are potentially part of an R…P alignment)

	A	D	C	N	S	R	Q	C	L	C	R	P	M
A	1										1	0	0
S					1						1	0	0
C			1					1		1	1	0	0
S					1						1	0	0
N				1							1	0	0
R						1					2	0	0
C			1					1		1	1	0	0
K											1	0	0
C			1					1		1	1	0	0
R	2	1	1	1	1	2	1	1	1	1	2	0	0
D	1	2	1	1	1	1	1	1	1	1	1	0	0
P	0	0	0	0	0	0	0	0	0	0	0	1	0

CHAPTER 2   INTRODUCTION TO BIOINFORMATICS

Table 2-11 Fourth Round of the Needleman-Wunsch Example
(Note the emergence of five potential alignment start sites)

	A	D	C	N	S	R	Q	C	L	C	R	P	M
A	1									2	1	0	0
S					1					2	1	0	0
C			1					1		3	1	0	0
S					1					2	1	0	0
N				1						2	1	0	0
R						1				2	2	0	0
C			1					1		3	1	0	0
K										2	1	0	0
C	2	2	3	2	2	2	2	3	2	3	1	0	0
R	2	1	1	1	1	2	1	1	1	1	2	0	0
D	1	2	1	1	1	1	1	1	1	1	1	0	0
P	0	0	0	0	0	0	0	0	0	0	0	1	0

column 3 to a fork at NxN and SxS (row 5, column 4; and row 4, column 5; respectively). At this point we must consider two possible alignments; one that matches the serines (S) and one that matches the asparagines (N). The choices, which receive equal scores, are constructed in Figure 2-20. Both possible solutions are depicted in sequence form at the bottom of the figure.

This discussion was designed to review the basic strategies used to align pairs of sequences. We will return to the topic in a later chapter to explore additional concepts, most notably multiple-sequence alignment. Multiple-sequence alignment strategies seek to build families where the best alignment is used as a family profile. This profile can be used for a variety of purposes, including searching sequence databases to identify

Table 2-12 Complete Needleman-Wunsch Example Matrix

	A	D	C	N	S	R	Q	C	L	C	R	P	M
A	8	7	6	6	5	4	4	3	3	2	1	0	0
S	7	7	6	6	6	4	4	3	3	2	1	0	0
C	6	6	7	6	5	4	4	4	3	3	1	0	0
S	6	6	6	5	6	4	4	3	3	2	1	0	0
N	5	5	5	6	5	4	4	3	3	2	1	0	0
R	4	4	4	4	4	5	4	3	3	2	2	0	0
C	3	3	4	3	3	3	3	4	3	3	1	0	0
K	3	3	3	3	3	3	3	3	3	2	1	0	0
C	2	2	3	2	2	2	2	3	2	3	1	0	0
R	2	1	1	1	1	2	1	1	1	1	2	0	0
D	1	2	1	1	1	1	1	1	1	1	1	0	0
P	0	0	0	0	0	0	0	0	0	0	0	1	0

additional members of the family, protein structure prediction, and gene location through open reading frame prediction. Prominent among multiple-sequence alignment strategies is the hidden Markov model (HMM), a statistical method that considers all possible combinations of matches, mismatches, and gaps to generate the best possible global alignment across all the members of the group. HMMs represent one of many possible solutions to such problems. We will also review other algorithms that can be used to identify coding regions, splice sites, and other important genomic features. A major theme of these studies is the leap from sequence to structure—a theme that we will return to many times throughout this book.

	A	D	C	N	S	R	Q	C	L	C	R	P	M
A	8	7	6	6	5	4	4	3	3	2	1	0	0
S	7	7	6	6	6	4	4	3	3	2	1	0	0
C	6	6	7	6	5	4	4	4	3	2	1	0	0
S	6	6	6	5	6	4	4	3	3	2	1	0	0
N	5	5	5	6	5	4	4	3	3	2	1	0	0
R	4	4	4	4	4	5	4	3	3	2	2	0	0
C	3	3	4	3	3	3	3	4	3	3	1	0	0
K	3	3	3	3	3	3	3	3	3	2	1	0	0
C	2	2	3	2	2	2	2	3	2	3	1	0	0
R	2	1	1	1	1	1	1	1	1	1	2	0	0
D	1	2	1	1	1	1	1	1	1	1	1	0	0
P	0	0	0	0	0	0	0	0	0	0	0	1	0

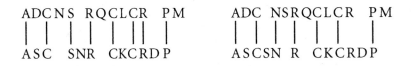

```
ADCNS RQCLCR PM        ADC NSRQCLCR PM
| | | | | | || |        | | | | | | |  |
ASC  SNR CKCRD P       ASCSN R CKCRDP
```

Figure 2-20 Two optimized paths through a Needleman-Wunsch solution matrix.

SUMMARY

This chapter was designed to be a foundation for many important topics that are presented throughout the book. We began with a discussion of contemporary database structure for bioinformatics, proceeded through a description of various options for linking and searching heterogeneous databases, and finally closed with the basics of sequence alignment—the most common type of bioinformatic database search. Each of the sections was designed to focus on basic theory with the intent of creating building blocks for future topics. The database infrastructure discussion included reviews of various coding schemes and database schema issues; the bioinformatic infrastructure section introduced three basic system configurations—federated, linked and indexed, and data warehouse; the XML database discussion was intended to demonstrate the power of markup languages and to describe specific life sciences vocabularies that can be used as data interchange standards; and the discussion of pairwise sequence alignment was presented with a view toward basic algorithms and concepts such as global versus local scoring systems. Each of these concepts and associated underlying strategies will become the basis for more advanced discussions, and most will appear repeatedly as we explore other contemporary topics in computational biology.

ENDNOTES

1. Brown, A. J. P., and Tuite, M. F. (Eds,). *Yeast Gene Analysis. Methods in Microbiology, Vol. 26*. Academic Press, New York, 1998.

2. DeRisi, J. L., Iyer V. R., Brown P. O. 1997. Exploring the metabolic and genetic control of gene expression on a genomic scale. *Science* 278: 680–686.

3. Pringle, J. R., Broach, J. R., and Jones, E. W. (Eds.). *The Molecular and Cellular Biology of the Yeast* Saccharomyces, *Vol. 3. Cell Cycle and Cell Biology*. Cold Spring Harbor Laboratory Press, Cold Spring Harbor, NY, 1997.

4. Walker, G. M. *Yeast Physiology and Biotechnology*. John Wiley and Son, Chichester, UK, 1998.

5. European Molecular Biology Laboratory Web site: www.embl-heidelberg.de/.

6. Berman H. M., Westbrook J., Feng Z., Gilliland G., Bhat T. N., Weissig H., Shindyalov I. N., Bourne P. E. 2000. The Protein Data Bank. *Nucleic Acids Research* 28: 235–242.

7. Benson D. A., Karsch-Mizrachi I., Lipman D. J., Ostell J., Rapp, B. A., Wheeler, D. L. 2004. GenBank Update. *Nucleic Acids Research* 32 (Database issue): D23-D26.

8. This limit was in place at the time of this writing, and may change over time.

9. Haas L. M., Schwarz P. M., Kodali P., Kotlar E., Rice J. E., Swope W. C. 2001. DiscoveryLink: A system for integrated access to life sciences data sources. *IBM Systems Journal* 40: 489–511.

10. Haas L. M., Schwarz P. M., Kodali P., Kotlar E., Rice J. E., Swope W. C. 2000. Integrating life sciences data—with a little garlic. Proceedings of the IEEE International Symposium on Biomedical Engineering, IEEE, New York.

11. Papakonstantinou Y., Garcia-Molina H., Widom J. 1995. Object exchange across heterogeneous information sources. Proceedings of the IEEE Conference on Data Engineering, Taipei, Taiwan; IEEE, New York. 251–260.

12. Tomasic A., Raschid L., Valduriez P. Scaling heterogeneous databases and the design of DISCO. 1996. Proceedings of the 16th International Conference on Distributed Computer Systems, Hong Kong; IEEE, New York.

13. Shan, M. C., Ahmed, R., Davis, J., Du,W., and Kent W. "Pegasus: A Heterogeneous Information Management System" in *Modern Database Systems*. (W. Kim, Ed.) ACM Press (Addison-Wesley Publishing Co.), Reading, MA, 1994.

14. Liu L., Pu C. 1995. The distributed interoperable object model and its application to large-scale interoperable database systems. Proceedings of the Fourth International Conference on Information and Knowledge Management, ACM, New York.

15. Adali S., Candan K., Papakonstantinou Y., Subrahmanian V. S. 1996. Query caching and optimization in distributed mediator systems. Proceedings of the ACM SIGMOD International Conference on Management of Data, Montreal, June 1996; ACM, New York. 137–148.

16. Goble A. A., Stevens R., NG G., Bechofer S., Paton N. W., Baker P. G., Peim M., Brass A. 2001. Transparent access to multiple bioinformatics sources. *IBM Systems Journal* 40(2): 532–551.

17. Incellico. *CELL Technical Overview v 1.6*. Incellico, Inc., 2002.

18. SRS User Guide version 7.0. Copyright Lion Biosciences AG.

19. Wang L., Riethoven J. J. M., Robinson A. J. 2002. XEMBL—distributing EMBL data in XML format. *Bioinformatics* 18(8): 1147–1148.

20. Gelfand M. S., Mironov A. A., Pevzner P. A. 1996. Gene recognition via spliced sequence alignment. *Proceedings of the National Academy of Sciences* 93: 9061–9066.

21. Farber R., Lapedes A., Sirotkin K. 1992. Determination of eukaryotic protein coding regions using neural networks and information theory. Journal of Molecular Biology 226: 471–479.

22. Reese, M. G., Harris, N., and Eeckman, F. "Large Scale Sequencing Specific Neural Networks for Promoter and Splice Site Recognition" in *Biocomputing: Proceedings of the 1996 Pacific Symposium* (L. Hunter and T. E. Klein, Eds.). World Scientific Publishing, Singapore, 1996.

23. "Back-translated" protein sequences are created by translating an amino acid sequence into its corresponding mRNA sequence. Likewise, any mRNA sequence can be readily translated into its corresponding DNA predecessor. Degeneracy in the genetic code prevents exact identification of the third base of each triplet.

24. Kent J. W., Zahler A. M. 2000. The intronerator: exploring introns and alternative splicing in *Caenorhabditis elegans. Nucleic Acids Research* 28(1): 91–93.

25. Ganjavi H., Malkin D. 2002. Genetics of childhood cancer. *Clinical Orthopedics* 401: 75–87.

26. Dayhoff, M. O. (Ed.), Schwartz, R., and Orcutt, B. C. "A Model of Evolutionary Change in Proteins" in *Atlas of Protein Sequence and Structure, Vol. 5, Suppl. 3.* National Biomedical Research Foundation, Washington, D.C., 1978. 345–352.

27. Altschul S. F. 1991. Amino acid substitution matrices from an information theoretic perspective. *Journal of Molecular Biology* 219: 555–565.

28. Altschul S. F. 1993. A protein alignment scoring system sensitive at all evolutionary distances. *Journal of Molecular Biology* 36: 290–300.

29. Henikoff S., Henikoff J. G. 1992. Amino acid substitution matrices from protein blocks. *Proceedings of the National Academy of Sciences* 89(22): 10915–10919.

30. Needleman S. B. and Wunsch C. D. 1970. A general method applicable to the search for similarities in the amino acid sequence of two proteins. *Journal of Molecular Biology* 48: 443–453.

Gene Structure

INTRODUCTION

Biologists, biochemists, religious leaders, and philosophers have been known to debate the criteria that define life. The question is not difficult for higher organisms—nobody would debate that humans and other animals are living creatures. However, as we move down the evolutionary tree from higher organisms to plants and bacteria and finally to viruses and prions (infectious agents composed of peptides), the question becomes more philosophical. Furthermore, the line that divides living from nonliving becomes blurred when one compares very simple organisms such as viruses with very complex chemical structures. The subtle differences that mark the transition from large complex chemical structures to simple organisms are without doubt one of the most difficult to nail down. Some might even argue that nonbiological structures such as mountains, oceans, and rivers are, in some sense, alive because they display some of the dynamic characteristics of living creatures.

Whereas the full debate is beyond the scope of this book, one view has important implications for our discussion. The view to which we refer holds that something can be considered "living" only if it contains the information necessary to code for its own structure. Whether we are discussing a virus, bacterium, or higher organism, that information is contained in a structure we have come to know as a genome. All genomes, from viruses to humans, are designed around linear sequences of nucleotides, and these sequences—with minor exceptions—share a universal code. One of the most significant achievements in molecular biology was the elucidation of the DNA code words. The principle approach involved synthesizing mRNAs containing repeating sequence patterns and observing the polypeptides that were created when these messages were translated in cell-free protein synthesis systems.

The code has a much more subtle meaning than the specification of a chain of amino acids because it is the final folded structure that confers biological activity upon a protein. The concept is fascinating because much of the information embodied in a nucleotide sequence is too subtle to be discerned by direct analysis of the sequence itself. It is not possible, for example, to predict the final folded structure of a protein by reading the base DNA sequence. In principle all the necessary information resides in the sequence, but the complex set of splicing reactions, translational variations, and post-translational modifications cannot be accurately predicted using any technology in existence today. However, as our understanding of nucleotide sequence features continues to advance, we move closer to having such predictive capabilities.

The present discussion focuses on the general structures that characterize coding regions and the biological processes that shape them. These processes include well-characterized transcriptional-splicing events in addition to physical alterations at the gene level. Our goal is to create a framework for understanding the intersection between features and processes that affect the information content of the genome and computational tools for their identification.

This discussion closes with a brief focus on high-throughput sequencing of whole genomes. Central to this important endeavor is a new class of algorithms designed to facilitate the assembly of millions of overlapping fragments into a single sequence. Moreover, complete genome assembly involves a portfolio of computational approaches including, but not limited to, multiple-sequence alignment, pattern discovery, and statistical techniques for judging sequence relatedness. In this regard, this discussion sets the stage for Chapter 4, which focuses on many of these techniques and strategies.

THE CENTRAL DOGMA OF MOLECULAR BIOLOGY

The elucidation of the structure of DNA predates the writing of this chapter by almost exactly 50 years. At that time, our understanding of the genome was limited to chemical structure; the first molecular biologists were x-ray crystallographers, physicists, and physical chemists—Francis Crick, Rosalyn Franklyn, James Watson, Maurice Wilkins, and others. The discovery of the double-helix structure of DNA led Watson and Crick to suggest a mechanism for its replication in their landmark paper published in the April 25, 1953 issue of *Nature* [1]. Structure suggesting function was to become a recurring theme in molecular biology. In 1953, the basic structure of the cell was well understood. Chromosomes, composed of DNA and presumed to be the genetic material, were known to be nuclear structures. Protein synthesis, however, was already known as a cytosolic process associated with structures known as ribosomes that have no relationship to the nucleus. A piece of the puzzle was missing. There had to be a mechanism for transferring information from the chromosomes inside the nucleus to the protein synthesizing machinery in the surrounding cytoplasm.

The proposed solution, one of the most insightful in the history of twentieth-century science, involved a messenger molecule. This messenger, it was believed, would somehow be transformed into a transcript of the chromosomal material prior to being transported outside the nucleus, where it would serve as a template for protein synthesis. Today the concept seems obvious; in the mid-1950s, when Sydney Brenner and his colleagues first proposed the mechanism, however, few biologists were willing to subscribe to such a wild theory. In those days, the concept of a flexible messenger molecule that could serve as a template for a gene sequence was very difficult to envision: The DNA code words had yet to be discovered, the protein synthesis process was shrouded in mystery, and the vision of DNA as a template for another molecule had yet to be articulated. However, what made this proposal unique was not its reliance on undiscovered biochemical processes, but its vision of information transfer. In 1953, long before the discovery of messenger RNA, Sydney Brenner and a small group of molecular biologists were already beginning to think about gene expression in terms of a process built on distinct information-transfer steps. Molecular biology was already transforming itself into an information science.

The discovery of messenger RNA (mRNA) was an important milestone because it allowed researchers to outline the basic flow of information from DNA to mRNA to protein. This flow is often referred to as the "central dogma" of molecular biology. Over the years, this dogma proved to be somewhat less than perfect because information can also flow in the reverse direction. Reverse transcription, the process that facilitates this reverse flow, depends on a class of enzymes called reverse transcriptases. Retroviruses use reverse transcriptase enzymes to synthesize viral DNA that becomes embedded in the host's chromosomes. (HIV is one of many deadly retroviruses.) However, despite such exceptions, the basic flow of information follows the central dogma.

The process flow from gene to protein has become a framework for discovery, and over the past 50 years virtually all the molecular-level details have been elucidated. The fact that sequences of DNA bases were the basic building blocks of genes was apparent many years before the mechanisms of transcription and translation were understood. Over the years, logistically brilliant experiments revealed much about the mechanisms of gene expression. These experiments included identification of the DNA code words, start and stop sequences, ribosomal binding sites for mRNA, splice sequences, and many other process control points. Bioinformatics, which lives at the core of each of these discoveries, has evolved to keep pace with our increasingly complex understanding of these processes.

THE GENETIC CODE

At the heart of bioinformatics are the three-letter DNA code words for the 20 amino acids. In the early days of molecular biology, the length and number of words in the code were unknown. It was also necessary to determine the direction of reading of the code. Today we take the polarity for granted and use a simple shorthand notation that reads left to right. It is assumed that the 5' end of the mRNA molecule is at the left and the 3' end at the right. (The residue on the left has a 5' phosphate group, and the one on the right has a free 3' hydroxyl.) Marshall Nirenberg and Philip Leder were the first to demonstrate the polarity of the system. They discovered, for example, that GUU codes for valine, whereas UUG codes for leucine. Likewise, the sequence AAAUUU codes for lysine-phenylalanine but not phenylalanine-lysine.

After the direction of translation was established, a series of ingenious experiments, carried out in the labs of Marshall Nirenberg, Har Gobind Khorana, and Severo Ochoa, was used to determine the sequence of bases in the code. A key strategy relied on synthetic polynucleotides that contained repeating dinucleotides and trinucleotides. For example, a polynucleotide containing repeating dinucleotide subunits such as UCUCU-CUCUCUCUCU contains two types of triplets: UCU and CUC. If the code is built on three-letter words, then this sequence should code for a polypeptide containing just two amino acids in alternating sequence. In this case, the encoded peptide is Ser-Leu-Ser-Leu-Ser. More interesting were the results obtained from sequences containing repeating sequences of trinucleotides. For example, poly UUC codes for three different polypeptides—polyphenylalanine, polyserine, and polyleucine. This result follows from the fact that poly UUC contains three different reading frames:

UUC-UUC-UUC-UUC-UUC
UCU-UCU-UCU-UCU-UCU
CUU-CUU-CUU-CUU-CUU

More complex examples were also synthesized and tested. Table 3-1 contains a list of these sequences, the resulting triplets across all reading frames, and the contents of the translated polypeptides. In this table, each sequence is built from repeating subunits of two, three, or four bases, and codes for a unique series of amino acids. Such experiments were used to help determine the DNA code words. Note the importance of reading frame alignment, a theme that persists in modern computational biology.

These and other experiments facilitated rapid progress, and by 1965 the combined results of the Nirenberg, Khorana, and Ochoa laboratories had been used to identify all the code words. Four important features of the code merit mention [2]:

• No punctuation or signal is necessary between the end of one word and the beginning of the next; reading frames must be correctly set at the beginning of each read. This fact underscores the requirement for an initiation signal in the mRNA sequence that the protein synthesizing machinery (the ribosome) can recognize as the beginning of a polypeptide.

Table 3-1 Synthetic Polynucleotides Used to Solve the Genetic Code

Repeating Subunits	Resulting Three-Letter Codes	Resultant Polypeptide Contents
UC	UCU, CUC	Ser, Leu
AG	AGA, GAG	Arg, Glu
UG	UGU, GUG	Cys, Val
AC	ACA, CAG	Thr, His
UUC	UUC, UCU, CUU	Phe, Ser, Leu
AAG	AAG, AGA, GAA	Lys, Arg, Glu
GAU	GAU, AUG, UGA	Asp, Met
GUA	GUA, UAG, AGU	Val, Ser
UAC	UAC, ACU, CUA	Tyr, Leu, Ser, Ile
UAUC	UAU, CUA, UCU, AUC	Tyr, Leu, Ser, Ile
UUAC	UUA, CUU, ACU, UAC	Leu, Thr, Tyr

- The code is degenerate in the sense that most amino acids are coded for by more than a single triplet. However, there is no code word that specifies more than one amino acid. The term *degenerate*, in this context, does not mean imprecise. Two amino acids, tryptophan and methionine, have only a single code word. The amount of degeneracy varies among the others.
- The third base is less specific than the others. In almost all cases, the degeneracy occurs in the third base. (Exceptions are arginine, leucine, and serine.) In addition, when two different amino acids share the same first two letters, the third position of one will consist only of purines (A or G) and the third position of the other only of pyrimidines (U or C). For example, histidine has two possible code words (CAU, CAC); glutamine shares the first two (CAA, CAG). In the case of histidine, the third

letter is always a pyrimidine (U or C), and for glutamine the third letter is always a purine (A or G).

- Of the 64 triplets, 3 do not code for amino acids: UAG, UAA, and UGA. These words are termination signals that mark the end of a protein sequence.

Table 3-2 displays the complete codon dictionary expressed as RNA triplets. In most cases the third base can vary for a given amino acid. Three exceptions—arginine, leucine, and serine—vary in other positions. Tryptophan and methionine have only a single code word. All codons are read in the 5' → 3' direction. Stop or termination signals are indicated in red. AUG (Met) is the start sequence resulting in an n-terminal methionine being present in all unmodified proteins.

Surprisingly, the nucleotide code words are preserved throughout evolution from the simplest bacterial cells through the most complex eukaryotes with relatively few exceptions. (Table 3-3 lists exceptions to the standard code; NCBI and other public data sources refer to numbered translation tables as part of the annotation for each sequence record. These references are preserved in the table.) This fact has been invaluable to computational biologists because it has allowed consistent measurements of evolutionary distances between organisms across the boundaries of both complexity and time. Statistical evaluations of the differences between nucleotide sequences are more sensitive than similar analyses of protein sequences because they contain more information (e.g., wobble base differences that do not alter the amino acid sequence and differences in noncoding regions).

Additional exceptions to the standard code continue to be discovered. For example, ACG has been found to initiate translation of certain proteins in adeno-associated virus type 2, and CUG is the initiation codon for one of the two alternative products of the human c-myc gene. These minor differences can become significant when they complicate the process of sequence-homology searching. NCBI and other public data sources typically refer to numbered translation tables as part of the database annotation for each sequence.

With today's gene-amplification technologies it is possible, in principle, to isolate ancient fossil DNA from extinct organisms and to compare conserved regions to measure the evolutionary distance between these and more modern creatures. The fact that all organisms seem to share the same genetic code also facilitated the launch of

Table 3-2 The 64 Triplets That Comprise the STANDARD GENETIC CODE

UUU	Phe	UCU	Ser	UAU	Tyr	UGU	Cys
UUC	Phe	UCC	Ser	UAC	Tyr	UGC	Cys
UUA	Leu	UCA	Ser	UAA	**Stop**	UGA	**Stop**
UUG	Leu	UCG	Ser	UAG	**Stop**	UGG	Trp
CUU	Leu	CCU	Pro	CAU	His	CGU	Arg
CUC	Leu	CCC	Pro	CAC	His	CGC	Arg
CUA	Leu	CCA	Pro	CAA	Gln	CGA	Arg
CUG	Leu	CCG	Pro	CAG	Gln	CGG	Arg
AUU	Ile	ACU	Thr	AAU	Asn	AGU	Ser
AUC	Ile	ACC	Thr	AAC	Asn	AGC	Ser
AUA	Ile	ACA	Thr	AAA	Lys	AGA	Arg
AUG	Met	ACG	Thr	AAG	Lys	AGG	Arg
GUU	Val	GCU	Ala	GAU	Asp	GGU	Gly
CUC	Val	GCC	Ala	GAC	Asp	GGC	Gly
GUA	Val	GCA	Ala	GAA	Glu	GGA	Gly
GUG	Val	GCG	Ala	GAG	Glu	GGG	Gly

Table 3-3 Exceptions to the Standard Genetic Code

Codon	Meaning	Comments
Standard Code Table (NCBI #1)		
CUG	Start	Occasionally used as start codon (Leu)
UUG	Start	Occasionally used as start codon (Leu)
Vertebrate Mitochondrial Code (NCBI #2)		
AGA	Stop	
AGG	Stop	
AUA	Met	
UGA	Trp	
AUU	Start	Homo sapiens
AUA, AUC, AUU	Start	Mus
GUG	Start	Coturnix, Gallus
Yeast Mitochondrial Code (NCBI #3)		
AUA	Met	
CUU,CUC,CUA,CUG	Thr	
UGA	Trp	
CGA, CGC		Absent

(continues)

Table 3-3 *(continued)*

Codon	Meaning	Comments
Mold, Protozoan, Coelenterate Mitochondrial Code, and Mycoplasma/ Spiroplasma Code (NCBI #4)		
UGA	Trp	
UUA, UUG, CUG	Start	Trypanosoma
AUU, AUA	Start	Leishmania
AUU, AUA, AUG	Start	Tetrahymena
AUU, AUA, AUG, AUC, GUG, GUA	Start	Paramecium
Invertebrate Mitochondrion (NCBI #5)		
AGA, AGG	Ser	
AUA	Met	
UGA	Trp	
AGG		Absent in Drosophila
AUA, AUU	Start	
AUC	Start	Apis
GUC	Start	Polyplacophora
UUG	Start	Ascaris, Caenorhabditis

Table 3-3 *(continued)*

Codon	Meaning	Comments
Ciliate, Dasycladacean and Hexamita Nuclear Code (NCBI #6)		
UAG	Gln	
Echinoderm Mitochondrial Code (NCBI #9)		
AAA	Asn	
AGA	Ser	
AGG	Ser	
UGA	Trp	
Euplotid Nuclear Code (NCBI #10)		
UGA	Cys	
Bacterial Code (NCBI #11)		
GUG, UUG, AUU, CUG	Start	No changes to amino acid code words
Alternative Yeast Nuclear Code (NCBI #12)		
CUG	Ser	

(continues)

Table 3-3 (continued)

Codon	Meaning	Comments
Ascidian Mitochondrial Code (NCBI #13)		
AGA, AGG	Gly	
AUA	Met	
UGA	Trp	
Flatworm Mitochondrial Code (NCBI #14)		
AAA	Asn	
AGA, AGG	Ser	
UAA	Tyr	
UGA	Trp	
Blepharisma Nuclear Code (NCBI #15)		
UAG	Gln	

Source: The National Center for Biotechnology Information, Bethesda, Maryland

molecular biology by allowing genes to be cloned in bacterial chromosomes. Bacterial gene cloning provided a critical advantage to early molecular biologists by providing a simple platform for growing and selecting clones based on well-characterized mutations that were linked to cloned sequences. The basic idea was to attach a bacterial sequence coding for a recognizable characteristic (e.g., temperature sensitivity) to the gene that was to be cloned. It then became straightforward to use the new characteristic to select cells from the culture that contained the newly cloned gene. Once selected, these cells could be grown in quantity as a source of the protein coded for by the cloned gene. However, this technique has drawbacks. most notably the lack of enzymes that catalyze many of the post-translational protein modifications that are common in higher organisms. In actuality, the differences are more complex and display variability between higher organisms as well. Responding to these challenges, molecular biologists have since created a number of different translation systems, including cell-free designs that contain all the essential intracellular components—enzymes, ribosomes, etc.—for protein synthesis. Table 3-4 lists various protein translation systems and their behavior with regard to key post-translational modifications.

It is important to note that the folding process for proteins is substantially different in lower and higher organisms. For the most part, folding is a post-translational event in higher organisms and a cotranslational event in lower organisms, meaning that bacterial proteins fold as they are translated on the ribosome, whereas eukaryotic proteins often complete the folding process after they detach from the ribosome. Eukaryotic systems are more complex and often employ both enzyme systems for post-translational modifications and "chaperones" (proteins that are involved in the folding process). We return to the folding process in Chapter 5, which is devoted to translation and the protein synthesizing machinery.

Table 3-4 Various Translation Systems and Their Characteristics

	Bacteria	**Yeast**	**Insect**	**Mammalian Cell Culture**
N-linked Glycosylation	No	High mannose	Simplified-no sialic acid	Complex
O-linked Glycosylation	No	Yes	Yes	Yes
Phosphorylation	No	Yes	Yes	Yes
Acetylation	No	Yes	Yes	Yes
Acylation	No	Yes	Yes	Yes
Y-carboxylation	No	No	No	Yes

STRUCTURE AND CONTENT OF THE GENOME

The human genome contains approximately 25,000 coding regions. This number is only an estimate, and as we have discussed previously, most coding regions contain six reading frames (three in each direction) in addition to multiple splice sites. This complexity has made it difficult to accurately count the number of coding regions. Over time, researchers will identify and sequence every human protein, matching each to a specific coding region. Only when this laborious task is complete will we have a completely accurate count. In the absence of a precise number, estimates have ranged from as few as 20,000 to as many as 100,000 genes. Various bioinformatic techniques for identifying open reading frames have helped reduce the range of possibilities, and today most researchers believe that the human genome contains approximately 25,000 coding regions.

Although the gene count remains imprecise, the number of bases of DNA does not—approximately 2.91 billion bases were identified in the human genome sequencing project that concluded in early 2001 [3]. On first glance the numbers seem counterintuitive—nearly 3 billion bases containing 25,000 coding regions, each approximately 1,000 bases in length, coding for 1 to 2 million proteins. Statistical analysis reveals that only 1.1% of the genome is composed of exons (protein-coding sequences), 24% of the bases are found in introns (intervening sequences), and 75% are located in intergenic regions. Furthermore, duplications of extremely long segmental blocks, sometimes nearly the length of whole chromosomes, are not uncommon. If these numbers are correct, the human genome is composed of approximately 32 million bases that directly code for protein and 2.9 billion bases that have other functions; perhaps structural or regulatory. It is important to point out that a large number of the variations responsible for the step up in complexity—the million plus proteins mentioned above—are post-translational modifications such as glycosylation, acetylation, methylation, and processing steps that remove n-terminal amino acids. However, the enzymes that catalyze these, and other genome-level biochemical reactions such as replication and transcription, are also included in the overall gene count. Subtracting these sequences from the total count would undoubtedly leave a surprisingly small number of coding regions.

REGULATORY MESSAGES

This picture of the genome is further complicated by the emergence of a new class of RNA molecule that provides purely regulatory functions [4, 5, 6, 7, 8, 9]. These messages are not translated into proteins but play an important role in modulating the rate of translation in addition to directly causing changes in chromosomal DNA (see the following sidebar). Such mRNAs may be spliced from other transcripts or directly coded for in the genome—a fact that further complicates the gene-counting process.

REGULATORY RNA MOLECULES

RNA, once viewed as an information shuttle between chromosomal DNA and the protein synthesizing machinery, has recently emerged as one of the most important regulatory molecules in the cell. The processes by which RNA molecules regulate gene expression are often referred to as RNA interference (RNAi). Two major pathways and classes of regulatory RNA molecules have been identified.

The first class, small interfering RNAs (siRNAs), function as mediators of sequence-specific degradation of mRNA molecules, preventing them from being translated into protein. The process involves an enzyme complex—RNA-induced silencing complex (RISC)—which uses an siRNA sequence as a template to identify complementary mRNA sequences for degradation before they can be translated into protein. Surprisingly, these special molecules have the property of inhibiting the very genes that they were originally transcribed from. The second class, microRNAs (miRNAs), exert their regulatory effects by directly blocking the translation process rather than through mRNA degradation. Small temporal RNAs (stRNAs), a subset of the miRNA class, appear during development—thus the term *temporal*. Like other miRNAs, stRNAs regulate development by mediating sequence-specific repression of mRNA translation.

Both siRNAs and miRNAs are small molecules, 20 to 30 bases in length. Because they are relatively small, both went undiscovered for many years; they were accidentally discarded during experiments that required purifying longer RNA species that code for protein. Both miRNAs and stRNAs are cleaved from larger double-stranded structures by an enzyme known as Dicer. Long (approximately 70 nucleotides) stretches of RNA that behave as substrates for the Dicer enzyme have the property of self-complementarity—they readily form double-stranded structures by folding into a hairpin shape, bringing two complementary sequences alongside each other. However, miRNAs and siRNAs display subtle mechanistic differences. Most notably, siRNAs are always exactly complementary to the sequences they inhibit, whereas miRNAs exhibit a small level of base-pair mismatch relative to their target sequences. The sequences that give rise to these molecules have been conserved through hundreds of millions of years of evolution, and it is believed that they originally evolved as a defense mechanism against RNA viruses in plants [10,11].

The two eukaryotic regulatory mechanisms are contrasted in Figure 3-1. In the figure, miRNAs and siRNAs are produced by the enzyme Dicer from longer, double-stranded RNAs. One pathway involves recognition and degradation of specific mRNA species by the RISC enzyme complex. A second pathway directly blocks translation into protein at the ribosome. This pathway only utilizes single-stranded RNAs for regulation (miRNAs), whereas the former can utilize double-stranded RNAs.

Small RNAs in general have been implicated in alterations at the chromosome level that result in long-term changes to gene-expression patterns. These effects are termed "epigenetic," meaning that they can cross generations but are not the result of changes to the chromosomal DNA sequence [12, 13, 14, 15]. Such structural changes are becoming critical to our understanding of developmental processes such as tissue-specific stem cell differentiation.

The enormous complexity associated with these control mechanisms is likely to revolutionize our understanding of the genome over the next several years. Coding regions have historically been defined by the protein sequences they contain. Not surprisingly, much of contemporary bioinformatics focuses on statistical methods for identifying traditional protein coding regions. However, as mentioned earlier, we now know that the portion of the genome that codes directly for proteins is extremely small. Consequently,

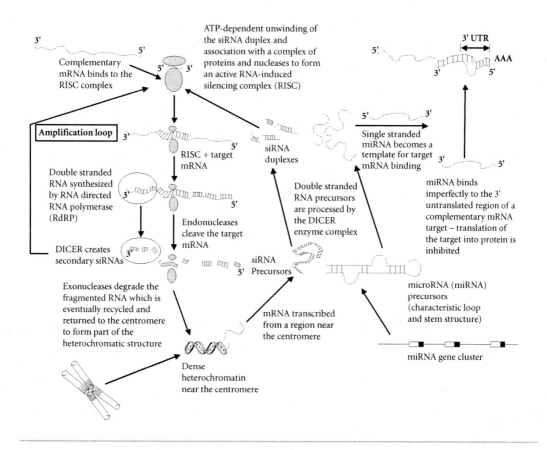

Figure 3-1 Two mechanisms for transcriptional regulation involving small RNA molecules. Micro RNA (miRNAs) and small interfering RNAs (siRNAs) are produced by the enzyme Dicer from longer, double-stranded RNAs. One pathway involves recognition and degradation of specific mRNA species by an enzyme complex known as RISC. A second pathway directly blocks translation into protein at the ribosome. This pathway only utilizes single-stranded RNAs for regulation (miRNAs), whereas the former can utilize double-stranded RNAs.

a new view consistent with a genome whose primary function is to code for molecules that regulate the expression of a relatively small number of coding regions is beginning to emerge.

Although we do not yet understand all of the DNA-level features associated with these control sequences, it is clear that certain structures, such as inverted repeat sequences, are a common theme. For example, a computational biologist, searching for siRNA or miRNA candidates, would undoubtedly begin by finding sequences of approximately 70 nucleotides that are flanked on each side by inverted repeat regions in the range of 20 to 30 bases [16]. Further statistical analysis on known small RNAs will enable researchers to further refine such a search. An example of such a sequence is the highly conserved let-7 gene displayed in Figure 3-2 [17]. The figure includes prespliced transcripts from three organisms. Each sequence contains a highly complementary segment that folds to form hairpin containing a stem and loop structure. Within the sequence is a highly conserved 21 to 23 nucleotide segment that represents the final processed transcript. This conserved transcript is generated by the Dicer enzyme complex, which recognizes and processes double-stranded stem and loop structures. After the final processed segment is released from the larger transcript, it becomes a template that binds to the 3' untranslated region (3' UTR) of complementary mRNAs, regulating their translation into protein. Because let-7 is a key regulator of developmental timing, and because its appearance is highly regulated by the cell cycle, it is classified as a small temporal RNA (stRNA).

CHROMOSOMAL STRUCTURE

It would be inappropriate to end this discussion without mentioning an often-neglected topic that has tremendous implications for gene expression: the three-dimensional structure of chromosomal DNA. Chromosomal DNA is often thought of as a database containing coded information about proteins and, more recently, regulatory messages. However, every DNA sequence contains a second, more subtle, layer of information related to its own secondary structure. More specifically, chromosomal DNA contains specific binding sites for various enzymes and proteins that facilitate a number of structural changes in the chromosomes themselves.

Chromosomal structure varies greatly across different phases of the cell cycle. Interphase chromatin, the form that exists between mitotic cell divisions, is a tangled mass that occupies most of the nucleus. Mitotic chromosomes are a stark contrast to interphase structures because they are well-organized compact entities with a reproducible ultrastructure. Chromosomes of both forms, and the transitional structures in between, are composed of a single folded duplex DNA fiber that runs the entire length of the

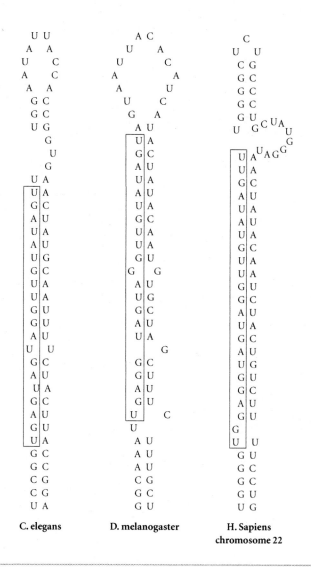

Figure 3-2 Prespliced let-7 stRNA sequences from three organisms. Note that each sequence contains a highly complementary segment that folds to form a double-stranded RNA. This double-stranded structure is recognized by the Dicer enzyme complex, which transforms stRNAs into single-stranded templates that ultimately regulate the translation of complementary target mRNAs. The enclosed region in each sequence correspond to the final processed let-7 transcript. This region, which is reliably 21 to 23 nucleotides long, is highly conserved among a broad range of higher organisms.

chromosome. Whether we are discussing interphase chromatin (the most relevant form for this book) or the mitotic chromosome, it is necessary to explain the packaging of a single, extremely long molecule of DNA into a form that can be transcribed or replicated and can become more or less compressed through various phases of the cell cycle.

Chromosomal DNA displays two major morphologies: euchromatin and heterochromatin. Euchromatin is relatively dispersed and occupies most of the nucleus. Heterochromatin is densely packed and resembles the DNA in mitotic chromosomes. It is typically found at the centromere (a constricted region of the chromosome that contains attachment points to the mitotic spindle) and passes through the cell cycle essentially unchanged. Specific DNA sequences are associated with the centromere and a small conserved fragment, known as CEN, can replace its counterpart on another chromosome with no apparent consequence. This region, which has been well characterized in yeast, is less well understood in higher eukaryotes. CEN is comprised of three segments, CDE-I, CDE-II, and CDE-III:

- CDE-I is a 9bp sequence, conserved with minor variations, at one boundary of all centromeres.
- CDE-II is an 80 to 90bp A-T rich (> 90% A-T) sequence found in all centromeres; its function may depend more on length than sequence.
- CDE-III is an 11bp highly conserved sequence located at the boundary opposite CDE-I of all centromeres. The length of CDE-III is not totally clear because flanking sequences, which are not totally conserved, may be required for function.

A sample CEN region is depicted in Figure 3-3.

With very few exceptions, heterochromatic DNA is not transcribed, meaning that it does not contain active genes. It remains completely condensed and transcriptionally repressed throughout the life of the interphase nucleus. Conversely, euchromatin contains all the active genes in a cell despite the fact that most of this DNA does not code for protein; location in euchromatin is required, but not sufficient for transcription.

Another important structure, the telomere, seals the end of all chromosomes. The term *seal* is significant because if the telomere is removed, the ends become sticky in the sense that they will react with other chromosomes. Telomeric DNA sequences are con-

TCACATGAT GATCTTATTATATTTAATCTAAAAAATTAAAAAAAATTTTTTTATAT...

AGTGTACTA CTAGAATAATATAAATTAGATTTTTTAATTTTTTTTAAAAAAATATA

CDE-I CDE-II

...ATATCTAAATATTATATATAATTTTATATTAAAATATATAAAATT **TGATTTCCGAA**

TATAGATTTATAATATATATTAAAATATAATTTTATATATTTTAA **ACTAAAGGGTT**

CDE-III

Figure 3-3 Three conserved regions are evident at the centromere of all eukaryotic chromosomes.

served from plant to human, so the structure seems to follow universal principals. Each telomere consists of a long series of short tandem repeats that can be described by the general form $C_n(A/T)_m$, where $n > 1$ and $m = 1$ to 4 on one strand, and the same formula with G substituted for C on the complementary strand. Furthermore, telomeres contain discontinuities in the form of single-stranded breaks whose structures prevent them from being recognized by the ligase enzyme that normally closes such gaps in a single DNA strand. The final portion of each sequence contains single-stranded DNA that is blocked, presumably by being organized into a hairpin structure, so that the very end is protected from attack by nucleases. (The protruding single-stranded portion is an extension of the G-rich strand.) Other, more complex stabilizing structures have been proposed that involve multiple hairpins and loops. These constructs can be modeled using algorithms that combine sequence information with the known physical properties of nucleotides.

Telomeres are dynamic structures. Failure to replicate to the end of the chromosome always results in the loss of bases. The enzyme telomerase corrects this problem by adding replacement fragments to the end of the DNA fiber. It is a reverse transcriptase enzyme that uses an mRNA template to lengthen the single-stranded segment at the end of the structure. This dynamic equilibrium is also maintained using a group of DNA binding proteins that regulate the overall length of the chromosome. The reverse transcriptase function of telomerase is depicted in Figure 3-4. It is very similar to other reverse transcriptase reactions such as those implicated in the replication of HIV and other retroviruses.

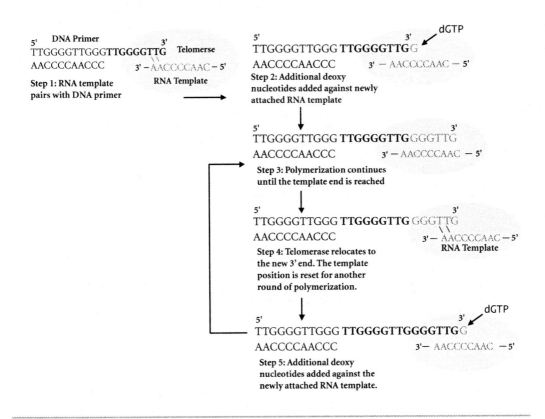

Figure 3-4 Telomerase functions by adding G and T bases at the end of a single-stranded sequence against a short complementary mRNA fragment. When polymerization reaches the end of the mRNA fragment, the message translocates and polymerization continues. The entire process is modulated by a group of proteins that function to regulate the length of the telomere. Various experiments with mutant phenotypes have revealed that telomere length is controlled by a cluster of binding proteins. Stability to the chromosome end is conferred by a closed-loop structure formed between the single-stranded 3' end and upstream double-stranded structures.

Nucleosomes

The compact nature of euchromatin renders most DNA sequences structurally inaccessible and functionally inactive. The difference between active and inactive regions is related to a hierarchical structure that exposes some sequences and not others. All higher organisms share these structural motifs. The primary structure is composed of nucleosomes, which contain approximately 200bp of DNA, organized around an octamer of small basic proteins called histones. The structure may be visualized as a cylinder with DNA wrapped around the outside. In almost all higher organisms, the length of DNA directly associated with the histone core is about 146bp. Core sections are connected by linker DNA, which can vary from as few as 8bp to as many as 114bp. The second level of organization is defined by the coiling of a series of nucleosomes into a helical array that is found in both interphase and mitotic chromosomes. A third level of organization involves further packing of the helical array—a structure that is present in heterochromatin and mitotic euchromatin. First-level structures have a packing ratio of approximately 6, second-level structures raise the number to about 40, and third-level structures achieve packing numbers as high as 10,000. Figure 3-5 depicts a typical nucleosome-DNA structure.

Both replication and transcription require unwinding of the DNA to allow access by various enzymes. This unwinding implies changes at all three levels of structure. Because the RNA polymerase enzyme complex is similar in size to the nucleosome, some change must take place in the DNA-histone complex to allow the polymerase to transcribe a nucleosome-associated DNA sequence. (Essentially, all transcription occurs across the surface of nucleosomes.)

This process is fairly well understood from a mechanical perspective. As the RNA polymerase complex moves along the helix, the DNA strand is displaced from the histone core. The polymerase moves rapidly through the first 30 base pairs on the nucleosome just before dramatically slowing down. Beyond this point, each base pair of movement creates significant positive supercoiling pressure on the helix because it is still fastened to the nucleosome. The structure is analogous to a coiled telephone wire fastened at one end and free at the other. An object sliding along the wire will tend to tighten the coils in its path—this tightening is known as positive pressure. At the halfway point, positive supercoiling forces cause the helix to eject the histone octamer and the transcription process suddenly accelerates. Through a process that is not totally understood, the histone complex stays in contact with the DNA strand and re-associates behind the RNA polymerase complex. Figure 3-6 mechanistically depicts this process.

Heterochromatin and Epigenetic Inheritance

The formation of heterochromatin is not strictly defined by sequence. Various processes such as translocation and transfection / integration by retroviruses can transfer genes to positions adjacent to heterochromatin. These genes often become inactive as a result of their new location. The closer a gene lies to an existing heterochromatic region, the greater the chance that it will be inactivated.

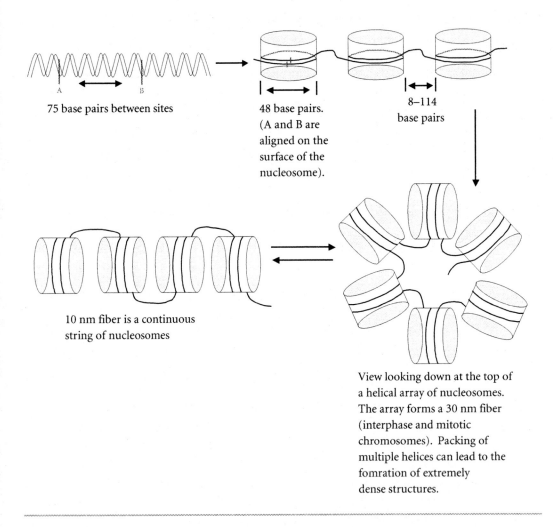

75 base pairs between sites

48 base pairs. (A and B are aligned on the surface of the nucleosome).

8–114 base pairs

10 nm fiber is a continuous string of nucleosomes

View looking down at the top of a helical array of nucleosomes. The array forms a 30 nm fiber (interphase and mitotic chromosomes). Packing of multiple helices can lead to the fomration of extremely dense structures.

Figure 3-5 Nucleosome structure can bring distant markers in the genome into close proximity. Primary constructs are formed when DNA coils around a core structure composed of histone proteins. Additional coiling of the primary structure leads to the formation of extremely dense heterochromatin characteristic of mitotic structures. Further packing of these helices can form extremely dense tertiary structures.

Step 1: RNA polymerase advances toward the nucleosome structure

Step 2: Histone complex displaced by forward supercoiling pressure from the advancing polymerase

Step 3: Histone complex dissociates from the DNA helix relieving built up supercoiling pressure

Step 4: Histone complex reattaches to the helix behind the polymerase reestablishing the original secondary structure

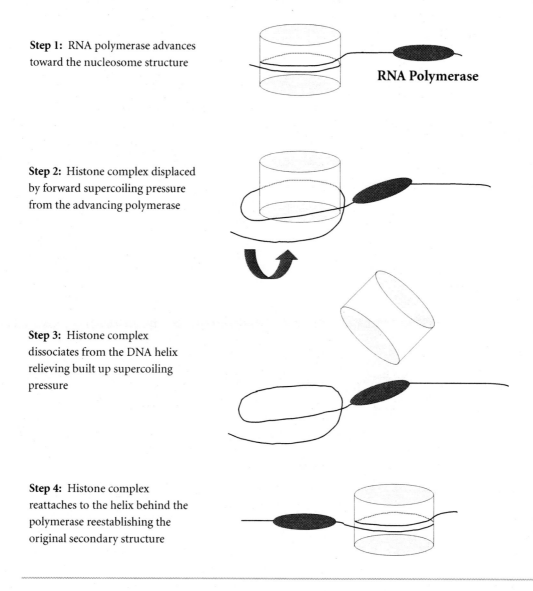

RNA Polymerase

Figure 3-6 RNA polymerase displaces DNA from the histone complex as it moves along the DNA helix during the transcription process. Positive supercoiling pressure displaces the histone complex, which reattaches behind the polymerase. Finally, the DNA strand winds around the histone complex, forming a new nucleosome. The coiled nucleosome structure can cause some DNA residues to be inaccessible to binding proteins, nucleases, polymerases, and other components of gene expression.

The formation of heterochromatin is considered to be a two-stage process. The first step involves a nucleation event that occurs at a specific sequence; the second involves propagation of the heterochromatin structure along the chromosome. The growth of heterochromatin is a polymerization process involving several proteins—some bind to the DNA directly and some to histones in the nucleosome complex. The length of the heterochromatin structure is not predetermined, and there are no known boundary conditions. The process is thought to involve a variety of stochastic and environmental parameters, such as the availability of specific structural proteins required to form the heterochromatic structure. When a gene is silenced in this manner, its state is inherited by all progeny. This phenomenon, known as position effect variegation, results in genetically identical cells displaying different phenotypes in the same organism. (The cells are genetically identical despite the fact that some of the genes are silenced.)

Histones are also modified by enzymes that add (or remove) important functional groups—acetyl, methyl, and phosphate. These reactions define a second genetic code, a regulatory code that operates at the histone level. Various combinations of these functional groups fine-tune transcription and other cellular processes by regulating access to the underlying DNA and recruiting other specific binding proteins. The results affect DNA replication and repair, recombination, progression of the cell cycle, chromosome stability, and the plasticity of stem cells [18]. During replication, modified and unmodified histone octamers are distributed to daughter cells. Because we know that the epigenetic effect is reliable, it is assumed that the modified histones provide some type of signal that causes the unmodified histones to become substrates for the methylase, acetylase, or phosphorylase that catalyze the change. The details surrounding this mechanism remain obscure at the time of this writing.

Direct methylation of DNA can silence genes in a way that persists through cell division into future generations. Most DNA-attached methyl groups are found on cytosines contained in CG "doublets," and most CG doublets are, in fact, methylated. In most cases, the C residues on both strands of the palindrome are methylated, creating the structure shown in Figure 3-7.

A palindrome containing complementary methylated cytosines is known as a fully methylated site. When this site is replicated, each daughter cell will contain one methylated and one open cytosine. Such a structure is known as hemimethylated. Restoration to the fully methylated state is accomplished by a maintenance methylase enzyme. If

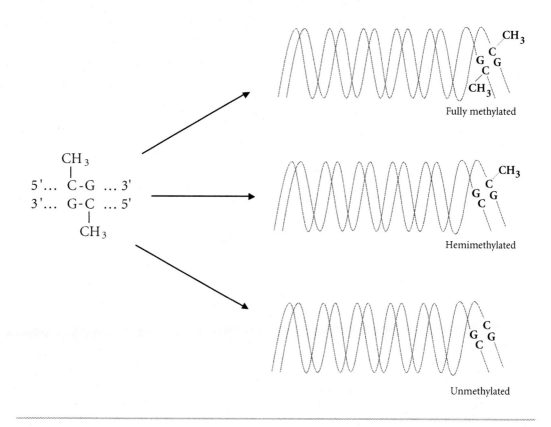

Figure 3-7 Methylated CG palindromic pair. Both strands of the DNA are methylated at cytosine, and the alteration is perpetuated in the next cellular generation through an enzymatic reaction that identifies the palindrome and adds a missing methyl group to the replicated strand.

another cycle of replication occurs before restoration to the fully methylated state, however, the hemimethylated state will persist in one daughter cell and the other will be completely unmethylated. The complete system is built on three enzymatic functions: A de novo methylation creates new methylated sites (presumably through specific sequence recognition); maintenance methylation restores the fully methylated state; and demethylation removes all methyl groups, completely unblocking the DNA. Figure 3-8 depicts the three enzymatic reactions.

Maintenance methylation is critical to survival: Mouse embryos in which the maintenance methylase gene is disrupted do not survive past early embryogenesis.

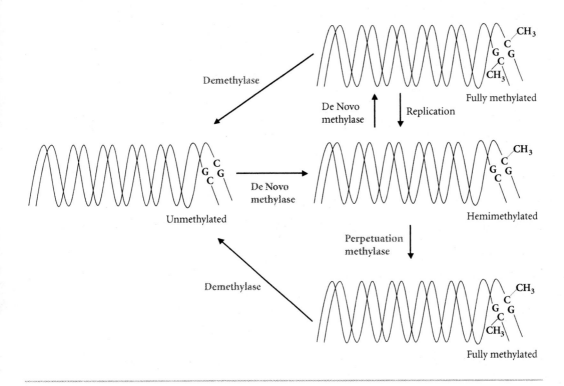

Figure 3-8 Three enzymes are responsible for maintaining the state of methylation: A de novo methylase adds methyl groups to unmethylated DNA; a perpetuation methylase maintains the fully methylated state; and a demethylase removes methyl groups. During replication, each daughter cell receives a single methylated strand; a perpetuation methylase is required to maintain the fully methylated state.

COMPUTATIONAL TECHNIQUES FOR THE IDENTIFICATION OF GENOMIC FEATURES

The tremendous explosion in both the volume and quality of genomic data (human and otherwise) has created a backdrop for discovery that begins with the basic process of gene identification [19, 20]. Although this process might appear to be straightforward, it is actually one of the most difficult challenges in contemporary bioinformatics. Even today, with the human genome sequences and associated information generally available to the scientific community, researchers continue to debate the exact number of genes. Superimposed on this discussion are the larger issues of control structures and genes that are suppressed through chemical modification (methylation, acetylation, and phosphorylation) or translocation into heterochromatic regions. Each of these topics involves the analysis of genomic sequence information; the most basic components being sequences that code for protein.

The fact that approximately 25,000 genes ultimately code for as many as 2 million different proteins hints at the enormous complexity of the gene-identification problem. The identification of coding regions is a complex process that requires transforming the basic biology of gene expression into a mathematical problem. Before we can discuss that problem, it makes sense to review the basic structure of coding regions with a view toward the underlying themes that will become the foundation of modern bioinformatics.

Much of the complexity we have been discussing arises from the basic structure of eukaryotic genes. As mentioned previously, bacterial (prokaryotic) genes are composed of an uninterrupted stretch of nucleotides, whereas gene-coding sequences of higher organisms contain coding regions (exons) that are interrupted by long noncoding intervening sequences (introns) that are spliced out in the final mRNA transcript. This process involves the creation of a primary mRNA transcript that is then spliced by a complex of RNA processing enzymes before the final version, the one that will be translated into a protein, is transported across the nuclear membrane into the cytoplasm.

Alternative splicing of primary transcripts is the primary driver of complexity in the human organism because it increases the diversity of the gene-expression process by allowing different proteins to be produced from the same gene. The splicing process has also become a driver of evolution and biodiversity because it facilitates genetic recombination among introns accelerating the evolution of new proteins that are assembled from lengths of preexisting amino acid sequences. These sequences, which have become the basic building blocks for proteins across all organisms, have been cataloged and extensively studied in recent years [21, 22, 23].

All introns contain well-characterized "consensus" sequences at their 5' (donor) and 3' (acceptor) ends. However, the enzymatic splicing mechanism that removes introns is somewhat error prone; it is sometimes unable to distinguish between alternative pairings, which leads to the production of new splice variants. This process, although important from an evolutionary perspective, is not the primary mechanism for producing a variety of proteins from a single message. A more directed mechanism for RNA splicing involves regulatory molecules that control the splicing machinery's access to portions of the transcript. It is important to note that the fidelity of the process must be very high because shifting the reading frame by a single base completely destroys the protein.

Another important transcriptional feature in higher organisms involves the addition of a poly-A tail to the end of each message. This addition is mediated by a special-purpose RNA polymerase enzyme, poly-A polymerase, and occurs at a specific site that can be identified by the sequence AAUAAA, approximately 20 nucleotides upstream of the cut site at the 3' end of a newly translated message. The poly-A tract is recognized by a poly-A binding protein (PABP). One PABP monomer is bound every 10 to 20 bases of the poly-A tail. The complete structure has a protective effect. Messages that lack bound PABP are degraded. The poly-A tail also provides an important regulatory function. In some cases, various mRNA species are stored in their nonpolyadenylated form and poly-A is added when translation is required. In other cases, an already adenylated species is de-adenylated and its rate of translation is subsequently reduced.

Also, during the transcription process, at about the 30 nucleotide stage, a "cap" composed of a methylated G nucleotide is added to the 5' end (the end where transcription begins). Addition of the cap can be represented as a chemical condensation between GTP and the original 5' triphosphate terminus of the mRNA. The new G residue is added to the 5' end of the chain (which typically contains a purine residue—A or G) in the reverse orientation from all other nucleotides, and thus

$$5' \text{ G}\mathbf{ppp} + 5' \text{ pppApNpNp} \rightarrow 5' \text{ GpppApNpNp} + \mathbf{pp} + \text{p}$$

Although different methylation states are possible, all eukaryotes contain a methyl group at position 7—the seventh carbon—of the terminal guanine. This modification, catalyzed by the enzyme guanine-7-methyltransferase, is referred to as cap 0. Another methyl group may be added to the 2'-O position of the next base (originally the first base of the chain). This structure, catalyzed by 2'-O, methyltransferase, is referred to as cap 1. Cap 1 structures with an adenine in position 2 are sometimes recognized by another enzyme that adds an additional methyl group to position N^6 of adenine residues, which already contain a 2'-O methyl. Cap 1 structures already containing two methyl groups are often modified by the addition of a methyl at the 2'-O ribose position of base 3 (base 2 in the unmodified chain).

The 5' methylated cap is an important structure; it protects the end of the transcript from nucleases and serves as a recognition site for the ribosome during translation of the message into protein. Upon binding, the ribosome begins "scanning" the message until it encounters the first AUG sequence—the codon for methionine. All eukaryotic proteins begin with an n-terminal methionine, which is often enzymatically removed after translation. The translation mechanism is another source of sequence diversity because the ribosome sometimes fails to recognize the first AUG start codon and skips to the second, producing a completely different protein. This process is called leaky scanning. Both the proximity to the cap and nucleotide composition of sequences that surround the start codon determine the efficiency of the recognition process [24].

Upstream of the complex of introns and exons are promoters and other regulatory elements that control transcription. Transcription in higher eukaryotes involves the assembly of a protein complex composed of "general transcription factors" that functions to induce the binding of RNA polymerase II at the promoter site. The promoter site almost always contains the sequence TATA, which is recognized by one of the general transcription factors. The TATA sequence, often referred to as a TATA box because of its palindromic nature, usually resides 25 nucleotides upstream of the point where transcription will begin. Another conserved sequence, CCAAT, is associated with transcription start sites in higher organisms and appears in approximately 50% of vertebrate promoters. The CCAAT sequence is normally found upstream from the TATA box.

After the general transcription factors and RNA polymerase II are bound at the promoter, transcription of the gene begins. The transcription rate is tightly regulated by control proteins that bind to sites scattered across a very large area associated with each gene—often as wide as 50,000 nucleotides, upstream and downstream of the promoter and even the gene itself. This effect, often referred to as control at a distance, is a common theme in the human genome. Thousands of different proteins bind to these regulatory sites; some "up regulate" and some "down regulate" the transcription process. The regulation mechanism seems to be based on loop structures in the DNA that bring control regions into contact with the promoter.

Each cell type has a different population of regulatory proteins to match its gene-expression pattern. The present discussion refers to one of three RNA synthesizing enzymes, RNA polymerase II. The other major RNA polymerases, I and III, are primarily responsible for synthesizing RNA molecules which have structural or catalytic roles within the cell, mostly related to the protein synthesizing machinery used for translation: RNA polymerase I synthesizes large ribosomal RNAs; RNA polymerase III synthesizes the transfer RNAs, amino acid carriers for translation, and the small structural

5S ribosomal RNA. Conversely, the thousands of genes coding for proteins and the small catalytic RNAs often referred to as snRNPs (small nuclear ribonucleoproteins) are all synthesized by RNA polymerase II. The present discussion focuses on genes that code for proteins and, therefore, RNA polymerase II [25].

An accurate view of transcription reveals a relatively small coding sequence (the actual gene) surrounded by a much larger region of nucleotides that contains a promoter, binding sites for regulatory proteins, structural sequences that cause the DNA to fold into loops, consensus sequences that facilitate RNA splicing, sequences that signal the 3' cut site where the poly-A tail is added, and a ribosomal binding site near the 5' end of the molecule (the site where the methylated guanine cap is added). Each of these elements provides a piece of information that can be used algorithmically in gene-finding experiments.

SEARCHING THE GENOME

Unfortunately the protein synthesis process, which begins with a DNA sequence and ends with a folded protein, cannot be completely described, most notably with regard to the specific signal sequences required for recognition and processing of the components. For example, although most promoters contain the signature TATA box, 30% do not, so this signal is not a completely reliable mechanism for locating transcription start sites. Furthermore, there is no specific set of rules for unambiguous identification of introns, and even if such rules were defined, there is no precise way to predict for a given gene which introns will be spliced into a final message.

Despite these complexities, bioinformaticians have succeeded in developing a combination of approaches to gene identification that have proven to be reliable. These approaches can be grouped into the following categories [26]:

- **Content-based**—Analysis based on statistical parameters of a sequence, such as the frequency of occurrence of particular codons and periodicity of repeated sequences. DNA sequences can also be translated into amino acids and scored against weighting functions that use a statistical basis to predict the formation of basic protein features—alpha helix, beta sheet, and reverse turn structures.

- **Feature analysis**—Methods based on the identification of donor and acceptor splice sites at the ends of introns, long poly adenine sequences that signal the 3' end of a transcript, binding sites for transcriptional factors, and start/stop codons that signal the beginning and end of an open reading frame (ORF). Open reading frame analysis based on identification of a 3' end start codon (ATG, the code for methionine) and a 5' end stop codon (TAA, TAG or TGA) is perhaps the most straightforward method for gene identification. However, the complexities of the splicing process can obscure start and stop codons with interruptions in the prespliced mRNA or add invalid stop codons by shifting the reading frame after the start.

- **Database comparison**—These methods rely on sequence-homology studies that search databases containing thousands of known protein sequences. In many cases, the protein sequences are subdivided into small motifs used to populate dictionaries of known structures. Amino acid sequences in the dictionary are back translated into their corresponding nucleotide sequences, the correct strand is then assembled and scanned against the complete DNA data. Many of these sequences are conserved throughout evolution and have served as the basis for annotation of the human genome. Sequence-homology algorithms use various measures of complementarity to compare the data, which almost always contain inexact matches, frame shifts, spaces, and "wildcard" characters representing degeneracy in the sequence; as mentioned previously, the genetic code is somewhat degenerate in the sense that most amino acids may be specified by more than one nucleotide triplet [27, 28].

Regardless of the algorithm used, it is important to remember that every gene-coding region contains six possible reading frames, three that commence at positions 1, 2, and 3 on one DNA strand and a corresponding set of three beginning at the 5' end of the complementary strand. Modern bioinformatic programs are designed to examine all six possible reading frames. The realization that a single gene-coding region can contain multiple reading frames superimposed on a large number of splice variants with open reading frames on both strands of the DNA helix has added tremendous complexity to the gene-finding process. Not surprisingly, modern gene-identification programs are designed to scan both strands in each of the three reading frames in the 5' to 3' direction.

Furthermore, algorithms that scan DNA sequences must take into account the fact that splice sites within the coding region almost always shift the reading frame while separating nucleotides that are destined to be joined in the final transcript. One such program, Artemis, is freely available to the public through the Sanger Center. It includes a genome viewer and annotation tools that allow visualization of sequence features and the results of various analyses within the context of the sequence. As one might expect, Artemis is designed to search, translate, and visualize all six reading frames. It is also compatible with a variety of standard file formats—most significantly those used by EMBL and GenBank—and can handle sequences output by other bioinformatic programs such as FASTA. These issues are especially critical for researchers using sequence-homology algorithms because the sequences being compared may be sparse and differ with regard to the specific lengths of intervening segments. Problems of this nature have driven the development of unbounded pattern-discovery programs that can identify sparse and complex patterns.

Approximately 50 years of statistical analysis has contributed to an understanding of the relative frequency of codon usage in various genomes, most recently the human genome [29, 30]. Table 3-5 depicts the distribution of codons in the human genome.

Two content-based statistical approaches have been used for ORF identification in genomes. The first is based on an unusual property of coding sequences; every third base tends to be duplicated more often than would be expected by random chance alone [31]. This observation holds true for all coding sequences in all organisms and is a result of the nonrandom nature of protein structure. The second approach involves comparing the distribution of codons in the test region to the known distribution for coding sequences in the rest of the organism [32, 33, 34, 35].

Feature identification as a tool for genomic analysis is at least 25 years old and has advanced as rapidly as molecular biology itself. Today there are many popular algorithms, most in the public domain, designed to identify the various features associated with coding sequences—introns, exons, promoter sites, etc. Most use tables and weighting functions along with some type of sequence specific statistical analysis to predict the presence and frequency of key features [36, 37]. Notable examples include GenScan (MIT) and TwinScan (Washington University). Each uses a probabilistic model based on known structures and compositional properties of genomic DNA for a particular group of organisms. Such feature-analysis techniques are much more powerful when

Table 3-5 Frequency of Each Codon per 100,000 Codons in the Human Genome

UUU	16.6	UCU	14.5	UAU	12.1	UGU	9.7
UUC	20.7	UCC	17.7	UAC	16.3	UGC	12.4
UUA	7.0	UCA	11.4	UAA	0.7	UGA	1.3
UUG	12.0	UCG	4.5	UAG	0.5	UGG	13.0
CUU	12.4	CCU	17.2	CAU	10.1	CGU	4.7
CUC	19.3	CCC	20.3	CAC	14.9	CGC	11.0
CUA	6.8	CCA	16.5	CAA	11.8	CGA	6.2
CUG	40.0	CCG	7.1	CAG	34.4	CGG	11.6
AUU	15.7	ACU	12.7	AAU	16.8	AGU	11.7
AUC	22.3	ACC	19.9	AAC	20.2	AGC	19.3
AUA	7.0	ACA	14.7	AAA	23.6	AGA	11.2
AUG	22.2	ACG	6.4	AAG	33.2	AGG	11.1
GUU	10.7	GCU	18.4	GAU	22.2	GGU	10.9
CUC	14.8	GCC	28.6	GAC	26.5	GGC	23.1
GUA	6.8	GCA	15.6	GAA	28.6	GGA	16.4
GUG	29.3	GCG	7.7	GAG	40.6	GGG	16.5

Source: GenBank Release 128.0 [15 February 2002], http://www/kazusa .or.jp/codon

combined with known information about protein and genetic structure. Such information is housed in public databases such as the National Center for Biotechnology Information (NCBI) GenBank DNA sequence database [38, 39]. One such algorithm, PROCRUSTES, forces a fit between a test DNA sequence and potential transcription products that have already been sequenced. A spliced-alignment algorithm is used to sequentially explore all possible exon assemblies in an attempt to model the best fit of gene and target protein. PROCRUSTES is designed to handle situations where the query DNA sequence contains either partial or multiple genes [40].

Another approach involves using neural networks that have been trained to recognize characteristic sequences of known exons, intron-exon boundaries, and transcription start sites in a particular organism. Such networks, once trained, are often capable of discerning complex and subtle relationships between sequence elements that are not otherwise detectable [41, 42]. The popular gene locator known as GRAIL (Gene Recognition and Assembly Internet Link), maintained by Oak Ridge National Laboratory, is based on neural network technology. The GRAIL database contains gene models for five different organisms: human, mouse, *Arabidopsis*, *Drosophila*, and *Escherichia coli*. Users can run the software across the internet and retrieve a list of possible exons, their positions, reading frames, and scores for a submitted list of sequences.

Finally, a new class of probabilistic algorithm has emerged that is capable of locating genes by identifying repeating sequence patterns. GenScan, TwinScan, and Glimmer are popular examples of such programs—each is publicly available. Glimmer, one of the most flexible gene locators, uses interpolated Markov models (IMMs) to locate coding regions and distinguish them from noncoding DNA. Although Glimmer was designed primarily for microbial systems, a special version—GlimmerM—has been used to find all the genes on chromosome 2 of the malaria parasite, *P. falciparum* [43]. Markov models, a well-known tool for analyzing biological sequence information, are covered in Chapter 4. In general such models can be envisioned as predicting the next residue in a sequence using a fixed number of preceding bases. For example, a fifth-order Markov model uses the five previous bases to predict the next base. (GeneMark, another popular gene-finding program, is based on a fifth-order Markov model.) Although the accuracy of a particular Markov model generally tends to increase in proportion to the length of the sequences used, fixed-order models can sometimes demonstrate statistical inconsistencies. IMMs overcome many of these problems by combining probabilities from contexts of varying lengths. Only contexts for which sufficient data are available are used for comparison. For example, a typical genome may contain an insufficient number of certain 6mers to allow next-base calculations, whereas some 8mers may occur with enough frequency to provide reliable estimates [44]. Glimmer and GlimmerM are designed to exploit this advantage of interpolated Markov models.

HIGH-THROUGHPUT GENE SEQUENCING

High-throughput genome sequencing has become a reality over the past few years. Among the most significant achievements of this era has been the determination of the complete sequence of the genomes of several higher organisms—mouse, rat, fruit fly, zebrafish, and human—in addition to more than 100 microbial species. The key enabling technique, shotgun sequencing, uses computer programs to reconstruct long sequences from large numbers of small fragments. The basic form of the shotgun sequencing process, now used across entire genomes, is outlined here:

1. Chromosomal DNA segments are fragmented using restriction enzymes or sonication. Relatively long fragments—in the range of 100,000 bases—are separated from the mixture using gel electrophoresis. Meticulously executed, the technique will produce a normally distributed collection of fragments with a variance of approximately 10%.

2. Size-selected fragments are inserted into the DNA of a genetically engineered bacterial virus. (Bacteriophage M13 is a common choice.) The new virus is referred to as a vector. Dilution protocols are designed to prevent multiple insertions per virus; the number of vectors containing more than one fragment is typically less than 1%. The insertion point is called the cloning site; the fragments are now referred to as inserts; and the collection of inserts is known as a library.

3. A bacterium is infected with a single vector. The bacterium reproduces to form a colony containing millions of copies of the vector and its associated insert. The procedure continues until enough copies are produced for sequencing.

4. The ends of the cloned fragments are sequenced starting just to the left or right of each cloned fragment's insertion point. The first 300 to 900 bases of each fragment are sequenced.

5. Assembly algorithms are used to reconstruct the sequence of each fragment; the known orientation of each fragment is used to build a complete sequence for the genome one chromosome at a time. To maximize the length of each sequence used, most experiments involve sampling fragments whose length is longer than the reasonable maximum read length of the sequencing machine. The technique, known as scaffolding, requires a large population of fragments containing many overlaps.

The basic strategy for DNA sequencing has changed little since its emergence in the early 1970s. In its most common form, a biochemical process is used to generate a collection composed of all possible lengths—sometimes referred to as prefixes—of the starting DNA segment. The collection of fragments is chemically treated to allow identification of the last base of each fragment. The prefixes are separated by electrophoresis, a process that involves passing them through a semipermeable gel in an electric field. Having relatively constant charge, the lengths of DNA are separated according to their length (or actually the diameter of the sphere carved out in three-dimensional space as the molecules tumble n the electric field). The prefixes exit the gel in size order. The final base of each is determined using a laser, charge-coupled detector; computer software facilitates the analysis of the emitted spectra.

The results are automatically uploaded to a central database along with detailed information about the spectra used to identify each residue and other relevant information about the chemical processes and environmental conditions associated with each read. This associated information is maintained in a data structure known as a trace file [45, 46]. Because the ratio of molecular weights for very long fragments approaches 1, the process becomes error prone as the length of the reads increases. For example, the ratio of molecular weights (or lengths) of a dinucleotide and a trinucleotide is 2/3, whereas the same ratio for sequences of length 1,000 and 1,001 respectively is 1,000/1,001. Because the migration time through the gel for each sequence is proportional to its length, the first pair would be much easier to resolve than the second. However, in this regard it is important to note that a gel of much lower density and much longer length would resolve the 1,000:1,001 case but not the 2:3 case, which would comigrate well ahead of the much longer sequences. In such cases, gradient gels containing increasing densities can be used to separate multiple size classes. Modern sequencing machines, which use gel formulations optimized for particular fragment lengths, can operate efficiently up to the 1,000 bp range.

For a source strand of 100 kilobases (kb), it would be realistic to generate and sequence 1,500 overlapping fragments with an average length of 500 bases. This strategy would result in sequencing a total of 750 kb; each base would, on average, be read 7.5 times. Using the standard syntax for describing genome sequencing experiments, researchers would refer to these results as providing 7.5x coverage of the base sequence. High-coverage models reduce the chance of misreading an individual base and increase the chance of completing an accurate assembly of the entire sequence [47].

The most difficult fragment-assembly problem to solve involves placement of repeat sequences. The genomes of higher organisms contain long sequences composed of repeating elements that are notoriously difficult to place, especially when some of the sequence data lacks overlap with nonrepeat regions. (This occurs when a sequenced fragment lies completely within a repeat region.) The problem is illustrated in Figure 3-9. Regions A, B, and C of the sequence have unique characteristics that can be used to create alignments, However, the repeated sequence X appears in two locations— between regions A and B and between regions B and C. Although an exhaustive set of fragments was produced, some of the fragments are contained completely within the region X, more specifically within the central region of X labeled X2. Lack of overlap with other regions of the sequence makes orientation of these fragments difficult. Because X1 and X3 overlap with nonrepeating sequence elements on the borders— AX1, X3B, BX1, and X3C—they are easily placed. The central region, X2, is easily missed by programs designed to produce the shortest possible assembly. As a result, region X is overcompressed in some solutions; the central region, X2, is missing in these alignments.

One important addition to the shotgun technique involves selecting segments that are twice as long as those normally used and sequencing both ends of the insert. This process gives rise to pairs of reads known as mates, oriented opposite each other and separated by the length of the insert. This technique, sometimes called double-barreled shotgun sequencing, is crucial to the process of aligning large fragments into a chromosomal map. The complete solution to the assembly problem involves other pieces of

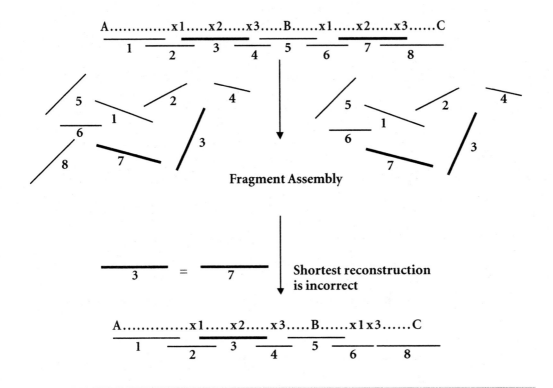

Figure 3-9 The repeat sequence problem in genome assembly. Regions A, B, and C of the sequence are interrupted by intervening sequence X, which is repeated. The intervening sequence contains three regions: X1, X2, and X3. Fragments spanning A-X1, X3-B, B-X1, and X3-C are sufficient to place X1 and X3 in both regions. Conversely, fragments comprised exclusively of X2 sequence elements cannot be properly placed, and some assembly algorithms overcompress the sequence, entirely removing X2.

information as well: known sequence information from other genomes, previously identified markers, expressed tags from back-translated mRNA species, protein sequences, and other information contained in public databases. For example, one useful technique involves aligning sequenced fragments with the complementary strand bearing the same sequence in another genome. If a very strong alignment is found, gaps between sequence elements (contigs) can be filled by using the polymerase chain reaction to copy the complementary strand across the gaps. Such gaps, due to the presence of unclonable regions, are a common problem. An alternative approach relies on comparing back-translated known protein sequences when a gap occurs in a coding region [48].

SUMMARY

This chapter reviewed the basic concepts surrounding gene structure. The discussion included both concepts related to the organization of chromosomal information and computational techniques for the identification of genomic features. In the process, this chapter covered algorithmic and statistical processes that can be used to identify various sequence elements. The chapter closed with a discussion of one of the most important advances in contemporary molecular biology: high-throughput sequencing of entire genomes. Several new algorithms have been developed for aligning sequence fragments into long gene segments. This alignment process, which has come to be known as genome assembly, represents one of the most computationally intense problems in modern science. The ability to sequence whole genomes is already having a significant impact on personalized medicine.

As previously mentioned, this book is organized around the flow of biological information from gene to transcript to protein to phenotype. This chapter and the one that follows are intended to create a framework composed of computational techniques for analyzing sequence information. They serve as a backdrop to Chapter 5, which focuses on the next step in the process—transcription. As you shall see, the computational tools for transcriptional profiling build on sequence-analysis algorithms in the same way that the biological process builds on chromosomal structure.

ENDNOTES

1. Watson J. D., F. H. C. Crick.1953. Molecular structure of nucleic acids. *Nature* April 25, 1953: 737.

2. Lehninger, A. *Biochemistry*. Worth Publishers, New York, 1972. 959–965.

3. Venter J. C., Adams M. D., Myers E. W., et al.2001. The sequence of the human genome. *Science* 291: 1304–1351.

4. Couzin, J. 2002. Breakthrough of the year: small RNAs make big splash. *Science* 298: 2296.

5. Sharp P. A., Zamore P. D. 2000. RNA interference. *Science* 287: 2430.

6. N. C. Lau, et al. 2001. An abundant class of tiny RNAs with probable regulatory roles in Caenorhabditis elegans. *Science* 294: 858.

7. G. Ruvkun. 2001. Glimpses of a tiny RNA world. *Science* 294: 797.

8. V. Ambros. 2001. Dicing up RNAs. *Science* 293: 811.

9. Lee R. C., Ambros V. 2001. An extensive class of small RNAs in Caenorhabditis elegans. *Science* 294: 862

10. Zamore P. D. 2002. Ancient pathways programmed by small RNAs. *Science* 296: 1265.

11. Plasterk R. H. A. 2002. RNA silencing: the genome's immune system. *Science* 296: 1263.

12. Jenuwein T. 2002. An RNA-guided pathway to the epigenome. *Science* 297: 2215.

13. Allshire R. 2002. RNAi and heterochromatin—a hushed-up affair. *Science* 297: 1818.

14. Hall I. M., et al. 2002. Establishment and maintenance of a heterochromatin domain. *Science* 297: 2232.

15. Taverna S. D., et al. 2002. Methylation of histone H3 at lysine 9 targets programmed DNA elimination in tetrahymena. *Cell* 110: 701.

16. Lagos-Quintana M., et al. 2001. Identification of novel genes coding for small expressed RNAs. *Science* 294: 853.

17. Pasquinelli A. E., et al. 2000. Conservation of the sequence and temporal expression of let-7 heterochromic regulatory RNA. *Nature* 408: 86–89.

18. Jenuwein T., Allis C. D. 2001. Translating the histone code. *Science* 293: 1074–1079.

19. International Human Genome Sequencing Consortium. 2001. Initial sequencing and analysis of the human genome. *Nature* 409: 860–921.

20. Venter C., et al. 2001. The sequence of the human genome. *Science* 291: 1304–1351.

21. Rigoutsos I., Floratos A., Ouzounis C., Gao Y., Parida L. 1999. Dictionary building via unsupervised hierarchical motif discovery in the sequence space of natural proteins. *Journal of Proteins: Structure, Function and Genetics* 37(2): 264–277.

22. Martí-Renom M. A., Stuart A., Fiser A., R. Melo S. F., Sali A. 2000. Comparative protein structure modeling of genes and genomes. Annual Review of Biophysics and Biomolecular Structures 29: 291–325.

23. Pieper U., Eswar N., Stuart A. C., Ilyin V. A., Sali A..2002. MODBASE, a database of annotated comparative protein structure models. *Nucleic Acids Research* 30: 255–259.

24. Kozak, M. 1999. Initiation and translation in procaryotes and eukaryotes. *Gene* 234: 187–208.

25. Alberts B., Bray D., Lewis J., Raff M., Roberts K., and Watson J. *Molecular Biology of the Cell, Third Edition*. Garland Publishing, 1994.

26. Baxevanis A., and Ouellette F. *Bioinformatics a Practical Guide to the Analysis of Genes and Proteins*. John Wiley and Sons, 2001. 235–242.

27. Claverie J. M. 1998. Computational methods for the identification of genes in vertebrate genomic sequences. *Human Molecular Genetics* 6: 1735–1744.

28. Claverie J. M. 1997. Exon detection by similarity searches. *Methods in Molecular Biology* 68: 283–313.

29. Mount D. 2001. *Bioinformatics—Sequence and Genome Analysis.* Cold Spring Harbor Laboratory Press, 2001. 337–373.

30. Sharp P. M., Li W. H.1987. The codon adaptation index—a measure of directional synonymous codon usage bias, and its potential applications. *Nucleic Acids Research* 15: 1281–1295.

31. Fickett J. W. 1982. Recognition of protein coding regions in DNA sequences. *Nucleic Acids Research* 10: 5303–5318.

32. Uberbacher E. C., Mural R.J. 1991. Locating protein-coding regions in human DNA sequences by a multiple sensor-neural network approach. *Proceedings of the National Academy of Sciences* 88: 11261–11265.

33. Uberbacher E. C., Xu Y., Mural R. J. 1996. Discovering and understanding genes in human DNA sequence using GRAIL. *Methods of Enzymology* 266: 259–281.

34. Burge C. B., and Karlin S. 1998. Finding genes in genomic DNA. *Current Opinion in Structural Biology* 8: 346–354.

35. Burste M., Guigo R. 1996. Evaluation of gene structure prediction programs. *Genomics* 34: 353–367.

36. Chen Q. K., Hertz G. Z., Stormo G. D. 1995. MATRIX SEARCH 1.0: A computer program that scans DNA sequences for transcriptional elements using a database of weight matrices. *Computer Applications in Biosciences* 11: 563–566.

37. Prestridge D. S. 1991. SIGNAL SCAN: A computer program that scans DNA sequences for eukaryotic transcriptional elements. *Computer Applications in Biosciences* 7: 203–206.

38. Gish W., States D. J. 1993. Identification of protein coding regions by database similarity search. *Nature Genetics* 3: 266–272.

39. Kolchanov N. A., et al.1999. Integrated databases and computer systems for studying eukaryotic gene expression. *Bioinformatics* 15: 669–686.

40. Gelfand M. S., Mironov A. A., Pevzner P. A. 1996. Gene recognition via spliced sequence alignment. *Proceedings of the National Academy of Sciences* 93: 9061–9066.

41. Farber R., Lapedes A., Sirotkin K. 1992. Determination of eukaryotic protein coding regions using neural networks and information theory. *Journal of Molecular Biology* 226: 471–479.

42. Reese, M. G., Harris, N., and Eeckman, F. "Large Scale Sequencing Specific Neural Networks for Promoter and Splice Site Recognition" in *Biocomputing: Proceedings of the 1996 Pacific Symposium* (L. Hunter and T. E. Klein, Eds.). World Scientific Publishing, Singapore, 1996.

43. Salzberg S. L., Pertea M., Delcher A. L., Gardner M. J., Tettelin H. 1999. Interpolated Markov models for eukaryotic gene finding. *Genomics* 59: 24–31.

44. Salzberg S. L., Delcher A. L., Kasif S., White O. 2003. Microbial gene identification using interpolated Markov models. *Nucleic Acids Research* 26(2): 544–548.

45. Maxam A. M. and Gilbert W. 1997. A new method for sequencing DNA. *Proceedings of the National Academy of Sciences* 74: 560–564.

46. Sanger F., Nicklen S., Coulson A. R. 1977. DNA sequencing with chain-terminating inhibitors. *Proceedings of the National Academy of Sciences* 74: 5463–5467.

47. Meyers G.1999. Whole-genome DNA sequencing. *IEEE Computational Engineering and Science* 3(1): 33–43.

48. Chen T., Skiena S. 2000. A case study in genome-level fragment assembly. *Bioinformatics* 16(6): 494–500.

4

Computational Techniques for Sequence Analysis

INTRODUCTION

This chapter builds on concepts introduced in the previous discussions of gene structure and associated feature-identification techniques. Our goal is to introduce several contemporary approaches to sequence alignment/comparison and pattern discovery (both bounded and unbounded). Neural networks and their more primitive antecedents, perceptron algorithms, figure prominently in this discussion because they have emerged as valuable tools for comparing sequence information. Single nucleotide polymorphisms (SNPs), the most abundant type of DNA sequence variation in the human genome, are also central to this discussion, and we will review the statistical approaches used by population geneticists to identify and study SNPs.

This discussion begins with a particular class of probabilistic algorithms that has emerged as an important tool for locating genes by identifying repeating sequence patterns. GenScan, TwinScan, and Glimmer are popular examples of such programs—each is publicly available. Glimmer, one of the most flexible gene locators, uses interpolated Markov models (IMMs) to locate coding regions and distinguish them from noncoding DNA. Although Glimmer was designed primarily for microbial systems, a special version—GlimmerM—has been used to find all the genes on chromosome 2 of the malaria parasite, *P. falciparum* [1]. Markov models, a well-known tool for analyzing biological sequence information, are covered in the next section; we will focus on a specific form of the model—the profile Markov model—because it has proven particularly valuable for analyzing genomic data. In general such models can be envisioned as predicting the next residue in a sequence using a fixed number of preceding bases. For example, a fifth-order Markov model uses the five previous bases to predict the next base (Gene-Mark, another popular gene-finding program is based on a fifth-order Markov model). Although the accuracy of a particular Markov model generally tends to increase in proportion to the length of the sequences used, fixed-order models can sometimes demonstrate statistical inconsistencies. IMMs overcome many of these problems by combining probabilities from contexts of varying lengths. Only contexts for which sufficient data are available are used for comparison. For example, a typical genome may contain an insufficient number of certain 6mers to allow next base calculations, whereas some 8mers may occur with enough frequency to provide reliable estimates [2]. Glimmer and GlimmerM are designed to exploit this advantage of IMMs.

HIDDEN MARKOV MODELS

The past several years have seen dramatic improvements in the design of algorithms for pattern recognition. These advances are enabling researchers to detect subtle and complex relationships between seemingly unrelated sets of sequence data. Several different areas of mathematics and computer science have been involved—most notably statistical analysis, probability theory, and artificial intelligence. One of the most significant advances in this space has been the development of hidden Markov models (HMMs). HMMs have been used in such diverse fields as speech recognition and computer vision, where they are particularly useful for analyzing time-synchronized sequential data. These areas share an important characteristic with biological sequence analysis: History provides the context upon which next-state probabilities are predicted.

An HMM is a finite state machine built on a set of predefined probability distributions that govern transitions between the states. A complete model contains a set of states, output alphabet, transition probabilities, output probabilities, and initial state probabilities. This discussion focuses on a particular application of HMMs to sequence alignment. For this purpose, it is useful to think of an HMM as a statistical model that considers all possible permutations of matches, mismatches, and gaps, and ultimately generates the best possible alignment of a set of sequences. The model is heuristic in the sense that it must be "trained" on a set of well-characterized sequences. Once trained, the data represent an HMM profile that can be used to identify additional members of the same sequence family or create an optimized alignment for a large number of sequences.

The HMM technique embodies several advantages over other statistical methods. Most notably, it is insensitive to the presentation order of the sequences and gap and insertion penalties are not required. Two HMM programs are readily available: Sequence Alignment and Modeling Software System (SAM) and HMMER [3, 4]. HMMER can be downloaded from a Web site hosted by Washington University, and you can obtain SAM in similar fashion from the University of California at Santa Cruz. The HMM modeling technique involves generating sequences with various combinations of matches/mismatches, insertions, and deletions. Each event is assigned a probability that depends on various parameters that form the basis for the model. The process involves adjusting these parameters in a recursive way until the model mirrors the observed variation in a group of related proteins. Once trained, the model is capable of providing statistically significant multiple-sequence alignments for a collection of related sequences.

A special case of the hidden Markov model, known as the profile HMM, is depicted in Figure 4-1. Profile HMMs imply a specific structure that allows for position-dependent gap penalties. The model consists of a linear sequence of nodes with begin (B) and end (E) states. A typical model may contain hundreds of nodes. Each node between beginning and end states corresponds to a column in a multiple-sequence alignment. Nodes are characterized by three states—match (M), insert (I), or delete (D)—with position-specific probabilities for transitioning into each state from the previous node. In addition to a transition probability, the match state also has position-specific probabilities for containing a particular residue. Likewise, the insert state is assigned a probability for inserting a residue. The probability of a blank node is specified by the transition to the delete state. Blank nodes are placeholders for positions in the sequence where some of the sequences contain a mismatch that must be skipped in order to complete the alignment. Match probabilities are generated in a column-specific way; each box contains a distribution of amino acids based on the probability of finding each residue in that particular column in the sequence family used to construct the model. Similarity scores are defined by the most probable path through an HMM that is used to generate a sequence [5, 6].

P * F S A
P * F S A
P🔵F S A
R * F - A

PⒼFSA can be traced through the model as:
BEG - M1 - I1 - M2 - M3 - M4 - END

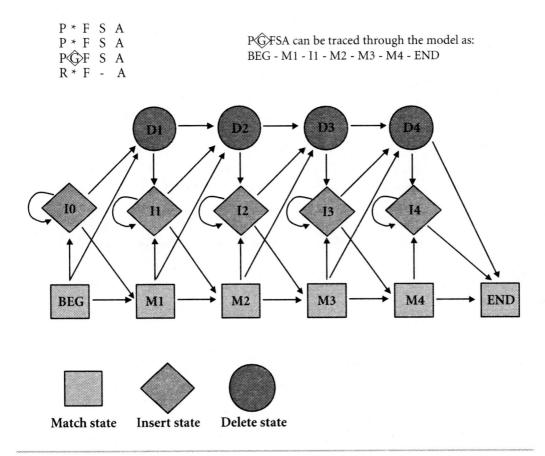

Match state   Insert state   Delete state

Figure 4-1 Hidden Markov Model representation of a sequence alignment. Each sequence can be traced through the model as a series of matches, inserts, and deletions. Each transition in a path has an associated probability, and these are used to build an overall model that predicts the most likely path for any given sequence.

Figure 4-1 is built on a trivial case containing only four sequences of five amino acids each. Each column in the alignment may include matches or mismatches, insertions, or deletions. The HMM is a probabilistic representation of the multiple-sequence alignment. Each column in the model represents the probability of a match, insert, or delete in each position of the alignment. Specific sequences can be generated from the HMM by starting at the beginning (B) state and following any path through the model, proceeding through a variety of positional state transitions and terminating at the end state. It is important to emphasize that any sequence can be generated by the model because, in principle, every amino acid has a finite probability of occurring at each position. Likewise, any position may be substituted with an insert or a deletion to correct the alignment—each potential event can be represented by a finite probability.

Although each match state contains accurately characterized amino acid distributions, each insert state does not. In the past, researchers often used random amino acid distributions for the insert state that assigned equal probability to all residues. More recently it has become customary to use accurate distributions for each specific organism or cell type. Circular delete states produce a deletion in the alignment with an associated probability of 1. A logical way to generate the sequence P – G – F – S – A would be to navigate the sequence B – M1 – I1 – M2 – M3 – M4 – E. Because the sum of the probabilities associated with the possible transitions at each state is 1, the average for a single transition when there are three possibilities should be 0.33. M4 and D4 are exceptions because each only presents two possible transitions resulting in an average probability of 0.5. If each match state contained a uniform distribution across all amino acids, the probability associated with any particular match would be 0.05. (There are 20 amino acids.) Using average probable values of 0.33 for each transition, 0.5 for the M4/D4 transitions, and 0.05 for each amino acid in each state, the probability of the sequence P – G – F – S – A becomes the product of all the transitional probabilities in the path multiplied by the probability that each state will produce the corresponding amino acid in the sequence. This result can be expressed as $(0.33 \times 0.05) \times (0.33 \times 0.05) \times (0.33 \times 0.05) \times (0.33 \times 0.05) \times (0.33 \times 0.05) \times .5 = 6.1 \times 10^{-10}$. One consequence of serially multiplying several numbers that are each smaller than 1 is that the final result is guaranteed to be very small. The solution is to express amino acid distributions and transition probabilities as log odds scores and to add the logarithms to yield the final score.

Several options exist for creating the amino acid distributions used in the match state part of the calculation. The first, and most obvious, involves determining the distribution of each amino acid in each position of the alignment by analyzing the sequence family used to build the model. In practice this task is accomplished by finding every possible pathway through the model that can produce the training sequences, counting the number of times each transition is used and identifying the amino acids required by each match state. This training procedure effectively embeds a virtual copy of the sequences in the model and improves the accuracy of the predictions. The model in our example, once defined, should return the highest probability for the match – insert – match – match – match combination. Likewise, the highest probability path for every other sequence in the training set should be the path that corresponds to the original alignment used in the training set (e.g., that last sequence in Figure 4-1 should be optimized as match – match – delete – match). Each sequence defines a Markov chain because downstream states depend on upstream states in the sequence. Only the outcome is visible to the external observer (the sequence and associated states and probabilities are buried within the model)—thus the name "hidden."

PSEUDOCOUNTS

Estimating match state probability distributions from a small number of amino acids can result in statistically insignificant results. This problem is known as overfitting. For example, consider a scenario that contains just two sequences, both with histidine in position 2. The statistical distribution for this match state would contain a probability of 1 for histidine and 0 for all other amino acids. Following the HMM methodology and multiplying values across the chain would result in a probability score of 0 for any sequence that contains any residue other than histidine in position 2. (The log odds would technically become minus infinity.)

It is clearly necessary to avoid this sort of statistical anomaly. The most common solution is to use pseudocounts—incrementally adjusted scores that do not allow any amino acid to be assigned a positional probability of zero. The most straightforward method involves adding 1 to every count. Instead of setting the probability to 2/2 for histidine and 0/2 for the 19 other amino acids, both numerator and denominator would be adjusted as if 20 new sequences were added, each one with a different amino acid in position 2. There would now be 3 sequences containing histidine in position 2, yielding a probability of 3/22 for histidine and 1/22 for all nonhistidines. The process is repeated for each position in the sequence, summing real and artificial counts to create new numerators and denominators.

The arithmetic is depicted in Figure 4-2. However, even this adjustment embodies some misrepresentation because it assumes that the other 19 amino acids are equally likely to occur in position 2. Because there are significant differences in the distribution of the 20 amino acids in any protein, it makes more sense to adjust the size of each

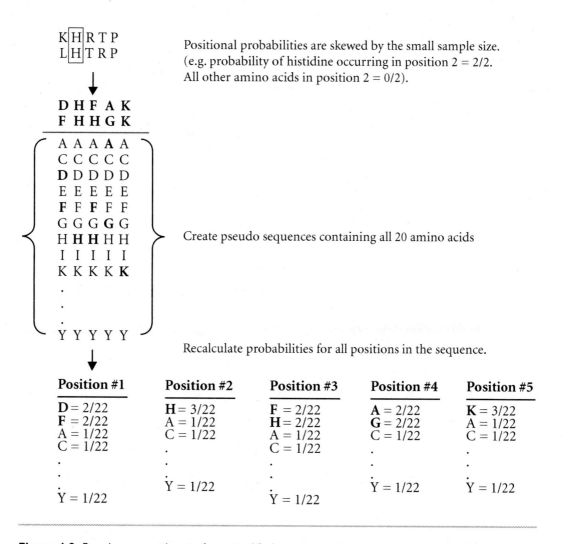

KH RT P
LH T R P

Positional probabilities are skewed by the small sample size. (e.g. probability of histidine occurring in position 2 = 2/2. All other amino acids in position 2 = 0/2).

D H F A K
F HH G K

A A A A A
C C C C C
D D D D D
E E E E E
F F F F F
G G G G G
H H H H H
I I I I I
K K K K K
.
.
.
Y Y Y Y Y

Create pseudo sequences containing all 20 amino acids

Recalculate probabilities for all positions in the sequence.

Position #1	Position #2	Position #3	Position #4	Position #5
D = 2/22	H = 3/22	F = 2/22	A = 2/22	K = 3/22
F = 2/22	A = 1/22	H = 2/22	G = 2/22	A = 1/22
A = 1/22	C = 1/22	A = 1/22	C = 1/22	C = 1/22
C = 1/22	.	C = 1/22	.	.
.	.	.	.	.
.	Y = 1/22	.	Y = 1/22	Y = 1/22
Y = 1/22		Y = 1/22		

Figure 4-2 Pseudocount arithmetic for a simplified case containing two sequences, both of which contain a histidine residue at position 2. The distribution calculations for histidine and the other 19 amino acids is shown.

pseudocount to represent an observed frequency for that amino acid in a representative frequency. Another rational approach involves using distributions that mirror the type of amino acid known to be preferred in that position (i.e., hydrophobic, hydrophilic, etc.). Chemically defined substitution matrices are often used for this task.

Although it is always preferable to train the model on a large number of sequences, small numbers—fewer than 50—can be effective if an accurate amino acid distribution is used as prior information. One such set of mixtures, Dirichlet mixtures, have proven particularly useful [7]. The mixtures, which are built from components known as Dirichlet densities, are created through position-specific statistical analysis of amino acid distributions across large numbers of proteins. A Dirichlet density is a probability density over all possible combinations of amino acids appearing in a given position. A particular Dirichlet density, for example, might assign a high probability to conserved distributions where a single amino acid predominates over all others. Alternatively, a high probability might be assigned to amino acids with a common identifying feature (e.g., hydrophobic or hydrophilic character). Final pseudocounts for each amino acid are calculated from a weighted sum of Dirichlet densities and added to the observed amino acid counts from the training set. HMMs built using Dirichlet mixtures are unique in the sense that they embody an enormous amount of structural information about a specific class of protein. Such models are often used to represent amino acid distributions that are favored in certain chemical environments.

The process of designing substitution methodologies is sometimes considered more art than science. Success requires an unusual blend of algorithmic exactness and chemical/biological insight. Like many other mathematical techniques that combine scientific insight with mathematical rigor, HMMs are an important research tool whose power depends on the skill of the researcher.

PERCEPTRONS AND NEURAL NETWORKS

A perceptron is a mathematical construct, a weighting function, designed to embody a set of rules that can be applied to information represented in the form of a sequence with discrete and meaningful positions. Perceptrons are equivalent to single-layer neural networks where input and output layers are directly connected without additional "hidden" layers. (We will return to the neural network concept later in this section as it builds on the design of the simpler perceptron.) Both neural networks and perceptrons are useful tools for identifying a variety of position-specific structures associated with families of sequences. Algorithmically, perceptrons are relatively simple. Most often they are used to identify a feature that is associated with a specific characteristic through a process that involves examining a large number of sequences, some that exhibit the characteristic and some that do not. The goal is to write a weighting function that embodies this knowledge and can be used to predict which group a new sequence, outside the training set, will fall into.

The weighting function is developed through an iterative process. When applied to one of the sequences, the function will give a value and the magnitude of that value must be greater than 1 for all sequences that contain the feature and less than −1 for all sequences that do not. The iterative process, which involves examining the sequences, generating scores, and adjusting weighting function values, continues until the program arrives at a function that can be used to mathematically separate the sequences into two distinct groups. After these criteria are achieved, the function can be applied to new sequences to predict which group each is most likely to be a member of—the one that contains the feature or the one that does not.

Prior to scoring, each sequence is encoded in a matrix that mirrors the structure of the weighting function. Scores are determined by multiplying each element in a sequence matrix by its corresponding element in the weighting function and adding together the sum of all the products. If the calculated score for a sequence on the "positive" list is greater than 0, or the score for a sequence on the "negative" list is less than 0, the matrix is left unchanged. If the sum of the products is too low or too high, the weighting function must be adjusted. This adjustment is accomplished by incrementing each position in the weighting function that corresponds to a residue in the encoded sequence matrix for sequences on the positive list, or decrementing these positions for sequences on the negative list. The process ends when each sequence receives an appropriate positive or negative score.

Figure 4-3 contains a flow diagram that illustrates the sequence-encoding process, scoring of encoded sequences against a weighting function, and the process of making modifications to the weighting function. Learning is envisioned as taking place in "epochs." Each epoch involves a single pass through both lists of sequences, alternating between positive and negative. When an epoch can be completed without any changes to the weighting function, the process is complete. It is important to recognize that a final weighting function represents one of many possible solutions to a given set of sequences. In our example, the weighting function is initialized with the number 1 in each position. These assignments are strictly arbitrary and, in principle, any random set of initialization scores will work just as well. The algorithm always finds the closest solution among a family of weighting functions and, given a sufficient number of epochs, a solution is always found if one exists.

Positive	Negative
P1 AATTAC	N1 CATTAC
P2 AATTAG	N2 AATTGG
P3 ATATAG	N3 TTATAG

```
        1 2 3 4 5 6                 1 2 3 4 5 6
     A | 1 1     1    |          A | 1 1 1 1 1 1 |
     T |     1 1   1  |    ×     T | 1 1 1 1 1 1 |      = 6
     C |              |          C | 1 1 1 1 1 1 |
     G |              |          G | 1 1 1 1 1 1 |
         Sequence P1                Initial weighting function
```

↓ No changes

Positive	Negative
P1 AATTAC	**N1 CATTAC**
P2 AATTAG	N2 AATTGG
P3 ATATAG	N3 TTATAG

```
        1 2 3 4 5 6                 1 2 3 4 5 6
     A |   1     1    |          A | 1 1 1 1 1 1 |
     T |     1 1      |    ×     T | 1 1 1 1 1 1 |      = 6
     C | 1         1  |          C | 1 1 1 1 1 1 |
     G |              |          G | 1 1 1 1 1 1 |
         Sequence N1
```

↓ Changes required

Positive	Negative
P1 AATTAC	N1 CATTAC
P2 AATTAG	N2 AATTGG
P3 ATATAG	N3 TTATAG

```
        1 2 3 4 5 6                 1 2 3 4 5 6
     A | 1 1     1    |          A | 1 0 1 1 0 1 |
     T |     1 1      |    ×     T | 1 1 0 0 1 1 |      = 2
     C |              |          C | 1 1 1 1 1 1 |
     G |           1  |          G | 1 1 1 1 1 1 |
         Sequence P2
```

↓ No changes

Positive	Negative
P1 AATTAC	N1 CATTAC
P2 AATTAG	**N2 AATTGG**
P3 ATATAG	N3 TTATAG

```
        1 2 3 4 5 6                 1 2 3 4 5 6
     A | 1 1         |          A | 1 0 1 1 1 1 |
     T |     1 1      |    ×     T | 1 1 0 0 1 1 |      = 3
     C |              |          C | 1 1 1 1 1 1 |
     G |         1 1  |          G | 1 1 1 1 1 1 |
         Sequence N2
```

Figure 4-3 The perceptron algorithm. Sequences are first separated into two lists (positive and negative). Each sequence is then encoded in a matrix that facilitates scoring against a weighting function. If the resulting score is too low or too high, modifications are made to the weighting function. When all sequences achieve appropriate scores, the process terminates. The final weighting function can be used to make predictions about new sequences that were not included in the training set.

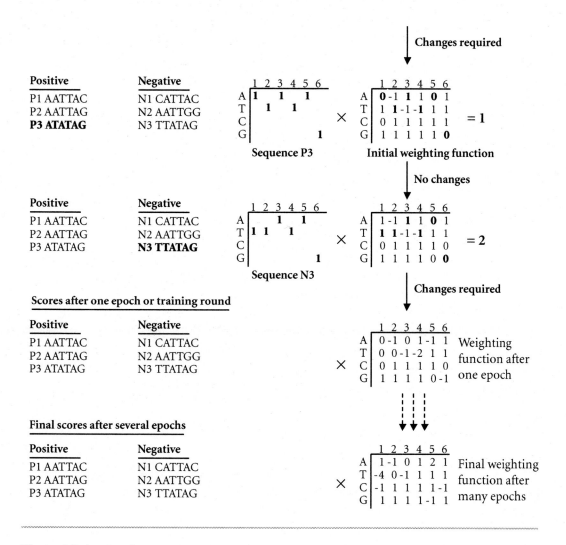

Figure 4-3 *(continued)*

It is sometimes possible to examine the weighting function and identify features based on large negative or positive scores. Unfortunately, this is often not the case, and even simple examples such as the one depicted in Figure 4-3 often result in complex weighting functions that do not lend themselves to human interpretation. Despite the fact that our example contains only three positive and three negative sequences, each only six residues long, the final weighting function embodies a complex set of rules. Additionally, initialization values sometimes persist in the weighting function, and these values can obscure the final results (e.g., score of 1 for a G in position 1 of our example).

Subtracting these persistent scores can often be helpful. For example, removing the score of 1 for G in position 1 of our final weighting function helps highlight the fact that all positive sequences contain an A in this position and negative sequences contain either a T or C. However, the strong (−4) score for a T is misleading because only one sequence displays this feature. Conversely, the low positive score for A in position 1 is undoubtedly related to its presence in one of the negative sequences. Such interpretation is likely to be misleading for larger sets containing relatively long sequences. A more direct approach involves constructing test sequences containing well-characterized features and scoring these sequences against the final weighting function. Alternatively, data-visualization techniques can be used to summarize weighting functions in a way that highlights the features and rules they embody.

Although the scoring technique is position-dependent, there is no requirement that sequences precisely align on feature boundaries. This flexibility is related to the heuristic quality of the algorithm. Misalignments between features are automatically handled in the weighting function with incremented scores in all columns that contain features. However, lack of precision with regard to feature alignment can make it difficult to create meaningful weighting functions; the results can be difficult to interpret. Misalignments can also disguise features and make it difficult to write a function that mathematically separates all positive and negative sequences.

Some of these issues can be addressed by combining the techniques of sequence alignment and pattern discovery. One could envision optimizing a multiple-sequence alignment with HMM and using the aligned sequences as input for the perceptron algorithm. Figure 4-4 illustrates the effects on the weighting function of a small (one base) sequence misalignment. Although such effects often grow out of proportion to the magnitude of the misalignment, even a single base-pair shift can completely disrupt the

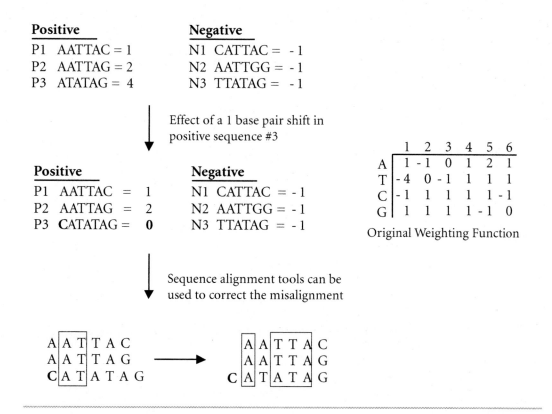

Figure 4-4 The effect of a one-level sequence misalignment on a perceptron weighting function. Even a small change can be disruptive. Any misalignment can be complex and confusing to interpret. The solution is to combine sequence-alignment and pattern-recognition tools and to adjust alignments of individual sequences while examining the effects on the weighting function.

solution. The problem is twofold—small sequence shifts can be disruptive enough to render the problem unsolvable, and other changes that do not completely disrupt the solution can be confusing and complex to interpret. Furthermore, the perceptron algorithm embodies a certain level of resourcefulness in the sense that any differences between positive and negative sequences will be exploited to create a solution. This characteristic of the technique can attach significance to differences that are not truly meaningful. One solution to this problem is to train the perceptron against a large number of negative sequences that are likely to contain all possible permutations of sequences that do not contain the feature in question. If a weighting function cannot be found, individual sequences creating the problem can be removed or realigned. Perceptron algorithms used in this way often serve as excellent alignment tools. One powerful strategy involves successively adjusting alignments and examining weighting functions to minimize the number of columns in the function that require changes and the number of epochs required to find a solution.

IDENTIFICATION OF TRANSLATION INITIATION SITES IN E. COLI

The use of weighting functions as pattern discovery engines dates back to the early 1980s when they were used to identify translation initiation sites in E. coli [8]. Shine and Dalgarno had previously sequenced the 3' end of the 16S ribosomal RNA and found that it was complementary to a short sequence upstream of the initiation codon for several genes. At the time it was not known whether the Shine/Dalgarno sequence in concert with the start codon (AUG) was sufficient to trigger ribosomal binding and translation into protein [9]. Additional data suggested that other sequence or secondary structure features were required. A large database was constructed of sequences that were known to contain a ribosomal binding site. Various rules-based and statistical approaches were applied to the problem with the goal of identifying a set of features sufficient to guarantee translational initiation. Because the level of complexity and variability of the rules was unknown, it was not clear whether a simple set of rules would suffice. Additionally, it was likely that the process involved secondary structure that could be coded in a number of different sequences—the fact that sequence-based approaches to finding rules had failed hinted that this might well be the case.

Further analysis revealed that sequences around and within the binding site were highly biased. It was proposed that individual residues in key locations could interact with the ribosome and that translational initiation depended on the sum of all contributing interactions exceeding a threshold [10]. Additional studies on the level of conservation of these positions further contributed to the view that initiation depended on the sum of various effects. Thus was born the concept of a weighting function that could embody a mathematical representation of the positional rules for predicting such interactions. The perceptron algorithm seemed perfectly suited to such a task, and early results produced weighting functions that exhibited the ability to accurately identify initiation sites in sequences that were not included in the training set—the ultimate test of a pattern-discovery system [11, 12].

FROM PERCEPTRON TO NEURAL NETWORK—SOLUTION TO THE "EXCLUSIVE OR" PROBLEM

The simplicity of the perceptron algorithm makes it appealing for many pattern-discovery problems in bioinformatics. However, the technique has limitations that are important to understand because they have led to the development of more sophisticated constructs known as neural networks. More specifically, perceptrons are designed to solve problems that are linearly separable, meaning that the problem can be visualized in a Cartesian plane where the perceptron defines a line or "hyperplane" in a higher-dimensional space that separates all output >0 from all output <0. As mentioned before, multiple solutions (weighting functions) exist; each represents a different line through the Cartesian space. Problems that are not linearly separable—that is, separable by a single hyperplane—cannot be solved using this method. These differences are illustrated in Figure 4-5. The left half of the figure depicts a linearly separable problem based on a simple AND condition (i.e., thymine (T) in positions 3 AND 5 of a sequence). The right side depicts a logical XOR (exclusive or), which can be represented only by a nonlinear solution. Sequences that fall into this category might contain a T in position 3 or a T in position 5, but not both.

Figure 4-6 contains sequence analogs of each of these logical constructs. The first pair of sequences embodies the logical AND case. Each member of the positive group contains a T in positions 3 and 5. Members of the negative group may contain any residues in positions 3 or 5 with the exception that both positions cannot contain a T. A weighting function capable of separating both lists is displayed in the figure along with scores for each of the sequences in both groups.

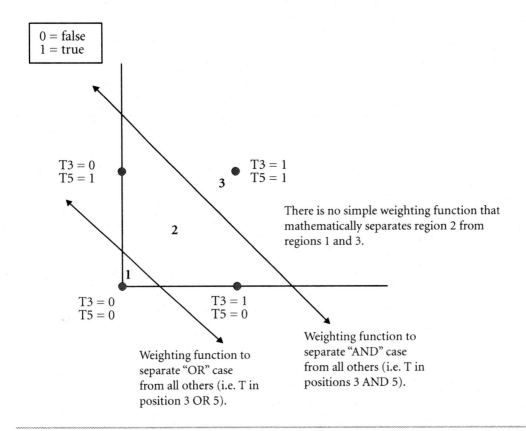

0 = false
1 = true

T3 = 0
T5 = 1

T3 = 1
T5 = 1

3

There is no simple weighting function that
mathematically separates region 2 from
regions 1 and 3.

2

1

T3 = 0
T5 = 0

T3 = 1
T5 = 0

Weighting function to
separate "OR" case
from all others (i.e. T in
position 3 OR 5).

Weighting function to
separate "AND" case
from all others (i.e. T in
positions 3 AND 5).

Figure 4-5 Diagrammatic representation of linear and nonlinear sequence-analysis problems. The Cartesian coordinate system contains 3 regions, numbered I through 3. Region I represents the NOT condition—T is not present in position 3 or 5. Region 2 represents the XOR condition—T in position 3 or 5, but not both. Region 3 contains the AND condition—T in both positions 3 and 5. A linear function does not exist that can separate region 2 from regions I and 3. Nonlinear function that can isolate the XOR condition must be represented by two arrows in the Cartesian plane.

The second pair of sequences embodies the logical XOR condition. Each member of the positive group contains a T in position 3 or 5, but not both. Members of the negative group may contain any other sequence combinations with the exception of those that fit in the positive group. (Note that a sequence containing a T in both positions 3 and 5 would fall into the negative group.) The perceptron algorithm cannot be used to construct a weighting function to solve the XOR condition.

Logical AND Condition

	1	2	3	4	5	6
A	0	0	-2	0	-2	0
T	0	0	1	0	1	0
C	0	0	-2	0	-2	0
G	0	0	-2	0	-2	0

Positive Group   **Negative Group**

Positive Group	Negative Group
A A T C T A	A A C C T A
A T T A T C	A T A A T C
C T T A T C	C T T A G C
G A T G T C	G A T G A C
T A T C T A	T A C C T A
T A T A T A	T A A A C A
G T T T T C	G T A T C C
A A T A T A	A A C A T A
T T T T T T	T T A T T T

Logical AND Weighting Function:

Positive Group = T in positions 3 and 5

Negative Group = Any combination of A, C, or G in positions 3 and 5

Logical XOR Condition

Positive Group	Negative Group
A A T C A A	A A T C T A
A T C A T C	A T T A T C
C T T A A C	C T A A G C
G A T G G C	G A T G A C
T A C C T A	T A C C G A
T A A A T A	T A T A T A
G T G T T C	G T T T T C
A A T A C A	A A C A G A
T T T T A T	T T T T T T

Logical XOR Weighting Function cannot be constructed using a single layer Perceptron

Positive Group = T in position 3 or 5 but not both

Negative Group = Any other combination including T in both positions 3 and 5

Figure 4-6 Sequences displaying logical AND and logical XOR characteristics. The first pair of lists (logical AND example) can be separated using a single weighting function derived using the perceptron algorithm. The second pair of lists (logical XOR example) cannot be separated with a single weighting function. The first problem is considered linear, and the second is considered nonlinear.

The solution to the XOR problem is to add additional weighting functions in a second layer, often referred to as a hidden layer. These additional functions and layers form the syntactic difference between a perceptron and a neural network. The basic design of a neural network (or multilayered perceptron) contains discrete input, output, and hidden layers, and is built on two fundamental principles: back propagation and feed-forward activation. The architecture, however, is considerably more complex.

Neural networks may contain any number of hidden layers, each composed of multiple weighting functions or units (neurons). Each neuron is directly connected to all of its counterparts in the previous layer; there are no interconnections within a layer. Three parameters define each neuron—the connection weights of its input connections, the threshold that controls its output, and the connection weights of its output connections. In a feed-forward system, individual units receive their input from the previous layer and output their results to the next layer. Individual connections are characterized by input and output weights (WI and WO) and thresholds (T). When the sum of the weighted inputs exceeds the threshold for a particular neuron, the output is set at the value defined as WO. If the sum falls below the threshold, the output is set at 0. This design is inspired by the biological neuron, where many inputs converge on a single brain cell that only fires when the sum of all inputs exceeds a preset threshold. Both systems learn by adjusting firing thresholds and connection strengths.

As in the perceptron algorithm, sequences from both lists are alternatively presented to the network for analysis. Training the network involves adjusting the weights and type of each connection until the network output correctly distinguishes between the two datasets used for training. Each time a sequence is examined, either in the positive or negative group, the network performs a feed-forward calculation, and the output is confirmed. As in the case of a single-layer perceptron, sequences in the positive group should receive a positive score, and sequences in the negative group should receive a negative score. If the magnitude and sign of the score is incorrect, the program propagates changes backward through the network, starting at the output layer, by examining the output value at each layer and neuron and adjusting connection weights and thresholds as appropriate. The magnitude of each change is controlled by a variable set within the program. The value of this variable ultimately determines the rate at which the network learns. The process of working backward from the output layer in a deterministic way, adjusting connection weights and thresholds to obtain the desired result, is known as back propagation. The basic design of a neural network is depicted in Figure 4-7.

WO input layer = WI hidden layer

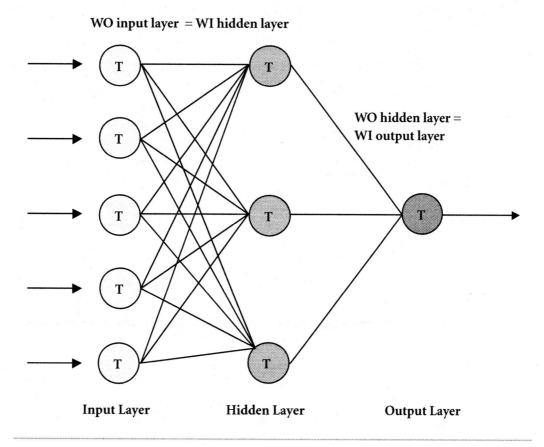

WO hidden layer =
WI output layer

Input Layer   **Hidden Layer**   **Output Layer**

Figure 4-7 Architecture of a neural network. The design allows for any number of hidden layers, and any number of units within each layer. Each unit is connected to all units in the previous layer. Units are not connected to each other within a single layer. Activation of the network proceeds from the input units, layer by layer, through the output units. (This network contains a single hidden layer, which is the most common design.) In feed-forward activation, units of the hidden layer compute their activation and output values and pass these to the output layer. The output layer produces the network's response to the original input. Individual connections are characterized by weights (denoted as WI for input weight and WO for output weights) and thresholds (denoted as T). When the sum of the weighted inputs exceeds the threshold for a particular neuron, the output is set at the value defined as WO. If the sum falls below the threshold, the output is set at 0.

By stacking perceptrons in multiple connected layers, we can create a system with enough flexibility to solve the XOR problem. The neural network that embodies this solution can be thought of as containing two distinct neuronal types within the hidden layer—logical OR and logical AND. Both biological and computerized neural networks can contain special function neurons, and both can be logically defined by their firing thresholds and connection design. However, computerized neural networks display an important architectural difference; every neuron is normally connected to each of its counterparts in the previous layer. Biological systems are more flexible with regard to their connection architecture. Moreover, biological systems display plasticity in the sense that the connection architecture is dynamic and can change over time. Computerized

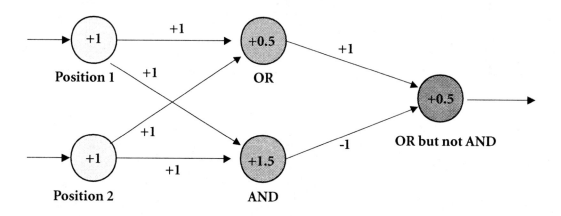

Position 1	Position 2	Hidden Layer (OR) Output	Hidden Layer (AND) Output	Output Layer Output
1	0	1	0	1
0	1	1	0	1
1	1	1	-1	0
0	0	0	0	0

Figure 4-8 Neural network solution to the XOR problem.

neural networks are not normally rewired due to the complexity of rewriting the software—plasticity is limited to adjusting connection weights between adjacent layers.

Figure 4-8 depicts the solution to the XOR problem for a simple two-residue problem. The goal is to create a design that outputs a positive value when one, but not both, of the sequence positions contains a thymine (T). In the case where both, or neither, of the residues are thymine, the output should be negative.

In the figure, the solution is composed of two special-purpose neurons—logical AND and logical OR. The logical OR neuron outputs a +1 when at least one of the two positions contains a T. The logical AND neuron outputs a –1 when both positions contain a T. If both logical OR and logical AND conditions are true (logical XOR), the sum of inputs to the output neuron will be 0. Because the output neuron has a threshold of 0.5, the final layer will output a 0. Conversely, if one of the positions, but not both, contains a T, the threshold of 1.5 will not be reached at the logical AND neuron—output from this neuron will be 0. The logical OR neuron will be above its threshold of 0.5 and output will be +1. The sum of inputs to the final layer will be +1, exceeding the threshold of 0.5, and the final output from the system will be +1. In the case where neither residue is a T, all inputs to the hidden layer are 0 and none of the neurons in the system will reach threshold. The final output will thus be 0.

These operations are described in Table 4-1, which lists output values for all possible XOR conditions.

Neural network technology, like HMMs, relies on a combination of scientific insight and algorithmic rigor. The process of constructing training sets is the most conspicuous example. Researchers often use biological knowledge to justify making exceptions to a

Table 4-1 Truth Table for the XOR Condition

Residue 1	Residue 2	Output Value
A,G,C	T	1 (true)
T	A,G,C	1 (true)
T	T	0 (false)
A,G,C	A,G,C	0 (false)

specific set of selection criteria. These decisions along with various tunable parameters associated with the software are critical to the success of any neural network experiment.

PATTERN DISCOVERY, SINGLE NUCLEOTIDE POLYMORPHISMS, AND HAPLOTYPE IDENTIFICATION

Single nucleotide polymorphisms (SNPs) are the most abundant type of DNA sequence variation in the human genome [13]. A SNP is a DNA site in which a single base varies between individuals. Such variations can serve both as a physical landmarks and genetic markers whose transmission can be followed from generation to generation. Recent years have seen a massive effort to correlate the appearance of SNPs with specific diseases. These studies typically involve sequencing portions of DNA from large populations including affected and nonaffected individuals. Furthermore, genetic markers (haplotypes) that are found in close proximity to a mutation responsible for a disease are often found to exhibit strong correlations with that disease. The phenomenon, known as linkage disequilibrium, results from the close physical proximity of the disease marker to the mutation. The concept of linkage disequilibrium is illustrated in Figure 4-9.

THE SNP CONSORTIUM

On April 15, 1999, ten pharmaceutical companies in conjunction with Britain's Wellcome Trust announced that they had set up a joint nonprofit venture known as The SNP Consortium (TSC). Although the original goal was to identify 300,000 SNPs, the consortium succeeded in creating a library of more than 1.5 million. The entire dataset has been placed in the public domain. SNPs have been implicated in many diseases and often have far reaching impacts on the efficacy of drugs. It is known, for example, that a SNP in the gene for the enzyme N-acetyl transferase is associated with a high incidence of peripheral neuropathy for patients being treated with isoniazid, an antituberculosis drug.

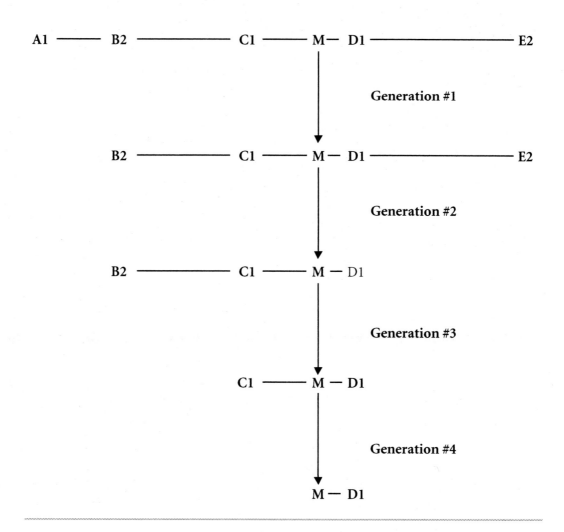

Figure 4-9 Linkage disequilibrium is the basis for association studies that compare the frequency of occurrence of specific haplotypes and positionally related genetic diseases. In this example, a mutation (M) is initially found on a chromosome with the A1-B2-C1-D1-E2 haplotype. Recombination events between generations reduce the strength of the associations between M and various other markers that make up the haplotype. After several generations, only markers that are physically close to each other remain associated. These tightly linked markers are said to exist in linkage disequilibrium. (Source: Kwok P. and Gu Z. [1999]. Single Nucleotide Polymorphism Libraries: Why and How Are We Building Them? *Molecular Medicine Today*, 5, 538–543)

This molecular/population genetic approach provides a new way to identify genes associated with diseases and is often the only way to study the molecular events leading to the development of a specific disease.

Population genetic approaches to understanding diseases are complex and rely on statistics that describe the expression of many markers in large numbers of individuals. In the genome-wide mapping approach, two groups of patients are identified, disease and control. The groups are matched for as many variables as possible, including demographic background, age, ethnicity, etc. Genetic profiles are then established using a set of markers that are evenly distributed throughout the genome. Statistical tests are used to identify haplotypes associated with the disease. The number of individuals required varies, but it is estimated that 60,000 markers at 50kb spacing will be needed to complete an association study with 1,000 individuals. Such a study will require 60 million genotyping assays. Another approach, candidate-gene mapping, relies on educated guesses regarding the key genes involved in a disease. It is generally agreed that five markers are sufficient for an individual gene [14]. Both approaches involve the identification and sequencing of large numbers of markers in relatively close proximity to each other. SNPs are perfect candidates for such studies for the following reasons [15]:

- The mean density of SNPs is approximately 1 per 1,000 bases in the genome. This density allows construction of a library that will meet most of the needs of association studies.
- The intergenerational SNP mutation rate is very low. (Mutations confound statistical analyses of population studies.)
- Because many mutations that cause Mendelian disorders result from a single polymorphism in a gene that controls an important cellular function, it is likely that many SNPs are direct contributors to disease states.
- High-throughput genotyping methods now make SNP identification possible on a large scale at reasonable cost.

A new code has been adopted by the NCBI to describe SNPs. The syntax includes additional letters to represent various options for known polymorphisms. Although such a code is necessary, substitutions and wildcards are always a problem for the bioinformaticist because they reduce the precision of any search or comparison. Table 4-2 contains the new codes.

Table 4-2 Extensions to the Genetic Code for Managing Single Nucleotide Polymorphisms (SNPs)

IUPAC Code	Meaning
A	A
C	C
G	G
T	T
M	A or C
R	A or G
W	A or T
S	C or G
Y	C or T
K	G or T
V	A or C or G
H	A or C or T
D	A or G or T
B	C or G or T
N	G or A or T or C

Source: National Center for Biotechnology Information—Entrez SNP

Multiple-sequence alignment tools and perceptron algorithms are a powerful combination for identifying features that display positional integrity. However, these tools must be used carefully in situations where multiple SNPs or other features are separated by hundreds or even thousands of bases. Generally speaking, weighting functions that are built from very long sequences embody rules that are not statistically significant. One solution is to populate the negative group with many more sequences to increase the statistical relevance of repeating sequence elements. An alternative approach involves synthesizing random sequences to expand the size of the negative group, effectively using these as a filter to highlight significant repeating features on the positive side.

Another approach to increasing the statistical significance of such comparisons is to decrease the length of the sequences. It is inherently more difficult to find statistically significant differences between relatively short sequences because they contain fewer positions that can be used to make adjustments to the weighting function. An obvious approach involves dividing the sequences into short segments and running separate comparisons on each. Finally, SNPs and other features that occur in coding regions are statistically easier to work with than noncoding features because coding regions tend to be identical between different individuals. In such cases, the perceptron algorithm would likely set all positions in the weighting function to 0 and increment/decrement only those that directly correspond to the specific difference—the unknown feature or SNP.

Unfortunately, not all features are contained within known boundaries. Most repeating elements of the genome appear in control regions, and it is often difficult to assert that a specific region contains a feature. Even if a specific region is known to contain an important, but unidentified sequence element, the process of aligning a large number of such sequences may be problematic if that feature is relatively small and other longer, positionally variant, sequence elements dominate the alignment. In such cases, the small feature would ultimately appear in different positions of the alignment, and algorithms such as perceptron would not be able to build a useful weighting function. (In principle it would not even be possible to construct meaningful positive and negative lists from the sequence data where the positive list contained the sequence element and the negative list did not.) Situations where positionally variant large sequence elements dominate a multiple-sequence alignment and mask a small but significant feature can be solved only by testing different alignments.

One notable weakness of most alignment strategies is that they are designed to focus on the best fit and can miss subtle features. Figure 4-10 includes an alignment example

```
ATTCGCTAGCTCGATCCGTATACTG GT GG
ATTCCGATGCTACAGCTTACTGATC AG CT
ATTCGTCAGACTGCTTTACTGACCG GC AC
GTTCCGATCTCGAGCTCAGTACTAT AG TA
ATTTACTGGACTCGAAGCTACGCAC GG GT
ATTCACGCCGGATGCCGTGATATGA GC CC
ACTCATGCGCGCGATGGCGATATCG AG TT
ATTCATGCACGGTAGCGCGCATGGA GT GG
ATCCATGCGGGACATTGGATCTACC GA AA
ATTCATGCTCGCTATGCTCGAGATT GA CT
ATTCATCGCGATATCGCGCGATAGC GT TG
```

Alignment based on ATTC in positions 1-4
misses the G in position 26 or 27.

```
ATTCGCTAGCTCGATCCGTATACTG G TGG
ATTCCGATGCTACAGCTTACTGATCA G CT
ATTCGTCAGACTGCTTTACTGACCG G CAC
GTTCCGATCTCGAGCTCAGTACTATA G TA
ATTTACTGGACTCGAAGCTACGCAC G GGT
ATTCACGCCGGATGCCGTGATATGA G CCC
ACTCATGCGCGCGATGGCGATATCGA G TT
ATTCATGCACGGTAGCGCGCATGGA G TGG
ATCCATGCGGGACATTGGATCTACC G AAA
ATTCATGCTCGCTATGCTCGAGATT G ACT
ATTCATCGCGATATCGCGCGATAGC G TTG
```

New alignment based on G in position 26 or 27.

Figure 4-10 Sequence alignment containing major and minor structural features. Note that a major feature dominates the alignment, obscuring a more-subtle but potentially important sequence element.

that embodies this problem. Note that the major structural feature, the one that dominates the alignment, hides a more subtle but potentially important SNP and linked sequence element.

Sequence elements of the form displayed in Figure 4-10 are a common theme in any genome; the lack of context often makes them seem completely position-independent. Because multiple-sequence alignment strategies and rules-based algorithms such as perceptron are insufficient for identifying new out-of-context elements, a new class of pattern-discovery algorithm is required. Solutions belonging to this class must be capable of detecting all existing patterns in a set of input sequences without using alignments or enumerating the entire solution space [16, 17]. All reported patterns should be as specific as possible. For example, if the sequence A-(x)-T-G appears in several positions within the input set, then it makes no sense to report the pattern A-(x)-(x)-G if the second pattern appears in the same position as the first and nowhere else. Furthermore, all patterns should be maximal. (A pattern, p, is maximal if there is no other pattern, q, that contains the pattern p as a subsequence and has the same number of occurrences as p.) For example, given two patterns, ABCD and ABCDE, pattern ABCD is considered maximal only if it occurs more often than ABCDE. The task of identifying maximal patterns is readily accomplished by combining elementary patterns into progressively larger ones until all repeating patterns are identified regardless of size [18].

The mathematical basis of this class of algorithms has matured over the past several years, and it is now possible to discover repeating patterns in unbounded sequence regions regardless of size or intervening space between repeating elements [19]. These techniques are especially valuable because they transcend the sort of alignment problem depicted in Figure 4-10 and are capable of identifying even the most subtle relationships over varying distances. Figure 4-11 depicts a hypothetical example.

The basic strategy for discovering such patterns involves building a dictionary that contains all maximal variable-length patterns from a set of input sequences or a single long sequence, and using this dictionary as a reference for scanning new sequence data that were not part of the original training set. Dictionary sequences are built up in a recursive process that involves multiple scans through the test data. Most approaches involve setting parameters that include a minimum threshold for the number of occurrences of a sequence element in addition to a number of rules for using wildcards. It might not be appropriate, for example, to capture all occurrences of A-(x)-A in the

5' AGTCGATGAATCGATAGATCGCTAGATCGCGCAATAGAGGTGATAGCGCTAGA
GATGAGCTCCGAGATAGAGAGAAACCGCGGTGATGCGCTAGAGAAATCGCGGTGAGATC 3'

5' AGTCGATGAATCGATAGATCGCTAGATCGCGC**AA.....GT**GATAGCGCTAGA
GATGAGCTCCGAGATAGAGAGA**AA.....GT**GATGCGCTAGAGA**AA.....GT**GAGATC 3'

Pattern is a 5 residue space
bounded on the 5' side by AA
and on the 3' side by GT

Figure 4-11 A hidden repeating genomic feature. Note that the feature is relatively invisible in the upper diagram but visible when highlighted in the lower diagram. Such features are normally discovered using unbounded pattern-discovery techniques rather than perceptron-style algorithms.

genome unless that pattern occurs in numbers that exceed their statistical likelihood by a significant ratio. (This pattern should occur once in every 16 triplets by purely random chance.) Alternatively, if a particular pattern is found to be statistically linked to the appearance of another well-characterized sequence or structure, it might be considered a valid addition to the dictionary. It is clear that these decisions involve a mix of biological knowledge and statistical inference in addition to purely mathematical pattern discovery.

This discussion points to the need to establish different parameters and thresholds for various data types. For example, protein sequence data is unlikely to suffer from the repetition issues that plague nucleotide sequences because the data can contain any of 20 different residues in each position. For example, whereas a 3-letter nucleotide sequence might have no significance outside of its ability to code for a specific amino acid, a 3-letter amino acid sequence in a protein has only a 1/8,000 chance of appearing randomly. An amino acid triplet that appears twice in the same protein sequence is mathematically equivalent to a repeating sequence of nine consecutive nucleotides, including substitutions for variability in the codon table. However, although one might be tempted to translate coding region sequences into their corresponding amino acid sequences, this strategy is confounded by the presence of noncoding introns. It is also important to remember that less than 1% of the genome codes for protein and most of

5'   GTGTTCACAGATGCCGCGTTCGGCATGCTAGTACTGCTAAATGCGC
ACGAATCCTGATCTACTAGTTGTTCTCGGCAGCTAGGTTCCCTATGATCA 3'

> Begin pattern search at the 5' end by identifying
> GT as a potential pattern

5'   **GTGT**TCACAGATGCCGC**GT**TCGGCATGCTA**GT**ACTGCTAAATGCGC
ACGAATCCTACTA**GT**T**GT**TCTCGGCAGCTAGGTTCCCTATGATCA 3'

> Extend all occurrences of GT

5'   **GTGTT**CACAGATGCCGCGTTCGGCATGCTA**GTA**CTGCTAAATGCGC
ACGAATCCTGATCTACTA**GTTGTT**CTCGGCAGCTA**GGT**TCCCTATGATCA 3'

> Remove nonrepeating sequences GTG, GTA
> from the list

5'   GT**GTT**CACAGATGCCGC**GTT**CGGCATGCTAGTACTGCTAAATGCGC
ACGAATCCTGATCTACTA**GTTGTT**CTCGGCAGCTAG**GTT**CCCTATGATCA 3'

> Extend occurrences of GTT

5'   GT**GTT**CACAGATGCCGC**GTT**CGGCATGCTAGTACTGCTAAATGCGC
ACGAATCCTGATCTACTA**GTTGTTC**TCGGCAGCTAG**GTTC**CCTATGATCA 3'

> Remove nonrepeating sequence GTTG from list

Figure 4-12 Step-by-step buildup of a pattern dictionary for a small DNA sequence. Patterns smaller than four-based are not considered and a given pattern must repeat at least three times to be added to the dictionary. Sequences of all lengths are considered up to one third the length of the input sequence.

the areas that will be searched have regulatory or structural functions—nucleotide sequences in these areas do not correspond to amino acid sequences.

Figure 4-12 illustrates the process of building a sequence dictionary. In keeping with the spirit of our previous discussion, we have decided to set a minimum threshold of

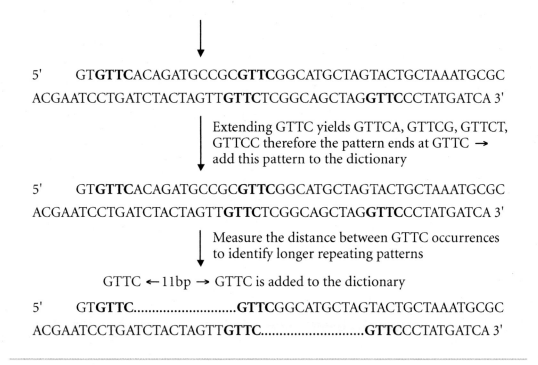

5'   GTGTTCACAGATGCCGCGTTCGGCATGCTAGTACTGCTAAATGCGC
ACGAATCCTGATCTACTAGTTGTTCTCGGCAGCTAGGTTCCCTATGATCA 3'

Extending GTTC yields GTTCA, GTTCG, GTTCT,
GTTCC therefore the pattern ends at GTTC →
add this pattern to the dictionary

5'   GTGTTCACAGATGCCGCGTTCGGCATGCTAGTACTGCTAAATGCGC
ACGAATCCTGATCTACTAGTTGTTCTCGGCAGCTAGGTTCCCTATGATCA 3'

Measure the distance between GTTC occurrences
to identify longer repeating patterns

GTTC ←11bp → GTTC is added to the dictionary

5'   GTGTTC..........................GTTCGGCATGCTAGTACTGCTAAATGCGC
ACGAATCCTGATCTACTAGTTGTTC..........................GTTCCCTATGATCA 3'

Figure 4-12 *(continued)*

four nucleotides for the length of a maximal sequence and three repeats as the minimum number of times the pattern must appear. Because a pattern must repeat at least three times, the longest sequence that is evaluated is one third the length of the total input string. If we had been studying longer sequences, we might have set a lower threshold for the minimum number of bases and a higher threshold for the number of times the pattern must be repeated.

We have now reviewed the basic theory behind three broad classes of algorithms that form cornerstones of modern bioinformatics—hidden Markov models, perceptrons, and unbounded pattern discovery. HMMs provide a mechanism for aligning multiple sequences. Such algorithms can be thought of as extensions to more basic methods for aligning individual pairs of sequences. In many cases, the extension to pairwise sequence alignment involves a process that recursively adds additional sequences to a growing alignment, aligning each new sequence in its turn. Perceptron algorithms and neural networks are designed to create weighting functions from previously aligned sequences. These weighting functions are designed to score new sequences that were not part of the original training set. Based on these scores we can accurately place a new sequence into one of the groups used in the training set. Pattern-discovery methods are used to identify new sequence features that will ultimately become part of other studies that utilize multiple-sequence alignments or neural network-based analysis techniques.

The algorithms and computational technologies we have reviewed represent important components of a large technology portfolio for comparing and managing genomic sequence information. When combined with algorithms for aligning and assembling sequence fragments, this toolkit forms the computational foundation for industrial-scale whole genome sequencing—the next topic in this discussion.

SUMMARY

This chapter built on the previous discussion, which included both concepts related to the organization of chromosomal information and computational techniques for the identification of genomic features. In the process, we explored additional algorithmic processes that can be used to identify particular sequence elements, mathematical techniques that have been developed to align large numbers of sequences, and various statistical methods for comparing sequence data, including the development of weighting functions that can be used to discriminate between two classes of sequence. Collectively these technologies are the foundation upon which the science of bioinformatics has been built.

The past two chapters were intended as a framework that will be extended in Chapter 5 with a discussion of algorithms and computational strategies for transcriptional profiling. The focus of this discussion, however, shifts from sequence analysis to technologies for detecting and accurately counting individual mRNA species. Collectively, these discussions of genomic analysis and transcriptional profiling will form a backdrop for understanding the diversity of the proteome. This diversity lies at the core of an exciting new science commonly referred to as systems biology.

ENDNOTES

1. Salzberg S. L., Pertea M., Delcher A. L., Gardner M.J., Tettelin H. 1999. Interpolated Markov models for eukaryotic gene finding. *Genomics* 59: 24–31.

2. Salzberg S. L., Delcher A. L., Kasif S., White O. 2003. Microbial gene identification using interpolated Markov models. *Nucleic Acids Research* 26(2): 544–548.

3. Krogh A., Brown M., Mian I. S., Sjolander K., Haussler D. 1994. Hidden Markov models in computational biology. Applications to protein modeling. *Journal of Molecular Biology* 235: 1501–1531.

4. Eddy S. R. 1998. Profile hidden Markov models. *Bioinformatics* 14: 755–763.

5. Burge C., Karlin S. 1998. Finding the genes in genomic DNA. *Current Opinions in Structural Biology* 8:3: 46–354.

6. Salzberg, S. L., Searls, D. B., and Kasif, S. (Eds.). "An Introduction to Hidden Markov Models for Biological Sequences" in *Computational Methods in Molecular Biology*. Elsevier Science, 1998. 45–63.

7. Sjolander K., Karplus K., Brown M., Hughey R., Krogh A., Mian I. S., Haussler, D. 1996. Dirichlet mixtures: A method for improved detection of weak but significant protein sequence homology. *Computer Applications in the Biosciences* 12: 327–345.

8. Stormo G. D., Schneider T. D., Gold L. M. 1982. Characterization of translational initiation sites in E. coli. *Nucleic Acids Research* 10: 2971–2996.

9. Shine J., Dalgarno L. 1974. The 3'-terminal sequence of Escherichia coli 16S ribosomal RNA: complementarity to nonsense triplets and ribosome binding sites. *Proceedings of the National Academy of Sciences* 4: 1342–1346.

10. Gold L., Prinbow D., Schneider T., Shinedling S., Singer B. S., Stormo G. 1981. Translational initiation in Procaryotes. *Annual Review of Microbiology* 35: 365–403.

11. Stormo G. D. 1988. Computer methods for analyzing sequence recognition of nucleic acids. Annual Review of Biophysics and Biophysical Chemistry 17: 241–263.

12. Stormo G. D., Fields, D. S. 1990. Consensus patterns in DNA. *Methods in Enzymology* 183: 211–221.

13. Cooper D. N., Smith B. A., Cooke H. J., Niemann S., Schmidtke J. 1985. An estimate of unique DNA sequence heterozygosity in the human genome. *Human Genetics* 69: 201–205.

14. Wang D.G., et al. 1998. Large-scale identification , mapping, and genotyping of single-nucleotide polymorphisms in the human genome. *Science* 280: 1077–1082.

15. Kwok P., Gu Z. 1999. Single nucleotide polymorphism libraries: why and how are we building them? *Molecular Medicine Today* 5: 538–543.

16. Burgard A., Moore G., Maranas C. 2001. Review of the Teiresias-based tools of the IBM bioinformatics and pattern discovery group. *Metabolic Engineering* 3: 285–288.

17. Rigoutsos I., Floratos A. 1998. Combinatorial pattern discovery in biological sequences: the Teiresias algorithm. *Bioinformatics* 14: 55–67.

18. Wepsi A., Dacier M., Debar H. 1999. An intrusion detection system based on the Teiresias pattern discovery algorithm." *EICAR Proceedings*.

19. Brazma A., Jonassen I., Eidhammer I., Gilbert D. "Approaches to the Automatic Discovery of Patterns in Biosequences." Technical report, Department of Informatics, University of Bergen, Norway, 1995.

5

Transcription

INTRODUCTION

Although, in principle, the genome contains all the information one would need to understand a complex metabolic pathway or disease, the information is encoded in a combination of physical and logical constructs that make interpretation very difficult. As you saw in Chapter 3, genes are found in six different reading frames running in both directions and, more often than not, they contain intervening sequences that are subsequently spliced out of the final transcript. Genes are also embedded in multilayer three-dimensional structures. The primary unit of structure, the nucleosome, is composed of chromosomal DNA coiled around a histone protein complex. The location of individual genetic elements within this structure significantly impacts both transcription and replication. The positional effects are subtle because they are related to the topology of a helix coiled around a cylinder. Residues exposed to the interior face of the nucleosome are not accessible to enzymes involved in transcription or replication. Conversely, residues exposed on the surface of the structure and residues contained in the segments that connect nucleosomes are fully accessible. Enzymatic digestion experiments have revealed a level of variability in the structure, and it is now known that protein-coding regions can be hidden or made available for transcription in a time-dependent fashion that relates to the cell cycle. Furthermore, epigenetic factors such as methylated DNA and translocated genes can affect gene expression across multiple generations; as a result, genetically identical cells often exhibit different phenotypes. The combined effect of these genome-level variations makes it difficult to predict the expression of a particular gene and even more difficult to predict the sequence of a final spliced transcript.

Unfortunately, very few physical states or disease conditions are monogenic in nature. Even if a physical state were controlled by a single gene coding for a single protein, the up regulation of that gene would perturb the broader system—many coding regions would be affected. Biology is a systems problem, nonlinear in nature, and the expression of a single gene has very little meaning outside the context of the web of interactions that describes a metabolic state. Each stage in the gene-expression pipeline provides important information about the factors that ultimately determine a phenotype:

- Base sequence information can be used to identify conserved sequences, polymorphisms, promoters, splice sites, and other relevant features that are critical to a complete understanding of the function of any given gene.
- Information about the up and down regulation of closely related messages, mRNA interference, life expectancy, and copy count of individual messages can help build a transcriptional view of a specific metabolic state.
- Despite much analysis, it is not yet possible to predict the three-dimensional folded structure of a protein from its gene sequence. Furthermore, the final protein is often a substrate for any of a number of post-translational modifications—acetylation, methylation, carboxylation, glycosylation, etc. The enzymes that catalyze these reactions recognize structural domains that are difficult to infer using exclusively genomic data.
- Intermediary metabolism is the result of millions of protein:protein interactions. These interactions are context sensitive in the sense that a given protein can exhibit different characteristics and serve completely different functions in different environments. The complex networks that describe these interactions are routinely referred to as systems biology.

The genome-centric view of molecular biology is slowly being replaced by a more comprehensive systems view. One of the most important elements of this approach is a comprehensive understanding of the transcriptional state of all genes involved in a specific metabolic profile. This picture is complicated by the fact that many species of RNA that will be identified as playing an important role in the profile are never translated into protein. As previously discussed in Chapter 3, many messages are degraded by the RNA silencing machinery within the cell and others are prevented from engaging in protein translation. These control mechanisms can cause a high copy-count message, one that is highly abundant within the cell, to be translated into a very small number of protein molecules. Regulatory messages (miRNA, siRNA) are relatively straightforward to spot because they are reproducibly short and lack sequences that are normally associated with ribosomal binding. However, these small regulatory messages are spliced from longer transcripts that certainly have the potential to cause confusion.

Any technique used to study the transcripts within a cell must be capable of spanning the range from single digit copy counts to very large numbers, often in the thousands. Accuracy is important because at the single-digit level, small changes in the number of copies of certain messages can have significant effects on metabolism and disease.

This chapter specifically focuses on transcription—the process of creating a messenger RNA template from a gene sequence. The process has particular significance in the context of this book because it represents the first information-transfer step between gene and protein. In one sense, the step from gene to transcript represents a step up in complexity because many different transcripts can be created from a single coding region. Conversely, each transcript may be viewed as a simplification because much extraneous information has been removed from the raw gene sequence. This simplification is particularly apparent in situations where splicing operations create a message that is substantially different from the original chromosomal sequence. The structural link between mRNA transcript and protein is much more direct than the link between gene and protein. Furthermore, the appearance of a message in the cytoplasm is a clear indication that a particular gene has become involved in a cell's metabolism. This direct link between the appearance of a transcript and metabolic changes within the cell has given rise to a new emerging discipline known as transcriptional profiling.

This discussion begins with a review of the different types of transcripts and their roles in gene expression. The goal is to lay a foundation for the remainder of the chapter, which focuses on various techniques for identifying and counting individual species of mRNA. Transcriptional profiling depends on these techniques in addition to a portfolio of algorithms for data analysis. Over the past few years, the size of a typical expression-profiling experiment has grown to include thousands of transcripts. The result has been a corresponding increase in the level of sophistication of the statistical methods used to analyze the results. These methods are the focus of much of this discussion.

THE TRANSCRIPTOME

If we were to take an inventory of all the messages involved in the creation of a single protein, we would need to include those that code for enzymes that catalyze post-translational modifications—methylases, acetylases, carboxylases, glycosylases, and other enzymes that remove amino acids from the amino or carboxy terminus. We would also need to account for the various regulatory messages, mentioned earlier, in addition to a large number of mRNA species that code for basic cellular processes. The messages present in the cell at any given time span a broad range of maturation; some represent early prespliced messages, and some have been spliced into final transcripts. These different versions would also need to be included in our analysis. If we were to continue this process for every transcribed coding region, we would eventually account for every message in the cell—both coding and regulatory. The complete inventory of transcribed elements within a cell has come to be known as the transcriptome.

Despite the fact that at any given moment the complete set of existing RNA transcripts represents only a small percentage of those coded for by the genome, the transcriptome is far more complex in diversity and structure. Figure 5-1 displays the various species that comprise the transcriptome.

Unlike the genome, which remains mostly static throughout the life of a cell, the transcriptome varies tremendously over time and between cells that have the same genome. Moreover, various disease states have a dramatic impact on the gene-expression profiles of different cells. Tumor cells, for example, would naturally be expected to display characteristic gene-expression profiles that could ultimately act as signatures for various disease subtypes.

One of the most important goals of the emerging discipline known as information-based medicine is to use these profiles to create more precise patient stratifications. Many diseases that are currently classified according to their clinical symptoms (phenotype) will soon be defined by a combination of gene-expression profile and clinical symptoms, or gene-expression profile alone. Furthermore, expression profiles for many

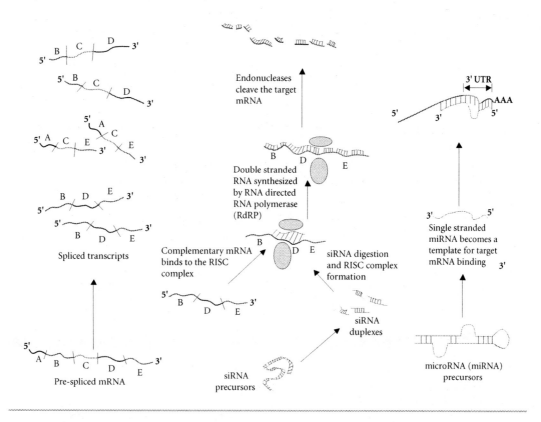

Figure 5-1 Diagrammatic representation of the transcriptome, including various species of RNA: messenger RNA, miRNA, siRNA, prespliced mRNA, and double-stranded RNA. Many processes contribute to the variety of RNA species present in a cell, and the production of a single protein involves expression of several different genes, including some that code for enzymes involved in post-translational modifications.

cell types will be helpful in establishing safe doses even after a disease is well characterized and the correct treatment is established. The ability to monitor the state of the transcriptome, both in health and disease, is paving the way for a new era in medicine. Remarkably, this new era will benefit from a mix of technologies that cross both basic science and clinical medicine. The tools of information-based medicine include disease-specific databases of expression profiles linked to clinical and demographic information in addition to sophisticated search and data-mining tools.

MAPPING A COMPLETE TRANSCRIPTOME

Because the transcriptome displays tremendous variability, both between individuals of the same species and between different cells within a single individual, mapping a complete transcriptome is a tremendously complex undertaking—more ambitious, perhaps, than mapping a complete genome. Such a project has been launched. As in the genome mapping project, the effort is based on a technical collaboration; in this case the alliance is between Affymetrix, Inc. and the U.S. National Cancer Institute (NCI). The stated goal of the project is to build a complete transcriptional map of the genome at a resolution approaching individual nucleotides. The core infrastructure for the project is composed of DNA microarray technology from Affymetrix in conjunction with sophisticated gene-clustering algorithms and data-mining software. By marrying the results to information gleaned from whole genome sequencing and annotation projects, researchers will be able to gain a thorough understanding of all issues related to transcription, including structural modifications of the chromosomal material, identification of transcription factor binding sites, DNA modifications such as methylation, and origins of replication. Accomplishing these impressive goals will require interrogating the genome with millions of small, very closely spaced probes, which can reveal subtle differences within single coding regions. At the time of this writing, an important milestone in the project had recently been achieved: the release of a complete transcriptional map of human chromosomes 21 and 22 [1].

The results are illustrative of this discussion. Collectively, the two chromosomes contain 770 well-characterized and predicted genes. Coding and noncoding regions were interrogated using DNA microarrays containing small probes spaced approximately 35 base pairs apart across the entire chromosome. Surprisingly, it was discovered that the number of RNA species present in the cell that corresponded to sequences on these chromosomes exceeded the number of characterized and predicted coding regions by an order of magnitude. Approximately 50% of these positive probes were found to be located less than 300 base pairs distant from the nearest identified coding region. Table 5-1 summarizes the results.

The fact that the total number of transcripts dramatically exceeds the number of protein-coding regions is consistent with the emerging view of gene expression that we have been describing. It is important to remember that the additional transcripts represent regulatory messages in various stages of splicing (including double-stranded RNA)

Table 5-1 Relative Proportion of Probes Found in Coding and Noncoding Regions on Chromosomes 21 and 22

Cell Lines	Total Positive Probes	Positive Probes Found in Exons
1 of 11	268,466	17,924
5 of 11	98,231	10,903

Source: Kapranov P., et. al. (2002) "Large-Scale Transcriptional Activity in Chromosomes 21 and 22." *Science* 296, 916–919

in addition to prespliced protein-coding messages. In some sense, the problem can be simplified by defaulting to a completely mathematical representation that compares expression profiles in the form of images rather than sequences. The expression profile for a given metabolic state could be envisioned as a collection of mathematical entities that are up or down regulated in a reproducible pattern. After the pattern is discovered, a representation of the pattern linked to a phenotypic description of the state, disease, or clinical symptoms is stored in a database. Eventually such a database would be populated with millions of patterns and phenotypic descriptions. Medical researchers would then be able to search for matches to their patients' own profiles and clinical records with the goal of predicting the course of a disease or possible treatment outcomes. It is important to point out that a complete description of even a single pathway is complex, and a complete system-level model remains beyond the capabilities of today's information technologies.

EXPRESSION PROFILING

Expression profiling has already yielded important results and academic research centers are beginning to populate large databases with specific patient information. At the time of this writing, a project of this nature had recently been announced between NuTec Sciences in Atlanta, the Winship Cancer Center associated with Emory University Medical School, and IBM in Armonk New York. Four specific areas of cancer were selected for study: breast, colorectal, lung, and prostate. Information gathered from expression profiling of various tissues and body fluids of affected patients is being analyzed in the context of clinical and demographic history. The goal of the project is to make treatment decisions based on the newly discovered correlations. Such projects can serve a multitude of purposes, including drug rescue for compounds that might fail clinical trial if tested on a patient population that is genetically too broad. Herceptin is a perfect example of a compound that is only effective for certain patient populations. Overexpression of the HER2/neu oncogene (also known as c-erbB2) is a frequent molecular event in many human cancers. The humanized anti-HER2/neu antibody, Herceptin has proven to be effective in patients with metastatic breast cancer who over-express the HER2/neu oncogene. Herceptin could not pass a clinical trials test in a patient population that was not genetically defined [2].

The linkage between databases of expression data, target identification, and clinical trials is important because it has the potential to revolutionize the drug discovery and delivery process. The same databases that support target identification, a pure research activity, will certainly support clinical trials as well as medical diagnostics for clinical use. It is likely that diagnostics companies of the future will deploy the same databases as researchers and use them to make treatment recommendations. In the not-too-distant future, treatment decisions will be made through a process that combines initial genetic data (DNA sequence information) with mRNA expression data and information from an individual's medical record—the exact same information that will be used by researchers to identify targets and test the efficacy of new therapeutics. The trend toward molecular-based personalized medicine will, therefore, drive closer ties between each step of the drug discovery pipeline and clinical medicine.

Some of the RNA species contained within the stored patterns would represent immature unspliced versions of other transcripts also contained within the image. Others would represent regulatory messages that appear in the transcriptome because they modulate the translation of newly expressed messages. The expression levels of these associated messages, especially the regulatory ones, can be important data points. In each case, the balance between a regulatory or immature unspliced message and its corresponding protein-coding sequence has potential as an important diagnostic. For example, a highly up regulated message might not result in an increased level of expression for a particular protein if increased appearance of the message is matched with a high level of regulatory sequences that prevent translation. Likewise, an increase in the appearance of immature unspliced messages has true biological significance because it implies an expression ramp up that exceeds the cell's RNA-processing capabilities. After a recurring pattern is identified, chemical analysis can be used to unravel expression-level details for each coding region represented in the pattern [3]. New algorithms are also being used to identify statistical correlations between genes and clusters of genes to help identify related traits and further refine the profiling technique.

Gene-expression levels are time-dependent in a very sensitive way, and in many contexts it will become important to store transcriptional information as a function of time. An example might include drug response at a metabolic level for a specific population of cells. Medical science has historically relied on time-dependent assays in many areas (e.g., endocrinology), and time-dependent transcriptional analysis could certainly become part of the diagnostic arsenal.

As data-analysis tools become more sophisticated, researchers are beginning to take a systems approach to understanding the complex web of interactions that define cellular pathways. Recent approaches have included modeling a pathway where components were analyzed using DNA microarrays, quantitative proteomics, and databases of known physical interactions [4]. Transcription maps are central to such analysis. In one specific project conducted at the Institute for Systems Biology, a global model was constructed based on 20 systematic perturbations of a system containing 997 messenger RNAs from the yeast galactose-utilization pathway. The experiments provided evidence that 15 of 289 detected proteins are regulated post-transcriptionally, and the model that emerged identified explicit physical interactions governing the cellular response to each perturbation [5]. Such experiments are an important milestone in the history of drug discovery because they demonstrate that it is possible to develop and test complete systems models, which have the potential to rapidly advance the cause of predictive medicine. It is also important to note that the effort brings together contemporary tools of molecular biology and the latest information technologies—structure and pathway databases, expression array profiles, and data-mining/cluster-analysis software. The construction of a complete system-level description of a cell is the ultimate goal of systems biology. Such a description is considered a "grand challenge" problem in molecular biology. One prerequisite for completion of this project is a fully descriptive map of the transcriptome. Describing a single pathway is complex, and a complete system-level model remains beyond the capabilities of today's information technologies.

Because the transcriptome is composed of all messages within the cell—coding, noncoding, and immature—its content is highly dynamic. A complete map of the transcriptome is a collection of millions of expression profiles that represent snapshots of the cell as it responds to various stimuli over time. The map for an entire organism would be comprised of a similar collection of snapshots across thousands of different classes of cells. It is reasonable to assume that time-dependent multicell transcription profiling will ultimately form the basis of any complete analysis of gene expression—the ultimate goal being a complete system-level description of a cell. Efforts to build such maps have become a principal driver of the development of tools for transcriptional profiling.

In the next section, we will begin to examine the technologies behind transcriptional profiling. In addition to their role as a research tool, these technologies are rapidly becoming important diagnostic tools. As with any diagnostic tool, successful deployment depends on the availability of standards. Research efforts that create RNA profile maps for various cellular states are beginning to form the basis of this new diagnostic science.

TECHNOLOGIES FOR TRANSCRIPTIONAL PROFILING

As previously discussed, the development of a complete molecular-level picture of health and disease involves understanding metabolic processes at four distinct levels: genome (DNA sequence), transcriptome (mRNA profile), proteome (protein structure and interactions), and metabolic pathway. The research toolkit required to build this picture has evolved significantly over the past several years and currently includes a variety of technologies that complement each other:

- DNA sequence information is directly relevant to the development of genetic tests for illnesses that exhibit a pattern of inheritance. DNA sequence information also provides a context for understanding polygenic diseases and complex phenotypes. Complexities associated with the splicing process make it important to interpret DNA sequence information in the context of phenotype—a single mutation can affect many proteins to create a complex phenotypic change.
- Messenger RNA profiles are important diagnostics that can delineate a pattern of up and down regulation of a large number of related genes. This information can be

used experimentally to help drive the target-discovery process or as a clinical diagnostic to predict the onset or progression of disease. It is important to note that many messages serve a regulatory function and are not translated into protein.

- Proteomics is a discipline focused on understanding the structures and interactions of the millions of proteins encoded in the genome. Final protein structures are normally achieved only after post-translational modifications (acetylation, glycosylation, methylation, removal of n-terminal amino acids, etc.); it is not currently possible to predict these modifications from DNA or mRNA sequence information. However, computational modeling of protein structure can be a useful tool for predicting potential sites for post-translational modification, as well as the extent of change to protein folding that is likely to result from those modifications.

- Systems biology is an attempt to study the complex and subtle relationships between the millions of proteins that make up an organism. Systems experiments often involve perturbing a system at the mRNA level and measuring the complex downstream results. Modeling of biological systems is a complex bioinformatic challenge that has recently become feasible because of rapid advances in information technology [6].

Messenger RNA profiling technologies are emerging as standard tools in all the areas mentioned above, both for research and clinical use. On the research side, transcription profiling has five major applications:

- Clarification of details surrounding the splicing process for sequenced coding regions
- Identification of key messages for previously unidentified proteins (Many of these protein are minor messages present in small copy numbers and previously unidentified.)
- Delineation of metabolic pathways through "perturbation" experiments
- Identification of regulatory sequences that are not translated into protein
- Analysis of molecular-level responses to various stimuli—i.e., stress, drugs, hormone signals, genetic mutations, etc.

On the clinical side, transcription profiling is beginning to play a role in identifying patients for clinical trial, predicting the onset of disease, and customizing treatment regimens for individual patients. Central to these advances are pattern-matching technologies that facilitate rapid large-scale database-similarity searches. The task is similar to that of scanning a database containing millions of fingerprint records for patterns that are similar to a reference fingerprint. In the vast majority of situations, in which thousands of genes are involved, it is necessary, for a given set of expressed genes, to correlate up and down regulation patterns with treatment outcomes as measured by phenotypic changes. Over the next several years, such techniques are likely to become core components of clinical medicine.

Over the past several years, it has become apparent that the "one gene at a time" approach to understanding complex metabolic events is simply not adequate. Some estimates indicate that as many as 10% of the 10,000 to 20,000 mRNA species in a typical mammalian cell are differentially expressed between cancer and normal tissues. As a result, several technologies have been developed for quantifying the expression of many genes in parallel. One of the many technologies, the DNA hybridization array, has become dominant because of its low cost and flexibility. (DNA hybridization arrays are also referred to as microarrays, expression arrays, and gene chips.)

EXPRESSED SEQUENCE TAGS (ESTs)

Identification of the expressed messages within a particular population of cells has always been an important research goal for cell and molecular biologists. Prior to the advent of high-throughput techniques such as microarrays, researchers typically purified and sequenced complementary DNA (cDNA) for this purpose. Because it is reversely transcribed directly from mRNA, cDNA represents a direct source of spliced and coding sequences of genes. Therefore, sequencing of cDNA has become a well-established and accepted technique that is complementary to genome sequencing efforts in many important ways.

In 1991, the first application of high-throughput sequencing of cDNA clones was described, where clones from human brain were randomly selected and partially sequenced. These partial sequences, which represented genes expressed in the tissue at key time points, were referred to as expressed sequence tags or ESTs. Similar approaches for different tissues and organisms were soon to follow. ESTs provide the largest amount of information possible per sequenced base. The vision of rapid identification of all human genes has led to the development of several commercially financed data banks containing EST sequences [7].

EST sequences taken from a random cDNA pool can also yield a statistical picture of the level and complexity of gene expression for the sample tissue. The influence of environmental factors and tissue-specific gene expression can therefore be studied. Furthermore, the gene sequences obtained can be efficiently used for physical mapping by determining their chromosomal position. They also contribute to an understanding of intron and exon boundaries and are often used to predict the transcribed regions of genomic sequences.

DNA MICROARRAYS

Because microarray analysis is highly parallel in nature, typical experiments produce thousands, sometimes millions, of data points. Microarrays are often referred to as gene chips because they are built on technologies adapted from the semiconductor industry—photolithography and solid-phase chemistry. Each array contains densely packed oligonucleotide probes whose sequences are chosen to maximize sensitivity and specificity, allowing consistent discrimination between closely related target sequences. A typical pharmaceutical microarray experiment involves the following steps [8, 9]:

1. A microarray is constructed (or purchased) containing thousands of single-stranded gene fragments, including known or predicted splice variants and potential polymorphisms. The sequences are selected to support a large number of cross comparisons to confirm complex results.
2. mRNA is harvested from selected cells in treated and untreated individuals. (Untreated samples will be used as an internal control in the array.)
3. mRNA is reverse transcribed into more stable cDNA with the addition of fluorescent labels; green for cDNA derived from treated cells, and red for cDNA derived from untreated cells. (The labels are composed of 5-amino-propargyl-

2'-deoxyuridine 5'-triphosphate coupled to either Cy3 or Cy5 fluorescent dyes: Cy3-dUTP or Cy5-dUTP).

4. Samples of fluorescently labeled cDNA are applied to the array and exposed to every spot. A sequence match results in binding between the cDNA test sequence and a complementary DNA sequence on the array. Each match contains a double-stranded fluorescently labeled spot that results from the combination of the two fluorescent dyes and the amount of dye containing cDNA in each of the samples.

5. A laser fluorescent scanner is used to detect the hybridization signals from both fluorophores, and the resulting pattern of colored spots is stored in a database: red for strongly expressed genes in the treated sample, green for weakly expressed genes in the treated sample, yellow for genes that are equally expressed in both samples, black for sequences that are not expressed in either sample. Because the sequence of every spot in the chip is known, the identity of each expressed cDNA can be determined, and the amount and source (treated or untreated sample) inferred from the color and intensity of the spot.

6. Differences in intensity correspond both to expression levels of the genes in the sample and to exactness of the match. Similar sequences containing various combinations of single and multiple base changes are used as internal controls to provide more precise sequence information about genes expressed in the test sample. For example, the identity of a single base can be deduced by measuring the binding affinity of a test sequence to four slightly different probes that vary only at the position of the base in question. (Each contains one of the four possible bases.) Figure 5-2 outlines the steps involved in a typical two-color microarray experiment.

Microarray production has evolved from a low-density technology based on robotically placed spots to a high-density technology based on the same masking and photolithography technologies used by the computer industry in the manufacture of microprocessors. Consequently, there is little need to conserve on the number of genes to be scanned in a single experiment. For example, the Affymetrix Human Genome U95 (HG-U95) set consists of five microarrays, the first of which contains nearly 63,000

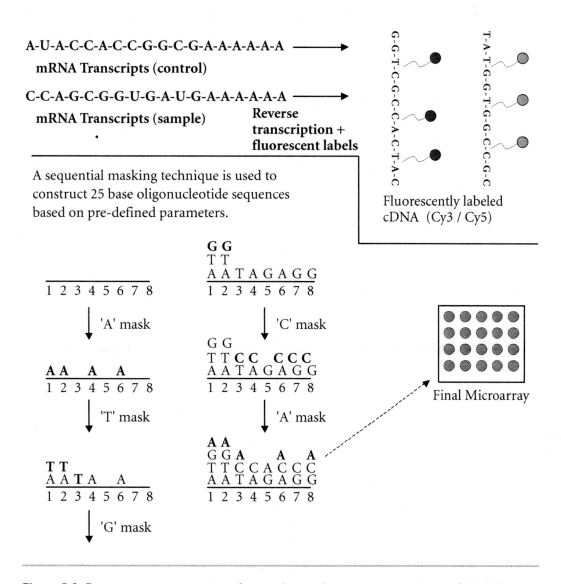

Figure 5-2 Diagrammatic representation of a typical two-color microarray experiment. DNA derived from treated cells is labeled with a green fluorescent marker. DNA from control cells is labeled with a red fluorescent marker. Both samples are applied to every cell in the array. Complementary sequences bind to the array forming fluorescent spots, which are detected using a laser scanner. The color and intensity of each spot reveals information about the relative strength of the match between each test sequence and the sequence stored in the array.

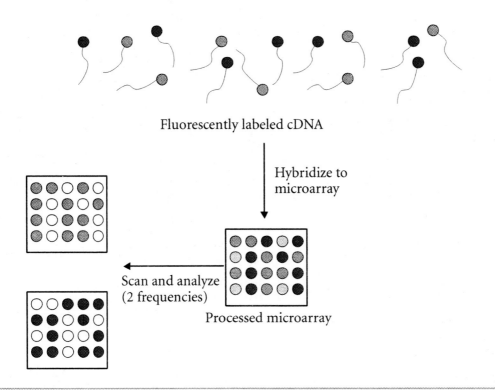

Figure 5-2 *(continued)*

probe sets interrogating approximately 54,000 clusters derived from the UniGene database. These probes are estimated to represent approximately 10,000 full-length genes. As costs continue to decline, high-density oligonucleotide arrays will become the standard tool for comprehensive transcriptional profiling.

Efforts to directly compare samples are almost always complicated by the fact that each profiling experiment requires a separate array. Results must therefore be normalized in order to make meaningful interarray comparisons. Additionally, fabrication techniques limit the length of each probe to approximately 25 bases. To adequately represent each gene, Affymetrix microarrays typically include a set of 16 to 25 25-mers that uniquely represent each coding region and can be expected to hybridize under the same general conditions. Every set of perfect-match (PM) probes for an mRNA sequence has a corresponding set of mismatch (MM) probes. An MM probe is constructed from the same nucleotide sequence as its PM counterpart, with the exception that one base (usually number 13 in the sequence) has been replaced to cause a mismatch. The combination of a PM and its MM counterpart is referred to as a probe pair. There are two reasons for including probe pairs for each sequence. First, at very low concentrations (low copy counts) of the target, the PM probes are operating near the lower limit of their sensitivity, and MM probes display a higher sensitivity to changes in concentration. Second, MM probes are thought to bind to nonspecific sequences with the same affinity as PM probes. This property allows MM probes to serve as internal controls for background nonspecific hybridization.

One drawback of microarray analysis is related to its inability to distinguish very low-abundance transcripts, those present in single-digit copy counts where the copy range is very large. A more common problem involves the quantification of mRNA species from a large population of cells where the species of interest is present only in a small sub-population. In such situations, the species of interest is likely to be diluted beyond the detection limit by more abundant transcripts appearing across the broader population. Increasing the absolute amount of the hybridized target is not usually helpful because it is the relative abundance of each transcript within the RNA pool, coupled with probe characteristics, that determines the sensitivity of the array for each sequence [10]. Unfortunately, it is also difficult to identify transcripts that are up regulated by less than 50%, a significant problem for researchers in areas such as oncology and neuroscience where subtle changes in gene expression are critical to understanding the differences between disease and health.

However, the downstream effects of subtle changes in gene regulation are often more dramatic and straightforward to measure. Many of the minor messages that are difficult to detect are likely to be regulatory genes, and microarray analysis can still reveal the more pronounced levels of up and down regulation associated with more downstream members of these gene pathways—the messages most likely to code for druggable targets. Additionally, several new techniques are being developed to solve the minor message problem with the goal of detecting and precisely counting the number of molecules of every transcript in the cell, including those with copy counts in the single-digit range. The next section discusses other RNA quantification techniques.

The major goal of microarray data analysis is to identify statistically significant differences between genes expressed in the control and test samples. One of the most straightforward and commonly used analysis techniques involves construction of a simple scatterplot where each point represents the expression level of a specific gene in two samples, one assigned to the x-axis and one to the y-axis. For each point, its position relative to the main diagonal (the identity line) directly relates the ratio of expression levels for the test and control sequences. Messages with identical expression levels in both samples appear on the identity line, whereas differentially expressed sequences appear at some point above or below the diagonal as determined by the level of expression on each axis. Points that appear above the diagonal are overexpressed in the sample represented by the y-axis; conversely, points that appear below the diagonal are overexpressed in the sample represented on the x-axis. The overall expression level for any gene can be determined by measuring the absolute distance from the origin. Figure 5-3 depicts a microarray scatterplot.

HIERARCHICAL CLUSTERING

Scatterplots are excellent visual representations because they facilitate rapid and simple comparisons of two datasets. However, it is frequently necessary to identify groups of genes with similar expression profiles across a large number of experiments. The most commonly used technique for finding such relationships is cluster analysis, which is often used to identify genes that may be functionally related. Such clusters often suggest biochemical pathways. Like many other mathematical tools, cluster analysis generates meaningful results only when combined with biochemical insight.

Hierarchical clustering, the most frequently used mathematical technique, attempts to group genes into small clusters and to group clusters into higher-level systems. The resulting hierarchical tree is easily viewed as a dendrogram [11, 12].

Most studies involve comparing a series of experiments to identify genes that are consistently coregulated under some defined set of circumstances—disease state, increasing time, increasing drug dose, etc. A two-dimensional grid is constructed with each row corresponding to a different gene sequence and each column to a different set of experimental conditions. Each set of gene-expression levels (each row in the matrix) is compared to every other set of expression levels in a pairwise fashion, and similarity

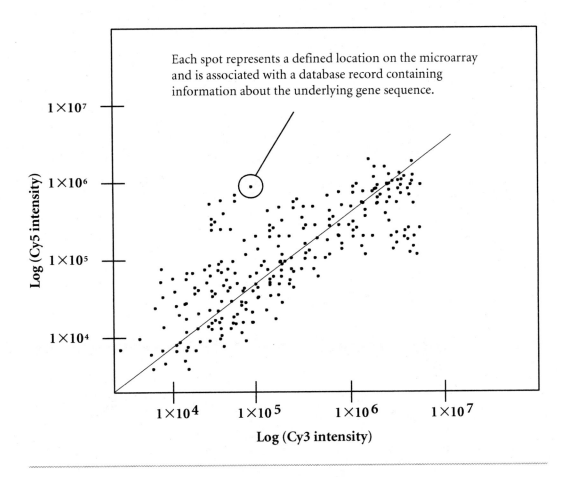

Each spot represents a defined location on the microarray and is associated with a database record containing information about the underlying gene sequence.

Figure 5-3 Microarray scatterplot for two samples. For each point, the position relative to the main diagonal indicates the relative expression levels for test and control sequences. Points that appear above the diagonal are overexpressed in the sample plotted along the y-axis. Likewise, points that appear below the diagonal represent genes that are overexpressed in the sample plotted on the x-axis. Messages that are identically expressed in both samples are plotted directly on the diagonal. The overall expression level for any gene is determined by measuring the absolute distance from the origin. (Adapted from: Jeffrey Augen, "Bioinformatics and Data Mining in Support of Drug Discover," *Handbook of Anticancer Drug Development.* D. Budman, A. Calvert, E. Rowinsky, eds. Lippincott Williams and Wilkins. 2003)

scores are produced in the form of statistical correlation coefficients. These correlation coefficients can be thought of as representing the Euclidean distances between the rows in the matrix. The correlations are ordered, and a node is created between the highest-scoring (geometrically closest) pair of rows—the two gene sequences that were most nearly coregulated across each of the experiments. The matrix is then modified to represent the joined elements as a single node, and all distances between the newly formed node and other gene sequences (rows) in the matrix are calculated. It is not necessary to recalculate all correlations because only those involving the two rows joined in the new node have changed. Typically, the node is represented by a link in the dendrogram, the height of the link being directly proportional to the strength of the correlation. The process of creating proportional links and joining genes into clusters continues until all genes in the experiment have been joined into a single hierarchical cluster through links of appropriate length. If more than two nodes are related by the same correlation coefficient (same geometric distance), the conflict is resolved according to a predetermined set of rules.

Advantages of Hierarchical Clustering

It is sometimes meaningful to cluster data at the experiment level rather than at the level of individual genes. Such experiments are most often used to identify similarities in overall gene-expression patterns in the context of different treatment regimens—the goal being to stratify patients based on their molecular-level responses to the treatments. The hierarchical techniques outlined earlier are appropriate for such clustering, which is based on the pairwise statistical comparison of complete scatterplots rather than individual gene sequences. The data are represented as a matrix of scatterplots, ultimately reduced to a matrix of correlation coefficients. The correlation coefficients are then used to construct a two-dimensional dendrogram in the exact same way as in the gene-cluster experiments previously described.

The overall process of constructing a two-dimensional dendrogram using hierarchical clustering data is depicted in Figure 5-4. The example in the figure embodies all the principles of the technique but in a vastly simplified form; expression-profile experiments typically include hundreds, sometimes thousands of genes, and the analysis is almost always more complex than this illustration.

Messenger RNA profiling techniques have become a cornerstone of modern disease classification. These advances are especially significant in areas such as oncology and neuroscience, where complex phenotypes have recently been found to correlate with specific changes in gene expression, the result being more precise patient stratification

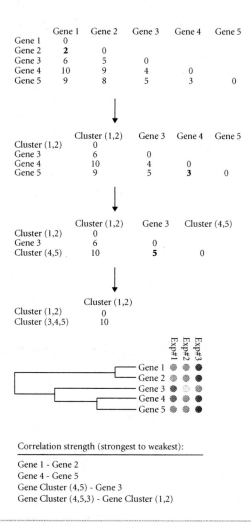

	Gene 1	Gene 2	Gene 3	Gene 4	Gene 5
Gene 1	0				
Gene 2	2	0			
Gene 3	6	5	0		
Gene 4	10	9	4	0	
Gene 5	9	8	5	3	0

	Cluster (1,2)	Gene 3	Gene 4	Gene 5
Cluster (1,2)	0			
Gene 3	6	0		
Gene 4	10	4	0	
Gene 5	9	5	3	0

	Cluster (1,2)	Gene 3	Cluster (4,5)
Cluster (1,2)	0		
Gene 3	6	0	
Cluster (4,5)	10	5	0

	Cluster (1,2)
Cluster (1,2)	0
Cluster (3,4,5)	10

Correlation strength (strongest to weakest):

Gene 1 - Gene 2
Gene 4 - Gene 5
Gene Cluster (4,5) - Gene 3
Gene Cluster (4,5,3) - Gene Cluster (1,2)

Figure 5-4 Construction of a two-dimensional dendrogram representing a hierarchical cluster of related genes. Each column represents a different experiment, each row a different spot (oligonucleotide sequence) on the microarray. The height of each link is inversely proportional to the strength of the correlation. Relative correlation strengths are represented by integers in the accompanying chart sequence. Genes 1 and 2 are most closely coregulated, followed by genes 4 and 5. The regulation of gene 3 is more closely linked with the regulation of genes 4 and 5 than any remaining link or combination of links. The strength of the correlation between the expression levels of genes 1 and 2 and the cluster containing genes 3, 4, and 5 is the weakest (relative score of 10). (Adapted from: Jeffrey Augen, "Bioinformatics and Data Mining in Support of Drug Discover," *Handbook of Anticancer Drug Development.* D. Budman, A. Calvert, E. Rowinsky, editors. Lippincott Williams and Wilkins. 2003)

both for clinical trials and treatment. A significant example that illustrates the utility of hierarchical clustering involves the identification of distinct tumor subclasses in diffuse large B-cell lymphoma (DLBCL). Two distinct forms of DLBCL have been identified using hierarchical clustering techniques, each related to a different stage of B-cell differentiation. The fact that the cluster correlates are significant is demonstrated by direct relationships to patient survival rates [13].

Disadvantages of Hierarchical Clustering

Despite its proven utility, hierarchical clustering has many flaws. Interpretation of the hierarchy is complex and often confusing; the deterministic nature of the technique prevents reevaluation after points are grouped into a node; all determinations are strictly based on local decisions and a single pass of analysis; it has been demonstrated that the tree structure can lock in accidental features reflecting idiosyncrasies of the clustering rules; expression patterns of individual gene sequences become less relevant as the clustering process progresses; and an incorrect assignment made early in the process cannot be corrected [14]. These deficiencies have driven the development of additional clustering techniques that are based on multiple passes of analysis and utilize advanced algorithms borrowed from the artificial intelligence community. Two of these techniques, k-means clustering and self-organizing maps (SOMs), have achieved widespread acceptance in research oncology where they have been enormously successful in identifying meaningful genetic differences between patient populations.

When discussing clustering algorithms, it is essential to recognize the limitations of two- and three-dimensional representations of individual gene-expression values across a collection of experiments. Figure 5-5 depicts a simple analysis composed of two experiments. Each experiment is represented by a dimension in the grid, and clusters of the genes are readily apparent.

Representations of two or three experiments are relatively straightforward to visualize because they can be plotted on the axes of a simple graph (either x and y axes or x, y, and z axes). Results from more than four experiments are difficult to represent because they cannot be visualized in three dimensions. Figure 5-6, which depicts the results from three experiments, represents the most complex case that can be easily visualized on the axes of a graph. As in the two-dimensional case, each gene occupies a unique position on the graph determined by its fluorescence ratio in each of the three experi-

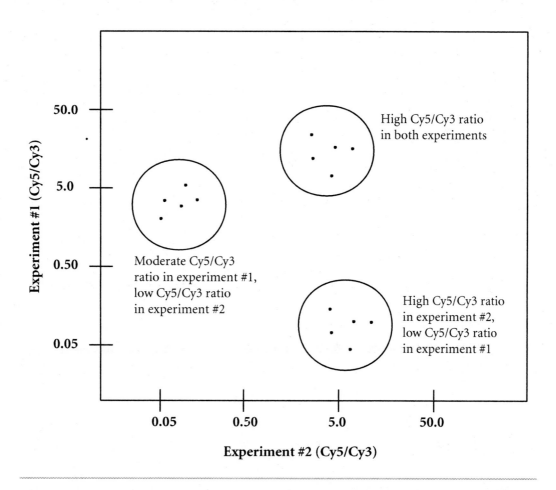

Figure 5-5 Visual representation of two gene-clustering experiments. For each transcript, the fluorescence ratio (Cy5/Cy3) is plotted on one of the two axes; y-axis for experiment 1 and x-axis for experiment 2. Genes with high fluorescence ratios in both experiments appear farthest from the origin. Genes with similar behavior across the two experiments are closely clustered on the graph. Three different clusters are evident in diagram.

ments. For example, a gene that exhibits Cy5/Cy3 fluorescence ratios of 3,5, and 4.5 in the three experiments would be represented by a single point plotted at the coordinate 3,5,4.5 in the graph. As in the two-experiment model, absolute distance from the origin correlates with the Cy5/Cy3 ratio, and the distance between points in three-dimensional

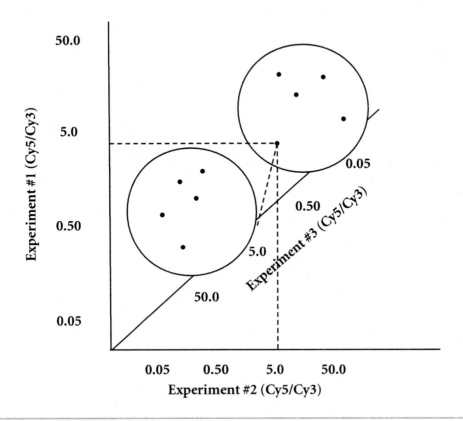

Figure 5-6 A three-dimensional (three experiment) gene-clustering analysis containing ten different sequences. Each axis in the drawing represents a different experiment, and each set of expression levels is represented by a single vector defined in three dimensions. As in the two-dimensional case, grouping of the sequences is accomplished by determining the geometric distance between each vector. Higher-dimensional models representing more than three experiments cannot be visualized as single vectors, and so different graphical techniques must be used.

space is representative of the likelihood that the genes they represent are coregulated across the three experiments.

The ten genes used in these experiments are clustered into readily recognizable groups. As mentioned previously, higher-dimensional representations, those containing more than three sets of experimental results, are much more complex to imagine because absolute distances between individual genes and gene clusters do not lend themselves to visual representation. However, despite the complexities associated with visual representation of microarray data across large numbers of experiments, it is always possible to calculate a single vector to represent all the expression values for any gene sequence regardless of the number of dimensions/experiments. It is the distance between these vectors that determines the degree to which a pair of genes is coregulated.

Regardless of the graphical technique used, clustering algorithms can be collectively viewed as a mechanism for defining boundaries that partition vectors into meaningful groups. Datasets with many dimensions are often visualized in a simple two-dimensional plot—time or experiment number on the x-axis and expression ratio on the y-axis. (Expression ratios are normally represented logarithmically.) When many different gene sequences are shown on the same grid, it is often possible to visually identify groups. A two-dimensional grid containing expression-level information for several different genes measured across ten different time points is displayed in Figure 5-7. Although many of the expression curves overlap and individual sequences are difficult to dissect out from the mix, it is clear that the data fall into three distinct clusters of coregulated genes. Representations of this type are often used to set starting conditions for more complex algorithmic clustering procedures such as those described next.

K-MEANS CLUSTERING

K-means clustering is most useful when the number of clusters that should be represented is known. An example might include microarray classification of a group of patients that have morphologically similar diseases that fall into three clinically distinct categories (k=3). The clustering process would proceed as follows [15]:

1. Each expression vector is randomly assigned to one of three groups or clusters (k=3).
2. An average expression vector (called the center) is calculated for each group, and these vectors are used to compute the distances between groups.
3. Each gene-expression vector is reassigned to the group whose center is closest. Expression vectors are allowed to remain in a cluster only when they are closer to the center of that cluster than to a neighboring one.

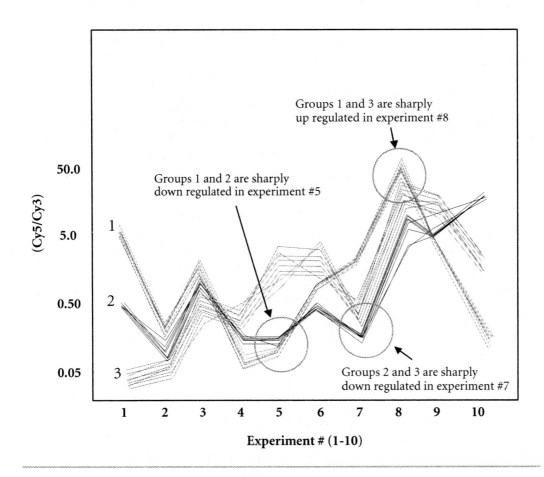

Figure 5-7 A two-dimensional grid containing expression-level information for a large number of genes measured across ten different time points. The expression data represented in these ten experiments reveal three distinct clusters of coregulated genes (1, 2, and 3). (Adapted from: Jeffrey Augen, "Bioinformatics and Data Mining in Support of Drug Discover," *Handbook of Anticancer Drug Development*. D. Budman, A. Calvert, E. Rowinsky, editors. Lippincott Williams and Wilkins. 2003)

4. Inter- and intracluster distances are recomputed, and new expression vectors for the center of each cluster are calculated.

5. The process is repeated until all expression vectors are optimally placed. At this point, any additional changes would increase intracluster distances while decreasing intercluster dissimilarity.

The Advantages of K-Means Clustering

K-means clustering has proven to be a valuable tool for identifying coregulated genes in systems where biochemical or clinical knowledge can be used to predict the appropriate number of clusters. The tool is also useful when the number of appropriate clusters is unknown if the researcher experiments with different values of k.

The Disadvantages of K-Means Clustering

Despite these advantages, the unstructured nature of the k-means clustering technique tends to proceed in a local fashion, and this effect intensifies as additional clustering centers are added to the analysis. Excessive locality eventually leads to incorrect groupings, and important gene associations can be lost. It follows that as the number of clustering centers is increased, initial placement of the centers becomes increasingly critical; for analyses that involve large numbers of clustering centers, it makes sense to use more-structured techniques. Algorithms based on self-organizing maps solve many of these problems and have demonstrated tremendous utility in anticancer drug discovery and research oncology.

SELF-ORGANIZING MAPS

The SOM analysis technique bears much resemblance to k-means clustering because both techniques involve an iterative approach to locating the center of each cluster. However, SOM analysis is much more structured, and the user must initialize the system with a specific geometric construct representing the initial location of each cluster center. (SOM cluster centers are referred to as a centroids.) More than a simple list of locations, the construct is a complete topology where centroids are part of a symmetrical structure. Initial mapping of nodes into the structure is random followed by an iterative process that organizes the map. The SOM process is tantamount to selecting a gene-expression vector and adjusting reference vectors for nearby centroids to make them more compatible with the selected gene; the nearest centroid is adjusted by the largest amount, and other local centroids are moved toward the selected gene by smaller amounts depending on their proximity to the selected point. More specifically, each iteration involves randomly selecting a data point (P) and moving the all nodes in the direction of (P) by an amount that is inversely proportional to the distance between the two points. The process typically continues for many thousands of iterations until a well-organized map is complete. A large number of iterations is necessary to achieve a stable map because typical experiments involve many genes, and each point (gene) in the map migrates a relatively small distance during each iteration of the algorithm.

Many successful experiments have been conducted utilizing a simple two-dimensional 3×2 rectangular grid of centroids as the starting point. Alternative structures based on hexagonal rings, grids, and lines have also been used, and each has a pronounced effect on the outcome of the analysis. More structured than k-means clustering and far less rigid than hierarchical techniques, SOM is emerging as the technique of choice for analyzing complex datasets with high-dimensional character and many gene sequences [16].

An eight-node SOM based on two experiments is depicted in Figure 5-8.

A seminal paper on use of SOMs to profile a specific disease state was recently published by Golub and Slonim. The research compared expression profiles from tissue samples recovered from patients with acute myeloid leukemia and acute lymphoblastic leukemia (AML and ALL respectively) using the Affymetrix HU6800 GeneChip [17]. The goal was to identify a gene or small number of genes that are consistently up regulated in one disease class and down regulated in the other. After such a grouping is located, cluster analysis can be used to locate "nearby" genes that behave in similar fashion. The array contained probes for 6,817 different human genes, and final results revealed 1,100 that were coregulated in one of the disease classes. Each of these can be thought of as providing a "weighted vote" based on its statistical significance in the analysis. The system is tested on a well-characterized sample (known disease class) that is not included in the training set for the SOM. Of the 1,100 genes identified, 50 that had the highest correlation with class distinction were selected as predictors. These predictors were tested against 38 carefully diagnosed patients. Of the 38 samples, 36 were correctly assigned as belonging to either the AML or ALL group strictly on the basis of up or down regulation of these 50 genes. Two of the 38 predictions were statistically uncertain. The selection of 50 genes was arbitrary in the sense that more than 50 genes displayed expression patterns that were well correlated with one of the disease states. Further refinement of the technique might include additional genes; in practice it often makes sense to adjust the predictor set after the function of each of the genes is known. Such an approach links microarray analysis to further biochemical experimentation and

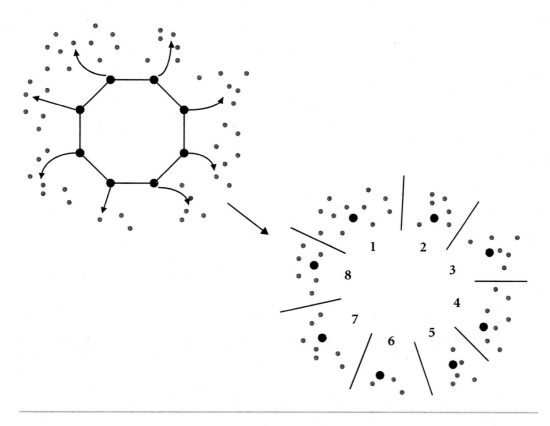

Figure 5-8 A simple SOM analysis composed of 8 centroids, 51 genes, and 2 dimensions (2 sets of experimental conditions). Large dark spots denote centroids, and small spots represent gene-expression vectors. Successive iterations of the system generate a migration trajectory for each centroid until the best fit is found. Additional experiments require additional dimensions and are difficult to visualize in a drawing. Many other topologies—hexagonal rings, lines, and complex grids—are also possible and have a pronounced effect on the outcome.

may require extensive analysis to identify functions for previously unknown genes. Conversely, if a gene is found to be a strong correlate with a specific disease state, and if the function of that gene is not currently known, it makes excellent scientific sense to select that particular sequence for further analysis. Approaches of this sort are driving the use of microarray analysis as a core component of research oncology.

Two additional procedural points are important to note:

- All expression data should be passed through a variation filter to remove genes that do not show significant up or down regulation. This additional step prevents centroids from being attracted to groups of inactive genes.
- Expression levels must be normalized across all experiments to focus attention on the shape of the expression curves rather than absolute expression levels.

SUPERVISED NEURAL NETWORKS

As previously discussed, neural networks are algorithmic approaches to machine learning that are designed to simulate the input/output structure of biological neurons. Like their biological counterparts, neural networks learn by adjusting weighting functions and combining outputs to create trigger situations when inputs exceed certain thresholds. SOM clustering algorithms are members of a broad class of "unsupervised" machine learning algorithms intended to provide an alternative to more rigid "supervised" approaches built on specific sets of assumptions. The system proceeds through thousands of iterations of learning until a solution is discovered that optimally places the centroids in the centers of gene clusters.

Supervised neural networks (SNNs) are similar in their iterative approach to learning, but proceed until a predefined endpoint determined by the user is reached. The simplest case of a SNN is the single two-dimensional matrix, referred to as a perceptron, which we reviewed in Chapter 4 [18]. Values contained in the matrix are used as the basis of a scoring system whose ultimate goal is to distinguish between two sets of data. An iterative process is used to score individual members of each dataset and make modifications to the matrix until a satisfactory endpoint is reached. More complex systems use multiple layers of perceptrons; scores in the first layer are combined and used as triggers for the second layer, and so on through as many layers as are built in to the system. Modern neural networks often use three layers of perceptrons—an input layer, a hidden layer that combines data from the input layer, and a final output layer. Each iteration involves comparison to the predetermined endpoint, and a decision is made regarding modification of one of the layers.

One of the most important features of multilayer perceptron-based SNNs is that they can be designed to perform multiset classifications of complex datasets. Recent experiments have demonstrated the utility of this approach for studying gene-expression signatures from multiclass microarray data. The data represented gene clusters for major metabolic pathways. One of the most intriguing outcomes of the research involved the detailed examination of "false positives"—results that seemed to artificially cluster genes not thought to be directly related. However, deeper analysis revealed that these false positives were found to represent related metabolic pathways with overlapping enzymatic reactions [19]. Biological systems are logistically complex in the sense that transitivity rules often fail: If genes A and B belong to the same class and genes B and C are also of the same class, then it does not necessarily follow that A and C belong to the same class.

This effect can confound the learning process for neural networks. The problem is one of separating two distinct classes of expression profiles when those profiles both display some level of overlap with a third biologically distinct class. For example, consider three genes—A, B, and C—belonging to three distinct biological classes. If the class that includes gene A is considered to be the positive group, and the class that contains gene C is the negative group, then, in effect, when the network learns the signature of the class that includes A it will also learn the signature of gene B; thus genes with expression profiles similar to that of B but belonging to the biological class containing gene C may be erroneously identified as a member of the class that includes gene A. This result amounts to identification of a false positive.

A false negative can also occur in the reverse direction if gene B is mathematically recruited into the solution set built around the class containing gene C (the negative group in the learning exercise). The resulting network would likely identify certain members of the class containing gene A as belonging to the class containing gene C, thus providing a false negative result.

It is important to note that any recognition problem that can be solved by a neural network can be solved in three layers. However, neural networks containing more than three layers can sometimes converge on a solution more quickly if provided with a sufficient amount of training data.

SERIAL ANALYSIS OF GENE EXPRESSION (SAGE)

Serial Analysis of Gene Expression (SAGE) is a sequence-based gene-expression analysis tool that incorporates both a discovery engine and a mechanism for quantification of the level of expression. Microarray technology necessarily relies on a large body of sequence information that must be used to direct construction of the physical array. In situations where new sequences are likely to be discovered, the array must be constructed with an extremely large number of sequences, possibly covering the entire genome. Because most microarray experiments involve very short sequences, several per known coding region, the number of spots required for an unbounded experiment is likely to be enormous. Clustering enormous numbers of spots can be difficult and confusing. For these and other reasons related to time, cost, and complexity, it is often desirable to use a technique such as SAGE that can reveal the identity of every relevant message regardless of the number of transcripts produced. This information can then be used to construct more focused microarray experiments that contain only relevant sequences.

SAGE is designed to measure the expression of a small "tag" rather than the entire transcription product of a gene. The tag, defined as a ten-base-pair region directly adjacent to the 3'-end of the first occurrence of the sequence CATG, is generated through a process of well-defined enzymatic digestions and oligonucleotide purification steps. The complex process of generating SAGE tags is as follows [20]:

1. In the first step, double-stranded cDNA is made from purified mRNA using a biotinylated oligo (dT) primer. The result is a length of double-stranded cDNA with an exposed 3' end and a biotin moiety attached at the 5'end. Digestion with the endonuclease Nla III is then used to expose a defined location—5'...CATG...3' —within each cDNA that will be used for excision of the adjoining SAGE tag. (Nla III cleaves DNA immediately adjacent to the 3' side of the sequence CATG.) Ultimately, the SAGE tag will be the ten bases immediately adjoining the Nla III cut site.

2. Biotinylated 3' cDNAs are then bound to streptavidin-coated magnetic beads and affinity-purified.

3. The 5' termini of the purified cDNAs are separated into two pools and attached to adaptors at their 5' ends using oligo duplexes that encode the Nla III CATG cohesive overhang, a type IIs recognition sequence (which will be recognized by another restriction enzyme and used to release the tag), and a polymerase chain reaction (PCR) primer sequence.

4. The adapted cDNAs are then digested at the type IIs recognition sequence with BsmFI (also known as a tagging enzyme). BsmFI cleaves 14 to 15 base pairs 3' of its recognition sequence, releasing the linker-adapted SAGE tag from each cDNA.

5. The linker-adapted SAGE tags from each pool are then repaired using DNA polymerase, combined, and ligated using T4 DNA ligase. The resulting linker-adapted "ditags" are amplified by PCR and digested one more time with Nla III to release the primer adaptors .

6. The SAGE ditags are purified prior to being polymerized using T4 DNA ligase. Repaired ditags are then size-selected and cloned into a high-copy plasmid vector-pending sequencing.

Figure 5-9 illustrates these steps.

Because each tag represents a small (ten-base-pair) portion of an existing transcript, SAGE analysis is strongly dependent on the availability of high-quality genome sequence data. Newly identified and sequenced tags have little meaning outside the context of such data. High-throughput sequencing of whole genomes is, therefore, an important adjunct to the SAGE technique. High-quality sequence data combined with SAGE represents a powerful strategy for identifying and counting transcripts within a population of cells. Ultimately the number of tags counted for each gene will be proportional to the number of copies of each message present in the original sample.

The simplicity of SAGE analysis makes it an excellent tool for measuring the appearance and disappearance of a small number of highly regulated transcripts under a well-characterized set of conditions. Table 5-2 displays the results of such an experiment. Each entry in the table corresponds to a transcript whose expression is up regulated in the presence of an active p53 oncogene (data from rat fibroblast cells). P53, known to be inactive in many human cancers, has become the subject of intense scrutiny. Although expression of the gene is known to induce either stable growth arrest or programmed

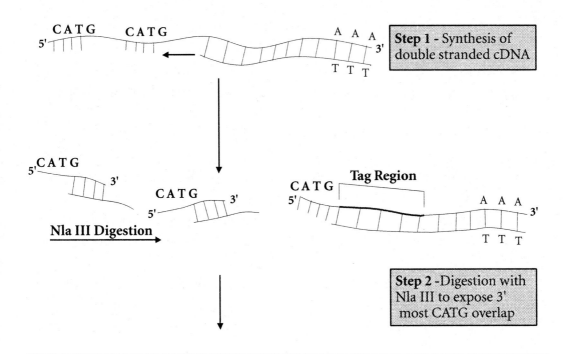

Figure 5-9 Serial analysis of gene expression (SAGE). A complex series of biochemical reactions is required to produce a sequence composed of short (ten base pair) tags derived from each transcript in the mix. The steps are: (1) Synthesis of biotinylated double-stranded cDNA; (2) Restriction enzyme digestion of cDNA and exposure of the 3' most CATG fragment; (3) Addition of adaptors and primer sequences for PCR coupled with excision of a ten-base-pair tag from each cDNA sequence; (4) formation of ditags (sequences containing two adjoining tags) followed by amplification and removal of the adaptors and primer sequences; (5) Concatenation of all tags into a single double-stranded DNA followed by sequencing.

cell death (apoptosis), the mechanism underlying development of p53-dependent apoptosis remains incompletely understood [21]. SAGE is an appropriate technique for such analysis because the transcripts each come from well-characterized genes that have been completely sequenced. In addition, each of the ten genes identified in the experiment is up regulated by at least twofold (200%). As in other expression-profiling techniques, SAGE is most effective when the quantification spans a limited range.

> **Step 3** - Addition of adaptors and PCR primer sequences coupled with excision of a 10bp tag from each cDNA sequence.

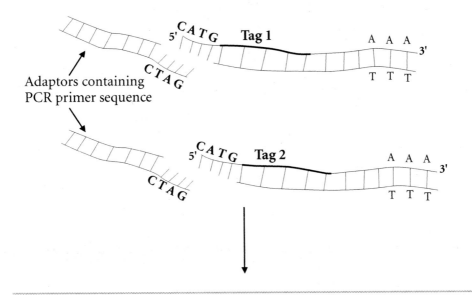

Figure 5-9 *(continued)*

Similar studies in humans have revealed the up regulation of 14 transcripts, 8 of which are known to code for proteins involved in cellular responses to oxidative stress. These observations stimulated additional biochemical experimentation that ultimately suggested a three-step process for p53-induced apoptosis: (1) transcriptional induction of redox-related genes; (2) formation of reactive oxygen species; and (3) oxidative degradation of mitochondrial components. Leakage of calcium and proteinaceous components from the damaged mitochondria stimulate caspases that are ubiquitously activated during the apoptotic process. Table 5-3 lists these transcripts.

The use of a single relatively short tag to identify each transcript often creates ambiguity; exactly the reason that SAGE results must be interpreted in the context of other biochemical information. As one might expect, the tags used to identify p53-induced genes are occasionally found in more than one coding region. For example, the

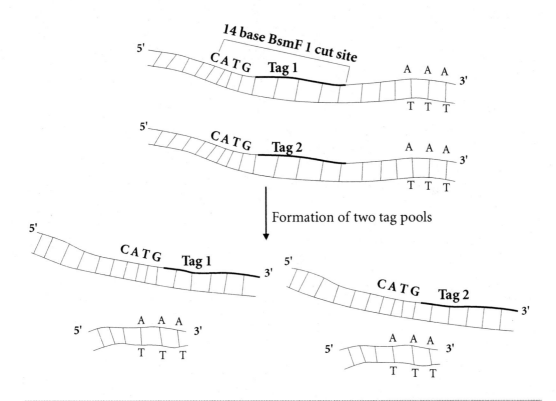

Figure 5-9 (continued)

sequence GAGGCCAACA, which identified PIG3 (NADPH quinone oxidoreductase homologue), is associated with three different GenBank accession numbers (see Table 5-4).

The fact that SAGE and microarray analyses can complement each other has not escaped notice. One popular strategy involves using SAGE to design custom microarrays in lieu of prefabricated designs with predefined target cDNA sequences. This approach has been used effectively to identify genes that are differentially expressed in primary breast cancers, metastatic breast cancers, and normal mammary epithelial cells [22]. In addition to identifying known cancer markers—HER-2/neu and MUC-1—the combination of techniques revealed several new genes and pathways not previously linked to breast cancer. Moreover, the new analysis generated significant information about

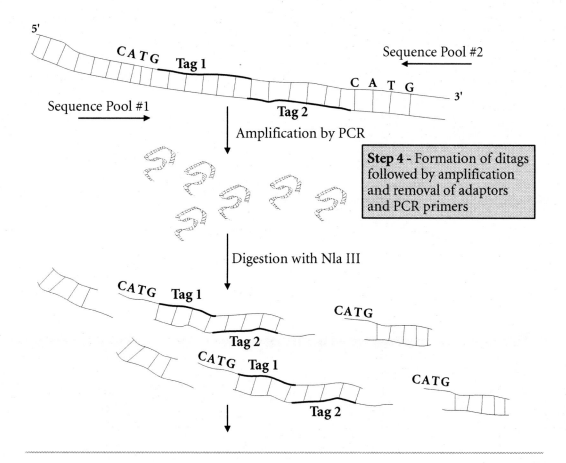

Figure 5-9 *(continued)*

expression-level differences between primary and metastatic disease. These differences have become important clinical markers, thus bridging research and clinical environments. It is likely that complete transcriptional maps will eventually enable researchers to construct families of microarrays containing all relevant sequences for each disease and metabolic state. Accomplishing this goal will take time; SAGE and other analysis techniques are likely to play an important role in the identification of sequences that will become the basis of a complete transcription-level picture of each relevant metabolic state.

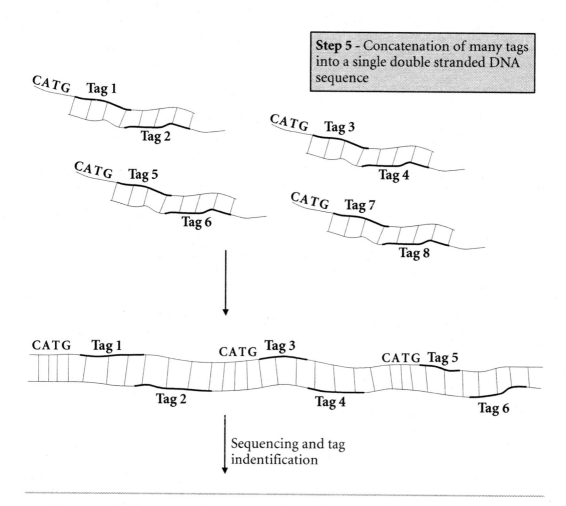

Step 5 - Concatenation of many tags into a single double stranded DNA sequence

Sequencing and tag indentification

Figure 5-9 *(continued)*

MASSIVELY PARALLEL SIGNATURE SEQUENCING

Researchers at Lynx Therapeutics have developed a technology that generates accurate and precise copy counts for every transcript in a sample regardless of the number of transcripts or the range of copy counts. This patented technology was invented by Sydney Brenner, whose goal was to be able to obtain an accurate accounting of the com-

Table 5-2 SAGE Analysis of Genes Induced in the Presence of an Active Form of p53 in the Rat Fibroblast

Gene	Percent Up Regulation (+p53 / –p53)
MDM2	300%
HSP70	500%
WAF1	>500%
Cyclin G	2500%
BAX	200%
CGR11	1200%
CGR19	>500%
EGR1	3000%
Shabin 80	>2000%
Shabin 123	>500%

Source: Madden, et. al. (2000) *Drug Discovery Today* 5(9), 415–425

plete transcriptional profile of a cell—major and minor messages, transient messages, short-lived transcripts, and control sequences.

The strategy involves several innovative approaches to amplifying, cloning, and sequencing millions of transcripts in parallel [23, 24 , 25]. Two new technologies form the basis of this approach. The first, Megaclone, allows a cDNA copy of each message to be cloned onto the surface of a 5um microbead. More specifically, each microbead, through amplification and selection processes that will be described, is ultimately decorated with 100,000 copies of the same sequence. For example, a message present in 20 copies will appear on 20 different microbeads—100,000 copies per microbead. The second, Massively Parallel Signature Sequencing (MPSS), uses sequence-dependent fluorescent signatures to successively identify four base-pair segments, and ultimately construct sequences from the microbead-bound cDNA. With more than one million microbeads

Table 5-3 Eight Genes Significantly Up Regulated in the Presence of the p53 Oncogene in Human Epithelial Cancers Cells

Gene	Function and Reactive Oxygen Species (ROS) Effect
p21	CDK inhibitor (induced by ROS)
PIG1	Galectin 7 (enhancer of superoxide production)
PIG3	Quinone oxidoreductase homologue (ROS generator)
PIG4	Serum amyloid A (induced by ROS)
PIG6	Proline oxidase homologue (glutathione biosynthesis)
PIG7	TNFa-induced mRNA (ROS induces TNFa)
PIG8	Etoposide-induced mRNA (quinone-causing ROS)
PIG12	GST homologue (induced by ROS)

Source: Polyak, et. al. (1997) *Nature* 389, 300–305

Table 5-4 SAGE Tags Often Display Redundancy

Tag Sequence	Accession	Description
GAGGCCAACA	AF010309	PIG3 (NADPH quinone oxidoreductase homologue)
GAGGCCAACA	H42923	yo10e11.s1 (EST name) Soares adult brain N2b5HB55Y *
GAGGCCAACA	W07320	za94c09.r1 (EST name) Soares fetal lung NbHL19W *

* Library constructed by Bento Soares and M. Fatima Bonaldo
Source: sagenet.org, NCBI

immobilized in a single layer array inside a flow cell, solvents and reagents can be washed over the samples in each cycle of the process (hence the designation "massively parallel"). Sequence data are ultimately matched against more-complete well-characterized entries in the public database infrastructure.

The combination of Megaclone and MPSS represents a complete departure from analog detection techniques; each transcript in the cell is separately cloned, amplified, and sequenced. Moreover, the technique is fully digital in the sense that each transcript is guaranteed to be sequenced as many times as it appears in the cell without any dependence on comparisons or extrapolations. Because the technique involves precise counting, accuracy is maintained across a very broad range of copy counts. Furthermore, the digital nature of the Megaclone-MPSS strategy facilitates precise comparisons between experiments and eliminates the need to make final adjustments to expression values.

Megaclone

The first half of the process—sequence-specific microbead preparation—is outlined here and graphically depicted in Figure 5-10.

1. All mRNA transcripts contained in the sample are reverse transcribed into cDNA.
2. A complex mixture of conjugates between cDNA templates and prefabricated oligonucleotide tags is prepared, where the number of different tags is at least 100 times larger than the number of cDNA templates. (The large ratio ensures that every template in the sample is conjugated to a unique tag.) The available tag library includes more than 16.7 million distinct 32mers.
3. The sample is amplified by PCR, after which the tags are rendered single stranded and combined with a population of microbeads that have attached on their surfaces the complete set of complementary tags or anti-tags. (Each microbead displays a single anti-tag.) Each template-tag combination will find and bind to its corresponding anti-tag microbead in the mixture. Because the population of tags bound to template cDNAs represents only 1% of the total number of tags, only 1% of the microbeads will be loaded with template molecules. This small population of cDNA-loaded microbeads is separated from the remaining unloaded microbeads with a fluorescence-activated cell sorter (FACS).

Each loaded microbead displays between 10^4 to 10^5 identical copies of one of the transcripts.

4. Using a specially fabricated flow cell, as many as two million microbeads are immobilized for sequencing. Because the position of each microbead remains fixed throughout the process, as many as two million distinct sequencing operations can be carried out in parallel. The design of the flow cell provides enough

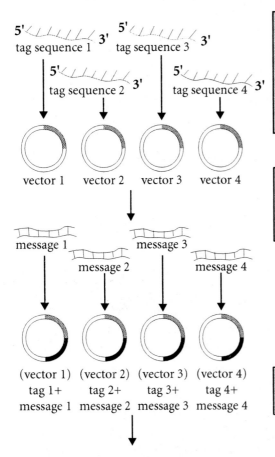

Step 1 - Eight rounds of combinatorial synthesis using four base long nucleotide words are used to construct a library of random tags, each 32 bases long.
Tags are converted into double stranded cDNA molecules and inserted into proprietary cloning vectors.

Step 2 - cDNA templates are prepared from cellular mRNA and inserted into the cloning vectors alongside the 32 base tags.

Step 3 -Tagged sequences are amplified using fluorescent primers.

Figure 5-10 The Megaclone system for creating a large microbead-based cDNA library representing all mRNA transcripts in a cell.

head space for reagent flow across the microbeads while maintaining an intact monolayer. The strategy involves iterative sequencing reactions and position-specific fluorescence measurements. (Ultrafine positional control is achieved through new scanning technology and software that tracks each microbead as sequencing proceeds.)

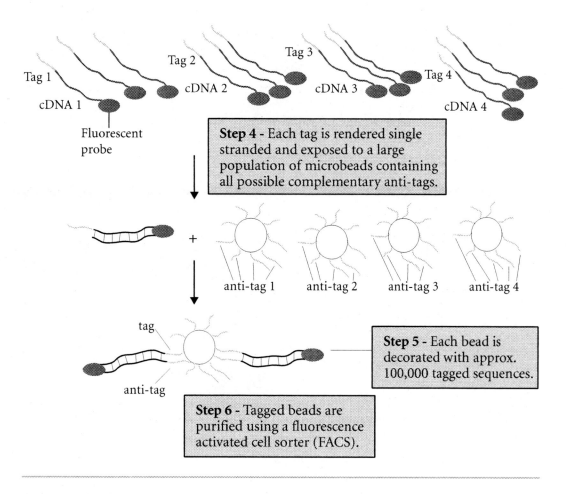

Tag 1

Tag 2

Tag 3

Tag 4

cDNA 1

cDNA 2

cDNA 3

cDNA 4

Fluorescent probe

Step 4 - Each tag is rendered single stranded and exposed to a large population of microbeads containing all possible complementary anti-tags.

+

anti-tag 1   anti-tag 2   anti-tag 3   anti-tag 4

tag

anti-tag

Step 5 - Each bead is decorated with approx. 100,000 tagged sequences.

Step 6 - Tagged beads are purified using a fluorescence activated cell sorter (FACS).

Figure 5-10 *(continued)*

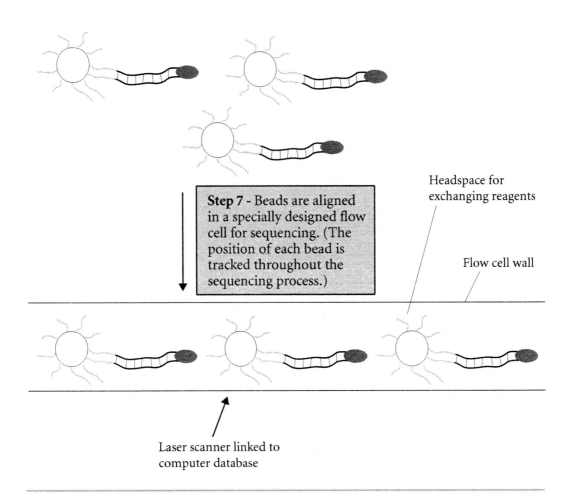

Step 7 - Beads are aligned in a specially designed flow cell for sequencing. (The position of each bead is tracked throughout the sequencing process.)

Headspace for exchanging reagents

Flow cell wall

Laser scanner linked to computer database

Figure 5-10 *(continued)*

MPSS

MPSS relies on successive iterations of oligonucleotide digestion, ligation of specially coded adaptors, and probe hybridization. More specifically, the process involves digesting the bound cDNA template to expose a four-base single-stranded overlap sequence; ligation of a series of encoded adaptors, each specific for a single residue and one of the four exposed positions; hybridization of one of 16 fluorescent probes to each of the 4 bound adaptors; and identification of the four bound probes and thus the sequence of the four-base overhang. The process is repeated until each of the bound cDNA templates has been sequenced from the first digestion site to the bound 32-base oligonucleotide tag securing the cDNA template to the microbead. The partial sequences are for identification purposes only; they are ultimately used to search publicly available data sources that contain more complete gene sequences. MPSS, depicted in Figure 5-11, is outlined here:

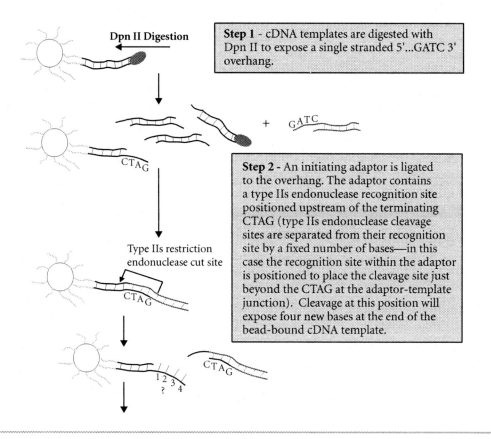

Dpn II Digestion

Step 1 - cDNA templates are digested with Dpn II to expose a single stranded 5'...GATC 3' overhang.

+ $_G$ATC

CTAG

Step 2 - An initiating adaptor is ligated to the overhang. The adaptor contains a type IIs endonuclease recognition site positioned upstream of the terminating CTAG (type IIs endonuclease cleavage sites are separated from their recognition site by a fixed number of bases—in this case the recognition site within the adaptor is positioned to place the cleavage site just beyond the CTAG at the adaptor-template junction). Cleavage at this position will expose four new bases at the end of the bead-bound cDNA template.

Type IIs restriction endonuclease cut site

CTAG

CTAG

1 2 3 4
?

Figure 5-11 Massively Parallel Signature Sequencing (MPSS). Sequences of up to two million microbead-bound cDNA templates are determined in parallel using an iterative process of enzymatic cleavage to expose a four-base single-stranded overhang, encoded adaptor ligation, and sequence interrogation by encoded hybridization probes. Sequencing chemistry steps are executed simultaneously across all microbeads in a specially designed flow cell that maintains the positional integrity of each bead while providing enough head space for the flow of solvents and reagents. The dynamic range of MPSS scales from fewer than 10 transcripts per million (tpm) to as many as 50,000 tpm.

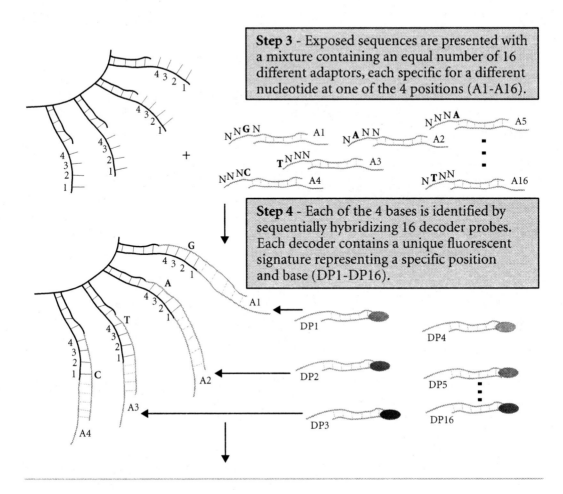

Step 3 - Exposed sequences are presented with a mixture containing an equal number of 16 different adaptors, each specific for a different nucleotide at one of the 4 positions (A1-A16).

Step 4 - Each of the 4 bases is identified by sequentially hybridizing 16 decoder probes. Each decoder contains a unique fluorescent signature representing a specific position and base (DP1-DP16).

Figure 5-11 *(continued)*

1. Microbead-bound cDNA templates are digested with the restriction enzyme Dpn II to reveal a single-stranded GATC overhang. (Dpn II cleaves on the 3' side of the sequence 5'...GATC 3'.)

2. An initiating adaptor ending in the complementary sequence 3'...CTAG...5' is ligated to the overhang. This adaptor also contains a type IIs endonuclease recognition site positioned upstream of the terminating CTAG. Recall that type IIs endonucleases have the unusual property of their cleavage site being separated

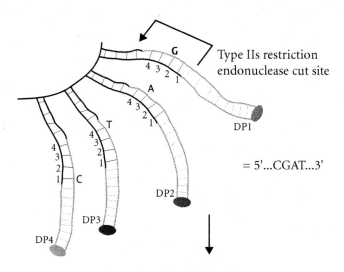

Type IIs restriction endonuclease cut site

= 5'...CGAT...3'

Step 5 - The process is repeated beginning with another round of type IIs endonuclease cleavage to expose the next 4 bases.

Figure 5-11 *(continued)*

from their recognition site by a fixed number of bases—in this case, the recognition site within the adaptor is positioned to place the cleavage site just beyond the CTAG at the adaptor-template junction. Cleavage at this position will expose four new bases at the end of the bead-bound cDNA template.

3. Digestion with the appropriate type IIs endonuclease exposes the first four bases of the cDNA template at the adaptor-template junction. The four exposed bases are presented on a single-stranded overhang, and the initiating adaptor is released by the digestion.

4. A mixture of encoded adaptors is used to determine the identity of each of the four exposed bases. Each adaptor is specific for one of the four possible DNA bases in one of the four positions of the overhang. Consequently, the exposed

four-base single-stranded overhangs can each be expected to attach one of four adaptors. The presence of a large homogeneous population of cDNA templates on each bead guarantees that a significant (and approximately equal) number of each of the four appropriate adaptors will be attached to the templates.

5. The identity and order of the exposed bases is determined by hybridizing, one at a time, each of 16 decoder probes to the ends of the adaptors. Because four adaptors were bound to the cDNAs, four decoder probes will hybridize—each one will represent a specific base in one of the four positions. Moreover, each of the 16 probes contains a unique fluorescent marker that can be detected by the laser scanner. Because the bound adaptors are specific both for a DNA base and one of the four positions, the fluorescent signatures on each bead will reveal the order and identity of the exposed bases in the overhang.

6. As in the case of initiating adaptors, each encoded adaptor contains a type IIs restriction endonuclease site upstream of the four bases being interrogated. The position of the site is set to guarantee that cleavage by the appropriate type IIs endonuclease will expose a new overhang containing the next four bases. The process of binding base and position-specific encoded adaptors and matching fluorescent probes is repeated to determine the next four bases in the sequence.

7. The process continues until every remaining base in the microbead-bound cDNA templates is identified. As a result, for each cDNA template all bases between the CATG cut site and the tag sequence securing the template to the microbead are identified. This information is subsequently used to search other databases for more sequence and functional information about the transcripts. Because all beads were sequenced in parallel, a complete transcriptional map of the sample is revealed. During the sequencing chemistry steps, a database containing information about each microbead was constructed. Counting identical sequences present in the database reveals information about the number of copies of each transcript in the original sample.

Perhaps the most compelling feature of the Megaclone-MPSS strategy is the immortality of the data. As previously discussed, one of the central goals of transcriptional profiling is the creation of a central repository containing expression data from thousands of different cell types under a variety of conditions. Megaclone-MPSS facilitates the construction of such repositories because copy counts can be directly compared between experiments. Furthermore, complete annotated sequence information is not a clear need if the goal is to build transcriptional profiles that can serve as diagnostic tools. The diagnostic simply becomes a pattern of up and down regulation of signature sequences that serve as proxies for complete transcripts. Because the length of an MPSS sequenced transcript is typically in the range of 16 to 20 bases, each signature sequence is likely to represent a unique transcript—it is very unlikely that the same signature sequence will be cleaved from two different transcripts and, therefore, disguised in the sequencing process. SAGE, discussed earlier, is built on a similar strategy of constructing tags of limited length that are later used to query databases containing complete annotated sequences.

The Megaclone-MPSS technique is not without drawbacks. One notable issue is its inability to provide complete information regarding SNPs and other polymorphisms. Because each signature sequence represents a final Dpn II digestion product (the length of cDNA between the bead-bound tag and the first CATG), any additional sequence information existing beyond the Dpn II cut site is automatically lost. An up regulated transcript containing an SNP outside the signature sequence will simply appear to be up regulated, and the fact that a polymorphism is present will be lost in the analysis. One could envision a more complex situation where a disease group associated with the up regulation of a specific gene contains two different subpopulations: one with a SNP in the gene, and one without. The up regulation would be quantified by MPSS, but the SNP might fall outside the signature sequence region. These data would not be helpful in explaining the presence of two subgroups, but might have some diagnostic value for the overall disease. Moreover, if the subgroups required two distinctly different treatment regimens, MPSS alone would fail as a complete diagnostic. By comparison, microarray analysis would likely identify both the SNP and the up regulation event but might have other problems related to dynamic range if key transcripts were up or down regulated across a broad range of copy counts.

As with all biochemical techniques, Megaclone-MPSS has strengths and weaknesses. In general, if the goal is to achieve very accurate copy counts for all transcripts across a very broad range, then MPSS is likely to be a valuable tool. Conversely, if the goal is to interrogate every gene at the single nucleotide level, possibly to identify SNPs or other small aberrations, microarray technology is likely to represent a better fit. Many situations require both sets of capabilities. The fact that MPSS data is often used to search public databases populated with more complete sequence information obtained through microarray analysis supports this view. The reverse is also true in the sense that microarray analysis can be used to identify interesting transcripts, which can then be quantified at the single-copy-count level with MPSS.

THE SPLICE-VARIANT PROBLEM

Messenger RNA splice variants have the capability of confounding almost any high-throughput expression-profiling technique. SAGE and Megaclone-MPSS are especially vulnerable because they rely on partial sequences to identify expressed transcripts. Splice variants that vary outside the region being studied cannot be distinguished by these techniques. Even when splice variants are distinguishable, subtle differences outside the region of study will not be revealed. Furthermore, using SAGE- or MPSS-derived sequences as probes to search large gene-sequence databases is unlikely to help because basic sequence data is not useful as a predictor of transcriptional splicing. After SAGE or MPSS has revealed the presence of a specific gene, microarray technology can be used to enumerate the complete set of splice variants.

However, it is important to point out that microarray results can also be difficult to interpret in this context because each spot in the array corresponds to a short—approximately 25 bases—portion of a transcript. Although overlaps between the short cDNA templates contained in the array can be used to assemble complete sequences, the presence of unspliced messages and message fragments removed during splicing can confuse the interpretation. In general, it is almost impossible to use microarray, or any other high-throughput technique, to unambiguously identify the specific combinations of exon variants that occur together in individual mRNA molecules [26]. The problem of correctly orienting mRNA fragments into splice variants is depicted in Figure 5-12.

Unambiguous identification of individual mRNA isoforms can be obtained only by using low-throughput approaches based on amplification and end-to-end sequencing of individual transcripts. Nuclease protection assays (NPAs) are often used in this context to test for the presence of individual sequence elements in an isolated transcript or population of transcripts. NPA is based on hybridization of single-stranded, well-

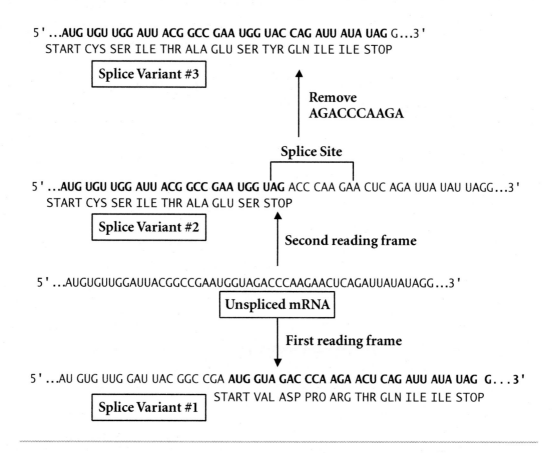

5'...AUG UGU UGG AUU ACG GCC GAA UGG UAC CAG AUU AUA UAG G...3'
START CYS SER ILE THR ALA GLU SER TYR GLN ILE ILE STOP

Splice Variant #3

Remove
AGACCCAAGA

Splice Site

5'...AUG UGU UGG AUU ACG GCC GAA UGG UAG ACC CAA GAA CUC AGA UUA UAU UAGG...3'
START CYS SER ILE THR ALA GLU SER STOP

Splice Variant #2

Second reading frame

5'...AUGUGUUGGAUUACGGCCGAAUGGUAGACCCAAGAACUCAGAUUAUAUAGG...3'

Unspliced mRNA

First reading frame

5'...AU GUG UUG GAU UAC GGC CGA AUG GUA GAC CCA AGA ACU CAG AUU AUA UAG G...3'
START VAL ASP PRO ARG THR GLN ILE ILE STOP

Splice Variant #1

Figure 5-12 The splice-variant problem. Various combinations of mRNA fragments derived from long unspliced transcripts must be assembled and correctly oriented to correctly identify final mRNA species. The fact that some of the fragments represent shifted reading frames further complicates the analysis. Splice variants 1 and 2 result from a single base frame shift. Removal of the sequence AGACCCAAGA from splice variant 2 eliminates a stop codon that overlaps the 5' side of the splice site and exposes a new stop codon further downstream. As a result, splice variant 3 contains elements from both reading frames. High-throughput analysis techniques would reveal the presence of mRNA sequence elements from all three splice variants even if the cell did not express all three versions of the gene.

characterized antisense probes to an RNA sample. After hybridization, remaining unhybridized probes and sample RNA are removed by digestion with a mixture of nucleases. After nuclease inactivation, the remaining double-stranded probe:target hybrids are precipitated and purified for further sequence analysis. NPAs can reveal the presence of specific exons in a mixture of mRNA species. The combination of high-throughput pro-filing approaches—SAGE, MPSS, microarray, etc.—with a carefully planned sequence of NPAs, can be a powerful solution to the problem of comprehensive mRNA profiling. These approaches are complemented by a growing base of transcription profiles and complete transcriptome maps that are rapidly becoming part of the public database infrastructure for bioinformatics.

SUMMARY

Essentially all diseases and metabolic states are polygenic. Even if a physical state were controlled by a single gene coding for a single protein, the up regulation of that gene would perturb the broader system, and many coding regions would be affected. As a result, the genome-centric view of molecular biology is slowly being replaced by a more comprehensive systems view. One of the most important elements of this approach is a complete understanding of the transcriptional state of all genes involved in a specific metabolic state. As a result, technologies for gene-expression profiling have become central to molecular biology and diagnostic medicine.

Any technique used to study the transcripts within a cell must be capable of spanning the range from single-digit copy counts to very large numbers, often in the thousands. Accuracy is important because at the single-digit level, small changes in the number of copies of certain messages can have significant effects on metabolism and disease. This discussion focused on various technologies for transcriptional profiling, including both physical techniques and mathematical algorithms. Because different technologies are appropriate for different types of experiments, this chapter presented a balanced view that does not particularly favor any one approach. Likewise, this review of the basic classes of clustering algorithms is designed to highlight different approaches with a focus on the theoretical differences. Moreover, readers are encouraged to consider the differences presented here when reviewing experimental results. These differences are intended to form a backdrop for the next phase of our discussion, which focuses on protein translation.

ENDNOTES

1. Kapranov P., Cawley S. E., Drenkow J., Bekiranov S., Strausberg R. L., Fodor S. P. A., Gingeras T. R. 2002. Large scale transcriptional activity in chromosomes 21 and 22. *Science* 296: 916–919.

2. Slamon D. J., Godolphin W., Jones L. A., et al. 1989. Studies of the HER-2/neuproto-oncogene in human breast and ovarian cancer. *Science* 244: 707–712.

3. Sze S. H., Roytberg M. A., Gelfand M. S., Mironov A. A., Astakhova T. V., Pevzner P. A. 1998. Algorithms and software for support of gene identification experiments. *Bioinformatics* 14: 14–19.

4. Augen J. 2002. The evolving role of information technology in the drug discovery process. *Drug Discovery Today* 7(5): 315–323.

5. Ideker T., Thorsson V., Ranish J., Christmas R., Buhler J., Eng J., Bumgarner R.,Goodlett D., Aebersold R., Hood L. 2001. Integrated genomic and proteomic analysis of a systematically perturbed metabolic network. *Science* 292: 929–934.

6. Ideker T., Thorsson V., Ranish J., Christmas R., Buhler J., Eng J., Bumgarner R., Goodlett D., Aebersold R., Hood L. 2001. Integrated genomic and proteomic analysis of a systematically perturbed metabolic network. *Science* 292: 929–934.

7. Adams M. D., Kelley J. M., Gocayne J. D., Dubnick M., Polymeropoulos M. H., Xiao H., Merril C. R., Wu A., Olde B., Moreno R. F., et al. 1991. Complementary DNA sequencing: expressed sequence tags and human genome project. *Science* 252:1651–1656.

8. Friend S., Roland S. 2002. The magic of microarrays. *Scientific American* 286(2): 44–49.

9. Shalon D., Smith S. J., Brown P. O. 1996. A DNA microarray system for analyzing complex DNA samples using two-color fluorescent probe hybridization. *Genome Research* 6: 639–645.

10. Mimics K., Middleton F., Lewis A., Levitt P. 2001. Analysis of complex brain disorders with gene expression microarrays: schizophrenia as a disease of the synapse. *Trends in Neuroscience* 24: 479–486.

11. Kuklin A., Shah S., Hoff B., Shams S. 2002. "Data Management in Microarray Fabrication, Image Processing, and Data Mining," in *DNA Arrays: Technologies and Experimental Strategies* (Elena Grigorenko, ed.). CRC Press, 2001, 115–128.

12. Eisen M. B., Soellman P. T., Brown P. O., Botstein D. 1998. Cluster analysis and display of genome-wide expression patterns. *Proceedings of the National Academy of Sciences* 95: 14863–14868.

13. Alizadeh A. A., Eisen M. B., Davis R. E., Ma C., Lossos I. S., Rosenwald A., Boldrick J. C., Saber H., Tran T., Yu X., Powell J. I., Yang L., Marti G. E., Moore T., Hudson J. Jr., Lu L., Lewis D. B., Tibshirani R., Sherlock G., Chan W. C., Greiner T. C., Weisenburger D. D., Armitage J. O., Warnke R., Levy R., Wilson W., Grever M. R., Byrd J. C., Botstein D., Brown P. O., Staudt L. M. 2000. Distinct types of diffuse large B-cell lymphoma identified by gene expression profiling. *Nature* 403: 503–511.

14. Tamayo P., Slonim D., Mesirov J., Zhu Q., Kitareewan S., Dmitrovsky S., Lander E., Golub T. R., 1999. Interpreting patterns of gene expression with self-organizing maps: methods and application to hematopoietic differentiation. *Proceedings of the National Academy of Sciences* 96: 2907–2912.

15. Quackenbush J. 2001. Computational analysis of microarray data. *Nature Reviews / Genetics* 2: 418–427.

16. Kohonen T., Huang T. (Ed.), Schroeder M. (Ed.). *Self Organizing Maps, Third Edition*. Springer-Verlag, Berlin, Heidleberg, New York, 2001.

17. Golub T. R., Slonim D. K., Tamayo P., Huard C., Gaasenbeek M., Mesirov J. P., Coller H., Loh M. L., Downing J. R., Caligiuri M. A., Bloomfield C. D., Lander E. S. 1999. Molecular classification of cancer: class discovery and class prediction by gene expression monitoring. *Science* 286: 531–537.

18. Rosenblatt F. 1958. The perceptron: a probabilistic model for information storage in the brain. Psychological Review 65: 386–407.

19. Mateos A., Dopazo J., Jansen R., Yuhai T., Gerstein M., Stolovitzky G. Systematic learning of gene functional classes from DNA array expression data by using multi-layer perceptrons. (manuscript in preparation). Bioinformatics unit, Centro Nacional de Investigaciones Oncologicas, Madrid, Spain; Department of Molecular Biophysics and Biochemistry, Yale University, New Haven CT; IBM Computational Biology Center, York Town Heights, NY.

20. Madden S., Wang C., Landes G. 2000. Serial analysis of gene expression: from gene discovery to target identification. *Drug Discovery Today* 5(9): 415–425.

21. Polyak K., Xia Y., Zweier J., Kinzler K., Vogelstein B. 1997. A model for p53-induced apoptosis. *Nature* 389: 300–305.

22. Nacht M., et al. 1999. Combining serial analysis of gene expression and array technologies to identify genes differentially expressed in breast cancer. *Cancer Research* 59: 5464–5470.

23. Brenner S., et al. 2000. Gene expression analysis by massively parallel signature sequencing (MPSS) on microbead arrays. *Nature Biotechnology* 18: 630–634.

24. Brenner S., et al. 2000. In vitro cloning of complex mixtures of DNA on microbeads: Physical separation of differentially expressed cDNAs. *PNAS* 97: 1665–1670.

25. Reinartz J., et al. 2002. Massively parallel signature sequencing as a tool for in-depth quantitative gene expression profiling in all organisms. *Briefings in Functional Genomics and Proteomics* 1(1): 95–104.

26. Roberts G., Smith C. W. J. 2002. Alternative splicing: combinatorial output from the genome. *Currrent Opinion in Chemical Biology* 6: 375–383.

6

Overview of the Proteome and the Protein Translation Process

INTRODUCTION

The sequence of chapters in this book was chosen to parallel the flow of information from gene to transcript to protein. It seems only natural to follow such a path because genes code for proteins, and proteins are the basic building blocks from which all organisms are constructed.

This chapter begins with an overview of protein translation and the biochemical mechanisms that introduce variability into this process. The mechanisms responsible for translating a message into a protein represent a metabolic control point as well as a step up in complexity. Surprisingly, subtle variations in the process can cause a single mRNA species to code for more than one protein. These variations are closely related to the statistical chance of a particular start codon becoming a ribosomal binding site. Many factors are involved—downstream secondary structure, the context in which a start codon is found, the location of nearby open reading frames, and slight variability in the ribosomal scanning mechanism. The combination of transcriptional splicing and translational variation provides higher organisms with a remarkable level of genetic flexibility. It is this level of flexibility that allows organisms with very similar base gene sequences to display strikingly different phenotypes.

As a consequence of its variability, the proteome in its fully enumerated form is far more complex than the transcriptome, which we reviewed earlier. This discussion closes by reviewing specific clinical examples where variations in the protein translation process can cause or prevent a specific disease.

RIBOSOMAL STRUCTURE AND THE PROTEIN TRANSLATION PROCESS

Translation, like the other processes discussed thus far, cannot be fully understood without a view of the information-based components of the gene-expression system.

THE RIBOSOME

Central to the translation process is the ribosome, a complex catalytic machine that performs four key functions. In logical order, they are as follows:

1. Scanning for a protein start codon (usually AUG) after locating and binding to a ribosomal binding site. A select group of mRNAs are transcribed under conditions of high stress—hypoxia, serum deprivation, irradiation, apoptosis, etc. These unusual messages include survival factors, oncogenes, and proteins that regulate apoptosis. Such messages contain internal ribosome entry sites (IRES), which replace the normal 5' cap-based recognition mechanism for initiation.

2. Reading and interpreting each three-letter RNA code word advancing the reading frame by three letters prior to each read operation.

3. Facilitating polymerization of the protein molecule by physically attaching a transfer RNA (tRNA) holding the proper amino acid for each reading frame. Each used tRNA is automatically ejected in preparation for the next read operation.

4. Identifying termination codons and stopping the translation process.

Sequences, codes, and various forms of conformational information are central to the translation process as are a large number of protein-protein and protein-RNA interactions. As such, the ribosome can be thought of as a nano-scale robot capable of reading, interpreting, and acting on sequence information.

Ribosomes are composed of several active centers, each constructed from a particular set of proteins associated with a region of ribosomal RNA (rRNA). These centers provide both catalytic and structural functions. The catalytic activities are dependent on the structure of the ribosome; they cannot be duplicated with isolated proteins and rRNA outside the context of the complete structure. The overall structure of a ribosome is characterized by two major subunits, known by their sedimentation constants: 60S and 40S (S = Svedberg sedimentation coefficient). The smaller subunit contains approximately 1,800 bases of rRNA and 33 proteins, the larger includes 49 proteins and approximately 5,000 bases of rRNA. Quality control, a key function of the translation system that is often taken for granted, involves molecular-level proofreading and editing. This high-fidelity process is the result of an intricate network of protein-RNA interactions that complement enzymatic specificity (e.g., the rejection of valine by isoleucyl-tRNA synthetase) [1]. Even the slightest lack of fidelity at the level of protein translation can result in an "error catastrophe" that ultimately kills the cell. Post-translational protein folding and the recognition/destruction of misfolded proteins are both active processes mediated by molecules known as chaperones, chaperonins, and a small 76–amino acid protein called ubiquitin. These pathways—all based on protein-protein interactions—act as a kind of intracellular immune system; the final step in achieving fidelity in the translation process.

THE TRANSLATION PROCESS

A purely biochemical view of translation misses many of the nuances that have the distinct flavor of an information science. Although a complete description of the translation process is outside the scope of this book, some elements are germane to this discussion. An overview of the eukaryotic mechanism includes the following steps:

1. An mRNA transcript is ready for translation when all introns have been removed and the ends contain a 5' methylated guanine cap and 3' poly-A tail. Such transcripts are stable in the cytoplasm for an extended period of time.

2. A series of protein-mRNA interactions disrupt secondary structure at the 5' cap region of the untranslated message. These structural changes pave the way for the attachment of ribosomal subunits and associated proteins.

3. An initiation complex forms. The complex is composed of the small 40S ribosomal subunit, initiator Met-tRNA (Met-tRNA$_i$), an associated binding protein—eIF2, and a GTP molecule. Met-tRNA$_i$ is structurally different from Met-tRNA$_m$ used for chain elongation; it has an unusual tertiary structure, and the 2' ribose of base 64 is phosphorylated. In prokaryotes, the initiator methionine has a formylated amino group. (The formyl group is removed after translation.) Although eukaryotes do not incorporate a formylated amino group on the initiator Met, they do use a unique Met-tRNA$_i$ that cannot add methionine in the middle of a growing chain. Unique structural features allow this tRNA molecule to initiate translation by entering the partially formed P site located on the small ribosomal subunit. After scanning is complete and an appropriate AUG start codon is located, the complete ribosomal structure forms, completing both A and P sites.

4. After bound at the 5' cap, the initiation complex begins to migrate down the length of the message scanning for the first AUG start site. The scanning process is capable of melting RNA secondary structure hairpins with stabilities < -30Kcal; more stable hairpin structures impede the scanning process.

5. The first AUG triplet is not always an initiation site. An evolutionary solution to this problem involves additional sequence elements that must be present to halt the scanning process. The correct initiation signal includes additional sequence elements, and the AUG triplet must be recognized in the context of these sequence elements. An optimal signal consists of the sequence 5'...GCC(A/G)CC**AUG**G...3'. Most significant are the purine residue—A/G—three bases upstream of the AUG start codon and the G found immediately downstream. Changes to these two critical elements can reduce translational efficiency by more than ten times. Although the vast majority of eukaryotic initiation events involve scanning from the 5' cap, another mechanism, mentioned earlier in this chapter, allows direct binding of the 40S ribosomal subunit directly

to an internal ribosome entry site (IRES). Many initiation sites are within 30 bases of the 5' cap. Such sites fall within the space covered by the small ribosomal subunit immediately upon attachment at the cap region. No scanning is necessary for these sites. Other mechanisms—reinitiation and context-dependent leaky scanning—also facilitate initiation events downstream of the first AUG triplet. (We return to these mechanisms later in this chapter.)

6. After a proper initiation site is located, ribosomal assembly is completed by the attachment of a large (60S) subunit. Completed assemblies contain two principal binding sites for tRNA molecules. The A (acceptor) site exposes a triplet representing the next amino acid to be added to the growing chain. An appropriate tRNA containing the next amino acid will bind to this site. The P (peptide or donor) site exposes the codon of the most recently added amino acid. The tRNA bound at the P site contains the growing polypeptide chain. In each case, the end of the tRNA that contains an amino acid is located on the large (60S) subunit, and the anticodon at the other end interacts with the mRNA bound by the small (40S) subunit. Both binding domains, P and A, extend across the entire structure.

7. An aminoacyl-tRNA molecule enters the A site of the ribosome. (The P site already contains a peptidyl-tRNA.) Elongation involves transfer of the polypeptide from the P site peptidyl-tRNA to the aminoacyl-tRNA at the A site with formation of a new peptide bond between the growing chain and the next amino acid. Elongation factors are involved in the addition of an aminoacyl-tRNA molecule to the A site. The reaction consumes phosphate bond energy in the form of GTP, and a GDP is released. Initiator tRNA (Met-tRNA$_i$) is not recognized by the elongation factors, and is consequently prevented from responding to internal AUG codons. (In prokaryotes, this mechanism is crucial because fMet-tRNA$_i$ contains a methionine with a blocked n-terminus that cannot support chain elongation.)

8. Translocation moves the ribosome downstream by one codon and places the new peptidyl-tRNA into the P site. The remaining deacylated tRNA leaves via a transitional tRNA binding domain sometimes referred to as the E (exit) site. In summary, a charged aminoacyl-tRNA enters the ribosomal structure through the A

site, translocates to the P site upon peptide bond formation, transfers the growing chain to a new tRNA bound at the A site, and exits via the E site. Figure 6-1
outlines this process.

9. The process continues until the ribosome encounters one of the three termination codons: UAG (amber), UAA (ochre), or UGA (opal)—the names have historical but not scientific significance. Eukaryotic release factor (ERF) binds to a
termination codon at the A site and begins the termination process, which
involves release of the completed polypeptide from the last tRNA, expulsion of
the tRNA from the ribosome, and dissociation of the ribosome from the mRNA.

Like other components of the gene-expression system, the ribosome is designed to
read and translate information into structure. These structures—namely proteins—also
contain information that allows them to properly fold into functioning macromolecules. Chapter 8 covers the folding process.

UNRAVELING THE COMPLEXITIES OF rRNA

The ribosome is a complex machine that strongly depends on rRNA secondary structure for its function. One method for unraveling the complexities of this structure
involves evolutionary comparisons between different organisms. In general, regions tend
to be conserved if they are important to the formation of secondary structure; maps of
these regions have proven useful for building descriptive models of the ribosome.
Through such studies it has become evident that the additional complexity of the
eukaryotic ribosome confers diversity of function. This diversity further complicates the
interpretation of genetic and transcriptional information.

For example, a final mRNA transcript—one that has been spliced and processed—
can still code for more than one polypeptide in a eukaryotic system. Two subtle mechanistic features give rise to this diversity—one at the n-terminus and one at the
c-terminus:

- **"Leaky" scanning**—The n-terminal AUG occurs in a weak context, and small ribosomal subunits occasionally proceed to the next downstream initiation site. Both

1. Formation of a ternary complex: (Met-tRNAi) + GTP + eukaryotic initiation factor complex (eIF2)

2. Ternary complexes bind to free 40S subunits, which attach to the 5' end of a message.

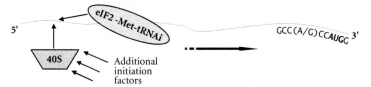

3. After scanning to a start site, a 60S ribosomal subunit attaches and translation begins.

4. Successive rounds of translocation and chain elongation continue until a stop codon is reached.

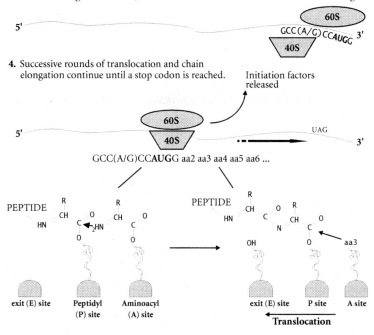

Figure 6-1 Ribosome-based protein synthesis involves three major steps: (1) Initiation—the formation of a complex consisting of the n-terminal aminoacyl-tRNA, mRNA, and a small (40S) ribosomal subunit; (2) elongation—the process by which a chain of amino acids is assembled—involves a series of aminoacyl-tRNA additions, peptide bond formations, and translocations; (3) termination releases both the new polypeptide chain and the ribosome from the mRNA template. Most messages are simultaneously translated by several ribosomes; the number of sites being proportional to the length of the message. As a result, longer messages appear to experience higher translation rates and produce more copies than shorter messages.

proximity to the 5' cap and nucleotide composition of sequences that surround the start codon determine the efficiency of the recognition process [2].

- **Reinitiation**—Ribosomes reassemble on the 3' side of a termination codon and initiate translation of a small downstream open reading frame. This process results in the production of two polypeptides; the first is unaffected, and the second is an artifact.

Conversely, in prokaryotic systems, translation always commences at the first AUG downstream of a well-characterized polypurine site known as the Shine-Dalgarno sequence (5' ... A G G A G G ... 3'). The distance between the AUG start codon and the Shine-Dalgarno sequence is typically less than ten bases. Translation continues until the first stop codon is located. The fact that leaky scanning and reinitiation appear not to occur in prokaryotic organisms is indicative of the reduced complexity of the prokaryotic ribosome. Furthermore, evolution tends to favor diversity, a theme that fits well with the complexity buildup we have been discussing. By extension, translation systems that embody a certain level of imprecision are likely to confer evolutionary advantages upon their hosts. Surprisingly, lack of translational fidelity appears to have an important biological function. Some of the secondary polypeptides that result from leaky scanning and reinitiation are known to have distinct metabolic functions, and some are thought to participate in regulatory feedback loops.

FIDELITY OF TRANSLATION

Considering the number of steps, interacting components, and overall complexity, translation is a remarkably accurate process. In fact, misincorporation of an amino acid normally occurs only once in about 10,000 codons. Even more remarkable is the high rate of accuracy exhibited by the system for amino acids with very similar structures (e.g., valine and isoleucine; the enzyme isoleucyl-tRNA synthetase rarely incorporates valine into an isoleucine tRNA). The tRNA synthetases, which have been well understood for nearly 30 years, are one of many checkpoints that ensure translational fidelity.

Mechanisms that increase translational fidelity can be considered as belonging to one of three broad mechanistic categories: The integrity of mRNAs and tRNAs is rigorously maintained by sequence-specific enzymatic reactions; correct matching of each codon and tRNA pair in the reading frame of the ribosome is mediated by several protein-protein and protein-nucleic acid interactions; and tRNA-amino acid matches are rigorously controlled.

Sequence-Specific Enzymatic Reactions

Aminoacyl-tRNA synthetases maintain a broad area of contact with transfer RNA molecules during the enzymatic reaction. This close contact (as much as 5600 Å^2) exposes the enzyme to a large amount of sequence information on the surface of the tRNA molecule. This high level of specificity reduces the likelihood that a tRNA will become linked to the wrong amino acid. Consequently, tRNA synthetases serve as an important control point because, in addition to their assembly role, they increase the fidelity of the translation process.

Protein-Protein and Protein-Nucleic Acid Interactions

However, amino acids are relatively small molecules, and it is often difficult to enzymatically distinguish between similar molecules. Two proofreading mechanisms have evolved that address this problem. The first involves hydrolysis of an ATP-activated, but incorrect, aminoacyl-tRNA synthetase before transfer to tRNA can be completed. (Prior to tRNA attachment, amino acids are activated in the presence of ATP to form an enzyme-bound aminoacyl-adenyiate.) In the case of isoleucyl-tRNA synthetase, this mechanism involves two different catalytic sites on the surface of the enzyme. The first uses structural constraints to filter most incorrect amino acids by size. Valine, however, is too small to be excluded. The second site becomes active when sequence-specific structural changes at the tRNA-enzyme junction cause the translocation of valine to the second catalytic site where hydrolysis of the activated valine-AMP (adenosine monophosphate) occurs [3]. As a result, substitution of valine for isoleucine occurs only once for each 3,000 isoleucyl-tRNAs synthesized. The second mechanism involves deacylation of a complete, but incorrect, aminoacyl-tRNA before translation. More specifically, a system of protein-protein and nonsynthetase enzymatic reactions are used to correct the mistake and manufacture a proper aminoacyl-tRNA. The combination of these processes, for example, reduces the valine-for-isoleucine mistake rate to the 1 in 10,000 level characteristic of translation.

245

tRNA-Amino Acid Control

It has also been noted that mRNAs containing premature termination signals rarely result in the production of truncated proteins. Such sequences normally result from "nonsense mutations" that insert or delete base pairs and shift a termination signal into the reading frame. Through a sequence-specific process that remains poorly understood, these truncated RNAs are recognized and destroyed [4]. Even when incorrect aminoacyl-tRNAs remain intact, kinetic effects at the A site of the ribosome do not favor their incorporation. This effect is thought to be the result of strained conformations of the elongation factor-tRNA-ribosome complex [5].

This theme of higher-order complexes driving kinetic effects is also evident in the context-specific initiation and termination processes previously discussed. Each of these processes involves sequence recognition by a large complex of proteins and nucleotides that must fit together properly. Slight imperfections lead to strained conformations and imperfect molecular fits. These strained conformations always cause one reaction to be favored over another; the final choice of tRNA, initiation site, or termination site can be viewed as the kinetic product of a very complex chemical reaction. Sequentially selecting the most favorable kinetic route can significantly lower the error rate in a multistage process such as translation.

SPECIAL FEATURES OF THE EUKARYOTIC-TRANSLATION PROCESS

Several unique features differentiate eukaryotic translation from that of lower organisms. Surprisingly, some of these differences increase the amount of variability exhibited by the system. For example, the "first AUG" rule is sometimes violated when a new upstream initiation site is created by mutation. Alternatively, mutations that remove an initiation site can cause translation to begin at a downstream AUG, even if it lacks proper sequence context. In the latter case, the original message is altered to produce an isoform that lacks the first start codon.

The mechanism for ribosomal binding at the second site varies—some messages contain a second initiation site that is not normally encountered during the scanning process; others involve an internal ribosome entry site (discussed later).

Table 6-1 contains a very brief list of some significant human genes known to exhibit this behavior. In each case, a new open reading frame is produced and the alternate protein product derived from this reading frame (the shortened isoform) has been isolated and characterized.

Initiation-site variability introduces a level of complexity analogous to mRNA splicing because a single sequence can code for more than one product. The two processes are closely related and sometimes overlap. The second gene listed in Table 6-1, estrogen receptor-α, is an excellent example. The alternative message contains a second translation initiation site downstream of the first, but the new site results from a transcription-level splicing event. The new codon defines a new open reading frame, and various translational events can silence or eliminate the original upstream start site to expose the second.

Interpretation of translational variants is confusing when the alternate initiation site lacks the normal sequence context. From a bioinformatics perspective, such sites can be located only using algorithms that find all AUG codons—including those that result from frame shifts—and analyzing the downstream sequences to determine whether they code for protein.

Following is a brief review of two major mechanisms that add translational variation by allowing initiation at secondary sites.

CONTEXT-DEPENDENT LEAKY SCANNING

When the first AUG occurs in a weak context (e.g., lacking both a purine in position −3 and G in position +4), some ribosomes initiate, but most continue scanning and initiate further downstream. Leaky scanning, as it is often called, allows the production of two separately initiated and structurally different proteins from the same mRNA. However, it is difficult to predict the outcome when the first start codon falls between extremes—i.e., (T/C)nn**AUG**G, (A/G)nn**AUG**(T/C), or (A/G)nn**AUG**A. It appears that downstream secondary structure plays a regulatory role by slowing the scanning process and increasing the amount of time available for ribosomal binding at the first start site. This mechanism, which serves to suppress leaky scanning, is dependent upon a critical distance of 13 to 15 nucleotides—half the diameter of the ribosome [6].

Table 6-1 Examples of Well-Characterized Human Genes That Contain Secondary Open Reading Frames

Gene	Comment	Reference
Tryptophanyl-tRNA synthetase		Tolstrup, et al. 1995. Transcriptional regulation of the interferon-γ-inducible tryptophanyl-tRNA synthetase includes alternative splicing. *Journal of Biological Chemistry* 270: 397–403.
Estrogen receptor-α	Long and short isoforms have distinctly different functions. Internal AUG site is the result of exonal splicing, not simply exposure of a previously silenced codon.	Denger, et al. 2001. Erα gene expression in human primary osteoblasts: evidence for the expression of two receptor proteins. *Molecular Endocrinology* 15: 2064–2077.
Dapamine regulated phosphoprotein		El-Rifai, et al. 2002. Gastric cancers overexpress DARPP-32 and a novel isoform, t-DARPP. *Cancer Research* 62: 4061–4064.
Erythroid membrane protein 4.1	Isoforms are expressed in distinctly different tissues.	Conboy, et al. 1991. Tissue and development-specific alternative RNA splicing regulates expression of multiple isoforms of erythroid membrane protein 4.1. *Journal of Biological Chemistry* 266: 8273–8280.
Water channel aquaporin 4		Lu, et al. 1997. The human AQP4 gene: definition of the locus encoding two water channel polypeptides in brain. *Proceedings of the National Academy of Sciences* 93: 10908–10912.
ZAC transcription factor		Bialnges, et al. 2001. Alternative splicing of the imprinted candidate tumor suppressor gene ZAC regulates its antiproliferative and DNA binding activities. *Oncogene* 20: 1246–1253.

The same regulatory principles apply when the first AUG codon is in a suboptimal context and initiation occurs at an upstream ACG, CUG, or GUG codon. Because such nonstandard codons represent weak start sites even in perfect sequence context, leaky scanning allows translation to begin at the first AUG (but second potential start codon). As expected, secondary structures located in the space between the two start sites can up or down regulate the use of the first (nonstandard) or second (AUG) start codon.

It is important to note that various combinations of optimal and suboptimal sites combined with varying secondary structures can support initiation at three sites on the same message. The c-myc gene is a known example of this phenomenon. The first AUG start codon supports translation of the predominant 65KDa protein product. A small quantity of slightly longer (68KDa) protein is translated from an upstream, nonstandard, CUG codon. Finally, a small number of ribosomes scan past the first AUG start site, despite the presence of an A in position −3, to initiate translation at another downstream AUG. (This event produces a small 50KDa c-myc isoform.) Modification of the first AUG start site from ACC**AUG**C to ACC**AUG**G eliminated translation of the small isoform entirely [7].

Leaky scanning beyond an AUG that exists in a strong but imperfect context can go unnoticed if the number of events is very small or the downstream AUG that might become a start site is normally out of frame. Mutations that shift a start site back into the reading frame can result in the production of a previously untranslated protein. Such is the case with certain antigenic peptides recognized by cytotoxic T-lymphocytes. A small degree of leaky scanning in a message for an intracellular peptide becomes significant when insertion of a provirus shifts a downstream AUG into the reading frame to create a new peptide that functions as a tumor-rejection antigen [8].

Like many of the processes discussed thus far, leaky scanning is an important biological dimension that must be comprehended by those seeking to develop algorithms for studying gene expression. Moreover, leaky scanning is not a random process. As we have seen, scanning past an AUG start codon is controlled by sequence-specific factors, including the context of the first start codon, the downstream RNA secondary structure, and mutations that shift the reading frame to expose a new start codon. Leaky scanning is important because it adds degrees of freedom to the gene-expression process. However, like other genomic subtleties, it tends to complicate the analysis process.

REINITIATION

Reinitiation is a cap-independent ribosomal binding process that allows translation to proceed from an internal ribosome entry site (IRES) located in the 5' untranslated region. A variety of stress conditions—hypoxia, serum deprivation, irradiation, apoptosis—lead to internal initiation because cap-dependent mechanisms are typically inhibited in such cells. IRES sites, however, are not viable substitutes for normal initiation sites because the resulting proteins are completely different. As a result, cells that are experiencing biochemical stress use reinitiation to express new proteins without changes to the underlying genes or messages. Furthermore, mRNAs containing IRES elements often encode factors involved in cellular proliferation such as growth factors and monogenic proteins. This bias is not surprising because IRES-mediated translation is inherently resistant to biochemical stress. It, therefore, makes evolutionary sense that key growth substances are encoded in a way that up regulates their expression under conditions of stress [9].

Reinitiation occurs with mRNAs that have small open reading frames near the 5' end of a transcript. Although the mechanism has not been completely delineated, some details are well understood. When the 80s ribosome reaches a termination sequence of the upstream open reading frame, the 60s subunit is released, and the 40s subunit remains bound to the message. Scanning continues until a new AUG start codon is encountered. The initiation complex reforms, and a new initiation event commences.

Control of reinitiation depends on several factors such as length of the upstream open reading frame (ORF), the secondary structure of the region, and the context in which the original AUG start codon appears. The latter is especially significant and very complex to analyze because a weak context often facilitates leaky scanning, which is easily confused with initialization at an IRES site. These complexities elevate the importance of extensive bioinformatic analysis. To understand reinitiation, you must combine information about the location of ribosomal binding sequences, termination codons, small reading frames, and RNA secondary structure with statistical information that relates each of these parameters. The complexity of this problem underscores the need for transcriptional information because the introns contained in gene sequences often include start and stop codons that can be interpreted as secondary initiation and termination sites. Furthermore, the processes we have been discussing—leaky scanning and reinitiation—tend to add upside to the overall gene count just as they add biological diversity. The diversity implied by multiple isoforms also raises a deeper question regarding the true meaning of a "gene count" by further uncoupling the number of genes from the number of proteins.

Human Thrombopoietin—A Special Case of Translational Complexity

The human thrombopoietin (TPO) gene produces a mixture of transcripts, all of which translate inefficiently because of an overlapping upstream open reading frame (ORF7). This low level of translation is normal; increasing the production of TPO causes a disease known as thrombocythaemia. Two factors act to prevent translation of TPO: The upstream AUG7 codon exists in a near optimal context (GCCGCCUCCAUGG) that prevents leaky scanning to the downstream TPO start codon (AUG8); the overlapping arrangement between ORF7 and the TPO start site inhibits reinitiation.

Various mutations can restructure the 5' untranslated region in ways that increase production of TPO and cause thrombocythemia. For example, a splice-site mutation can cause deletion of exon3 shifting initiation to the normally silent AUG9 present in exon 4. The resulting protein lacks only four amino acids and appears to function normally [10]. Still other scenarios involve mutations that restructure ORF7 in ways that up regulate translation beginning at the normal TPO start codon (AUG8). One example involves deletion of a G residue, which shifts ORF7 into the same reading frame as TPO. The result is overproduction of a slightly longer, but fully active protein [11]. Another case results from a G > T mutation in ORF7, which creates a premature termination codon 31 nucleotides upstream of AUG8. The resulting gap enables efficient reinitiation at AUG8 up regulating production of TPO [12]. Figure 6-2 outlines each of these translational variants.

MESSENGER RNA SEQUENCE ANOMALIES, TRANSLATIONAL EFFECTS, AND HUMAN DISEASE

Thrombocythaemia, discussed earlier, is one of many diseases caused by mutations that affect translation. The complexity of the translation process is mirrored in the large number of possible mutations, some surprisingly subtle, that can impact the process. In contrast to mutations that directly alter coding sequences, many translation-related diseases are caused by subtle alterations whose effects are amplified because they cause

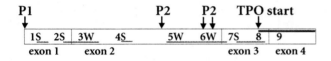

Upstream AUG#7 exists in a near perfect context and prevents translation of the TPO gene which overlaps ORF7.

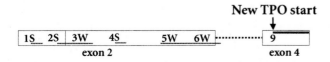

Deletion of exon 3 shifts start site to AUG#9 in exon 4. Only 4 amino acids are lost and the new gene product is functional.

Point mutation shifts ORF7 into the same reading frame as TPO producing a slightly longer, but active protein.

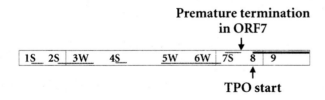

Point mutation in ORF7 causes premature termination leaving a 31 nucleotide gap. TPO translation readily proceeds via reinitiation.

S = strong context for an upstream ORF
W = weak context for an upstream ORF
P1/P2 = alternative promoters (P2 contains supports multiple start sites indicated by arrows)
Lighter lines indicate approximate lengths of upstream ORFs
Darker lines indicate the normal TPO gene product

Figure 6-2 Various mutations result in overproduction of the human thrombopoietin (TPO) gene product. (Underproduction is the normal state exhibited by healthy individuals). A small upstream reading frame (ORF7) normally prevents translation by overlapping the TPO start site. Various alterations in the structure of ORF7 can reverse the effect and cause overproduction of the gene product. This figure depicts three scenarios; many more have been identified.

insertion or deletion of new start or stop sites. Virtually every possible mechanism is represented. Among the most subtle are mutations in start codon flanking sequences that increase the likelihood of leaky scanning to a downstream start site. From a bioinformatics perspective, such mutations are difficult to understand because they exert their influence "at a distance." Less-subtle alterations include mutations that shift the reading frame to obscure a stop codon or insert a new upstream start site. A mechanistic understanding of these effects is important to those involved in developing algorithms for SNP identification. In the absence of such analysis, SNPs become pure statistical anomalies without context.

As mentioned previously, mutations that affect the context of an AUG start codon can increase the likelihood of leaky scanning to a downstream site. α-thalassaemia, for example, is caused by an A > C change in position −3 of the α-globin gene, and ataxia with vitamin E deficiency is caused by a C > T mutation in position −1 of the α-tocopherol transfer protein gene [13, 14]. Conversely, a positive context change in an upstream AUG can cause initiation to begin at a new site. However, if the new site terminates in a stop signal and reinitiation is supported, the effect on translation of the original signal may be minimized. Mutations that create a new 5'ward AUG start codon must be analyzed with a view of the surrounding context. A strong context can result in translation of a lengthened, possibly somewhat functional, protein. A weak context that supports leaky scanning might exhibit a limited effect.

Oncogenes are often characterized by such mechanisms. For example, the MDM2 oncogene experiences a twentyfold increase in translation when two upstream AUGs are eliminated. Likewise, the GLI1 oncogene becomes active when a basal cell carcinoma splicing event removes an upstream intron containing start codons that normally interfere with translation [15 , 16]. Expression of the HYAL1 oncogene is characterized by the opposite effect—retention of an upstream intron containing several AUGs renders the message untranslatable in squamous cell carcinomas [17]. A similar, but more complex effect is seen in some melanomas that have a small upstream ORF that overlaps the normal start codon for the CDKN2 gene. A (G > T) point mutation creates the new start site that is both upstream and out of frame. Individuals with this SNP cannot translate the CDKN2 gene product and are predisposed to melanoma [18].

INTERNAL RIBOSOME INITIATION AND THE REGULATION OF CELL DEATH

Cells that have been injured, infected with viruses, transformed into a malignant state, or otherwise compromised represent a risk to the organism. Apoptosis—programmed cell death—is the process that has evolved to maintain a balanced state between cell proliferation and cell death. Failure of the apoptotic mechanism is known to be associated with many disease states, including certain cancers and autoimmune diseases. Cap-independent translation processes that utilize internal ribosome entry sites are intimately involved in the regulation of apoptosis.

During the early stages of apoptosis, proteolytic activity is responsible for disrupting translation by cleaving the translation initiation factor eIF-4G. Additionally, the X-linked inhibitor of apoptosis protein (XIAP) has been shown to be translated by an IRES-mediated process in apoptotic cells. This particular mRNA is up regulated under conditions of cellular stress that typically signal the beginning of apoptosis, such as starvation and exposure to radiation. As a result, cells that have begun to head down the path of programmed cell death can continue to manufacture XIAP, a protein that inhibits the apoptosis process.

Synthesis of XIAP forms the basis of a mechanism for reversing the process and saving apoptotic cells from a committed death. The delicate balance of this control mechanism is further enhanced by IRES-mediated translation of another protein—Apaf-1—which plays a central role in the apoptosis pathway. After the onset of apoptosis, the precise balance of these opposing proteins forms the basis of an important regulatory pathway that ultimately determines the fate of a stressed cell. If the trigger is removed, the cell, through up regulation of XIAP, can return to its normal metabolic state. Conversely, continued stress is likely to shift the balance toward Apaf-1 synthesis and cell death. From an evolutionary perspective, it appears that mammalian cells have developed a multistep death process that begins with a shift away from protein synthesis during times of stress while maintaining a backup recovery mechanism. Such processes, for example, might prove valuable to cells that have become infected with a virus that cannot survive a shutdown of the protein synthesizing machinery.

Like leaky scanning and reinitiation, IRES-modulated apoptotic processes present unusual challenges to the bioinformaticist. Each involves a mixture of structure prediction, statistical analysis, and sequence comparison. Furthermore, as we have seen, the three are closely related. The most sensible bioinformatic approach to studying translation involves the following:

- Final protein sequences should be compared to base gene sequences to determine what features, if any, have been removed through splicing. The locations of features that are normally removed but contain start or stop codons are very important as are 5'ward segments that contain small open reading frames. The ultimate goal is to build a map of all features and known splice variants.
- The context of each AUG should be used to identify all potential start sites. Additional sequence analysis should be used to identify sites where single-point mutations, deletions, or insertions might create new start or stop codons.
- Analysis of downstream secondary structure can reveal features that affect the scanning process. Slower scanning rates increase the probability of initiation at upstream sites that have less-than-perfect context. This analysis is especially important in situations known to be characterized by leaky scanning or reinitiation.

Transcription and translation are intimately related in the sense that splicing events form a backdrop to translation. Bridging the gap from gene to protein requires a comprehensive view of all splice variants in addition to a thorough sequence-level understanding of the features contained in a given message. This sequence-level understanding must be extended to include predicted changes that occur as a result of small point mutations that can shift reading frames or create new start/stop codons.

SUMMARY

Just as the transcriptome represents a complete enumeration of all messages within a cell, the proteome represents a complete description of all translated proteins. Protein translation depends on the function of a complex catalytic machine, the ribosome, which performs four key information-based functions:

- Scanning for a protein start codon (usually AUG) after locating and binding to a well-defined binding site
- Reading and interpreting each three-letter RNA code word advancing the reading frame by three letters prior to each read operation
- Facilitating polymerization of the protein molecule by physically attaching a transfer RNA holding the proper amino acid for each reading frame
- Identifying termination codons and stopping the translation process

Sequences, codes, and various forms of conformational information are central to the process, as are a large number of protein-protein and protein-RNA interactions. The ribosome can be thought of as a nano-scale robot capable of reading, interpreting, and acting on sequence information. Considering the number of steps, interacting components, and overall complexity, translation is a remarkably accurate process. Misincorporation of an amino acid normally occurs only once in about 10,000 codons.

A purely biochemical view of translation misses many nuances that have a distinct informational flavor. For example, a complex of proteins called the initiation complex migrates down the length of the message scanning for the first AUG start codon. However, the first AUG triplet is not always an initiation site. The correct initiation signal includes additional sequence elements, and the AUG triplet must be recognized in the context of these features. Changes in RNA secondary structure can also affect the scanning rate. Slowing the scan provides additional time for ribosomal binding and can facilitate selection of AUG start codons that exist in less-than-perfect context. In this way, mRNA secondary structure can become a determinant of protein sequence.

Although the vast majority of eukaryotic initiation events involve scanning from the 5' cap, another mechanism allows direct binding of the 40S ribosomal subunit directly to an internal ribosome entry site (IRES). Other mechanisms—reinitiation and context-dependent leaky scanning—also facilitate initiation events downstream of the first AUG triplet.

Translational variations often have dramatic effects on health and disease. For example, the human thrombopoietin (TPO) gene produces a mixture of transcripts, all of which translate inefficiently in normal healthy individuals because of an upstream open reading frame that overlaps the TPO start site. Translational variations can increase the production of TPO causing a disease known as thrombocythaemia.

Cells that have been injured, infected with viruses, transformed into a malignant state, or otherwise compromised often lapse into a state of programmed cell death or apoptosis. Failure of the apoptotic mechanism is known to be associated with many illnesses, including certain cancers and autoimmune diseases. Cap-independent translation processes that utilize IRES sites are intimately involved in the regulation of the apoptotic state. Proteins that support cell death are also up regulated in the apoptotic state. The precise balance of these opposing forces forms the basis of an important regulatory pathway that ultimately determines the fate of a stressed cell.

Predicting translation products from gene sequences is a central goal of computational biology. Special features of translation—leaky scanning, reinitiation, internal entry sites, changes in mRNA secondary structure, and a broad variety of point mutations that shift reading frames or modify start/stop sites—all have the effect of complicating the predictive process. Algorithms designed to analyze DNA or mRNA sequences must take these effects into account. The analysis must comprehend RNA secondary structure, a variety of sequence-based features, and the possible effects of insertions, deletions, and point mutations. Furthermore, transcription and translation are intricately linked in the sense that splice variants often exhibit a broad scope of translational behavior. As a result, algorithms for predicting the structures of translation products must comprehend the effects that result from various intron-exon combinations. Such analysis is most valuable in the context of transcriptional profiling that enumerates the full set of splice variants.

ENDNOTES

1. Ibba M., Soll D. 1999. Quality control mechanisms during translation. *Science* 286: 1893–1897.

2. Kozak, M. 1999. Initiation and translation in procaryotes and eukaryotes. *Gene* 234: 187–208.

3. Silvian L., Wang J., Steitz T. A. 1999. Insights into editing from an Ile-tRNA synthetase structure with tRNA ILE and mupirocin. *Science* 285: 1074–1077.

4. Hentze M. W., Kulozik A. E. 1999. A perfect message: RNA surveillance and nonsense-mediated decay. *Cell* 96: 307–310.

5. Smith C. K., Baker T. A., Sauer T. 1999. Lon and Clp family proteases and chaperones share homologous substrate-recognition domains. *Proceedings of the National Academy of Sciences* 96: 6678–6682.

6. Kozak M. 2002. Pushing the limits of the scanning mechanism for initiation of translation. *Gene* 299: 1–34.

7. Spotts G. D., Patel S. V., Xiao Q., Hann S. R. 1997. Identification of downstream-initiated c-myc proteins which are dominant-negative inhibitors of transactivation by full-length c-myc proteins. *Molecular Cellular Biology* 17: 1459–1468.

8. Wada H., Matsuo M., Uenka A., Shimbara N., Shimizu K., Nakayama E. 1995. Rejection antigen peptides on BALB/c RL 1 leukemia recognized by cytotoxic T-lymphocytes: derivation from the normally untranslated 5' region of the *c-Akt* proto-oncogene activated by long terminal repeat. *Cancer Research* 55: 4780–4783.

9. Holcik M., Sonenberg N., Korneluk R. 2000. Internal ribosome initiation of translation and the control of cell death. *Trends in Genetics* 16(10): 469–473.

10. Weistner A., Schlemper R., Van der Maas A. P. C., Skoda R. C. 1998. An activating splice donor mutation in the thrombopoetin gene causes hereditary thrombocythaemia. *Nature Genetics* 18: 49–52.

11. Ghilardi N., Skoda R. C. 1999. A single-base deletion in the thrombopoietin (TPO) gene causes familial essential thrombocythemia through a mechanism of more efficient translation of TPO mRNA. *Blood* 94: 1480–1482.

12. Ghilardi N., Wiestner A., Kikuchi M., Ohsaka A., Skoda R. C. 1999. Hereditary thrombocythaemia in a Japanese family is caused by a novel point mutation in the thrombopoietin gene. *British Journal of Haematology* 107: 310–316.

13. Morle F., Lopez B., Henni T., Godet J., 1985. a-thalassaemia associated with the deletion of two nucleotides at positions −2 and −3 preceeding the AUG codon. *EMBO Journal* 4: 1245–1250.

14. Usuki F., Maruyama K. 2000. Ataxia caused by mutations in the a-tocopherol transfer protein gene. *Journal of Neurology, Neurosurgery, and Psychiatry* 69: 254–256.

15. Brown C. Y., Mize G. J., Pineda M., George D. L., Morris D. R. 1999. Role of two upstream open reading frames in the translational control of oncogene MDM2. *Oncogene* 18: 5631–5637.

16. Wang X. Q., Rothnagel J. A. 2001. Post-transcriptional regulation of the GLI1 oncogene by the expression of alternative 5' untranslated regions. *Journal of Biological Chemistry* 276: 1311–1316.

17. Frost G. I., et al. 2000. HYAL1[LUCA-1] , a candidate tumor suppressor gene on chromosome 3p21.3, is inactivated in head and neck squamous cell carcinomas by aberrant splicing of pre-mRNA. *Oncogene* 19: 870–877.

18. Liu L., et al. 1999. Mutation of the CDKN2A 5' UTR creates an aberrant initiation codon and predisposes to melanoma. *Nature Genetics* 21: 128–132.

Protein Structure Prediction

INTRODUCTION

Proteins occupy a unique position in the hierarchy of life. They represent the basic building blocks for every cellular structure from the smallest membrane-bound receptor to the largest organelle. Unlike most other macromolecules, proteins can fold into structures that have catalytic activity and mediate chemical reactions. Catalytic proteins, or enzymes, serve a crucial biological role—they lower the energy of activation for the chemical reactions that make life possible. They also provide a level of efficiency that could not be obtained in any other way, regardless of the amount of energy that one might be willing to use. The precise metabolic steps that are mediated by enzymatic reactions could not occur in their absence. Therefore, it is reasonable to state that all biological organisms are made of protein, and that the reactions that sustain them are driven by enzymes.

The complexity of the genome and the versatility of the processes that translate genomic information into proteins are remarkable in their efficiency. Describing the human organism at the metabolic level requires mapping the interactions of millions of proteins, yet describing that same organism at the gene level requires a relatively small catalogue of only 40,000 sequences. Previous chapters discussed the various control mechanisms that account for this order-of-magnitude increase in complexity. At the gene level, these include physical changes that affect transcription—secondary structure changes and epigenetic alterations. Additional versatility appears at the mRNA level where splicing events and RNA interference represent additional step ups in complexity. In addition, a variety of translation-level mechanisms such as leaky scanning and reinitiation allow a final spliced and assembled transcript to code for more than one protein. There is, however, one more step in the gene-to-protein continuum where a step up in diversity is experienced. That step is the final folding and post-translational modification of a protein.

In some sense, this final step is the most complex. All the information that one needs to interpret to make structural predictions is contained in the sequence of the protein. However, unlike gene sequences, which are built on standard code words, there is no straightforward code or set of rules that we can use to definitively predict the folded structure of a protein. Furthermore, the process is regulated. Misfolded proteins are rapidly identified and destroyed, whereas newly translated ones are often helped through the folding process by other proteins called chaperones.

The discovery of chaperones was somewhat of a blow to the long-standing view that protein folding is dictated entirely by the sequence of amino acids. This view, which grew out of pioneering research conducted in the lab of Christian Anfinsen, ultimately resulted in Anfinsen being awarded the 1972 Nobel Prize in Chemistry [1, 2]. The experiments involved chemically denaturing proteins by exposing them to high concentrations of urea or guanidine hydrochloride in the presence of the reducing agent B-mercaptoethanol, and then renaturing them by removing the chemicals with dialysis. High concentrations of urea or guanidine hydrochloride cause unfolding of the polypeptide chain, and B-mercaptoethanol reduces the intrachain disulfide links between cystine residues. More specifically, Anfinsen studied the denaturing and refolding of the enzyme ribonuclease. As expected, unfolding the protein chain and cleaving its four disulfide bridges resulted in complete disruption of all enzymatic activity. The activity returned, however, when the chemicals were removed by dialysis, indicating that even after being completely denatured the polypeptide chain still contained enough information to spontaneously refold into its catalytically active state. Particularly significant is the correct realignment of the four cysteine cross bridges. (On a strictly random basis, 8 cysteine residues in a single polypeptide chain can form 105 different sets of 4 disulfide bridges [3].)

The ribonuclease case is certainly not an exception; most proteins can fold properly after being denatured. Furthermore, the view that a protein's primary sequence embodies enough information to dictate its folded structure remains true even in cases where chaperones assist the folding process because chaperones recognize structural domains that form in the initial moments of folding. Without the information contained in the primary sequence, it would be impossible for a protein to fold into a configuration that could be recognized by a chaperone.

This chapter discusses various contemporary approaches to studying the folding process, focusing on methods that fit into two broad categories: *ab initio* and database driven. These strategies represent core components of process that is likely to join high-throughput gene sequencing and mRNA profiling as the next industrial-scale genetic science.

OVERVIEW OF *AB INITIO* AND DATABASE-DRIVEN APPROACHES

Ab initio methods seek to predict final folded structures by applying basic physical principles and a knowledge of the primary sequence. Such approaches follow directly from Christian Anfinsen's discovery that each polypeptide chain contains enough information to direct its own folding. *Ab initio* methods actually fall into two separate but related subcategories. The first—rules-based—seeks to identify a set of sequence-based guidelines that can consistently predict the native conformation of a given segment. Folded segments are then connected to construct the native conformation. The second relies on the use of physical principles to calculate the forces applied by each atom to each of its neighbors. Because the forces between atoms vary as the molecule folds, each set of calculations must be repeated over and over again until a final stable conformation is reached. Successive passes are represented by discrete time steps; smaller steps result in more accurate predictions. At the time of this writing, no computer on earth was large enough to completely fold a typical protein in a reasonable amount of time. We will return to a more detailed analysis of *ab initio* methods in the next section.

Database-driven approaches are fundamentally different from *ab initio* methods. They depend on building a dictionary of known conformations (also known as folds) and their underlying sequences. In recent years, high-throughput structure determination has driven exponential growth in the size of these dictionaries. Pattern-matching algorithms are used to compare experimental results with known structures. In principle, a researcher can determine the native conformation of a sequence by locating an exact or close match in the dictionary. Imperfect matches are managed by applying a basic understanding of the chemical properties of each amino acid.

Interestingly, the database-driven approach has been effective in another technical area—weather forecasting. A database containing thousands of days of weather history is constructed for a particular location. To predict tomorrow's weather, one would find a record whose characteristics are similar to today's. If the principle holds true, the next record in the database would be predictive of tomorrow's weather. Conversely, *ab initio* weather prediction would be based on cloud physics, atmospheric chemistry, and other physical principles related to wind currents, precipitation, and convection. As is the case with protein structure prediction, both approaches have merit.

The ultimate application of protein structure prediction is the modeling of interactions between proteins and ligands. Such modeling is critical to the drug-discovery process, which depends heavily on predicting the binding of lead compounds to targets. These experiments, often referred to as molecular docking, are central to the drug-discovery process. Early goals for structure-based drug design focused on *de novo* approaches where the outcome was a custom-designed lead compound. The proposed binding site of a protein was space filled with a custom-designed compound that had perfect charge complementarity and shape. Unfortunately, the approach relied on molecular docking software and, more specifically, energy and thermodynamics calculations that were not accurate enough predictors of the potency of various lead compounds. *In silico* approaches to lead-target binding have become more viable as increases in computational horsepower have fostered the development of more complex algorithms. Continued improvement is likely to drive the drug-discovery process in the direction of computer-simulated wet chemistry. Predicting the folding of proteins and *in silico* modeling of protein-small molecule interactions is the focus of the remainder of this chapter.

OVERVIEW OF PROTEIN STRUCTURE

During 1957 and 1958, John Kendrew and Max Perutz completed their study of the three-dimensional structure of myoglobin. Their worked marked a turning point in modern biochemistry—the first experimentally determined protein structure. Perutz and Kendrew shared the 1962 Nobel Prize in chemistry for their groundbreaking work. These early experiments were tedious and took many years to complete. Since that time, decades of research have been marked by dramatic improvements in the techniques for determining such structures and, today, it is reasonable to discuss "high-throughput" x-ray structure determination. Structures are also studied using other techniques such as NMR spectroscopy. Much has been learned about protein structure and a four-tiered framework has evolved. The tiers—primary, secondary, tertiary, and quaternary—are well-defined constructs:

- Primary structure refers to the amino acid sequence of a protein.
- Secondary structure refers to local conformations formed by individual segments of a protein as a direct result of the interactions between amino acids. These structures are well defined and named (i.e., alpha helix, beta sheet, and reverse turn or loop).
- Tertiary structure refers to global conformations that result from folding together secondary structures. Interactions of amino acid side chains are the predominant drivers of tertiary structure.
- Quarternary structure results from the interactions of multiple independent polypeptide chains. Proteins containing multiple chains of amino acids are referred to as having multiple subunits.

Protein conformations are not random. Since the early days of Kendrew and Perutz, an important focus of the crystallography community has been the documentation and cataloging of tertiary structures (also known as folds). As a result, dictionaries of folds have become an important tool for both crystallographers and bioinformaticists.

PRIMARY STRUCTURE

Proteins were definitively shown to be composed of linear polymers of amino acids as early as the 1920s. Fred Sanger, a pioneer in sequence determination for both proteins and nucleic acids, was the first to demonstrate the link between a protein's function and its amino acid sequence [4]. Figure 7-1 depicts the general structure of the 20 standard amino acids found in proteins. Each is composed of a free carboxyl group and a free unsubstituted amino group attached to the alpha carbon atom. In addition, each contains a side chain, also attached to the alpha carbon, known as the R group. Different R groups distinguish the amino acids from each other. Proline, whose structure is also shown in Figure 7-1, stands out as the only exception to these rules.

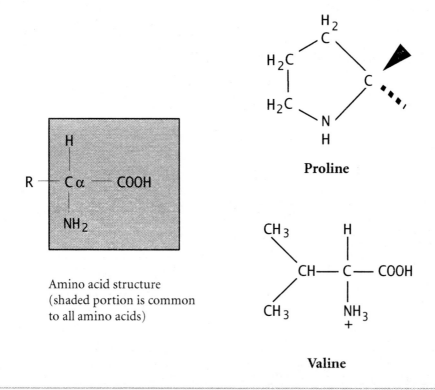

Amino acid structure
(shaded portion is common
to all amino acids)

Proline

Valine

Figure 7-1 General structure of the 20 standard amino acids found in proteins. Each contains carboxy and amino groups in addition to a unique side chain. Proline stands out because its R group is a substituent of the amino group.

The standard amino acids are grouped together based on the chemical properties of their side chains. These properties are critical determinants of protein structure. Basic groupings include amino acids with nonpolar or hydrophobic R groups, uncharged polar R groups, positively charged (basic) R groups, and negatively charged (acidic) R groups. Historically, these designations have been useful for classifying amino acid structures although many other chemical and physical properties are also important. We will return to a discussion of these properties in our review of the pairwise molecular interactions that drive protein folding. Figure 7-2 shows the structures and corresponding groupings of the 20 standard amino acids.

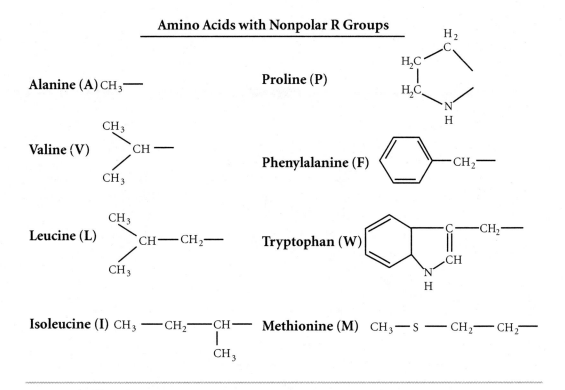

Figure 7-2 The 20 standard amino acids of proteins grouped according to their chemical properties. Side chains (R groups) are either polar, hydrophobic, positively charged, or negatively charged.

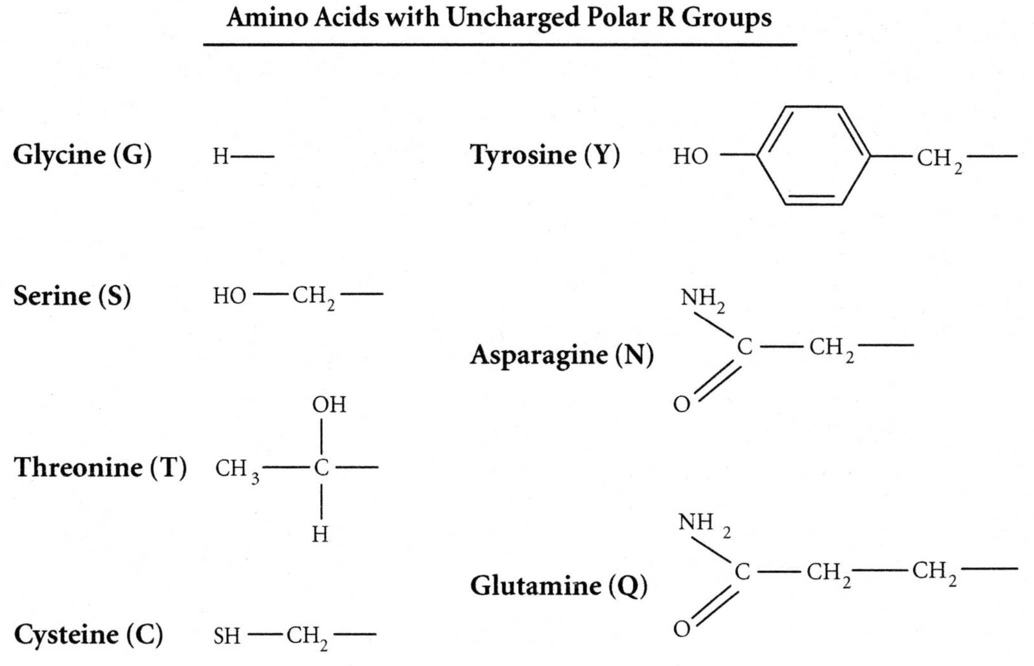

Amino Acids with Uncharged Polar R Groups

Glycine (G)   H—

Tyrosine (Y)   HO —⟨benzene ring⟩— CH_2—

Serine (S)   HO —CH_2—

Asparagine (N) NH_2 \ C —CH_2— / O (double bond)

Threonine (T) CH_3—C— (with OH above and H below)

Glutamine (Q) NH_2 \ C —CH_2—CH_2— / O (double bond)

Cysteine (C)   SH —CH_2—

Figure 7-2 *(continued)*

   Amino acids form bonds with each other through a chemical reaction that links the amino group of one amino acid to the carboxyl group of the next. The links are referred to as peptide bonds. Physical characteristics of the peptide bond have important implications for protein folding. One important characteristic is the rigidity of the bond. This rigidity is caused by the relatively short length of the peptide (C-N) bond, which imparts a certain amount of double-bond character to the link. As a result, polypeptide chains are not free to rotate about the peptide bonds. Instead, they display rotational freedom about the bonds formed by the α-carbons. The two bonds are normally referred to as Cα-N (alpha carbon to amino group) and Cα-C (alpha carbon to carboxyl group). The rotational angles of these bonds are designated phi (ϕ) and psi (ψ) respectively. A typical peptide bond including phi and psi angles is shown in Figure 7-3.

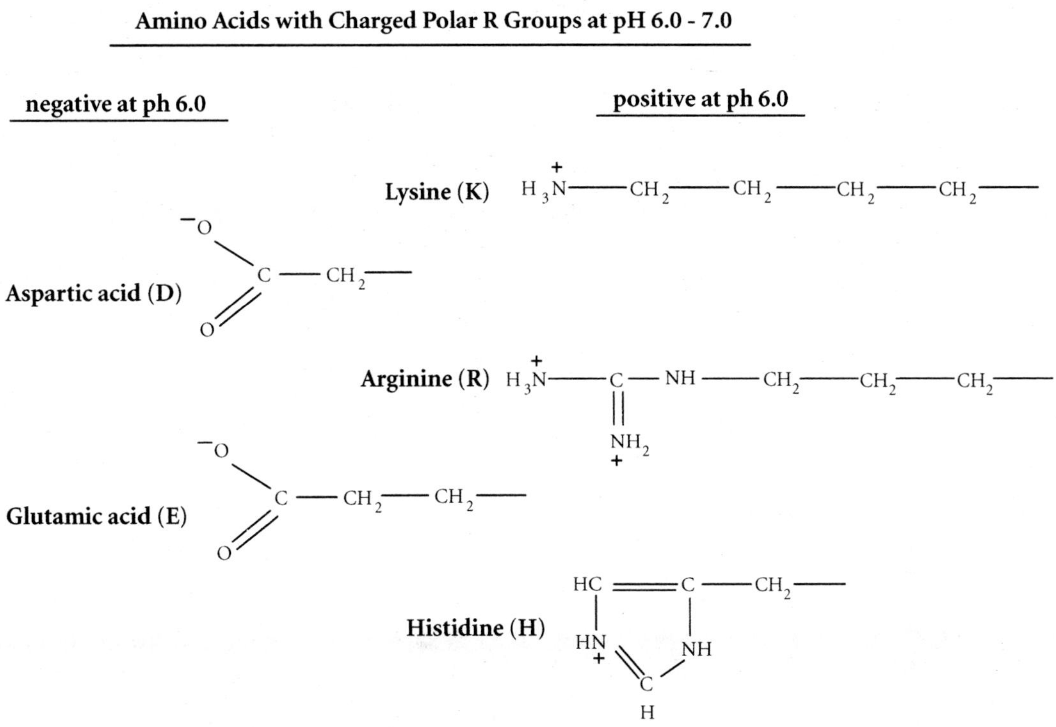

Amino Acids with Charged Polar R Groups at pH 6.0 - 7.0

negative at ph 6.0   **positive at ph 6.0**

Lysine (K) $H_3\overset{+}{N}$——CH_2——CH_2——CH_2——CH_2——

Aspartic acid (D) $\overset{-O}{\underset{O}{\diagup\!\!\diagdown}}C$——$CH_2$——

Arginine (R) $H_3\overset{+}{N}$——$\underset{\underset{+}{\overset{\|}{NH_2}}}{C}$——$NH$——$CH_2$——$CH_2$——$CH_2$——

Glutamic acid (E) $\overset{-O}{\underset{O}{\diagup\!\!\diagdown}}C$——$CH_2$——$CH_2$——

Histidine (H) $HC=C$——CH_2——
$\underset{+}{HN}$ NH
$\overset{C}{\underset{H}{}}$

Figure 7-2 *(continued)*

Phi and psi angles are somewhat limited by steric hindrance between amino acid side chains. These limitations reduce the number of allowable conformations for a polypeptide chain. The relationship between phi/psi angles and allowable configurations can be displayed using a map known as a Ramachandran plot [5]. Two amino acids, glycine and proline, complicate the analysis of phi/psi angles and steric hindrance. Glycine's R group, a simple hydrogen atom, provides little steric hindrance, whereas proline's rigid ring structure tends to further limit rotational freedom. Ramachandran plots, which are useful for delineating all allowable conformations of a polypeptide chain, are important

267

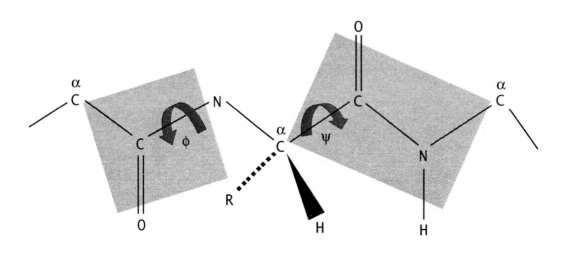

Figure 7-3 Peptide bonds are characterized by a lack of rotational freedom. However, proteins display rotational freedom about the bonds formed by the α-carbons. The two bonds are referred to as Cα-N (alpha carbon to amino group) and Cα-C (alpha carbon to carboxyl group). The Phi (φ) angle represents rotation about the Cα-N bond; the psi (ψ) angle represents rotation about the Cα-C bond. The shaded area in the figure is approximately planar and relatively rigid. The ψ angle is that subtended when the right-hand plane is rotated in the direction shown. Both angles may range from −180 degrees to +180 degrees. By convention both angles in the extended form (depicted below) are assigned the maximum value +180°. When φ approaches 0° and ψ approaches +180°, the carbonyl oxygen atoms overlap and prevent further rotation. Likewise, when ψ approaches 0° and φ approaches +180°, the hydrogen atoms attached to the peptide nitrogens overlap. When φ is approximately +120° and ψ is +180°, the N-H bond is trans to the Cα-H bond. When φφ is approximately +180° and ψ is +120°, the Cα-H bond is trans to the C-O bond.

to our discussion of secondary structure. The Ramachandran plot is displayed in Figure 7-4.

In the figure, allowed conformations of the polypeptide backbone are enclosed in solid black borders. Red borders denote the most stable areas. All other regions of the plot represent disallowed conformations. Right- and left-handed helix zones are marked with dotted lines. Configurations compatible with anitparallel beta sheet (β_A), parallel beta sheet (β_P), twisted beta sheet (β_T), right-handed alpha helix (α_P), left-handed alpha helix α_L),3_{10} helix (3), and pi helix (π) are also marked on the plot.

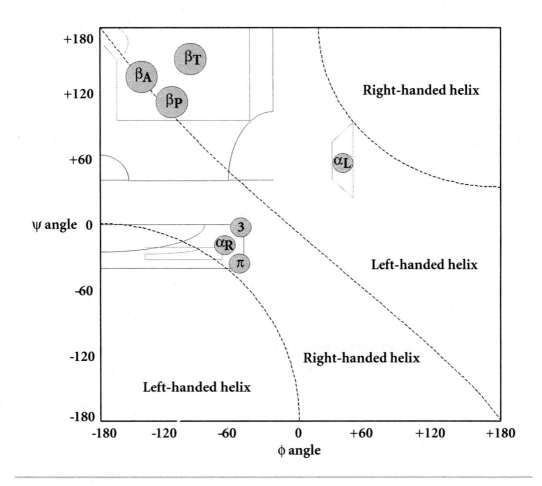

Figure 7-4 Ramachandran plot of φ versus ψ angles.

SECONDARY STRUCTURE

Secondary structure is more precisely referred to as local three-dimensional structure. The word *local* refers to effects that are directly related to interactions between amino acids along a length of the polypeptide chain. They do not include secondary effects caused by global folding of the protein. Two structures dominate the study of secondary structure: alpha (α) helix and beta (β) sheet. A second look at the Ramachandran plot in Figure 7-4 will reveal that φ/ψ angle combinations for α-helices and β-sheets fall into the two largest regions of allowed conformation. Because a-helix and b-sheet structures are stabilized by intrachain hydrogen bonds between residues in the backbone of the chain, they take the form of regular repeating structures. Secondary structures can also be irregular. Such structures, commonly referred to as loops, coils, or turns, typically serve as the links between more regular α-helices and β-sheets.

ALPHA HELIX STRUCTURES

Alpha helix structures are characterized by a regular repeating helical coil having approximately 3.6 amino acid residues per turn. (R groups extend outward from the helix.) A single complete turn of the helix, also known as the repeat unit, extends approximately .54nm (5.4 angstroms) along the long axis. The rise per residue is about .15nm. The dimensions of a typical α-helix are represented in Figure 7-5.

Other helical structures identified in the Ramachandran plot (e.g., π-helices, which have a 4.4 amino acid repeat distance) are less stable than the basic α-helix. As one might expect, various amino configurations tend to stabilize or disrupt an α-helix. Studies that combine information about the chemical properties of different amino acids with statistical data derived from protein sequencing experiments have been used to predict secondary structure directly from amino acid sequence [6]. The approach usually involves assigning a score to each residue based on its potential to contribute to α-helix, β-sheet, or reverse turn formation. Different approaches to using the scores have been applied. The most direct approach involves simply averaging or summing the scores along a segment of the polypeptide to predict conformations. Other methods rely on algorithms that use the scores to locate segments that are likely to form into one of the standard structures. Such algorithms, originally applied to the problem during the mid to late 1970s, have proven to be less reliable than originally believed [7, 8,9]. Decades of data collection have allowed researchers to refine the statistical basis of these algorithms, which are still considered a viable method for predicting secondary structure for many types of proteins.

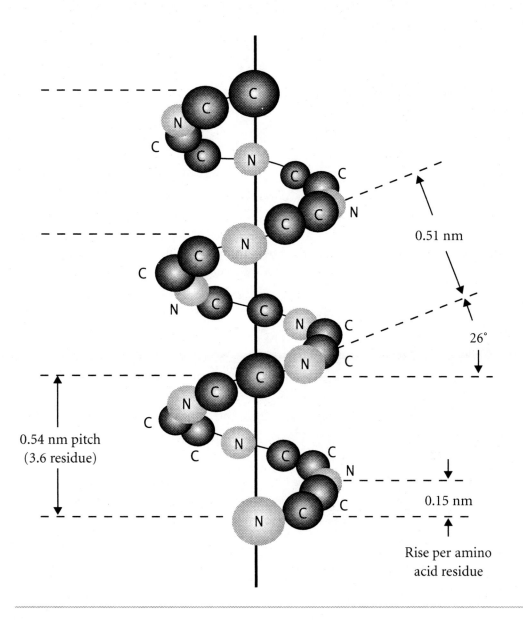

0.51 nm

26°

0.54 nm pitch
(3.6 residue)

0.15 nm

Rise per amino
acid residue

Figure 7-5 Dimensions of a typical right-handed alpha helix. Overall pitch is approximately 0.54nm (approximately 3.6 amino acids). The rise per amino acid is approximately 0.15nm.

Beta Sheet Structures

Unlike helices, β-sheet structures are stabilized by hydrogen bonds between adjacent polypeptide chains. Sections of the polypeptide chain that are involved in forming β-sheets are known as β-strands. In β–strands, φ and ψ angles are rotated approximately 180 degrees with respect to each other, producing a structure that resembles a pleated sheet. The R groups in this conformation are located in alternating positions on opposite sides of the sheet.

β-sheets are found in two configurations: parallel and antiparallel. Parallel configurations contain sheets that are oriented in the same direction with respect to their amino-terminal and carboxy-terminal ends. In antiparallel sheets, the orientations alternate so that a given strand always interacts with a segment running in the opposite direction. Mixed configurations composed of parallel and antiparallel segments are also possible. Most β-sheets exhibit a slight twist when viewed head on along an axis perpendicular to the polypeptide chains. All known naturally occurring conformations exhibit a right-handed twist. A diagram depicting the basic structure of a β-sheet appears in Figure 7-6.

Loops, Coils, and Reverse Turns

α-helix and β-sheet structures, which dominate the protein landscape, are normally connected by a less-stable construct known as a reverse turn, coil, or loop. These regions, which often occur near the surface of a protein, can be important in the formation of active sites for ligand binding or catalytic activity in proteins functioning as enzymes.

Several specific types of loop structures have been identified. Hairpin loops (reverse turns) form links between antiparallel β-strands and usually involve very few—four or five—amino acids. Other well-characterized structures are classified by the secondary structures and φ/ψ angles they connect. Long transitions are often referred to as omega (Ω) loops. These structures often involve side chains in addition to the polypeptide backbone. Although most loops are well ordered and achieve a stable structure, many are more random. These less-stable structures are referred to as random coils [10].

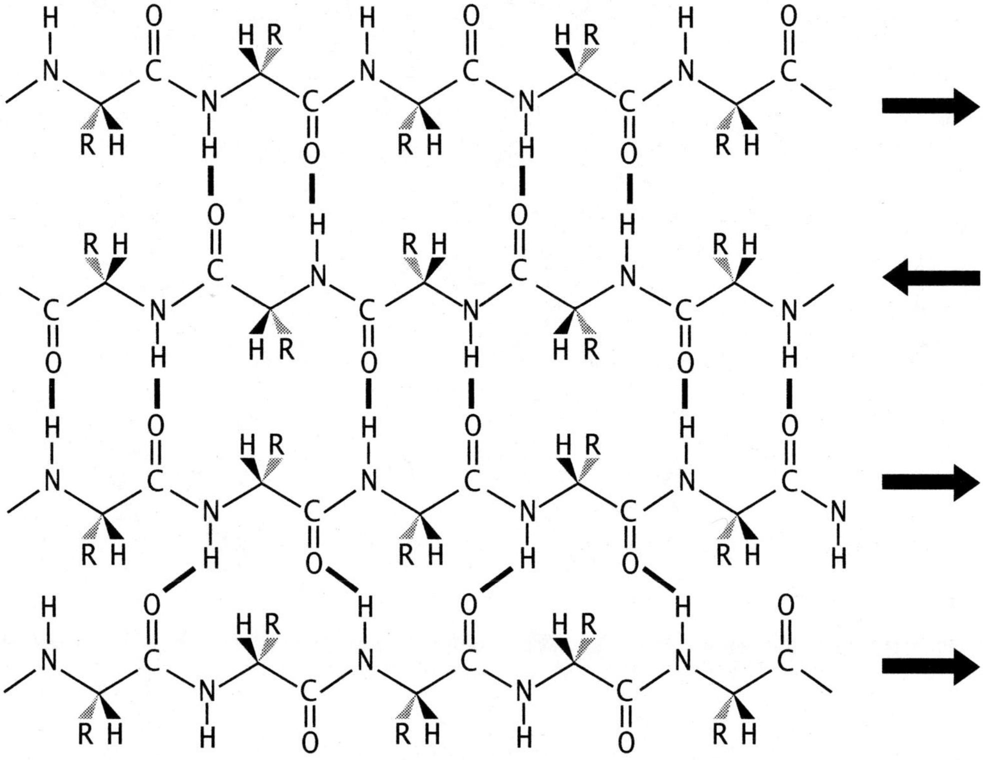

Figure 7-6 Structure of a β-sheet. Two configurations, parallel and antiparallel, are possible. In parallel configurations, hydrogen-bonded segments of the polypeptide chain run in the same direction with regard to their carboxy and amino terminals. Antiparallel structures are built from chains running in opposite directions. Mixed configurations are also possible.

TERTIARY STRUCTURE

Tertiary structure is defined as the global three-dimensional folding that results from interactions between elements of secondary structure. Various elements can combine to shape a protein in three dimensions. Although hydrogen bonding between backbone elements is the primary driver of secondary structure, interactions between side chains is the predominant driver of tertiary structure. Other factors such as hydrophilic/hydrophobic interactions with solvent molecules or interactions with lipids in a cell membrane can also become drivers of tertiary structure. For example, water-soluble proteins always fold to expose hydrophilic side chains on the outside surface of the molecule while keeping hydrophobic side chains on the inside. Membrane proteins tend to behave in the opposite way by exposing hydrophobic residues to the lipid-rich environment of the membrane interior. Proteins that span membranes are often folded to expose hydrophilic residues outside and inside the cell, and hydrophobic residues on surfaces that are buried inside the membrane. Some proteins achieve their final folded conformations only when exposed to these sorts of specific environmental conditions.

Interactions between charged ion pairs are also a common stabilizing influence within the hydrophobic core of a protein. The interaction occurs when a charged residue is paired with a neutralizing residue of opposite charge. The resulting chemical structure is referred to as a salt bridge. Surprisingly, despite the diversity of amino acid structure, only one type of covalent bond is possible between two residues: the disulfide (-S-S-) bridge. Disulfide bridges form between the thiol groups (-SH) of two nearby cysteine residues. However, the term *nearby* is deceptive because its meaning depends on the folded structure of the protein, and most cysteine residues do not participate in disulfide bridges.

Domains are folded sections of proteins that represent structurally distinct units. Many domains exhibit a specific function and will continue to do so even if removed from the rest of the protein. Motifs are smaller structures, usually composed of a small number of secondary elements that recur in many proteins. Despite their functional significance, individual motifs are rarely structurally independent. This distinction is important because it is fundamentally impossible to predict the folded structure of an individual motif outside the context of the rest of a protein.

A variety of post-translational modifications also contribute to the diversity of protein structure. Some modifications, such as the conversion of proline to hydroxyproline, have profound effects on tertiary structure. (The fibrous structure of collagen is stabilized by a large number of hydroxyproline residues.) Others, such as amino-terminal acetylation, glycosylation, carboxylation, and methylation, often have little to no effect on the final conformation, but alter the protein's chemical properties. In other cases a small cofactor, sometimes a metal atom such as zinc, is required to complete the folding process. One well-known example, the zinc-finger motif found in DNA binding proteins cannot fold properly without the covalent attachment of a zinc atom to a specific cysteine or cysteine-histidine combination [11].

The universe of possible combinations that can be obtained by folding together secondary structures is often referred to as fold space. Despite the number of contributing factors and the huge diversity of function, recent estimates put the total number of possible folds at somewhere around 1,000 [12]. The surprisingly low number is reflective of the evolutionary mechanisms that give rise to protein structure. Most folds are evolved incrementally from existing structures, and most domains are conserved because they have functional value to organisms. Furthermore, because tertiary structure is a product of evolutionary development, randomly constructed polypeptides rarely fold into the same ordered structures as naturally occurring proteins [13]. Even more surprising is the observation that completely different sequences can create the same folded structure and confer the same functionality to different proteins. Many such examples are evident in the Protein Data Bank (PDB) [14]. The fact that different amino acid sequences can fold into similar structures places a fundamental limit on the sensitivity of sequence-similarity-based searching, clustering, and analysis as a basic tool for protein structure prediction.

Fold Classification

Proteins can be roughly classified into three biochemical groups: globular, membrane, and fibrous. Globular proteins, normally found in aqueous environments, fold so that hydrophobic structures are on the inside. Membrane proteins, as mentioned earlier, normally fold the opposite way, exposing hydrophobic residues to the external environment. Fibrous proteins are built of elongated repeating structures, typically composed of a limited set of amino acids. Repeating units may contain well-defined, atypical, or no secondary structure. Over the past several years, many specific folds have been studied and characterized. Classification systems, built on a hierarchy of increasingly complex combinations of helices, sheets, and turns, have begun to emerge. We will return to the discussion of structure dictionaries and fold space classification in the section "Protein Structure Databases" later in this chapter.

QUARTERNARY STRUCTURE

Many globular proteins are oligomeric (i.e., they contain multiple independent subunits). Quarternary structure refers to the noncovalent, but stable, association of these subunits. Hemoglobin, which consists of four independent polypeptide chains, is a well-known example of a multisubunit protein. Each of the four chains is associated with an iron containing heme molecules—the site of oxygen binding. Therefore, each hemoglobin molecule can bind four oxygen atoms. The binding of oxygen to hemoglobin triggers significant changes to the molecule's quarternary structure, but no appreciable change to tertiary structure of the four individual chains. Large globular proteins with quarternary structure are complex to study. This complexity caused Max Perutz and his team to work for nearly 25 years to determine the structure of hemoglobin by x-ray crystallography. Even today in an era characterized by high-energy synchrotrons, super-computers, visualization software, and advanced algorithms for analyzing structural data, it would likely take several years to unravel the structure of something as complex as hemoglobin.

Most proteins are folded into conformations that do not readily react with other protein molecules. The formation of quarternary structure is, therefore, the result of very specific interactions between multiple chains. Regions involved in secondary-structure formation usually have surface areas that resemble the hydrophobic core of most soluble proteins (i.e., they contain a large percentage of nonpolar side chains in addition to residues that can form hydrogen bonds or disulfide bridges).

PROTEIN STRUCTURE DATABASES

Protein structure databases have their roots in the early 1970s when Margaret Dayhoff and others began to classify and store primary sequence in a central repository. The data were made available to the research community along with a variety of related algorithms. The original database, which came to be known as the Protein Information Resource (PIR), was stored at the National Biomedical Research Foundation (NBRF). Sequences were organized into families and superfamilies based on the degree of similarity. Various geometric methods were used to map the comparative distances between sequences based on amino acid substitutions.

Primary sequence was a natural place to begin because protein sequencing techniques were mature enough to facilitate steady data collection. Unfortunately, x-ray crystallography has always presented a number of technical challenges that slow the data-collection process. Even today, tertiary structure determination is a relatively slow process compared to protein sequencing. As a result, the number of available high-resolution structures lags behind the number of sequences by almost two orders of magnitude. However, the number of available tertiary structures has grown rapidly and, at the time of this writing, databases populated with those structures have emerged as a valuable biomedical resource.

Dramatic increases in the number of available structures has made possible the construction of multitiered classification systems. A variety of algorithms are used to compare and classify the structures. Most algorithms for structure comparison involve some sort of distance geometry analysis. The precise method used to encode the structures and the algorithms used to make the comparisons vary considerably among research labs. However, comparisons between protein superfamilies reveal a high degree of agreement between approaches [15].

Two databases have become particularly popular among researchers needing to classify new protein structures: CATH and SCOP. Each contains more than 1,000 well-characterized protein superfamilies representing more than 36,000 distinct domains. In 1993, when CATH was launched, fewer than 3,000 complete structures had been determined. At the time of this writing, the Protein Data Bank contained approximately 21,000 structures; new initiatives are forecasted to add between 30,000 and 100,000 additional structures over the next 5 years. This dramatic growth will undoubtedly test our assumptions about fold space. If today's models are correct, we can expect this growth to be contained within the current framework.

THE CATH DATABASE

CATH is a hierarchical classification composed of four major levels, and CATH is an acronym for the levels: Class, Architecture, Topology, and Homology [16]. (Database entries are based on the Brookhaven Protein Data Bank; only structures solved to less than 3.0 angstroms are included, and many are derived from a combination of x-ray crystallography and NMR.)

Class (C Level)

Class is determined by secondary structure and packing within the folded protein. In most cases, class can be automatically assigned using the method of Michie et al. [17, 18]. Manual inspection and literature reviews are used to make assignments for the remaining 10%. Three major classes are recognized; mainly-alpha, mainly-beta and alpha-beta. (Alpha-beta is a complex construct that includes both alternating alpha/beta structures and segregated alpha+beta structures as originally defined by Levitt and Chothia [19].) A fourth class composed of proteins with low secondary-structure content is also defined.

Architecture (A Level)

Architecture is a representation of the overall shape of the domain as a function of the orientations of individual secondary structures. Connections between secondary structures are not comprehended at this level. A-level designations are assigned manually using a simple description of the secondary-structure arrangement (e.g., barrel, roll, or three-layer sandwich). Automated procedures for identifying architectural structures are currently under development. CATH currently contains 30 major architectures. Check out the CATH public database Web site (www.biochem.ucl.ac.uk/bsm/cath/) for additional detail on these structures [20].

Topology (T Level)

At this level, structures are grouped into fold families depending on both the overall shape and connectivity of secondary structures. Assignments depend on the structure comparison algorithm SSAP (sequential structure alignment program) [21, 22]. SSAP adapts sequence-alignment algorithms to compare 3D structures. Structural environments are encoded using vectors that describe the relationships between residues in the polypeptide backbone. Structures that have an SSAP score of 70 where at least 60% of the larger protein matches the smaller protein are assigned to the same fold family. Highly populated fold families are further subdivided using a higher cutoff for the SSAP score (75 for some mainly-beta and alpha-beta families, 80 for some mainly-alpha families, together with a higher overlap requirement—70%). For further detail regarding SSAP vector encoding and comparison, refer to the original source publications of Taylor and Orengo [23, 24].

Homologous Superfamily (H Level)

This level groups together protein domains that are thought to share a common ancestor. Such proteins are described as being homologous. Similarities are first identified using sequence comparisons and subsequently by comparing structures using SSAP. Structures are clustered into the same superfamily if they satisfy one of the following criteria:

- Sequence identity >= 35% / 60% of larger structure equivalent to smaller.
- SSAP score >= 80.0 and sequence identity >= 20% / 60% of larger structure equivalent to smaller.
- SSAP score >= 80.0 / 60% of larger structure equivalent to smaller / domains that have related functions.

Structures within each H level are further clustered according to their level of sequence identity. Domains clustered in the same sequence families have sequence identities >35% with at least 60% of the larger domain equivalent to the smaller. This subclassification is referred to in the CATH hierarchy as S level (sequence level). The general structure of CATH is depicted in the images contained in Figure 7-7.

The first three tiers—class, architecture, and topology—are shown in the figure. The fourth class, homologous superfamily, is based on evolutionary links between proteins. These links are determined using a combination of structure and sequence-alignment algorithms.

Considerations for Structure Comparison in CATH

X-ray crystallography and related techniques, once slow and tedious, have evolved into high-throughput, industrial-scale sciences. As a result, high-quality structures are becoming available at rates that rival genome sequencing efforts. Unfortunately, matching and analyzing sequences is far more straightforward than matching structures. The problem is significant. The most powerful computers available today take several days to compare a long structure, such as a 300-residue architecture-level structure (i.e., TIM barrel, sandwich, or roll), against the entire database. This problem only worsens over time as more structures are added to the database. Because 50 to 100 new structures are being added each week, the problem is compounding faster than the growth in

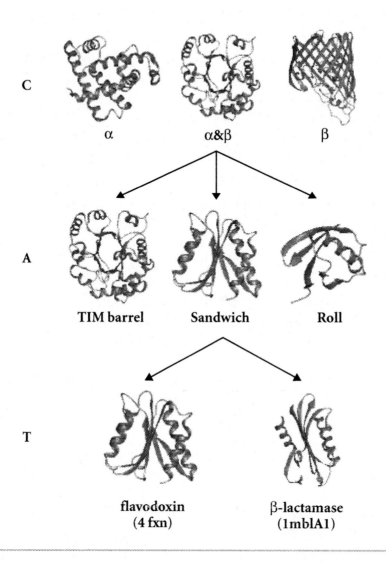

C

α   α&β   β

A

TIM barrel   Sandwich   Roll

T

flavodoxin   β-lactamase
(4 fxn)   (1mblA1)

Figure 7-7 Hierarchical structure of the CATH database. (Source: CATH Protein Structure Classification Web site, www.biochem.ucl.ac.uk/bsm/cath/)

computer horsepower. Furthermore, this number is likely to double or triple in the coming years.

This analysis leads to the counterintuitive conclusion that the process of populating structure databases could become a larger bottleneck than the actual determination of the structures. The result is not entirely surprising because hundreds of highly efficient labs are working to determine structures that all funnel into a very small number of databases. The solution generally adopted by researchers was to develop a new mechanism for rapidly filtering structures for computationally intense programs such as SSAP. One such program, GRATH (graphical representation of CATH structures), relies on comparisons between secondary structures rather than individual residues. Because there are an order of magnitude fewer secondary structures than individual amino acids, such an algorithm can perform a first-pass comparison of two proteins in a small fraction of the time required by SSAP. The best matches can then be passed on for further validation.

GRATH first abstracts secondary structures as vectors (depicted in Figure 7-8). Geometric relationships between pairs of vectors, such as the dot-product angle and dihedral angle are then defined along with information about chirality of the secondary structure. The geometric relationships between all the pairs of vectors are then used to construct a graph of the protein. The nodes of the graph are labeled by the type of secondary structure (α-helix, β-sheet, or turn), with each node representing a vector; edges are labeled according to the geometric relationships between the relevant vectors. In GRATH, the geometry is defined by the distance of closest approach between the vectors, the dot-product angle (tilt), the dihedral angle (rotation), and a representation of chirality [25, 26]. The algorithm then uses two matrices for structural comparison. The first, called the G1G2 matrix, contains information about secondary-structure matches between two domain graphs. The second, referred to as the correspondence matrix, details whether the geometric information in the two graphs is the same within a given tolerance.

Many studies have demonstrated the relationship between sequence and structure. As a result, proteins with more than 30% sequence similarity are commonly assumed to be members of the same superfamily. Fortunately, today's sequence-comparison algorithms are highly evolved and quite suitable for such comparisons. CATH uses Needleman-Wunsch alignments for global comparisons. However, small proteins (<100 residues)

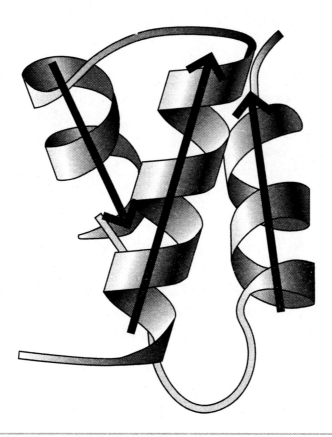

Figure 7-8 GRATH uses protein secondary structures represented as vectors. Each must then be associated with additional information depicting orientations and distances to complete a description of a protein as a graph. Protein graphs are then encoded into tables for rapid comparison.

sometimes cause confusion because unrelated sequences with nearly 30% sequence identity have been found. In response to this problem, the threshold for homologue detection has been raised to 35%. Furthermore, 80% of the larger protein must be aligned against the smaller protein. The power of these comparisons has been expanded considerably by adding sequence relatives from GenBank to the database. Adding these sequences has increased the size of the database by tenfold. The new data represent an intermediate sequence library that broadens the scope of each family and enhances the process of detecting distant homologues. Before expanding the database, 51% of distant

CALCULATING THE DOT PRODUCT AND THE CROSS PRODUCT

Assume two vectors U and V with endpoints represented by the coordinates a = (Ux, Uy) and (Vx, Vy) as depicted in Figure 7-9. The angle between the two vectors is designated ϕ, and the lengths of the two vectors are represented by their absolute values |U| and |V|, respectively.

The dot product U•V = COS ϕ |U| |V|. It can also be shown that this expression simplifies to (Ux * Vx) + (Uy * Vy), so the dot product U•V = (Ux * Vx) + (Uy * Vy). In Figure 7-9, the coordinates for vector U (Ux, Uy) are (2,3) and the coordinates for vector V (Vx, Vy) are (−1,5). The dot product U•V = (2 * −1) + (3 * 5) = 13.

The lengths of the vectors are simple to calculate: |U| = SQR(13) and |V| = SQR(26).

Rearranging terms, cos ϕ = (Ux * Vx) + (Uy * Vy) / |U| * |V|. The expression simplifies to 13 / (SQR(13) * SQR(26)) = 0.707 = COS 45°. Therefore, 45° is the angle between the two vectors. We can also calculate the dot product using this angle: COS ϕ |U| |V| = .707 * SQR(13) * SQR(26) = 13.

The magnitude of the cross product (UxV) = SIN ϕ |U| |V| where ϕ is the dot-product angle calculated above. The vector represented by the cross product is perpendicular to the plane containing the two vectors U and V. In Figure 7-9, the cross-product vectors are defined from vectors U and V and their midpoint vector M using the cross products UxM and VxM. As a result, information about the tilt and rotations of the vectors is included in the graphical descriptions. Data for these calculations are normally obtained from x-ray crystallography.

homologues were recognized by scanning against profiles derived from CATH. After inclusion of the new sequence libraries, that number rose to 82%.

A significant proportion of distant relatives (approximately 15%) can only be recognized by directly comparing the structures. Most of these situations represent evolutionary divergence where function is conserved and sequence is not. Because function is a product of structure, the folds have also been conserved. However, amino acid substitutions make sequence direct comparisons very difficult. The globin genes are one well-

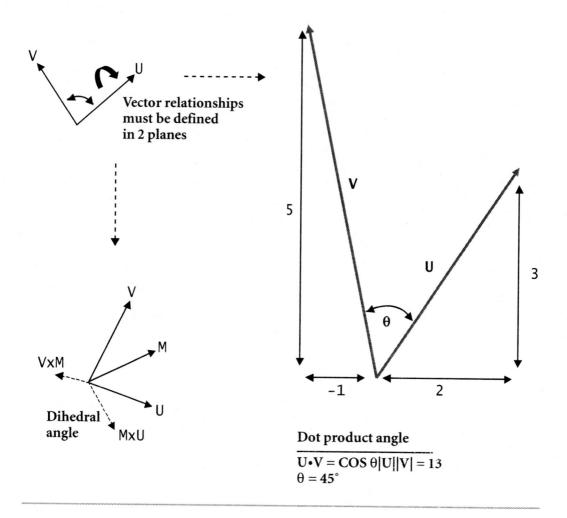

Figure 7-9 Dot-product angle and dihedral-angle calculations are central to defining vectors for encoding secondary structure. The dihedral-angle vectors are defined from vectors U and V and their midpoint vector M using the cross products UxM and VxM. As a result, information about the tilt and rotations of the vectors is included in the graphical descriptions. Data for these calculations are normally obtained from x-ray crystallography.

documented example; sequence homology can fall below 10% while oxygen binding function and 3D structure are both conserved. One approach to comparing such sequences involves allowing residue substitutions using amino acids with similar chemical and physical properties. A more-precise approach involves abandoning sequence comparisons in favor of the direct structural methods discussed earlier (SSAP, GRATH).

As fold space has been explored, the number of unique folds identified as a percentage of the number of new structures determined has continuously declined. When the systematic process of gathering and cataloging structures began in the early 1970s, the number was 100%—every newly determined structure represented new folds. By 1975, only one of every two newly determined structures represented a unique, previously unknown fold. The number has slowly declined since the early 1980s when approximately one of every five new folds was unique. Today fewer than 5% of new structures represent unique folds. This trend is a positive sign because if it continues we will eventually reach the point where virtually every newly determined structure fits a previously understood fold. Predicting the physical properties of a new structure will almost always be easiest in the context of similar, well-characterized structures.

For more detail regarding use and structure of the CATH database, refer to the CATH Web site at http://www.biochem.ucl.ac.uk/bsm/cath/.

THE SCOP DATABASE

The SCOP (Structural Classification of Proteins) database is another valuable resource for comparing and classifying new structures. The SCOP database is designed to provide a comprehensive description of the structural and evolutionary relationships between all proteins whose structure is known, including all entries in the Protein Data Bank. To make the database more accessible, it is available as a set of tightly linked hypertext documents.

Because existing automatic sequence and structure comparison tools cannot identify all structural and evolutionary relationships between proteins, SCOP classification of proteins has been constructed manually by visual inspection and comparison of structures. Some entries are classified by individual domains, others by complete multidomain structures.

SCOP and CATH share many similarities of data organization. The principal levels of structure are fold, superfamily, and family. The hierarchy is defined as follows:

1. Fold (major structural similarity)

Proteins are defined as having a common fold if they have the same arrangement of secondary structures with the same topological connections. Proteins grouped under the same fold category do not always share a common evolutionary origin. Similar but unrelated structures often arise from physical properties that favor particular packing arrangements and chain topologies. Such proteins may be grouped under the same fold category even if they do not share a common evolutionary origin. For convenience, different folds have been grouped into classes. The five distinct classes recognized in SCOP are similar to those of CATH—(1) all alpha, (2) all beta, (3) alpha and beta, (4) alpha plus beta, and (5) multidomain. Unusual entries— small peptides, designed proteins, and theoretical models—have been assigned to other classes [27].

2. Superfamily (probable common evolutionary origin)

Proteins that exhibit low levels of sequence homology, but whose structural and functional features suggest that a common evolutionary origin is likely, are grouped together in the same superfamily. For example, actin, the ATPase domain of the heat shock protein, and hexakinase together form a superfamily.

3. Family (clear evolutionarily relationship)

Proteins are clustered together into families when they share more than 30% sequence homology. As noted in the discussion of CATH superfamilies, similar functions and structures occasionally provide definitive evidence of common descent in the absence of high sequence identity. Globin structural variants are a well-characterized example of this phenomenon.

Current SCOP statistics are displayed in Table 7-1. The number of domains in the database has grown from 24,186 in February 2000 to 49,497 in March 2003. This growth is depicted graphically in Figure 7-10.

The explosive growth in structural genomics is generating a large number of experimental structures. Recent upgrades in the SCOP infrastructure were designed to help manage these new entries. These upgrades include a new set of identifiers designed to uniquely identify each entry in the hierarchy, a compact representation of protein

Table 7-1 SCOP Statistics: 18,946 PDB Entries / 49,497 Domains

Class	Number of Folds	Number of Superfamilies	Number of Families
All alpha proteins	171	286	457
All beta proteins	119	234	418
Alpha and beta proteins (a/b)	117	192	501
Alpha and beta proteins (a+b)	224	330	532
Multi-domain proteins	39	39	50
Membrane and cell surface proteins	34	64	71
Small proteins	61	87	135
Total	765	1,232	2,164

Source: SCOP Release 1.63 (March 1, 2003)

domain classification, and a new set of parseable files describing all SCOP domains [28]. Although SCOP is normally thought of as a hierarchy, logical cross links between nodes of the tree make it a computational graph, which allows complex relationships to be represented. This additional layer of complexity has facilitated the upgrade process. Because the original implementation of SCOP is based on description of the underlying data structure rather than the data itself, this abstraction makes addition of another level very straightforward—all that is needed is a modification of the description.

Like CATH, SCOP is a publicly available database. To familiarize yourself with its tools, references, and other resources, visit the SCOP Web site at http://scop.mrc-lmb.cam.ac.uk/scop/.

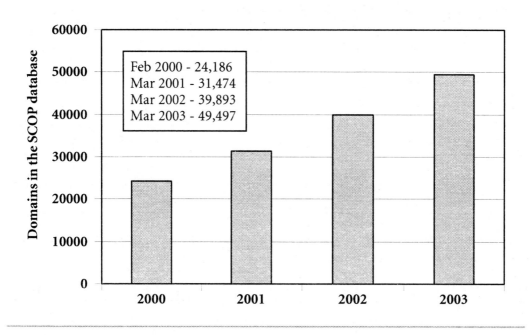

Figure 7-10 Growth in the number of domains represented in the SCOP database. (Source: Structural Classification of Proteins Web site, scop.mrc-lmb.cam.ac.uk/scop/)

AB INITIO STRUCTURE PREDICTION

Homology modeling has been the preferred method for predicting protein tertiary structure for decades. Explosive growth in the content of structure databases coupled with improvements in the algorithms used to compare sequences and structures has increased the value of these techniques. However, the ability to directly predict tertiary structure from primary sequence would be invaluable in many areas of research. For example, experiments that involve synthetic polypeptides or partially substituted sequences often produce new structures that do not exactly fit known models. Moreover, it is not always possible to experimentally determine a protein's structure—multi-subunit structures and membrane-bound proteins both represent difficult situations. Furthermore, structures stored in databases are typically obtained from proteins in the crystal state. Having the ability to use basic physical and chemical properties to predict the folded structure of a sequence will also enable researchers to predict the behavior of these structures in different environments. These predictions will be especially valuable for drug-interaction studies and other situations where x-ray structures do not adequately represent the native environment of a particular protein.

Progress in protein structure prediction is typically assessed by a community-wide experiment known as the Critical Assessment of Protein Structure Prediction (CASP) [29]. In CASP, protein sequences whose experimentally determined structures are soon to be released are made available to the public. Research groups compete with each other by using a variety of information sources and computer programs to predict the structures. Much progress has been made in recent years, and although no single algorithm has demonstrated consistent reliability, the essential challenges are now well understood. In this discussion, we will use the term *ab initio* to refer to experiments that begin without knowledge of globally similar folds and produce novel structures.

THE ENERGY LANDSCAPE

One of the earliest assumptions adopted by the protein-folding community is that, in the absence of large kinetic barriers, a polypeptide chain always folds into the lowest free-energy conformation for its sequence. Consequently, successful structure prediction requires a method for searching conformational space for energy minima. The goal is to develop an appropriate energy function that models folding behavior and can be used to locate energy minima. Ultimate success depends on being able to construct a detailed free-energy surface with a knowledge of the positions occupied by various transition-state intermediates. Figure 7-11 depicts such a surface. One important lesson of the diagram is that other slightly higher free-energy paths almost always exist just outside the border of any preferred path. Some of these involve alterations to secondary structure, others more subtle changes. Slight differences in temperature or solvent environment can push the folding process through one of these paths. The figure shows that different solvent conditions, amino acid substitutions, or other thermodynamic situations can reshape parts of the unfolded basin and affect rates and paths to the final conformation. Residual conformations may reside in some of these energy basins, and under certain circumstances different basins may or may not be occupied. Subtle free-energy changes can be significant. Most preferred paths are very close to others with slightly higher free energy. Small differences in temperature, for example, can drive the folding path in a different direction.

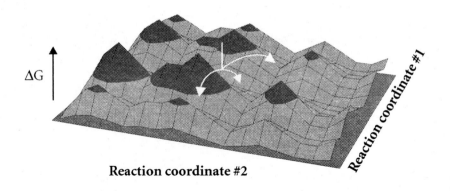

ΔG

Reaction coordinate #2

Reaction coordinate #1

Figure 7-11 Free-energy surface for a typical protein.

The energy landscape is often represented as a funnel. The most unfolded configurations are also the most numerous, but have the highest free energy. These species tend to exist near the rim of the funnel. Conversely, compact molecules with small configurational entropy are positioned near the center of the coordinate system. The theory predicts that favorable contacts lower the overall contact energy for more-compact proteins. The theory is also designed to comprehend solvent effects; hydrophobic interactions with amino acid side chains representing the dominant force. One way to account for these interactions is to ignore solvent molecules and assume increased interactions between hydrophobic residues. To fully understand the parameters that control the shape of the funnel and the free-energy surface, many parameters must be estimated, including the height of each kinetic barrier and its dependence on sequence, the solvent environment, and intermediate structures. As our understanding of the relationships between structure and function evolve, they will almost certainly shed light on the folding process. Conversely, a detailed understanding of the folding process is likely to facilitate structure and function predictions [30].

A detailed discussion of the kinetics and energetics of folding is beyond the scope of this book. For more information on these topics, refer to any one of many excellent sources that focus on these topics.

REDUCING THE COMPLEXITY OF THE PROTEIN-FOLDING PROBLEM

If unlimited computer power could be brought to bear against the protein-folding problem, brute-force methods would certainly prevail. At the extreme limit of such an approach would be the construction of a complete quantum mechanical model (QM) encompassing all the atomic interactions that occur between translation and a stable folded product. The problem would be divided into millions of very small time steps, and each calculation would need to be repeated for each step. Solvent effects would also need to be taken into account. Unfortunately, no computer on earth is powerful enough to support this many calculations. Worse still, the most powerful computer architectures in today's technology pipeline are many orders of magnitude too small to effect a complete quantum mechanical model. However, various approximations can make the problem more palatable.

These simplifications span a range of sophistication. At one end of the spectrum are lattice and bead-string models. These approximations tend to treat each amino acid as a point particle. Lattice models are somewhat constrained because each point must occupy a discrete site in a three-dimensional grid. This restriction is relaxed in beaded-string models. Lattice and beaded-string models are extremely useful because they can be exhaustively investigated with a modest amount of computer power.

A slightly more sophisticated view is provided by the united-atom model. As the name implies, united-atom models treat groups of atoms as single particles. The simulation typically takes place in a vacuum, also known as an implicit solvent. Implicit solvent approximations treat water molecules surrounding the protein as a continuum rather than as discrete molecules. For example, the dielectric properties of the solvent can be simulated as a varying force on the surface of the protein. The increased computational complexity of these models limits the number of simulations that can be run and variables that can be investigated.

All-atom models are next in sophistication. The term *all-atom* refers to the fact that this class of algorithm explicitly takes into account the effect of each solvent atom. Such explicit solvent models are computationally intensive because they are dominated by the interactions of millions of solvent molecules. Only complete quantum mechanical models that address the electronic wave functions of the system are more complex. Because of their computational complexity, QM models are most often used to study short time-frame processes; the catalytic properties of enzyme active sites are often revealed through this type of analysis. Furthermore, because most aspects of protein folding do not involve the making and breaking of covalent bonds—disulfide bridges stand as an obvious exception—simpler calculations based on Newton's equations of motion are entirely appropriate for modeling most of the process [31]. This approach has proven so powerful that it has become the standard for most of today's molecular dynamics (MD) computations.

All classical approaches rely on a model for interatomic interactions. This model is known as a force field because it can be used to compute the forces acting on all atoms in the system. The classical approach involves computing all forces acting on all atoms, and using this information to predict the positions of each atom a short time later. Repeated application of the algorithm reveals the trajectories of all atoms in the system. Time steps as small as 10^{-15} seconds are required to capture the fastest vibrations—those associated with hydrogen atoms in the protein and solvent. Applying this level of granularity to a rapidly folding protein—one that completes the process in 10^{-4} seconds—results in 10^{10} time steps. (Most proteins take longer than 10^{-4} seconds to fold and, therefore, require the calculation of many more time steps.) Each single atom trajectory typically requires the execution of approximately 5×10^6 machine instructions. For a very small protein, one with fewer than 100 amino acids in an environment of only about 6,000 water molecules, the calculation would include approximately 2×10^4 atoms.

Given these approximations, we can see that simulating the folding process for a very small protein will require 2×10^{21} individual machine instructions. The size of the computer needed to accomplish this task will depend on the length of time allotted to the experiment. For example, to complete the calculation in 20 days (1.7×10^6 seconds) would require a machine capable of executing 10^{15} floating-point instructions per second—a petaflop supercomputer. Table 7-2 depicts the computational complexity of the folding process for a very small protein in terms of time steps.

By comparison, at the time of this writing, the largest commercially available supercomputer can execute approximately 7.5 teraflops (7.5×10^{12} floating-point operations per second). Likewise, ASCI White, a U.S. government supercomputer designed to simulate and model nuclear explosions in three dimensions, is approximately 12 teraflops. These machines, despite their size and power, are two orders of magnitude too small to be useful for protein-folding simulations. Additionally, the reference protein we used for

Table 7-2 Computational Complexity of Protein Folding

Computational Parameter	Magnitude
No. of atoms	2×10^4
No. of instructions / atom / time step	5×10^6
No. of instructions / time step	1×10^{11}
Physical time for folding (sec.)	1×10^{-4}
Physical time step (sec.)	5×10^{-15}
No. of time steps needed	2×10^{10}
No. of instructions	2×10^{21}
No. of seconds in 20 days	1.7×10^6
No. of instructions per sec.	1×10^{15}

our calculations was very small—only 100 amino acids. Larger calculations containing an appropriate number of solvent molecules would require considerably more computing power and time.

The greatest challenge faced when modeling interatomic interactions is building a force field that correctly takes into account various bonded and nonbonded pairwise forces between atoms. Bond-stretch and angle-bending forces are usually small; torsional movements often represent significant displacements. Nonbonded forces consist of Coulomb interactions and Van der Waals forces. Coulomb, or charge-charge interactions, apply over the longest range. These forces tend to dominate many of the calculations. Coulomb interactions play a key role in defining the energy profiles of hydrogen bonds throughout the model. These interactions are ubiquitous because they occur intraprotein, intrasolvent, and between protein and solvent. Several reliable force fields are available for commercial or academic use—CHARM, AMBER, GROMOS, and OPLS-AA [32, 33, 34, 35].

Ab initio methods provide the greatest insight when used to model many trajectories rather than a single folding event. Used in this way, they become true *in silico* experimental technologies. Furthermore, multiple simulations of limited duration often provide more accurate information than a single long trajectory. Despite their many advantages, *ab initio* methods display one striking weakness: They always return the lowest possible energy conformation. For many polypeptides, this particular conformation—although eminently stable—is not the active state of the protein in solution. To truly explore the "conform-ome" of an amino acid sequence would require repeating the simulation under a variety of conditions (i.e., solvents, pH, temperature, etc.).

CHAPERONINS—ASSISTED FOLDING

As discussed previously, successful folding of a protein is a complex multistep process that often passes through many unstable transition states. Crowded intracellular conditions sometimes lead to protein aggregation and nonproductive folding. In addition, the sequential nature of translation often exposes slow-folding hydrophobic domains that fold differently during translation than they would if denatured and allowed to renature in the same environment.

The physical concepts surrounding spontaneous folding remain relevant, and they rightfully form the basis of *ab initio* approaches. However, large proteins composed of multiple domains often refold inefficiently. The folding mechanism for these molecules often involves many misfolded states that tend to aggregate into stable, but misfolded intermediates. These intermediates are often stable enough to prevent folding from proceeding to a biologically active structure. Many of these non-native states, though compact in shape, expose hydrophobic residues and unstructured segments of the polypeptide backbone to the solvent. As a result, they readily self-associate into disordered complexes driven by hydrophobic forces and interchain hydrogen bonding [36]. An important compensatory mechanism that relies on a class of proteins known as chaperones has evolved to assist the folding process for such proteins. However, a certain level of protein aggregation can occur in cells despite the presence of the chaperone machinery. These aggregates are thought to be the root cause of many serious illnesses such as Alzheimer's and Huntington's diseases.

A chaperone is a protein that selectively recognizes and binds to exposed hydrophobic surfaces of an unfolded protein to prevent aggregation. An ATP-dependent conformational change in the chaperone is responsible for release of the protein. Chaperones can also participate in the degradation of misfolded proteins. One mechanism apparently involves successive cycling through the chaperone system and failure of the protein to fold into the native state. By a mechanism that remains incompletely understood, such proteins are recognized by the ubiquitin system and processed into a form that is subsequently degraded by the proteasome. Data from the human genome project predicts that as many as 750 proteins may be involved in folding and degradation.

Chaperonins are a special subclass of multisubunit complexes that directly promote folding of certain proteins. An ATP binding mechanism drives large conformational changes that bury hydrophobic sites and initiate the creation of closed and open cavities. Unfolded proteins progress toward the native state while confined within these sites. This mechanism is responsible for the correct folding of many polypeptides, most notably cytoskeletal proteins such as actin and tubulin. At the time of this writing, potential folding mechanisms span a broad range. At one extreme is the simple confinement and protection from aggregation; the other extreme is characterized by more-complex mechanisms involving successive binding and release steps that ultimately allow the protein to freely refold in solution [37].

FOLDING OF MEMBRANE PROTEINS

Membrane proteins represent approximately 25% of all translated sequences. They play vital roles in transmembrane signaling, communication, and transport. The lipid content of a typical membrane makes the interior hydrophobic. This environment places certain constraints on the structures of associated proteins. More specifically, polypeptide chains that pass through a membrane normally have high percentages of hydrophobic residues and form structures that do not contain free hydrogen donor or acceptor atoms. As a result, integral membrane proteins normally consist of α-helix structures where all possible hydrogen bonds are present.

Early transmembrane structure-prediction programs relied exclusively on hydrophobicity scales built from a variety of physiochemical parameters [38]. Sequences are usually profiled within a sliding window of predetermined size, where physical properties of amino acids are averaged to obtain some type of structure-related score. Since the early 1990s, these techniques have been supplemented with *ab initio* calculations in addition to various machine learning techniques—for instance, hidden Markov models and neural networks trained on transmembrane protein segments with known topologies.

During the past decade, an almost endless variety of scoring strategies and discrimination functions were developed to leverage the ever-growing body of chemical knowledge. Refinements to these strategies have resulted in a class of algorithms that are very effective predictors of structure even in the absence of sequence similarity. One such algorithm, the dense alignment surface (DAS), has successfully recognized transmembrane helices in prokaryotic proteins despite a complete lack of sequence homology. The method was successfully applied to a set of sequences whose topologies had proven to be especially difficult to predict [39].

In the vast majority of cases, helical segments are oriented perpendicular to the membrane. The resulting structures can be classified into two broad groups: (1) channel-like proteins, where the channel is formed by identical helices from multiple polypeptides (homo-heteromer structure) arrayed in a regular shape, or by several helical segments of a single polypeptide chain; and (2) receptor-like proteins that have an irregular helix bundle containing segments of different orientations arrayed in antiparallel fashion. The latter arrangement has been shown to be energetically favorable [40].

Many transmembrane segments also contain hydrophilic residues. The fact that these residues must face the interior of the helix bundle creates geometric constraints that aid the structure prediction process. These constraints tend to stabilize the final folded structure inside the membrane. The purification of membrane-stabilized proteins is often difficult because detergents and surfactants used to create a hydrophobic environment do not always duplicate the stabilizing effects of the membrane. The problem is especially significant in enzyme purifications because catalytic activity is often lost if the enzyme cannot properly fold.

PREDICTING LEAD—TARGET INTERACTIONS

The ultimate goal of many structure-prediction experiments is to model the binding of target proteins and lead compounds—a central theme in drug discovery. An important part of target validation involves purifying and studying a specific receptor to identify the parameters most likely to affect lead compound binding. Pharmaceutical companies often rely on combinatorial chemistry and high-throughput screening to predict these interactions. During the past several years, *in silico* techniques for predicting these molecular events have advanced to the point where biotech companies are beginning to skip much of the lab bench work involved in combinatorial chemistry and synthesize only the most promising compounds based on a structural understanding of the receptor and associated ligands. Both target validation and lead compound optimization are enhanced by the use of programs that facilitate the prediction of three-dimensional structures of proteins and protein-ligand complexes.

Fortunately, many options are available to those using structure prediction as part of the target-identification process. In many cases, for example, the molecule being modeled is membrane bound, and the calculation is focused on the portion known, through chemical analysis, to be exposed outside the cell membrane. This approach has been helpful to researchers working to identify antibody targets on the surface of infected T-helper cells in HIV seropositive individuals. A recently created monoclonal antibody is believed to bind to a region of the gp41 transmembrane glycoprotein close to a transmembrane domain. This region is accessible to neutralizing antibodies and could form a useful target for vaccine design [41].

Another example involves using bioinformatic tools to predict which portion of a protein sequence is likely to be a biologically active binding site and to model the specific structure of that site. An interesting example is the gp120 glycoprotein, a cell surface protein that, like gp41, mediates HIV entry into target cells initiating the replication cycle of the virus. The crystal structure of the core of gp120 has recently been solved [42, 43]. It reveals the structure of the conserved HIV-1 receptor binding sites and some of the mechanisms evolved by HIV-1 to escape antibody response. The protein consists of three faces. One is largely inaccessible on the native trimer; two faces are exposed but apparently have low immunogenicity, particularly on primary viruses. The investigators modeled HIV-1 neutralization by a CD4 binding site monoclonal antibody. Results suggested that neutralization takes place by inhibition of the interaction between gp120 and the target receptors as a consequence of steric hindrance. Such structural knowledge is central to the discovery of new drugs across a variety of disease categories and is especially relevant to oncology, where cell-cell signaling plays a crucial role in disease progression [44].

Target modeling represents only half of the computational problem because a complete solution must also include correct identification of appropriate lead compounds. Furthermore, because compounds that bind to a target may still be toxic, absorption-distribution-metabolism-excretion (ADME) predictions are also a critical part of lead compound optimization. It is not possible to synthesize or even generate all the possible lead compounds; some estimates set the number of chemical structures in the molecular weight range of a typical pharmaceutical (under 500 daltons) at more that 10^{20} different molecules. As a result of this explosive diversity, pharmaceutical companies have built tremendous compound libraries containing tens of thousands of promising substances. Likewise, many data sources are now available that contain libraries of two- and three-dimensional structures. The National Cancer Institute's Drug Information System (NCI DIS) 3D database being one of the most significant examples [45].

The NCI DIS 3D database contains more than 400,000 compounds and is maintained by the Developmental Therapeutics Program Division of Cancer Treatment, National Cancer Institute, Rockville, Maryland. The structural information stored in the DIS represents the connection table for each drug—a list that details the connections between atoms in the compound. This information can be searched to find drugs that share similar bond patterns—often a predictor of biological activity. As mentioned previously, it is often possible to model the points of interaction between a drug and its target with only a small number of atoms. This geometric arrangement of atoms, typically referred to as a pharmacophore, can be used to search 3D structural databases to find compounds with similar biological activity (despite the fact that these compounds may have very different patterns of chemical bonds). A diverse set of lead compounds increases the chance of finding an appropriate drug with acceptable properties for clinical development [46]. Alternatively, if a lead compound has previously been identified, then similarity searches are often used to identify other small molecules with similar structures and chemical properties.

One problem with this approach is that three- or four-point pharmacophores are often too restrictive, and slightly more open-ended searches will usually return an unwieldy number of hits from a large structure database. Furthermore, it is often impossible to score or rank the hits. As a result, pharmacophore searches have a tendency to return "already known" solutions. A more sophisticated and unbiased approach involves exhaustive receptor-ligand docking experiments. Such experiments, which require that every compound in the library be tested for binding against the target structure, have been made possible by recent improvements in computer performance. (Target structures are determined experimentally using x-ray crystallography or NMR, or through *in silico* modeling.) Each docking event receives a score based on a calculation of the free energy of binding—typically based on the geometry of hydrogen bond contacts, lipophilic contacts, metal-binding contacts, and other factors related to entropic penalties that describe the freezing of ligand conformational flexibility upon binding [47].

In silico ADME modeling is often used to predict metabolic behavior of a drug prior to launching a clinical trial. Such modeling requires a detailed understanding of all related metabolic pathways and the effects the drug might have on the up and down regulation of key genes whose protein products modulate those pathways [48].

SUMMARY

Proteins represent the basic building blocks for every cellular structure from the smallest membrane-bound receptor to the largest organelle. Unlike most other macromolecules, proteins can fold into structures that have catalytic activity and mediate chemical reactions. Catalytic proteins, or enzymes, serve a crucial biological role—they lower the energy of activation for the chemical reactions that make life possible.

Protein structures are often divided into four categories. Primary structure refers to the amino acid sequence of the protein. Secondary structure refers to local three-dimensional structures that form as a result of charge interactions along the polypeptide chain. Two structures dominate the study of secondary structure: alpha (α) helix and beta (β) sheet. These structures are normally connected by a less-stable construct known as a reverse turn, coil, or loop. These regions, which often occur near the surface of a protein, can be important in the formation of active sites for ligand binding or catalytic activity in proteins functioning as enzymes. Tertiary structure is defined as the global three-dimensional folding that results from interactions between elements of secondary structure. Various elements can combine to shape a protein in three dimensions. Although hydrogen bonding between backbone elements is the primary driver of secondary structure, interactions between side chains is the predominant driver of tertiary structure. Finally, many globular proteins are oligomeric (i.e., they contain multiple independent subunits). Quarternary structure refers to the noncovalent, but stable, association of these subunits.

All the information that one needs to predict the tertiary structure of a protein is contained in its sequence. However, unlike gene sequences, which are built on standard code words, there is no straightforward code or set of rules that we can use to predict the native structure of a protein. Furthermore, the process is regulated. Misfolded proteins are often degraded, others are often helped through the folding process by other proteins called chaperones.

Many different approaches to predicting the folded structure of a protein are possible. *Ab initio* methods seek to predict final folded structures by applying basic physical principles and a knowledge of the primary sequence. *Ab initio* methods are computationally intensive, and a variety of approaches are used to reduce the complexity of the problem. At the extreme limit of such an approach would be the construction of a complete quantum mechanical model encompassing all the atomic interactions that occur between translation and a stable folded product. Unfortunately, today's largest computers are too small to support this many calculations.

Classical approaches to fold prediction rely on a mathematical model to represent interatomic interactions. This model is known as a force field because it can be used to compute the forces acting on all atoms in the system. The classical approach involves computing all forces acting on all atoms, and using this information to predict the positions of each atom a short time later. The greatest challenge faced when modeling interatomic interactions is building a force field that correctly takes into account various bonded and nonbonded pairwise forces between atoms. *Ab initio* methods provide the greatest insight when used to model many trajectories rather than a single folding event; multiple simulations of limited duration often provide more accurate information than a single long trajectory.

Another approach involves the use of structure databases containing information about experimentally determined conformations (also known as folds) and their underlying sequences. High-throughput structure determination has driven exponential growth in the size of these dictionaries. In principle, a researcher can determine the native conformation of a sequence by locating an exact or close match in the dictionary. Many protein structure databases have been created, each based on a slightly different structural hierarchy.

An important application of protein structure prediction is the modeling of interactions between proteins and ligands. Such modeling is critical to the drug-discovery process, which depends heavily on predicting the binding of lead compounds to targets. These experiments, often referred to as molecular docking, are central to the drug-discovery process.

Studying and predicting the structures of membrane-bound proteins is particularly difficult for a variety of reasons related to their physical chemistry. Early transmembrane structure-prediction programs relied exclusively on hydrophobicity scales built from a variety of physiochemical parameters. Since the early 1990s, these techniques have been supplemented with *ab initio* calculations in addition to various machine learning techniques—hidden Markov models and neural networks trained on transmembrane protein segments with known topologies. Recent years have witnessed the emergence of a new class of algorithms for predicting homologous structures, even in the complete absence of sequence similarity.

The ultimate goal of many structure-prediction experiments is to enable the modeling of target protein—lead compound interaction. During the past several years, *in silico* techniques for predicting these molecular events have advanced to the point where biotech companies are beginning to skip much of the lab bench work involved in combinatorial chemistry and synthesize only the most promising compounds based on a structural understanding of the receptor and associated ligands.

Bioinformatic tools are often used to predict which portion of a protein sequence is likely to be a biologically active binding site and to model the specific structure of that site. Such structural knowledge is central to the discovery of new drugs across a variety of disease categories and is especially relevant to oncology where cell-cell signaling plays a crucial role in disease progression. Target modeling represents only half of the computational problem because a complete solution must also include correct identification of appropriate lead compounds. Some estimates set the number of chemical structures in the molecular weight range of a typical pharmaceutical (under 500 daltons) at more that 10^{20} different molecules. As a result of this explosive diversity, pharmaceutical companies have built tremendous compound libraries containing tens of thousands of promising substances. Likewise, many data sources are now available that contain libraries of two- and three-dimensional structures; the National Cancer Institute's Drug Information System (NCI DIS) 3D database is one of the most significant examples.

The NCI DIS 3D database contains more than 400,000 compounds and is maintained by the Developmental Therapeutics Program Division of Cancer Treatment, National Cancer Institute, Rockville, Maryland. The structural information stored in the DIS represents the connection table for each drug—a list that details the connections between atoms in the compound. This information can be searched to find drugs that share similar bond patterns—often a predictor of biological activity. The geometric arrangement of atoms that models the interaction between drug and target is typically referred to as a pharmacophore. These structures can be used to search 3D structural databases to find compounds with similar biological activity. Such experiments, which require that every compound in the library be tested for binding against the target structure, have been made possible by recent improvements in computer performance.

ENDNOTES

1. Anfinsen C.B. 1973. Principles that govern the folding of polypeptide chains. *Science* 181: 223–230 (Nobel Prize lecture).

2. Anfinsen C.B., Haber E., Sela M., White F. W. 1961. The kinetics of the formation of native ribonuclease during oxidation of the reduced polypeptide domain. *Proceedings of the National Academy of Sciences* 47: 1309–1314.

3. Lehninger, A. *Biochemistry, Second Edition.* Worth Publishers Inc., New York, 1975, 140–141.

4. Sanger F. 1952. The arrangement of amino acids in proteins. *Advances in Protein Chemistry* 7: 1–67.

5. Ramachandran G.N., Sasisekharan V. 1968. Conformation of polypeptides and proteins. *Advances in Protein Chemistry* 23: 283–437.

6. Levitt M. 1978. Conformational preferences of amino acids in globular proteins. *Biochemistry* 17: 4277–4285.

7. Chou P.Y., Fasman G.D. 1978. Prediction of the secondary structure of proteins from their amino acid sequences. *Advances in Enzymology* 47: 45–148.

8. Nishikawa K. 1983. Assessment of secondary-structure prediction of proteins. Comparison of computerized Chou-Fasman method with others. *Biochimica Biophysica Acta* 748(2): 285–299.

9. Kyngas J., Valjakka J. 1998. Unreliability of the Chou-Fasman parameters in predicting protein secondary structure. *Protein Engineering* 11(5): 345–8.

10. Scheef, E. D., and Fink, L. "Fundamentals of Protein Structure" in *Structural Bioinformatics.* Edited by Philip Bourne and Helge Weissig. Wiley-Liss, Inc., New Jersey, 1995, 15–40.

11. Choo Y., Isalan M. 2000. Advances in zinc finger engineering. *Current Opinion in Structural Biology* 10(4): 411–416.

12. Wolf Y. I., Grishin N. V., Koonin E. V. 2000. Estimating the number of protein folds and families from complete genome data. *Journal of Molecular Biology* 299: 897–905.

13. Richardson J. S. 1992. Looking at proteins: representations, folding, packing, and design. *Biophysical Journal* 63: 1186–1209.

14. Berman H. M., et al. 2000. The protein data bank. *Nucleic Acids Research* 28: 235–242 (Reference is to Chapter 9 of the document).

15. Hadley C., Jones D. T. 1999. A systematic comparison of protein structure classifications: SCOP, CATH, and FSSP. *Structure* 7: 1099–1112.

16. Orengo C. A., Michie A. D., Jones S., Jones D. T., Swindells M. B., Thornton J. M. 1997. CATH—a hierarchic classification of protein domain structures. *Structure* 5(8): 1093–1108.

17. Orengo C. A., Martin A. M., Hutchinson E. G., Jones S., Jones D. T., Michie A. D., Swindells M. B., Thornton J. M. 1998. Classifying a protein in the CATH database of domain structures. *Acta Crystallography* D54: 1155–1167.

18. Michie A. D., Orengo C. A., Thornton J. M. 1996. Analysis of domain structural class using an automated class assignment protocol. *Journal of Molecular Biology* 262: 168–185.

19. Levitt M., Chothia C. 1976. Structural patterns in globular proteins. *Nature* 261: 552–558.

20. CATH public database Web site: http://www.biochem.ucl.ac.uk/bsm/cath/ The site includes references, algorithms, and a completely annotated set of three-dimensional protein structures.

21. Orengo C. A., Taylor W. R. 1996. SSAP: sequential structure alignment program for protein structure comparison. *Methods in Enzymology* 266: 617–35.

22. Taylor W. R., Flores T. P., Orengo C. A. 1994. Multiple protein structure alignment. *Protein Science* 3(10): 1858–70.

23. Taylor W. R., Orengo C. A. 1989. Protein structure alignment. *Journal of Molecular Biology* 208: 1–22.

24. Taylor W. R., Orengo C. A. 1989. A holistic approach to protein structure alignment. *Protein Engineering* 2(7): 505–19.

25. Harrison A., Pearl F., Mott R., Thornton J., Orengo C. 2002. Quantifying the similarities within fold space. *Journal of Molecular Biology* 323: 909–926.

26. Grindley H., Artymiuk P., Rice D., Willet P. 1993. Identification of tertiary structure resemblance in proteins using a maximal common sub-graph isomorphism algorithm. *Journal of Molecular Biology* 229: 707–721.

27. Murzin A., Brenner S., Hubbard T., Cyrus C. 1995. SCOP: A structural classification of proteins database for the investigation of sequences and structures. *Journal of Molecular Biology* 247: 536–540.

28. Conte L., Brenner S., Hubbard T., Chothia C., Murzin A. 2002. SCOP database in 2002. Refinements accommodate structural genomics. *Nucleic Acids Research* 30(1): 264–267.

29. Schonbrun J., Wedemeyer W. J., Baker D. 2002. Protein structure prediction in 2002. *Current Opinion in Structural Biology* 12: 348–354.

30. Gruebele M. 2002. Protein folding: the free energy surface. *Current Opinion in Structural Biology* 12: 161–168.

31. IBM Blue Gene Team. 2001. Blue gene: a vision for protein science using a petaflop supercomputer. *IBM Systems Journal* 40: 310.

32. Cornell W. D., et al.1995. A second generation force field for the simulation of proteins and nucleic acids. *Journal of the American Chemistry Society* 117: 5179–5197.

33. MacKerell A. D., et al. 1998. All atom empirical potential for molecular modeling and dynamics studies of proteins. *Journal of Physical Chemistry B* 102: 3586–3616.

34. Kaminski G. A., Friesner R. A., Tirado-Rives J., Jorgensen W. L. 2001. Evaluation and reparametrization of the OPLS-AA force field for proteins via comparison with accurate quantum chemical calculations on peptides. *Journal of Physical Chemistry B* 105: 6474.

35. Van Gunsteren W. F., Daura X., Mark A. E. 1998. GROMOS force field. *Encyclopaedia of Computational Chemistry, Vol. 2.*

36. Ulrich F., Hayer-Hartl M. 2002. Molecular chaperones in the cytosol: from nascent chain to folded protein. *Science* 295: 1852–1858.

37. Saibil H. R., Ranson N. A. 2002. The chaperonin folding machine. *Trends in Biochemical Sciences* 27(12): 627–632.

38. Crimi M., Degli Esposti M. 1991. Structural predictions for membrane proteins: the dilemma of hydrophobicity scales. *Trends in Biochemical Sciences* 16(3): 119.

39. Cserzo M., Bernassau J. M., Simon I., Maigret B. 1994. New alignment strategy for transmembrane proteins. *Journal of Molecular Biology* 243: 388–396.

40. Bowie J. U. 1997. Helix packing in membrane proteins. *Journal of Molecular Biology* 272: 780–789.

41. Zwick M. B., et al. 2001. Broadly neutralizing antibodies targeted to the membrane-proximal external region of human immunodeficiency virus type 1 glycoprotein gp41. *Journal of Virology* 75: 10892–10905.

42. Malenbaum S. E., Yang D., Cavacini L., Posner M., Robinson J., Cheng-Mayer C. 2000. The n-terminal v3 loop glycan modulates the interaction of clade A and B human immunodeficiency virus type 1 envelopes with CD4 and chemokine receptors. *Journal of Virology* 74: 11008–11016.

43. Ye Y. J., Si Z. H., Moore J. P., Sodroski J. 2000. Association of structural changes in the v2 and v3 loops of the gp120 envelope glycoprotein with acquisition of neutralization resistance in a simian-human immunodeficiency virus passaged in vivo. *Journal of Virology* 74: 11955–11962.

44. Poignard P., et al. 2001. GP120: Biologic aspects of structural features. *Annual Review of Immunology* 19: 253–274.

45. Milne, G. W. A., Nicklaus, M. C., Driscoll, J. S., Wang, S., Zaharevitz. D. 1994. The NCI Drug Information System 3D Database. *Journal of Chemical Information and Computer Sciences* 34: 1219–1224.

46. Ooms F. 2000. Molecular modeling and computer aided drug design. Examples of their applications in medicinal chemistry. *Current Medicinal Chemistry* 7: 141–158.

47. Waszkowycz B., Perkins T. D. J., Li J. 2001. Large-scale virtual screening for discovering leads in the postgenomic era. *IBM Systems Journal* 40(2): 360–376.

48. Augen J. 2002. The evolving role of information technology in the drug discovery process. *Drug Discovery Today* 7(5): 315–323.

8

Medical Informatics and Information-Based Medicine

INTRODUCTION

For centuries doctors have treated patients with a combination of knowledge, personal experience, and clinical observation. During the past 50 years, an accelerated understanding of sickness and health at the molecular level has dramatically advanced the field of clinical medicine by providing new and powerful diagnostics that extend the art of clinical observation.

Advances in information technology—most notably the infrastructure for storing and disseminating clinical information—are enabling a rapid acceleration of this trend. One of the most promising advances, grid computing, is likely to become a core component of the infrastructure that connects medical institutions to allow the sharing of clinical and research databases. Grid computing will become a true source of value creation for the medical community by providing three basic advantages: transparent access to geographically dispersed applications and computing resources, transparent access to geographically dispersed heterogeneous data, and multidisciplinary online collaboration.

This chapter discusses the infrastructure requirements that underlie a transition to information-based medicine. The chapter is intended as an introduction to the topic, which could easily fill the pages of a text devoted entirely to the subject. We will begin with a discussion of data-management frameworks and proceed to review the basic concepts underlying grid architecture. We have attempted to blend this discussion with a sense of the clinical issues surrounding electronic medical records and query systems for the clinical physician. This chapter closes with a forward-looking view of the potential benefits and complexities associated with presymptomatic disease testing.

THE CONTINUOUS EVOLUTION IN UNDERSTANDING THAT LEADS TO GENOMIC MEDICINE

In most sciences, as the body of knowledge expands so does the complexity of the overall picture. The life sciences are certainly no exception. In the early days of the genomic revolution, very little was known about the relationships between gene and protein sequences. Much of the puzzle has been unraveled; much remains to be discovered. Unfortunately, many of the most recent discoveries have accelerated the increase in complexity, and it has become clear that we still have a long way to go.

Some of the most recent discoveries have been the most surprising. For example, only three short years ago the one-gene-one-protein view of molecular biology was still intact and it was not yet apparent that both DNA strands contain protein-coding regions running in opposite directions. Today those views are outdated. This unique timeframe has witnessed many other fundamental shifts in our understanding as well. The list includes a complex regulatory network based on RNA interference; the role of translational variation and infidelity as a control point for protein structure; the realization that most messages in the cell are present in very low copy counts, and the recognition that small variations can have profound impacts on health and disease; the understanding that proteins are multifunctional, and that their activity is context-dependent; and the surprising abundance of single-nucleotide polymorphisms.

A slight expansion of our time horizon reveals many other substantial additions. These discoveries include, but certainly are not limited to, prions—small peptides capable of creating physiological state changes that ultimately cause a disease—and autocatalytic RNA molecules that can splice themselves into new forms. Each of these discoveries has added complexity to the overall picture while clarifying previously confusing observations. This expanding body of biological knowledge has begun to suggest both a data-management framework and a method for its growth.

TWO CLASSES OF RESEARCH

The taxonomy associated with this framework can be thought of as being built on two general classes: industrial-scale, high-throughput observation; and hypothesis-driven scientific research. Both categories are essential because, as we have seen, many sources of information are required to build a complete biochemical picture. Applications for combining and analyzing the information must also be comprehended in the design of the framework; these components are often referred to as components of a "tools" infrastructure. The framework must also include facilities for linking together disparate pieces of infrastructure, including a wide variety of heterogeneous databases.

High-throughput observation, the first major class, involves managing enormous amounts of data. Included are databases composed of gene and protein sequences, three-dimensional protein structures, mRNA expression profiles (microarray data), demographic data, and clinical medical records including medical images. Much of this information is generated using industrialized processes for gene sequencing, mRNA profiling, and x-ray crystallography; the majority of the clinical information is available as a consequence of medical record keeping. The second major class, hypothesis-driven scientific research, is composed of the constantly growing body of basic life sciences research results. The differences between the two are subtle but important. Industrialized processes are designed to systematically document a complete system; whole genome sequences are an obvious example. Conversely, quantification of the up and down regulation of a small population of messages in response to a specific treatment regimen would fall into the second category. Such experiments often generate a large amount of associated data and analysis; organizing and storing this information in a manner that facilitates retrieval represents one of the greatest challenges in modern biology.

Life sciences is unique in the sense that other sciences tend to be built almost entirely on a base of focused experimentation—high-throughput science is relatively rare. For example, astronomers frequently conduct spectral analysis of specific stars as part of focused research projects. However, there has never been an industrial scale project that gathered and stored spectral data from every observable star—today's database technologies cannot support a project of this magnitude.

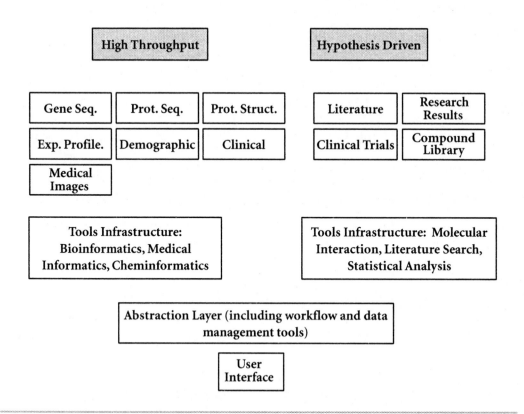

Figure 8-1 Data-analysis framework for information-based medicine. The highest level of the taxonomy includes two broad categories: high-throughput observation and hypothesis-driven scientific research. These data-storage categories are augmented with a tools infrastructure that includes bioinformatic algorithms and end-user applications for data analysis. Most end-user applications are linked to a specific data source (e.g., image-analysis software as part of a medical imaging database, sequence-alignment programs as part gene sequence database). The tools infrastructure must be "front-ended" with an interface that permits access across the full spectrum of data sources.

The combination of focused scientific research and high-throughput generalized observation has become a catalyst for building infrastructure for information-based medicine. A framework which embodies these concepts is depicted in Figure 8-1.

Implementing a data-management framework that supports the needs of both researchers and clinicians is logistically complex for several reasons:

- The data sources are heterogeneous in the sense that they include many different formats, structures, and data representations. Constructing a single interface to such a system is very complex. Furthermore, without some type of abstraction layer, individual researchers would need to become facile with several different query systems.

- The data sources that make up such an infrastructure are likely to be very large and geographically dispersed. The size and growth rate of these data sources makes duplication and distribution an unattractive solution.

- The distribution of clinical information across a widely available infrastructure presents difficult security challenges. Moreover, the system must be designed to defend against ingenious query strategies that can overcome many security measures. For example, a query that retrieves all patients over a certain age, with a certain illness, living in a particular zip code might refer to a single individual. Anonymity, in such a scenario, may be compromised regardless of the level of identity protection assigned to the record.

- The infrastructure must be designed to support computationally intense calculations. Examples include such diverse areas as medical image comparison, microarray analysis, and data-mining of clinical records. Because various parts of the infrastructure present different computational capabilities, the most effective solution is a grid design that can leverage the power of many machines regardless of physical location. (We see a more detailed discussion of grid infrastructure later in this chapter.)

- Many individual data sources are themselves distributed and must be combined into a single virtual view. A common example involves the virtualization of dispersed clinical databases that reside at multiple medical institutions. A researcher who needs to search these data sources must be presented with a single view that makes the geographical boundaries transparent.

- Standards for storing and retrieving medical data continue to evolve. Moreover, data structures and schemas are often proprietary and different equipment vendors adhere to different sets of rules.

- The vast amount of data spanning different phenotypes and genotypes is likely to create a combinatorial explosion that must be managed. The infrastructure must have enough capacity and bandwidth to handle experiments in the context of huge numbers of permutations.

The current state of computer and networking technology has allowed each of these challenges to be effectively addressed from a technical perspective. Unfortunately, many of the remaining barriers to the deployment of genomic medicine are political or economic in nature. The issues include such diverse problems as interinstitutional compensation, privacy, infrastructure cost, competitive pricing of clinical services, health insurance compensation, and ownership of the infrastructure.

RECENT TRENDS IN CLINICAL MEDICINE

Several forces and technical trends have come together to make possible this new approach to clinical medicine. Among the most significant are regular increases in density and decreases in the price of microarrays and other mRNA profiling technologies, the appearance of several promising high-throughput gene sequencing technologies, and the availability of new, fully digital diagnostic imaging systems (CAT, MRI, PET, x-ray, and diagnostic ultrasound systems). These advances have been accompanied by several new information technology trends such as ultra-low-latency networks, computer grids, advanced data-mining and pattern-discovery algorithms, and ultra-dense inexpensive storage.

As previously discussed, the past several years have witnessed unprecedented growth in the amount of available information about metabolic processes and the gene-expression patterns that control them. This information is having profound effects on the way patients are stratified and categorized, and diseases that appear phenotypically homogeneous are turning out to be very complex at the genetic level. Unfortunately, to date, this information explosion has had a very limited effect on the treatment of individual patients because there is no infrastructure to deliver the information and virtually no end-user tools to make the information accessible to researchers and clinicians. Even if the tools and infrastructure were to be made available, there are few standards for storing the information and no agreed-upon mechanisms for sharing data among medical institutions and research organizations.

The ability to mine databases of clinical and molecular-level information will be invaluable in creating new patient stratifications. Today most diseases are described phenotypically when, in reality, they are complex polygenic disorders with many subclasses. For example, psychiatric illnesses such as schizophrenia and depression should be thought of not as diseases but as phenotypes displayed by patients with many different gene-expression profiles, genome sequences, and medical histories. The specific combinations of these parameters will, someday, form the basis of a new classification scheme that will dramatically alter the meaning of health and disease with far-reaching implications for drug discovery and treatment. The first steps have already been taken, and it is time to begin building a shared infrastructure that promotes the practice of information-based medicine [1].

MOVING TOWARD INFORMATION-BASED MEDICINE

It is best to think about this shared infrastructure in phases. Phase one involves the definition and deployment of a fully paperless medical record. Despite the well-meaning efforts of many skilled architects and database experts, this initiative has not moved as quickly as one might imagine. The financial world, for example, has adopted a well-structured set of standards that enables recording, retrieving, and disseminating both financial information and money. Without these standards, it would not be possible to retrieve cash from an ATM machine or wire transfer funds between accounts. The medical community needs a similar set of standards for exchanging clinical and genomic information.

When a standard for paperless medical records becomes reality, the next phase will involve building links between institutions. These links are best described in terms of a communications and data-processing grid. After the links are in place, it will be possible to share large volumes of demographic and clinical information. Such sharing of information will soon become central to both treatment and research. Although information sharing has always been a core value in the research community, its virtues have not been as obvious on the treatment side. However, the ability to search large volumes of clinical information to compare treatment outcomes, demographic and clinical histories, and current disease parameters has the same potential to add value to the treatment side of the equation as to the research side. Realizing this value will require much in the way of pattern-discovery and related data-mining tools.

The next phase in the evolutionary timeline of information-based medicine involves linking clinical and research databases. The number of information resources that need to be included is impressive. All areas of biomedical research are appropriate because they are all interrelated. Many of these data sources include information about basic cellular processes in the form of gene sequences and expression profiles, protein interactions, known polymorphisms, protein structures, the results of ligand-binding experiments, and a variety of other biochemical and genetic details. On first glance it might appear that most of this information has limited clinical significance. However, that view is based on today's treatment regimens and patient stratifications rather than on tomorrow's more comprehensive metabolic-level views.

The scope and complexity of such systems coupled with a basic lack of standards necessitates that experiments proceed slowly. As a result, many academic research medical centers have begun to construct their own systems for delivering information-based medicine. Today these systems are important differentiators. As they become ubiquitous, however, we are likely to see broad acceptance and collaboration between institutions. Many technical challenges remain in closely related disciplines—one of the most significant being three-dimensional visualization of medical images and image processing across different modalities (e.g., PET, MRI, x-ray, and ultrasound).

The remainder of this chapter is devoted to various aspects of the problem with a focus on components of the infrastructure. We will begin at the core—electronic medical records.

ELECTRONIC MEDICAL RECORDS

Electronic medical records are central to the development of information-based medicine. The system architecture should comprehend three separate but related environments: clinical research, patient care, and clinical trials. Several characteristics are critical. For example, the record must be extensible in the sense that it can be upgraded with new information gathered with future technologies—most notably, high-throughput gene sequencing. Several promising low-cost, but rapid, DNA sequencing technologies have emerged; each has the potential to facilitate whole genome sequencing at the individual patient level. Likewise, dramatic reductions in microarray pricing are likely to fuel ongoing mRNA profiling. Because profiling will ultimately become part of a routine medical exam, records should be structured to allow for tremendous growth.

Unfortunately, the adoption of standards for digital medical records has been slow. Unlike other industries (e.g., financial, telecommunications, and broadcasting), a robust set of standards for storing, retrieving, and transmitting medical information has not emerged. Surprisingly, this problem is as pervasive in traditional areas of medicine as it is in new areas. The problem manifests itself in several ways. For example, although many of the newest imaging techniques generate large amounts of valuable raw data, it has become common practice to process these data into final images and subsequently discard the raw data. Unfortunately, much of the value embodied by the raw data is related to the variety of *in silico* experiments that are possible. As image-processing algorithms improve, the value of these experiments is likely to increase. This value can never be realized if the original information is lost.

The trend is not confined to clinical medicine. Gene sequencing experiments also generate large amounts of raw data in the form of "trace files" which contain the detailed spectral data from the sequencing machines. These data, which occupy large amounts of storage, are often destroyed after the sequence is confirmed. However, as in the earlier imaging example, there is no substitute for the raw data. Researchers can often benefit by returning to the original spectral data to verify a particular base. If the spectra are missing, the identity of the base can be determined only by resequencing.

THE NEED FOR STANDARDS

The clinical world, however, is not totally without data-management standards. Perhaps the most widely accepted clinical data messaging standard is Health Level-7 (HL-7). Initiated in 1986, HL-7 is a cooperative effort between healthcare providers and technology vendors. It describes a set of rules for moving clinical and associated administrative data (orders, referrals, test results, administrative information, etc.) between systems. Another widely adopted standard, Digital Imaging and Communications in Medicine (DICOM), represents a joint effort of the American College of Radiology and the National Electrical Manufacturers Association. DICOM is the underlying data-storage standard in most imaging systems routinely referred to as PACS systems (Picture Archiving and Communications Systems). In addition, the U.S. Department of Health and Human Services has recently agreed to license a medical vocabulary system known as SNOMED Clinical Terms (SNOMED CT) from the College of American Pathologists as a step toward establishing a common medical language. SNOMED contains terms for more than 340,000 medical conditions and concepts in addition to constructs that facilitate capturing, sharing, and aggregating health data across clinical specialties [2, 3].

These systems and designs represent excellent attempts at creating universally accepted standards, and they have advanced the field tremendously. However, the scope and extensibility required to support information-based medicine implies a much broader set of standards. Furthermore, whereas today's electronic medical records are designed around individual patients, future systems must be designed to support statistical analysis across patient groups. This single difference has become a significant barrier to institutions attempting to migrate from first-generation online clinical systems to more-complex designs that support information-based medicine. The major difference is that first-generation systems—those commonly used today—are designed to facilitate searching individual patient records. Such systems rarely support data-mining experiments across large populations of records. Even when cross-record queries are supported, the level of sophistication is often limited to very simple questions. Cross-database joins, free-text mining, and queries containing schema mismatches are unlikely to be supported by the majority of today's systems.

Figure 8-2 depicts the relative differences in complexity between current and next-generation electronic medical record systems. As you can see in the figure, current systems are designed to manage individual patient records. Next-generation systems are designed to support complex queries and constructs that span large populations of patient medical records.

LIMITATIONS OF TODAY'S ELECTRONIC MEDICAL RECORD SYSTEMS

Most of today's electronic medical record systems are computerized representations of paper records. In most cases, a patient's record is organized into screen pages, each corresponding to a category of information one would expect to find in a traditional paper medical record. The list of pages typically includes, but is not limited to, clinical history,

Find all patients:

Age 50 - 60
Evidence of aveolar bone loss
Elevated CRP, total cholesterol
Non-smoking
Alcohol consumption < 5 drinks/week
Blood pressure > 150 systolic, 95 diastolic
BMI - overweight
Elevated plasminogen activator

Sort by total serum cholesterol, BMI

Find all patients:

Admitted since Jan 2000
Age 50 - 60
Diagnostic history of aveolar bone loss
Diagnostic history of cardiovascular disease

Figure 8-2 Relative differences in complexity between supported queries in current and next-generation electronic medical record systems.

including diseases and allergies, vaccinations, medication history, physician encounter history, special alerts, family history, basic demographic information, lab results, and associated medical images. Additionally, most systems are designed to be extensible in the sense that they can contain ancillary information in the form of free text.

Unfortunately, these systems suffer from two major deficiencies: They are not designed to be extended with molecular-level information—gene sequences, mRNA profiles, and protein-interaction studies—and the underlying databases are not normally built with a robust set of relational links that can be used to discover subtle relationships between the records. These deficiencies must be addressed in the construction of databases that support more complex initiatives.

For example, consider the following representative (but highly unusual) query:

Find all patients with:

- Coronary artery disease
- Diabetes mellitus
- Nonalcoholic steatohepatitis
- Who had a breast biopsy
- In Zip code 55901, 55902, 55903, 55904
- Between 45 and 65 years of age
- Who are female
- And are alive

To execute such a search, an electronic medical record system would need to support a variety of constructs. First it must contain indices that link the records by disease categories—coronary artery disease, diabetes mellitus, and nonalcoholic steatohepatitis in the example. One might be tempted to solve this problem by creating individual databases for each major disease category and sorting patient records into the individual databases. Unfortunately, however, such hierarchies are inflexible and difficult to program around. In the example, we would be faced with the problem of choosing between coronary artery disease and diabetes mellitus as a primary category. A more-sensible approach involves structuring each record to support multiple diseases and building indices for each disease field.

The second requirement relates to linkages between patient records and other databases such as billing systems. The query refers to several nonmedical data items—age, sex, Zip code. Because a patient needs to have only a single Zip code, age, and sex on record, these pieces of information can be stored as part of a more-static record that stays constant in size but is routinely updated. Some of these items might appear in a billing database, for example. If such items are kept separate from the medical record, external joins between these data sources and the medical record must be supported.

Of course, the medical record must be accurate and up-to-date, even when the patient has not visited a medical institution for some time. Without such updates, it would be impossible to correctly respond to the query because we would not know whether the patient is still alive. Furthermore, reading each record in the database to answer each portion of the query is clearly inefficient.

OVERCOMING THE LIMITATIONS OF TODAY'S ELECTRONIC MEDICAL RECORD SYSTEMS

To overcome these limitations, the overall structure of an electronic medical record system must take into account the nature of the queries that are likely to be asked. These requirements imply a more-complex structure than would be appropriate for a first-generation online medical records system. Moreover, the structure must be flexible enough to respond to future research needs. The most logical approach involves building an abstraction layer that sits between the query tool and the databases. This abstraction layer should be designed to hide the complexity of the underlying system of databases and links.

Whether medical records are used for clinical comparison or scientific research, the data should be anonymized to protect each patient's privacy. Moreover, many jurisdictions have statutory requirements for the protection of patient privacy, and it typically makes sense to design systems that adhere to the most stringent standards. The anonymization scheme must be designed to preserve patient identities without compromising security by making these identities available through experimental queries. This confusing conflict stems from the need to balance the clinical needs of individual patients with the advantages that accrue from statistical studies. A simple solution to the problem involves building duplicate databases that do not contain unique patient identifiers. However, as mentioned previously, removing direct patient identifiers is sometimes insufficient to prevent positive identification through statistical analysis. The solution is to build an "obfuscation" layer into the query system that filters responses that uniquely identify an individual. Conversely, because medical care is provided under a variety of social, economic, and political systems around the world, privacy issues are highly variable.

A hypothetical structure that includes various links and interfaces is described in Figure 8-3.

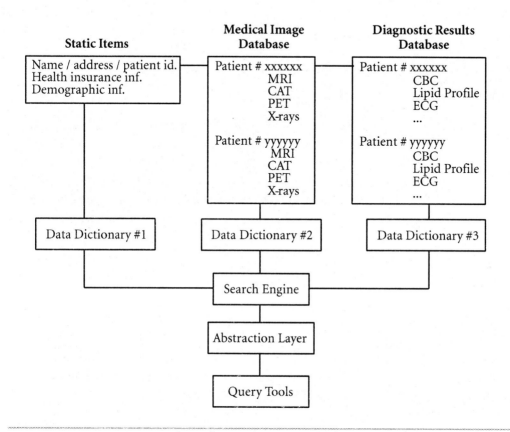

Figure 8-3 Logical structure of an online medical records system designed to support information-based medicine. Items that do not grow in size may become part of a more static database that is updated to reflect current status. Clinical items are included as part of an electronic record that grows substantially in size. Relational links between the records and a structure that permits external joins between data sources are central design points of the system. Query tools, an abstraction layer that hides logical complexity, and a data dictionary that supports the search engine are all central to the design.

HEALTH INFORMATION PORTABILITY AND ACCOUNTABILITY ACT

The U.S. statutory law for protection of personal privacy as it relates to medical records—HIPAA (Health information Portability and Accountability Act)—defines specific items that are considered confidential. The goal is to prevent "re-identification" of individuals through the analysis of multiple data items. All healthcare organizations will be required to comply with these regulations by April 15, 2005.

Examples of database items that must be anonymized under HIPAA rules include the following:

- Names must be removed or replaced with aliases.
- Addresses must not contain specific information about geographic subdivisions smaller than state.
- Statistical anomalies such that allow specific identification must be removed (i.e., if a town has three individuals born in 1900 and only one has a medical record, this record must not be identifiable).
- Date elements other than year that relate to a specific individual.
- Photographs, telephone numbers, social security numbers, e-mail addresses, medical record numbers, bank account numbers.
- Diagnostic-device serial numbers.

Compliance with HIPAA is challenging because the rules as stated are relatively broad and best-practices guidelines have not yet been developed. As a result, efforts are underway to develop technical standards that foster HIPAA compliance. Interestingly, one of the most visible is being driven by the National Institute of Standards and Technology (NIST). European nations and Canada have also created laws that govern the collection, use, and disclosure of personal medical information.

Although central to the overall system, databases of clinical records represent one of many data sources that combine to form a complex infrastructure. One important theme behind this design is connectivity between institutions. Even today's largest medical centers cannot treat a broad enough patient population to make their records the basis for a complete system. Information-based medicine must be based on millions of records spanning hundreds of disease categories. Patients must come from diverse backgrounds that span a broad range of genotypes, and for each genotype the system must include enough records to generate statistically significant information.

A necessary goal of personalized medicine is the creation of accurate patient stratifications. For each phenotype, there is likely to be a large number of genetically distinct subclasses. These subclasses are important because, although they might have the same disease, they are not likely to respond the same way to various treatments. For example, a melanocyte-specific gene, Melastatin (MLSN1), is known to show an inverse correlation between mRNA expression and metastatic potential in human melanoma cell lines [4]. Melastatin mRNA expression in primary cutaneous melanoma has also been found to correlate with disease-free survival. Like all correlations, the relationship is not perfect. However, it is clear that Melastatin mRNA expression correlates with melanocytic tumor progression, melanoma tumor thickness, and the potential for melanoma metastasis [5].

It also represents an important diagnostic for building patient stratifications. Melanoma patients expressing low levels of Melastatin are more likely to experience life-threatening metastases than patients with high levels. Expression levels of this one gene can form the basis of a stratification that helps define different treatments for patients who would otherwise be classified as having the same illness. For the analysis to be complete, however, many other parameters must also be compared. A complete picture is likely to include Melastatin mRNA levels along with a variety of other physical, clinical, and demographic parameters, including mRNA profiles for other related genes. It might, for example, also be important to understand intracellular responses to various classes of drugs after the decision has been made to follow an aggressive course of treatment. Furthermore, Melastatin gene expression can be regulated either at the level of transcription or mRNA processing; several different Melastatin mRNA species have been identified. Given enough data, these different species might also imply additional substratification of tumors and patients [6].

Each of these discoveries must be analyzed in the context of large amounts of clinical data collected from diverse patient populations. In addition, analyzing these data requires seamless connectivity to other data sources, many of which are in the public domain. The infrastructure for information-based medicine must support this connectivity. For a variety of reasons, which are outlined next, the design of choice is likely to be based on compute and data grids.

GRID COMPUTING AND MEDICAL INFORMATICS

A complex infrastructure will be required to make personalized medicine effective. Because information will be collected at hundreds of sites, the first step will be to connect computer resources at these sites in a grid-based design. A grid can be thought of as a collection of geographically distributed computing resources that are not under central control, but interact through open protocols and standards to accomplish real work.

Computer grids are emerging as an architecture for building large shared systems of heterogeneous computers, operating environments, and networks. There are two major classes of grid infrastructure: computational grids and data grids. Both will be required to support personalized medicine. For example, to store and distribute the millions of medical images that accumulate each year, a data grid that links large imaging systems at major medical centers must be made available. After the images are freely available to clinicians, it will be necessary to create a tools infrastructure containing software for comparing and analyzing images. This software is constantly evolving, and it will soon be possible to compare different modalities (e.g., PET and CAT scans) when making a diagnosis. The more images available, the more precise each diagnosis will be. Someday, in the not-too-distant future, doctors will compare medical images of their patients to millions of other images and fast pattern-matching algorithms capable of spotting similar images will be used in conjunction with other clinical information to identify close matches. Information contained in the medical records of these matching patients will be used to select the best treatment and predict outcomes.

Likewise, it will be necessary to obtain base sequence information and ongoing gene-expression patterns for patients—both healthy and ill. The collection of gene-expression profiles will occupy an enormous amount of storage space and, because data will be collected across many time points, algorithms for comparing mRNA expression profiles in a time-dependent fashion will form a core component of the clinical tool set. Doctors treating patients for specific illnesses will collect all relevant clinical, demographic, and gene-expression data and, using pattern-matching algorithms, identify patients that are similar. As previously mentioned, information at the DNA level will also be critical in such comparisons, especially polymorphisms that are known to be the basis for many disease states. During the next few years, high-throughput sequencing techniques supported by a new generation of fragment-assembly algorithms are likely to make the collection of complete genome sequences a reality for most individuals. The computer infrastructure to support this endeavor will be significant and local to each medical institution. Results from sequencing operations are likely to be shared in a data grid in the same way as the images mentioned previously.

The infrastructure must be designed to support both queries and updates to the records. However, although an individual medical record is transactional in nature, the majority of the data in the system can be updated at regular intervals. Two distinct design schemes are plausible:

- In the first scenario, each patient has a single medical record housed at one site. These local systems are both online and transactional. Local updates to each record are regularly replicated to a larger broadly available system with names and patient identifiers removed. The larger system includes older, nonactive records and other historical data. These larger databases, although local to each institution, are shared across a grid infrastructure. The fact that all data for an individual patient is housed at one site should be transparent to healthcare providers using the system to view and add data.

- In the second scenario, individual medical records are distributed across all institutions participating in the system. A patient's treatment records and test results reside at the various locations where service was rendered. In effect, this design mirrors today's nonelectronic medical record systems, where a patient may see many different healthcare providers and have as many different medical records. The number of locations and size of the records tends to grow over time. Individual caregivers, however, need not be aware of the distributed nature of the records because they are presented with a virtual view of the data that erases the perception of nonlocality. This virtual view can be accomplished in real time by linking the data sources under one interface, or all of the data for an individual patient can be gathered from various sites to create a temporary local record. New diagnostic data, images, and physicians comments are entered into the temporary local record prior to being distributed to appropriate remote sites and verified. After the system confirms all additions, the temporary record is erased. As in the first scenario, each site regularly replicates data to its larger research system, and the replication process renders each record anonymous by removing patient identifiers and names.

GRID INFRASTRUCTURE DESIGN CHARACTERISTICS

The term *grid* refers to a distributed computing infrastructure for solving advanced, computationally intensive problems or managing geographically distributed data. Both elements are present in solutions that support information-based medicine. Grids are built on a single underlying theme—coordinated resource sharing and problem solving in dynamic, multi-institutional virtual organizations. Unlike other physical and logical designs that focus on file sharing, grid computing is designed to provide direct access to computing resources, storage, and software. As one might expect, sharing is carefully controlled. What is shared, who is allowed access, and under what conditions that access can occur are some of the elements involved. The set of individuals and institutions defined by the sharing rules is typically referred to as a virtual organization (VO) [7].

The technologies for building and managing VOs complement many other networking and communications technologies. For example, elements of compute grids are often connected across the Internet. Because each institution connected by a compute grid is likely to pursue its own standards for platform design, grids tend to take on a highly heterogeneous nature with regard to hardware and operating environments. Furthermore, compute clusters containing distributed applications and databases often reside at various locations throughout the infrastructure.

Effective VO operation requires the establishment of effective data-sharing relationships between participants. These relationships must appear transparent to users regardless of the design of their local infrastructure. As a result, interoperability between heterogeneous systems quickly surfaces as the central issue that must be addressed in the design of a grid. Extending this thinking leads to the conclusion that a grid architecture is equivalent to a protocol architecture. Like many designs, grid architectures are layered. Each of the layers is described in the following sections.

Fabric Layer—The Interface to Local Control

The fabric layer is composed of computing resources: storage systems, catalogues, network devices, etc. Resources can be logical entities such as distributed file systems, or physical entities such as clusters of computers. Components of the fabric implement local, resource-specific operations that result from sharing operations at higher levels. Various mechanisms are embodied in the fabric layer, such as the procedures for starting and stopping programs, writing and reading files, reserving network devices, and issuing queries or updates to remote databases.

Connectivity Layer—The Basis for Efficient and Secure Communication

Grid-specific network transactions originate in the connectivity layer, which embodies rules for authentication and network-based transactions. Authentication protocols provide leverage communication services to provide encryption services and methods for verifying the identity of a particular user. Communication requirements include transport, routing, and naming. Authentication solutions for VO environments must include mechanisms that simplify access to shared resources. For example, users must be able to log on to the system once and gain access to shared data that spans multiple sites. It is particularly important for an individual user to be able to combine various sources into a virtual record without the explicit cooperation of the individual data providers. In addition, each site must be able to integrate with the security systems located at various points in the grid. Each user must also have the capability of launching a program or query that runs on his/her behalf. The program also must be able to access all resources authorized for the user.

Resource Layer—The Ability to Share Single Compute Resources

The resource layer builds on communication and authentication protocols to provide application programming interfaces (APIs) for secure initiation, monitoring, and access control at the single-device level. Resource layer protocols can be divided into two groups; information protocols and management protocols. Information protocols are used to obtain information about the structure and state of a device. This information might include the device's configuration, workload, or usage policy. Management protocols are used to negotiate access to shared resources. This access normally follows a set of rules that varies between individuals. Management protocols, which are used to negotiate access to shared resources, normally specify such resource requirements as advanced reservation or quality of service and a description of the operation to be performed (e.g., data access). Because management protocols are the point of instantiation of data-sharing relationships, they are also a logical gateway for the application of policies and rules.

Whereas the fabric layer embodies a broad set of standards that can vary across a large number of operating environments, connectivity and resource layers tend to be restricted to a much more concise set of definitions. The underlying layer (also known as the collective layer) exhibits a variety of services and application-specific behaviors. It also embodies a large number of protocols and standards relative to the connectivity and resource layers. As a result, diagrams describing the overall structure of a grid are often represented as an hourglass. The neck of the hourglass includes connectivity and resource layer protocols; fabric layer protocols describing resources sit below; and a wide range of services and application-specific behaviors reside at the top.

Collective Layer—Coordination of Multiple Resources

The collective layer contains protocols and services that are global in nature and designed to capture interactions across a variety of resources—hence the designation *collective*. The following list contains representative collective layer protocols:

- **Directory services** enable VO participants to discover the existence and properties of resources throughout the grid. Many directory services enable users to query for resources by name or description.

- **Scheduling services** enable users to request the allocation of one or more resources for a particular purpose, and to schedule a task for execution on those resources.
- **Data-replication services** support the management of virtual storage to maximize data-access performance.
- **Grid-enabled programming systems** are designed to support familiar programming models in a grid environment. Key services allow various programming systems to support resource discovery/allocation and grid-security policies.
- **Collaboratory services** support the coordinated exchange of information within the VO community (synchronous or asynchronous).
- **Security services** support authentication, authorization, confidentiality, nonrepudiation, audit, data integrity, and service availability (i.e., prevention of denial-of-service attacks).
- **System management services** provide facilities for managing data objects, business objects, exception handling, alerts, and backup/recovery operations.

Unlike resource layer protocols, which must be generalized to support a wide variety of systems, collective layer protocols tend to be specific to a service in the context of a specific VO environment. Most are highly domain- and application-specific. In some cases, collective layer functions are implemented as persistent services.

Application Layer—The End-User Environment

The application layer represents the top of the grid environment and the only component immediately visible to the end user. Grid applications are designed to call services defined by the lower layers, and many nongrid applications can be grid-enabled by adding references to specific interfaces defined at these levels.

Technical applications tend to fall into two broad classes that need to be addressed in the design of a grid: data-intensive and compute-intensive. Data-intensive applications are normally I/O bound because the largest fraction of their execution time is spent moving data across the grid. Data intensiveness can be evaluated by measuring "computational bandwidth"—the number of bytes processed per floating point or integer operation. As a reference point, large supercomputing applications often transfer seven bytes of data from memory for each floating-point operation. Well-balanced applications should be designed to balance memory bandwidth against CPU execution rate [8]. However, because memory often acts as a cache for disk storage, it is not uncommon for the transfer rates between disk and memory to be several hundred times smaller than the transfer rates between memory and CPU.

Unfortunately, even well-balanced data-intensive applications can be problematic in a grid infrastructure because the bandwidth of the grid is often insufficient to support large data transfers between systems. The solution is to intelligently distribute components of data-intensive applications so that they reside as close as possible to the storage systems they will be addressing. The simple task of searching a large database of patient medical records to create a data set that meets certain criteria is an excellent example of a data-intensive problem. The number and length of such records makes the data-transfer problem formidable, whereas the CPU time required to check each record against a set of simple criteria is unlikely to become a bottleneck. When such searches are conducted across a grid, the search application would perform best if launched on local machines at each site where records are stored. A central application at the end-user site must then consolidate the search results.

Conversely, compute-intensive applications tend to consume large amounts of CPU time, often on many different machines, but transfer relatively small amounts of data. Such applications may be composed predominantly of floating-point calculations (e.g., microarray analysis, protein folding, and molecular docking) or integer calculations (e.g., sequence comparison, text searching, and gene-expression pattern recognition). Because these applications normally do not require excessive disk/memory/CPU bandwidth, they are readily executed in a grid environment without regard to locality. Moreover, serial comparisons of sequences or expression array data can often be accelerated by distributing the calculation across many machines. In such situations, it makes sense to cache sequence data on each machine involved in the task. This strategy is often used to distribute sequence-homology problems across compute clusters.

Not surprisingly, such designs scale well in grid environments where the cluster is geographically dispersed because the limitations imposed by the bandwidth of the grid are not significant to the total time of the calculation. However, excessive division of such a problem across a very large number of machines can drive up the demand for bandwidth. The "graininess" of the solution should take several parameters into account (e.g., processing capability of each machine, complexity of the calculation, bandwidth of the grid, memory size available for caching, geographical distribution of the problem, and possibilities for redistributing the workload).

IMPLEMENTING SUCCESSFUL GRID COMPUTING

Because of their complexity, successful grid computing implementations are unlikely to result from the "vertically" oriented efforts of a single vendor. Recognizing the business value of collaboration, many hardware and software companies have teamed up to create a set of standards that defines every level of the architecture from simple switches and connections to high-level software components that manage traffic and computing resources. The effort is collectively recognized as a single organization—the Global Grid Forum (GGF). Working together, the members of GGF have produced a framework that has come to be known as the Open Grid Services Architecture (OGSA).

The OGSA represents an evolution toward a grid system architecture based on Web services concepts and technologies. It defines a uniform set of exposed service semantics (the grid service) and standard mechanisms for creating, naming, and discovering transient grid service instances. The architecture also supports location transparency and integration with a variety of underlying platform facilities.

A set of OGSA-compliant software tools—the Globus Toolkit—has also been developed. The tools, which are based on an open, broadly compatible architecture, include a set of set of services and software libraries designed to support grids and grid applications. Issues of security, information discovery, resource management, data-management, communication, and portability are all addressed by components of the Globus Toolkit [9]. Through the combined efforts of dozens of software and hardware vendors, OGSA and the Globus Toolkit continue to evolve. Projects building on the Globus toolkit range from scientific collaborations concerned with remote access to specialized experimental facilities. Grids have supported such diverse applications as earthquake simulation, theoretical particle physics, and the analysis of millions of digital mammograms.

Grid Computing in Drug Discovery

Despite its recent emergence, grid computing has already become a true source of value creation for the drug-discovery business. For example, scientists at the U.S. National Cancer Institute were recently able to combine the computational horsepower of more than 8,000 individual machines to create a virtual supercomputer that was used to evaluate the anticancer potential of more than 500 million molecules. The simulations identified several potential inhibitors of two proteins known to act as control points in cellular development.

The first protein, ras, is involved in signal transduction, normal proliferation, and cell-cycle progression. Mutated versions of the three human ras genes have been detected in 30% of all human cancers, implying an important role for aberrant ras function in carcinogenesis. Ras mutations are highly prevalent in pancreatic (90%), lung (40%), and colorectal (50%) carcinomas, and aberrant ras function is believed to contribute to the development of at least a major subset of these neoplasms [10].

The second protein, VEGFr (vascular endothelial growth factor receptor), is important for vascular development. Both the VEGFr full-length gene product and a variety of associated splice variants are known to play critical roles in angiogenesis; early mutations in the VEGFr gene result in lethality due to a disorganization of blood vessels and an overgrowth of endothelial-like cells. Because rapidly growing tumors are known to display a high degree of sensitivity to compounds that block vascular development, VEGFr has long been considered a promising antineoplastic target [11].

In all, 39 promising molecules were identified from the 500 million screened. Although researchers anticipated that fewer than 3% of the promising molecules would inhibit the growth of cancer cells, the actual success rate was much higher—more than 20%. In the future, information-based medicine initiatives will enhance this process by allowing researchers to further screen compounds for toxicity and efficacy against known gene-expression profiles both of the patient and tumor [12].

It is important to note that a true broad-based personalized medicine initiative on the scale we have been discussing will drive the generation of huge amounts of data and data-transmission traffic. For example, if 60% of women in the appropriate age range comply with recommendations to have an annual mammogram, at 160 megabytes per exam, the annual volume would exceed 5.6 petabytes (5.6×10^{15} bytes) in the United States alone. Furthermore, these data are likely to be stored at a large number of geographically dispersed locations. Because analysis of the information necessarily involves moving records among distantly connected systems, the demand for transmission bandwidth will scale with the number of researchers and physicians using the infrastructure.

The use of such systems to screen and test compounds represents an important aspect of the continuum from drug discovery to information-based medicine. However, such a system cannot realize its full potential in the absence of a large number of clinical records. The angiogenesis case described earlier is an excellent illustration of this concept because individual patients always differ with regard to their responses to any treatment. Correlating these responses with clinical, demographic, and genetic parameters is critical to proper patient stratification; such analysis is the ultimate determinant of the efficacy of a particular compound. At the time of this writing, more than 60 antiangiogenesis drugs are currently undergoing clinical trial. They include naturally occurring substances (mostly proteins), newly designed synthetics, traditional chemotherapeutic agents, and other medicines that have been unexpectedly discovered to have antiangiogenesis characteristics. Most of these compounds work best when used in concert with other chemotherapeutic agents.

Furthermore, different tumors respond differently for a variety of complex reasons. One of the most critical factors seems to be related to the developmental stage of the disease; complex relationships exist between the stage of a tumor and its sensitivity to certain compounds. A given drug can block early-stage development of some tumors and late-stage development of others. Conversely, a given tumor may display a high level of sensitivity to some drugs during early-stage development and others during later stages [13]. These complex relationships must also be superimposed on the broader metabolic and genetic differences that characterize each patient population.

Because the complete solution will require access to other data such as mRNA profiles and detailed clinical histories, the actual size of the required infrastructure will tend to grow exponentially over time. This dramatic growth is becoming a principal driver of grid infrastructure in the life sciences.

MODELING AND PREDICTING DISEASE

A complete description of almost any disease is likely to include clinical symptoms, relevant medical history, gene-expression data and base genotype, a wide variety of metabolic parameters, and treatment results expressed partly with regard to their effects on each of the above (with the possible exception of base genotype). Furthermore, the monitoring process should optimally begin long before the onset of disease. Such early monitoring provides a set of baseline measurements that ultimately becomes a valuable source of controls for the entire process. This approach is relevant regardless of the disease category; even infectious diseases are affected by various genotypic and metabolic parameters.

PRESYMPTOMATIC TESTING

Presymptomatic testing refers to a strategy for predicting the onset of metabolic diseases based on detectable, but subclinical, chemical changes and genetic predispositions. Such changes often involve increased levels of marker proteins or expressed messages. Not surprisingly, the same kinds of changes are often detectable between the time of initial exposure to a pathogen and the appearance of symptoms. Presymptomatic testing may be particularly valuable during this timeframe in situations where early intervention can prevent the disease. For example, an individual who has been exposed to variola virus—the pathogen responsible for smallpox—can be protected by vaccination within three days of exposure. (Vaccination within seven days of exposure will offer some degree of protection and reduce the severity of symptoms [14].) The initial process involves infection of macrophages and migration to regional lymph nodes. The virus then replicates at multiple sites, including spleen, lymph nodes, and skin.

This discussion has two focal points: identification of presymptomatic molecular events in an infected individual and the direct identification of microorganisms and other pathogens. Both are relevant to the deployment of information-based medicine. Fortunately, high-throughput sequencing initiatives have begun to drive the distribution of large amounts of sequence information for a variety of microorganisms and viruses. Furthermore, complete sequences are often not required. One excellent example is an initiative launched by Dupont Qualicon (a Wilmington, Delaware-based subsidiary of Dupont Inc.). The goal of this initiative is to collect and disseminate ribosomal DNA fingerprints for as many microorganisms as possible. The fingerprints are collected using restriction enzyme digestion and an automated system called ribotyping. In most cases, ribotypes are specific enough to distinguish between strains of bacteria that have undergone mutation—an important capability for tracking the migration of new bacterial strains around the globe and for treating individual patients who are infected with a drug-resistant organism. The latter is often the result of a newly mutated antibiotic-resistant bacterium finding its way to a new geographic location. A worldwide database of known pathogens that includes clinical information would be invaluable for treating such patients. Standard techniques are used to create new fingerprints, which are then matched against the database using pattern-identification software.

Presymptomatic Testing for Viral and Bacterial Infections

The identification of presymptomatic molecular events in infected individuals is likely to become relevant in situations where infection is suspected and the individual has a reason to be tested. In such situations, databases of diagnostic information that link a specific set of immune system parameters and other metabolic responses to a specific infection are likely to provide enormous value. Until the present time, such databases have not been widely available, and presymptomatic testing for viral and bacterial infections has been limited to simple diagnostic observations—various cell counts and antibody titers.

Presymptomatic Testing for Metabolic Diseases

Presymptomatic testing for metabolic diseases is complex because it involves measuring a large number of molecular-level parameters and their interactions. One might envision a straightforward process that includes initial genotyping, baseline measurements of key metabolic parameters, and ongoing measurement of these parameters based on a profile of known risk factors. More sophisticated analyses might include demographic history, family medical history, and a variety of environmental factors. Observed changes are used to track the progression from health to disease.

Surprisingly, access to a robust set of databases containing all relevant information and an appropriate set of search tools is insufficient to guarantee the success of presymptomatic testing. The reason is related to the level of precision that is required for meaningful comparisons. For example, mRNA profiles built using microarray technologies are subject to many sources of error. First, it must be noted that all measurements utilizing two-color fluorescence are measures of the relative gene-expression levels between control and experimental populations. Most researchers report results in terms of relative fold changes. The data can be normalized only if intensity measurements arising from both control and experimental samples are precisely proportional to the levels of each species of mRNA being measured. Unfortunately, such experiments embody many sources of systematic error, including background fluorescence, differences between the relative response to laser excitation of the two dyes used for control and experimental samples, differences in the incorporation frequency of the dye-labeled bases during reverse transcription, and quenching effects that reduce the signal when fluorescence intensity exceeds certain levels. Most of these errors can be quantified and corrected; however, one source of error that is difficult to manage involves cross hybridization between unrelated genes that share similar sequences. Furthermore, both protein- and gene-expression levels must be quantified across a relatively large dynamic range from individual molecules to tens of thousands of copies. Traditional tools are notoriously inaccurate across such ranges.

Making Presymptomatic Testing Work

The strategy of comparing gene- or protein-expression profiles to a database of known profiles can be effective only if all measurements involve a high degree of precision. One approach involves very precise control over all reagents and tools in addition to stringent rules regarding handling of samples. For any given disease, a diagnostic panel can be constructed that includes a large number of protein- or gene-expression levels. The logistics of constructing and using such a panel are outlined here:

1. Measurements of various protein and gene-expression levels are collected from a large population of individuals over an extended period of time. The data must span timeframes that include the transition into a disease state for a statistically significant number of patients. The transition is determined using standard clinical parameters.

2. When a clinical transition is detected, data for this patient and timeframe are set aside for further analysis.

3. Each individual data item is examined to determine whether its expression level correlates with the clinical transition. Some items will be up regulated and some will be down regulated. Most will not present a statistically significant correlation with the clinical transition in question.

4. A new panel is constructed using only those items that strongly correlate with the clinical transition.

5. The new panel is tested against a large population of healthy individuals with the goal of presymptomatically predicting the onset of disease. The results for each patient, including clinical records, are kept in a database along with the results for each panel at each point in time.

A similar strategy can be used to study drug responses. A typical panel might depict the rise and fall of various proteins or messages in response to exposure to certain drugs or treatment regimens. Additionally, drug responses are notoriously time-dependent, and each component of the panel is likely to display a unique set of time-dependent characteristics. Figure 8-4 depicts typical response curves for three different messages to a single dose of prednisone. The goal is to build a database containing a large number of panels composed of such response curves with direct links to clinical information. Such systems can be used to predict an individual's response to treatment with any drug that has been profiled in the database.

The process of reducing a large number of items down to a simple panel, which preserves only the most significant data items, is not completely straightforward because the up and down regulation of individual items may vary from one patient subclass to another. Part of the process, therefore, involves the identification of new disease groupings that can be distinguished using differences in the panels. The overall process is nearly identical to the various clustering methods previously described for use with microarray data. However, because the current discussion focuses on an unknown number of previously unclassified subgroups, the problem is significantly more complex.

An emerging strategy involves the use of pattern-recognition software to identify the most relevant items and subpopulations of patients. This strategy was recently used to

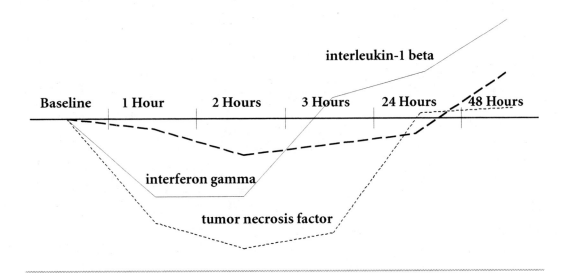

Figure 8-4 Typical response profiles for three circulating proteins—interleukin-1 beta (IL-1B), tumor necrosis factor (TNF), and interferon gamma (INFG)—following treatment with prednisone. Each displays a characteristic pattern of time-dependent changes. Databases containing clinical information linked to response patterns can be used as a diagnostic tool to predict efficacy of the drug in particular individuals. A typical panel might monitor dozens of proteins. (Source: Source Precision Medicine, Boulder, Colorado)

apply high-throughput proteomic profiling to the detection of early-stage ovarian cancers. Relevant serum-based protein levels were measured using mass spectrometry (surface-enhanced laser desorption ionization spectroscopy—SELDI), and self-learning pattern-recognition programs were used to identify the most relevant data items [15]. The preliminary training set was derived from analysis of serum samples obtained from 50 unaffected women and 50 clinically diagnosed patients. Using these data, the algorithm was able to unambiguously identify a proteomic pattern that completely discriminated between healthy and affected individuals. The discovered pattern was then used to classify an independent set of 116 masked serum samples: 50 from women with ovarian cancer, and 66 from unaffected women or those with nonmalignant disorders. The discriminatory pattern correctly identified all 50 ovarian cancer cases in the masked set, including 18 stage I cases. Of the 66 cases of nonmalignant disease, 63 were recognized as "not cancer." This result yielded a sensitivity of 100%.

Data-Management Infrastructure Design

Not surprisingly, presymptomatic testing and analysis of disease progression at the molecular level present important research opportunities, and the data-management infrastructure must be designed to support both. For example, with regard to this discussion, the systematic evaluation of changes in the protein constituency of a cell implies much more than just the generation of lists of proteins that display patterns of up and down regulation as a consequence of disease. An important research pursuit involves characterizing the information flow through protein pathways that interconnect the extracellular microenvironment with the control of gene transcription. Systems biologists often model such signaling pathways to gain an understanding of the complex relationships between events taking place within a cell. The fact that these events can represent both causes and consequences of the disease processes makes such analysis a valuable research tool [16].

Moreover, these signaling pathways are not confined to cells that are directly involved in the disease, but rather extend to the tumor-host interface—cancer is a product of the proteomic tissue microenvironment. For example, the tumor-host interface can generate enzymatic cleavage, shedding, and sharing of growth factors, so the microenvironment is a likely source of biomarkers that are ultimately shed into the serum proteome. It is these markers that will ultimately form the basis for early disease detection and therapeutic monitoring [17].

Of course, the process of parsing and analyzing large amounts of spectral data is computationally intensive. In some experiments, the number of possible patterns can be as high as 1.5×10^{24}. To explore each of these combinations one at a time would take a computer performing 1 billion operations per second more than 47 million years. However, these examples mentioned were solved using multidimensional clustering programs that calculate Euclidean distances between peaks identified in the spectra, and genetic algorithms to help select components that improve the fitness of each potential solution. Using these software technologies researchers were able to reduce the solution time to a few days.

MONOGENIC VS. POLYGENIC DISEASES AND THE CONCEPT OF *IN SILICO* CLINICAL TRIALS

Monogenic (single-gene) diseases are much easier to understand than complex polygenic disorders. At the time of this writing, more than 100 monogenic diseases have been identified. Two notable examples, cystic fibrosis and Huntington's disease, were direct beneficiaries of the human genome project. These illnesses are inherited in straightforward Mendelian fashion. If all diseases were caused by single (or multiple) mutations in a single gene, the drug-discovery process would proceed at a much more rapid pace. Unfortunately, even monogenic diseases generate a large number of downstream effects that must be thoroughly understood for effective disease management. However, the subtle differences in complexity are mostly irrelevant because virtually all diseases are polygenic. Moreover, differences in the complex interactions between various disease-related genes are the forces that give rise to the patient subclasses we have been discussing. These interactions, which result from the interplay between gene-expression and environmental factors, are present in all diseases—monogenic and polygenic. Gene- and protein-expression profiles are visual representations of those subclasses. Presymptomatic testing depends on this information to identify and classify susceptible individuals. It is also important to note that much of the variability we refer to occurs in regulatory (noncoding) regions of the genome.

The Search for Susceptibility Genes

Historically, three approaches have been adopted in the search for susceptibility genes: candidate-gene studies, whole genome searches, and the use of alternative human disease models.

Candidate-gene studies are based on the identification of single nucleotide polymorphisms (SNPs) in coding regions presumed to have some relationship to the disease under investigation. The frequency of occurrence of each polymorphism is then compared between healthy and affected individuals. Such studies are restricted by current biological knowledge regarding disease-associated biochemical pathways. Candidate-gene studies have been instrumental in building a molecular-level understanding of illnesses where a key mutation is directly involved in the disease state. Examples include type 1 diabetes and Alzheimer's. However, candidate gene studies rarely provide new insights into the underlying molecular events of complex diseases.

In whole genome searches, short sequences of DNA located throughout the genome are used to trace the inheritance of chromosomal regions in collections of families with multiple cases of the disease. If a marker is frequently found in affected individuals, the physical position of that marker is likely to lie close to a disease-susceptibility gene. The complete human genome sequence has become a tremendous asset for such experiments. Genome-wide searches using several hundred markers have been used to identify chromosomal regions harboring susceptibility genes for several diseases including asthma, rheumatoid arthritis, osteoarthritis, schizophrenia, bibolar disorder, type 1 and 2 diabetes, and Alzheimer's. Unfortunately, the effectiveness of the technique depends on the resolution of existing genetic marker maps. In many cases, an identified marker lies close to several coding regions and, in such situations, positional cloning experiments are often unable to isolate the correct susceptibility gene.

Alternative human disease modeling relies on rare but genetically simple diseases that mirror the early symptoms of the more common disease in question. In many cases, the genetically simple model involves a single point mutation that causes the same symptoms as the more common form of the disease. Such rare mutations have helped identify major genes involved in such illnesses as monogenic forms of type 2 diabetes, Alzheimer's, Parkinson's, and many congenital forms of heart disease. Unfortunately, genes identified in this way often represent a small subset of the problem and are unlikely to contribute much to the understanding of common forms of complex polygenic illnesses. However, such experiments often contribute important single points of insight into such illnesses. Insights gleaned from large numbers of such experiments can be pieced together to help elucidate the underlying pathways associated with the disease.

For example, in the case of Alzheimer's, mutations in three genes—β-amyloid precursor protein (APP), presinilin 1(PS1), and presinilin 2 (PS2)—account for 30% to 40% of early onset familial forms of the disease. These changes are suggestive of a disease mechanism: alteration in the processing of the APP protein such that an increased amount of the 42 amino acid variant of the amyloid beta peptide is produced. This peptide is fibrillogenic, and plaques in the brains of Alzheimer's patients are rich in the variant peptide. Combined with other evidence, these studies have implicated amyloid fibril-induced nerve cell death as a primary cause of Alzheimer's [18].

Each of these approaches to searching for susceptibility genes has been enhanced by the availability of microarray-based transcriptional profiling of clinical samples. Such experiments have generated a huge amount of data that has been used in the analysis of the molecular-level events that underlie the transformation into a disease state. Because blood is the most available tissue and one of the best sources of clinical samples, hematologic diseases are among the most widely studied. A wealth of information has been generated that is beginning to be used to predict the onset and study the progression of various forms of leukemia and lymphoma.

What Makes a Successful Clinical Trial?

Although it is not yet possible to replace the clinical trials process with an *in silico* equivalent, data-mining experiments that combine clinical information with gene- and protein-expression profiles are beginning to accelerate the entire drug-discovery process. One of the most important aspects of a successful trial relates to the precision used to screen patients. As disease-specific databases containing gene- and protein-expression profiles become available in a form that allows them to be linked to databases containing clinical and demographic records, the screening process will become much more precise. The process also works in the reverse direction because the same databases will be used to identify patients who are the best candidates for treatment with precisely targeted pharmaceuticals.

Recent examples point to the advantages of this approach. For example, the detection of either the bcr-abl translocation in patients with chronic myelogenous leukemia (CML) or activating mutations in the c-kit tyrosine kinase receptor in patients afflicted with gastrointestinal stromal tumors has identified excellent candidates for treatment with Gleevec. A large number of small molecules currently undergoing trial are targeted to growth factor receptors, angiogenesis promoters, cell-cycle regulators, and metastasis biomarkers. In addition, a new generation of antitumor antibodies is being tested as delivery vehicles for cytotoxic agents. These antibodies are often targeted at cell-surface receptors identified through high-throughput gene-expression analysis of tumors [19].

SUMMARY

Doctors have traditionally treated patients with a combination of knowledge, personal experience, and clinical observation. However, our understanding of sickness and health at the molecular level has accelerated during the past 50 years. The combination of molecular-level insight and sophisticated information technology infrastructure is enabling the launch of a new generation of diagnostic tools.

The taxonomy associated with this infrastructure can be thought of as being built on two general classes: industrial-scale, high-throughput observation; and hypothesis-driven scientific research. Data from both classes can be organized into a framework for information-based medicine. Applications for combining and analyzing the information are an important part of the framework, which also includes standards for connectivity and interfaces. These components are often referred to collectively as a "tools" infra-structure. The framework must include facilities for linking together disparate pieces of infrastructure, including a wide variety of heterogeneous databases.

Molecular medicine is supported by several technical trends. Among the most significant are regular increases in the density and accuracy of mRNA profiling technologies, the appearance of several promising high-throughput gene sequencing technologies, and the availability of new, fully digital diagnostic imaging systems (CAT, MRI, PET, x-ray, and diagnostic ultrasound systems). These advances are supported by several information technology trends such as ultra-low-latency networks, computer grids, advanced data-mining and pattern-discovery algorithms, and ultra-dense inexpensive storage.

Deployment of a fully paperless medical record is central to the development of information-based medicine. After a set of standards for paperless records has been adopted, the next phase will involve building links between institutions. These links are best described in terms of a communications and data-processing grid. When the links are in place, it will be possible to share large volumes of demographic and clinical information. Such sharing of information will soon become central to both treatment and research. The next phase in the evolutionary timeline of information-based medicine involves linking clinical and research databases into a single infrastructure. All areas of biomedical research are germane to this discussion because they are all interrelated. Many of these data sources include information about basic cellular processes in the form of gene sequences and expression profiles, protein interactions, known polymor-phisms, protein structures, the results of ligand-binding experiments, and a variety of other biochemical and genetic details.

Computer grids are emerging as a preferred architecture for building large shared systems of heterogeneous computers, operating environments, and networks. The term *grid* refers to a distributed computing infrastructure for solving advanced, computationally intensive problems or managing geographically distributed data. Both elements are present in solutions that support information-based medicine. Grids are built on a single underlying theme—coordinated resource sharing and problem solving in dynamic, multi-institutional virtual organizations. There are two major classes of grid infrastructure: computational grids and data grids. Both will be required to support personalized medicine. The infrastructure must be designed to support both queries and updates to the records. Different schemes for storing and retrieving records are possible.

A complete description of any disease is likely to include clinical symptoms, relevant medical history, gene-expression data and base genotype, a wide variety of metabolic parameters, and treatment results expressed partly with regard to their effects on each of the above (with the possible exception of base genotype). The monitoring process should optimally begin long before the onset of disease. Effective monitoring is the basis of presymptomatic testing for illness. The strategy typically involves building panels of disease-specific gene- and protein-expression profiles, and statistically linking these panels to clinical outcomes. Results are stored in disease-specific databases that ultimately form the basis of new diagnostics. The process of building gene- and protein-expression profiles is complex because it involves a time component. Furthermore, the process of reducing a large number of items down to a simple panel, which preserves only the most significant data items, is also computationally intensive. A variety of pattern-discovery algorithms and other artificial intelligence strategies are typically used to identify and cluster the most relevant data items. Finally, one of the most important uses of gene- and protein-expression panels is the identification of disease subclasses that are normally hidden behind indistinguishable phenotypes. These subclasses can be used to improve the accuracy of patient selection for clinical trials.

Presymptomatic testing also involves the identification and monitoring of individual susceptibility genes. Historically, three approaches have been adopted in this analysis: candidate-gene studies, whole genome searches, and the use of alternative human disease models.

Candidate-gene studies rely on the identification of single nucleotide polymorphisms (SNPs) in coding regions presumed to have some relationship to the disease under investigation. Whole genome searches involve the identification of chromosomal markers unique to affected individuals. Alternative human disease modeling relies on rare

343

but genetically simple alterations that cause the same symptoms as the more common form of the disease. Such rare mutations have helped identify major genes involved in such illnesses as monogenic forms of type 2 diabetes, Alzheimer's, Parkinson's, and many congenital forms of heart disease. Such experiments often contribute important single points of insight into such illnesses. Insights gleaned from large numbers of such experiments can be pieced together to help elucidate the underlying pathways associated with the disease.

Each of these techniques has been enhanced by the availability of microarray-based transcriptional profiling of clinical samples. Because blood is one of the best sources of clinical samples, hematologic diseases are among the most widely studied. A wealth of information has been generated that is beginning to be used to predict the onset and study the progression of various forms of leukemia and lymphoma.

Although it is not yet possible to replace the entire clinical trials process with an *in silico* equivalent, data-mining experiments that combine clinical information with gene and protein expression profiles are beginning to have a major impact on the overall process. Improvements in the infrastructure for information-based medicine are likely to accelerate all phases of the process over the next several years.

ENDNOTES

1. Augen J. 2003. The increasing importance of large-scale information systems for healthcare R&D. *Drug Discovery Today* 8(8): 329–331.

2. SNOMED International Web page at www.snomed.org.

3. Reuters press release 7/28/2003, U.S. moving toward "paperless" health system.

4. Melastatin is a trademark of Millennium Pharmaceuticals, Cambridge, MA, USA.

5. Deeds J., Cronin F., Duncan L. M. 2000. Patterns of melastatin mRNA expression in melanocytic tumors. *Human Pathology* 31(11): 1346–56.

6. Fang D., Setaluri V. 2000. Expression and up-regulation of alternatively spliced transcripts of melastatin, a melanoma metastasis-related gene, in human melanoma cells. *Biochemistry and Biophysics Research Communications* 279(1): 53–61.

7. Foster I., Kesselman C., Tuecke S. 2001. The anatomy of the grid: enabling scalable virtual organizations. *International Journal of Supercomputer Applications* 15(3): 1–24.

8. Moore, R., Chaitanya, B., Marciano, R., Rajasekar, A., and Wan M. 2002. "Data-Intensive Computing" in *The Grid: Blueprint for a New Computing Infrastructure.* (Ian Foster and Carl Kesselamn, Eds.) Morgan Kaufman Publishers, Inc. San Francisco, 1999. 105–129.

9. Foster I., Kesselman C., Tuecke S. 2002. Grid services for distributed systems integration. *IEEE Computer* 35(6): 37–46.

10. Cox A., Der C. 1997. Farnesyltransferase inhibitors and cancer treatment: targeting simply Ras? *Biochimica et Biophysica Acta / Reviews on Cancer* 1333: F51–F71.

11. Shibuya M. 2001. Structure and dual function of vascular endothelial growth factor receptor (Flt-1). *The International Journal of Biochemistry and Cell Biology* 33(4): 409–420.

12. Shread P. 2003. Grid project finds cancer growth inhibitors. Global Grid Forum Web page at www.gridforum.org.

13. Marx J. 2003. A boost for tumor starvation. *Science* 301: 452–454.

14. U.S. Centers for Disease Control Web page at www.bt.cdc.gov.

15. Petricoin E. F., Ardekani A. M., Hitt B. A., Levine P. J., Fusaro V. A., Steinberg S. M., Mills G. B., Simone C., Fishman D. A., Kohn E. C., Liotta L. A. 2002. Use of proteomic patterns in serum to identify ovarian cancer. *Lancet* 359 (9306): 572–577.

16. Petricoin E. F., Liotta L. A. 2003. Clinical applications of proteomics. Journal of Nutrition 133: 2476S–2484S.

17. Liotta L. A., Kohn E. C. 2001. The microenvironment of the tumour-host interface. *Nature* 411: 375–379.

18. Whittaker P. 2001. From symptomatic treatments to causative therapy? *Current Opinion in Chemical Biology* 2: 352–359.

19. Ross J., Ginsburg G. 2002. Integrating diagnostics and therapeutics: revolutionizing drug discovery and patient care. *Drug Discovery Today* 16: 859–864.

New Themes in Bioinformatics

INTRODUCTION

Several years ago dramatic advances in information technology and computer sciences made possible the launch of *in silico* biology. As the field matured, researchers became proficient at defining biological problems using mathematical constructs and building the computer infrastructure to solve those problems. Over time it became clear that most biological problems lend themselves to solution in a clustered environment after division into a large number of small pieces. This mathematical property of most biological problems has now become a principal driver of one of the most important trends in the information technology industry: the migration from large multiprocessing computers to clusters of commodity-priced machines. This migration is driving the development of a variety of tools for application integration and resource management that are further solidifying the role of clusters as the dominant force in high-performance technical computing.

The past 50 years have witnessed many revolutions in our understanding of the metabolic processes that collectively make up a living organism. Many of these changes were related to the chemical and physical techniques used to study these processes. One of the most significant involved the recognition that even simple biochemical processes are usually mediated by large numbers of interacting proteins. This evolution in thinking is significant to our discussion because it paved the way for the development of a new computational science—systems biology.

This chapter begins with a discussion of new computational motifs that are rapidly becoming mainstream components of the infrastructure driving research in bioinformatics. These include parallel computation on clusters of commodity-priced machines and new workflow-distribution mechanisms. Our discussion will include a description of the various classes of bioinformatic problems and the mechanisms used to distribute these in complex heterogeneous computing environments.

We have chosen to end our discussion with an introduction to systems biology—one of the most computationally intense areas in modern biology. Like other cutting-edge sciences, systems biology is maturing at a remarkable rate, limited only by the amount of computation available. The performance of today's computers continues to improve, and it will soon be possible for systems biologists to construct fully dynamic views of metabolic systems. Such analysis will include information about gene sequences, expression profiles, protein-protein interactions, and the reaction kinetics of a large number of metabolic intermediates.

OVERVIEW OF PARALLEL COMPUTING AND WORKFLOW DISTRIBUTION IN BIOINFORMATICS

Biotechnology differs from other technical disciplines because its computational component, bioinformatics, is built on a new class of computationally intense problem and associated algorithms that are still evolving. Furthermore, the emergence of new subdisciplines within biotechnology, such as systems modeling, high-throughput sequencing, and mRNA profile analysis, are likely to drive even more demand for unique and powerful IT platforms. Unlike more mature industries, the biological world is experiencing explosive growth with regard to both the amount and type of available data.

The designers of bioinformatic algorithms have been quick to take advantage of the atomic nature of many biological problems by building parallel infrastructure—most often Linux clusters composed of commodity-priced machines. These clusters have now become a dominant force in bioinformatics replacing large symmetric multiprocessing (SMP) systems whenever practical. Despite its recent emergence, bioinformatics is helping to shape one of the most important trends in information technology: the migration from traditional multiprocessing servers to clusters of commodity-priced machines.

Another property of most bioinformatic problems is that their solution requires a large number of discrete steps. Different algorithms, linked by their inputs and outputs, form the basis of the steps. Moreover the steps are connected by series of logical constructs—loops, conditionals, and branches. Taken together, the algorithms, connections, and flow logic make up a complete workflow that describes the underlying problem. When properly described, individual components of the workflow can often be executed in parallel with varying degrees of granularity.

Coordination of tasks in a workflow-based clustered environment has traditionally involved the development of simple scripts that distribute computing jobs across a cluster and manage the output. This approach has evolved and, today, vendors are beginning to offer tools that integrate and manage application workloads across a cluster. Three major tasks must be addressed if a cluster is to be used as a "virtual supercomputer": resource management, data management, and application management. These tasks differ substantially in a number of ways. For example, resource management is a universal problem, cutting across all computing disciplines and evolving rapidly as computer, communications, and storage technologies change. In contrast, both data management and application management are far more specialized, and the best solutions are likely to depend significantly on details specific to particular types of applications or vertical market segments. As a result, it seems unlikely that any single software system will emerge to address all three tasks at once.

Resource-management tools essentially address the question "Who may do what, and when and where may they do it?" These tools are designed to address job management, user authentication, and the allocation of facilities such as computers, storage, network capacity, etc. The most common type of resource-management tool is a batch queuing system. Frequently used batch queuing systems include open-source versions of the Portable Batch System (PBS) and Sun Grid Engine, as well as commercial versions of those two systems and Platform's Load Sharing Facility (LSF). A batch queuing system oversees execution of computing jobs that are submitted to it by users. However, such systems have drawbacks related to the fact that they are static and cannot dynamically manage and distribute workloads within a cluster. Complex jobs and computing environments are not static—their needs and capabilities change frequently. However, without information about the internal activities of the jobs, it is impossible for batch queuing systems to overcome the constraints of static resource allocation and respond effectively to dynamic changes. The problem is not a fundamental limitation of batch queuing; it can be fixed at the level of the scheduling algorithms that assign tasks to CPUs and allocate resources within a cluster. Sophisticated solutions are evolving which are capable of monitoring the performance of specific tasks in a cluster and making real-time changes to the way tasks are distributed.

Data-management tools address the accessibility and delivery of data, either from files or database systems. In a cluster (or grid) setting, two different types of data-management tools are widely used: database systems that both store large quantities of data and deliver it on demand in response to specific queries, and data-access systems that provide virtual integrated interfaces facilitating integrated access to and delivery of data that may be stored on a number of disjoint and distributed file and/or database systems. In both cases, data-management tools are responsible for user authentication for data access, reliable data delivery, data security and encryption, caching strategies to reduce access or delivery time and conserve network communication capacity, and other related issues.

Finally, most high-performance technical computing solutions involve many applications that must be integrated into a complete solution. Because resource- and data-management tools do not address application integration, new tools are evolving to address these needs by enabling users to integrate applications into a single managed workflow whose individual tasks are dynamically distributed across a cluster. The intelligent combination of resource-, data-, and application-management tools allows a typical cluster built of commodity-priced hardware to become a replacement for a traditional supercomputer.

PARALLEL COMPUTING FOR BIOINFORMATICS

The relationship between bioinformatics and computer science is unique among technical disciplines. Initially, technical improvements on the information technology side were the drivers of growth because they enabled the deployment and testing of new algorithms for *in silico* molecular modeling, pattern discovery, sequence matching, and other complex problems. Research organizations were quick to adapt; they quickly acquired skills that enabled them to define biological problems in computer science terms. Most of these problems are "embarrassingly parallel," meaning that they may be readily divided into many small pieces for solution. The designers of bioinformatic algorithms and programs were quick to take advantage of these attributes by building parallel infrastructure—most often clusters of commodity-priced computers. Support for this computing trend came from the academic community in the form of a new operating environment known as Linux. Unlike vendor-specific operating systems, Linux is developed in an "open-source" environment—a unique public domain structure that guarantees source code availability to anyone wanting to build custom enhancements. Both individuals and IT vendors are free to submit enhancements to the Linux community; these changes are then evaluated for inclusion in upcoming releases. The fact that millions of end users have access to Linux source code has allowed the relatively new operating system to mature at an impressive rate, and it has consequently become the de facto operating environment for clusters. These clusters have now become a dominant force in bioinformatics replacing large symmetric multiprocessing (SMP) systems whenever practical. As a result, bioinformatics has become an important segment of the Linux cluster market.

PARALLEL APPLICATIONS

In general, bioinformatics problems fit into one of two broad computing categories: floating point or integer. Floating-point problems are computationally intensive because they involve complex algorithms borrowed from physical chemistry and quantum mechanics. Molecular dynamics, protein folding, and metabolic systems modeling are representative floating-point problems. Integer-intensive problems—which are also computationally intensive—are typically built on algorithms that compare characters in sequences or search for matching phrases and terms. Most of contemporary molecular biology, including genome sequencing, is built on the solution to such problems. Gene sequence alignment and pattern discovery are relevant examples of high-speed integer-style problems. One of the most significant applications in this class is the assembly algorithm that was used to construct the human genome from millions of fragments obtained through "shotgun sequencing." The execution of this algorithm required enormous computer horsepower and represents one of the most complex logic problems ever solved.

Both classes of problem lend themselves to parallel computation because the operations they depend on are atomic in nature. The protein-folding case is an excellent example because the problem can be broken into individual time steps. During each time step, the forces acting between each pair of atoms in the molecule are calculated and a new transitional structure is generated. Even the smallest protein contains thousands of atoms and, despite a folding time of only tenths of a millisecond, an enormous number of time steps must be calculated—typically on the order of 10^{15} floating-point operations. The solution typically involves restricting the problem to the most relevant portion of the molecule and parsing the simulation across a large number of individual machines, an implementation perfectly suited to clustering.

Likewise, sequence-homology and pattern-discovery problems—both integer in nature—are well suited to solution in clustered environments. In most cases, a large number of sequences need to be matched against a single genome or a sequence database. Two different approaches exist for dividing the problem among a large number of machines. The first involves performing a different search on each node with the target sequence stored either locally or remotely in a central database; the second involves dividing the target sequence into many pieces, each of which is distributed to a different node in the cluster. Every node stores copies of all the search sequences, which are compared against the larger target fragment. Because each node contains only a portion of the target sequence, it is always possible for a particular search sequence match a region that spans two nodes. The overlap problem is relatively straightforward to solve by creating target fragments that overlap each other by at least as many residues as the longest search sequence. Search sequences that define an overlap will always be found on two nodes. Figure 9-1 illustrates the two approaches.

On a cost-per-calculation basis, clustered solutions are far superior for problems that consist of a large number of isolated calculations whether they are floating-point or integer intensive. Virtually every problem in bioinformatics gains a cost/performance advantage when engineered to run in a clustered environment. Most clustered bioinformatic solutions are coarse grained in the sense that division of the problem occurs at the application level; most such problems are readily divisible into pieces that can be assigned to individual nodes in a cluster. Conversely, traditional parallelism involves rewriting applications to create multiple executable threads that are designed to simul-

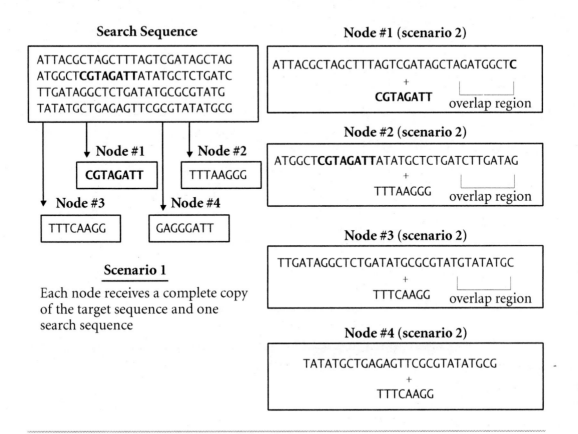

Figure 9-1 Two strategies for performing sequence searches in clustered environments. The first approach involves dividing up the problem in such a way that each node contains a complete copy of the target sequence and a single search sequence. The second involves division of the target sequence into relatively small pieces, each of which is compared to all search sequences. In the later case, each node contains a piece of the target and a copy of every search sequence. Node boundaries are managed by creating target fragments that overlap each other by at least as many residues as the longest search sequence.

taneously run on an SMP machine. Unfortunately, few such applications scale linearly beyond a small number of processors. Conversely, coarse-grained parallelism is easier to deploy, scales well in clustered computing environments, and often provides superior performance for bioinformatics applications.

THE NEW INFRASTRUCTURE

Building compute infrastructure specifically for the purpose of solving a large number of discrete, but closely related, problems is a challenging task. One particularly complex aspect of the problem is related to the requirement for heterogeneous hardware and operating system support. This requirement can be driven either by specific characteristics of individual applications or by the desire to optimize individual computing tasks. For example, many complete solutions involve database searches that perform best on "large memory" machines, sequence alignment tasks that can be divided among hundreds of processors exhibiting high clock speeds, and floating point calculations that are best executed on machines with fast floating point co-processors. The challenge is to design a flexible computing infrastructure that can accommodate a variety of processing characteristics.

Superimposed on the infrastructure design requirements is a need for efficient task distribution. Smoothly executed, this distribution is tantamount to the construction of a single "composite application." Unfortunately, design complexity also rises exponentially with the introduction of heterogeneous hardware. Additionally, many clusters exhibit an additional level of heterogeneity in the sense that they contain mixtures of traditional and nontraditional computing machines (instruments and other devices equipped with processors, memory, and operating environments). Such machines—spectrometers, sequencing devices, chromatography equipment, etc.—are rapidly becoming core components of the data-distribution and computing infrastructure.

One notable example are the systems currently being used to determine protein sequence using mass spectrometry. Proteins are enzymatically or chemically fragmented and the molecular weight of each peptide is accurately determined using mass spectrometry. A computer program is used to generate all possible amino acid combinations that might give rise to each fragment strictly on the basis of molecular weight. All permutations of amino sequences are generated for each fragment and screened against a database of known peptide or gene sequences to identify matches. Assembly programs are used to build the correct sequence of the original protein. The infrastructure for solving this problem includes large symmetrical multiprocessing database servers, Linux clusters where the calculations are divided among large numbers of nodes (sometimes referred to as worker machines), a workflow distribution hub, laboratory equipment such as mass spectrometers, and a variety of network hubs, routers, and switches. Moreover, in the future such problems are likely to be geographically distributed across a grid.

WORKFLOW COMPUTING

There is a general tendency to think about bioinformatic applications as standalone entities. However, most computationally intensive biological problems involve many distinct but interrelated steps, each requiring a different algorithm or application. The solutions to such problems are best visualized as workflows composed of discrete components linked by logical constructs (i.e., loops and conditionals such as if-then-else and do-while). Assembling the various components into a single logical solution and distributing the solution into a clustered computing environment is rapidly becoming an important focus across the bioinformatics community. Properly executed, the solution can become a true source of value creation for scientists who often spend large amounts of time attending to individual applications, building tables of results, iteratively searching public databases, and manually transforming the output of one application into a data type that can be used as the input for another. Additionally, many processing steps involve successive iterations that can readily be distributed for parallel processing on separate nodes of a cluster.

In an effort to address these inefficiencies, software vendors have begun to offer solutions for defining, managing, and distributing bioinformatic workflows in clustered and, more importantly, heterogeneous computing environments. The value of such solutions will continue to scale with the demand for computational horsepower, especially because that demand is currently outpacing the performance growth curve for traditional supercomputers. This trend has recently become a principal driver of one of the most important trends in contemporary computer science: the migration from large multiprocessing computers to clusters of commodity-priced machines. This migration is driving the development of a variety of tools for application integration and resource management that are further solidifying the role of clusters as the dominant force in high-performance technical computing.

A disproportionate number of problems in the life sciences are not only computationally intensive, but also involve passing large amounts of independent data from heterogeneous sources through a complex sequence of computational steps. Such problems are typical of the ones that benefit the most from parallel execution and workflow management.

An important problem for many bioinformatics researchers is the classification of groups of amino acid sequences into fine-grained categories (subfamilies) whose members have similar physical properties and may be metabolically related. For example, each of the sequences involved might be what is known as a structural domain of some protein in a certain protein family, and the goal might be to identify which of the sequences are likely to have similar function. For a typical problem, there may be tens of thousands of sequences involving millions of amino acids.

A number of approaches to this sequence classification problem are possible, but the one considered here creates the subfamilies by identifying "seed pairs" (highly similar pairs of sequences) and collecting other sequences around each seed pair based on a model of the nature of the similarity of the pair. Stated more precisely, the computation proceeds as follows:

1. Find a number of disjoint, highly similar pairs of sequences and designate each as the seed pair for a new subfamily.
2. For each subfamily, create a model that captures the nature of the similarities among all the sequences in the subfamily. This model is used to measure the similarity between the subfamily and any arbitrary sequence. For this example, the model will be what is known as a hidden Markov model (HMM), and the measurement process for an arbitrary sequence will assign to that sequence a score indicating the likelihood that the sequence should be placed in the subfamily.
3. Assess all the sequences against each subfamily model, and assign each sequence to the subfamily for which it achieves the highest score.
4. Iteratively repeat Steps 2 and 3 using the new set of subfamilies.

Although straightforward to describe, the preceding approach to solving the sequence classification problem involves a significant number of computationally intensive steps. Each step requires the use of a particular bioinformatics algorithm; some of the steps are very time-consuming. Following is a list of programs required to complete the sequence of calculations:

- **blastall**—A program from the National Center for Biotechnology Information (NCBI) that can rapidly assess the similarity of pairs of protein sequences. (Used to find seed pairs in Step 1.)

- **clustalw**—Another program from the NCBI that aligns two or more protein or DNA sequences so as to maximize the match between the aligned sequences. (Used to create the model for each seed pair in Step 2.)
- **hmmbuild**—A program that creates a hidden Markov model that describes a set of aligned sequences. (Used in Step 2.)
- **hmmcalibrate**—A program that optimizes hidden Markov models created by hmmbuild. (Used in Step 2.)
- **hmmsearch**—A program that scores the sequences in large sequence databases against a calibrated hidden Markov model. (Used for sequence assessment in Step 3.)

The sequence of operations described above implies a workflow with complex logical constructs—loops and conditionals. The following steps logistically describe the solution.

1. Set up input files and parameters for blastall so that it will compute the similarity score for each sequence against every other sequence in the entire set of sequences (a so-called all-to-all blastall). This step may require use of a number of auxiliary programs (such as NCBI's FORMATDB program) to properly format the input files.

2. Use a custom Perl script to sort through the output from blastall to find the set of disjoint sequence pairs that will be used as seed pairs. Create a new subfamily for each seed pair.

3. Align the members of each subfamily using clustalw.

4. Use hmmbuild to create a hidden Markov model from each clustalw alignment.

5. Optimize each HMM model using hmmcalibrate.

6. Use hmmsearch to score every sequence against each of the HMM models.

7. Use another custom Perl script to process the results from hmmsearch to assign each sequence to the subfamily corresponding to the HMM model for which it obtained the highest score. The result is a new set of subfamilies that replaces the previous set.

8. Repeat Steps 3 through 6 using the new subfamilies.

Today, the standard way to use these programs to solve the sequence-classification problem involves a process in which an end user (typically a scientist) must manually run a particular program, check its output, convert the output so that it may be used as input for the next program, run the next program, and so on. In many cases, an end user puts together a complex wrapper script to automate this process in the form of a batch job. Unfortunately, the process has many drawbacks:

- The scripts tend to make minimal if any use of data location and validation of data content; instead they depend on file-sharing capabilities such as NFS (with their inherent unreliability).
- Users and workflow developers are required to understand many details of the various programs and data sources. Using the output of one program as the input for the next may require complex data conversions or other manipulations based on knowledge of the internal details of the programs involved. With the growing number of different programs and databases, it has become nearly impossible for users to have this sort of knowledge.
- Perl scripts that address complex data processing and control flows are difficult to write, debug, maintain, and modify (even by their creators). Customization by end users (i.e., scientists) is nearly impossible because relatively skilled programming is required for even modest changes. As a result, workflows are not easily shared among researchers.
- There is no good strategy for scaling workflow performance as the problem size increases. Additionally, the concept of reuse is not intrinsic to the strategy. The required human interaction often represents a limiting factor in this regard. Additionally, Perl scripts make use of certain inherently serial technologies that are bound to single servers. The process does not scale well in large heterogeneous environments.

Software vendors have begun to design systems that include components for widely used programs such as blastall, clustalw, hmmbuild, hmmcalibrate, and hmmsearch. Also available are utility components for such common tasks as displaying results in HTML for viewing in a Web browser, or storing various types of computational results in the data repository. In addition to the standard components listed above, complete systems must include workflow-specific methods that connect individual software packages. These methods define the input/output structure and logical relationships between individual components of the workflow. Because it is often possible to execute individual tasks in parallel, specialized components that divide datasets into appropriately smaller subsets are used to facilitate parallel processing. The corresponding operation involves combining and reorganizing results into a single solution. End users typically describe their workflow plan using some type of graphical tool that also serves as the front end to a centralized workload distribution hub. The hub contains control logic for dividing and distributing datasets and applications, and collecting and resequencing processed results. Intermediate results are also returned to the hub where they are redistributed in the correct order as the workflow proceeds.

The ability to manage, distribute, and optimize bioinformatic workflows is likely to become a central theme in life sciences computing. Additionally, the computer infrastructure implied by such solutions is extensible in the sense that it can be scaled to meet the demands of most applications. This design has already begun to pave the way for a new generation of computationally intense applications. Programs used to model complex dynamical systems represent one of the most prominent members of this group. Such applications are discussed in greater detail in the next section.

HIGH-PERFORMANCE COMPUTING AND SYSTEMS BIOLOGY

Workflow management, parallel computing, grid infrastructure, and virtual supercomputing have collectively paved the way for solving a new generation of computationally intense biological problems. Many of these challenges have been enumerated throughout the previous chapters. They include high-throughput gene sequencing, transcriptional profiling, predictive protein folding, and a variety of analytical techniques such as x-ray crystallography and protein NMR. However, the most complex problems typically involve the analysis of large numbers of interacting components that collectively form a complete metabolic system. Although it is not yet possible to simultaneously model all the interactions that take place in a cell, many large dynamical systems have been described. The science of building these models has come to be known as systems biology.

It is important to note that the systems representation to which we refer is much more than an understanding of the logical relationships between genes and proteins. These constructs, which form an important information base, are much too static to embody a complete system-level picture. What we seek is a complete understanding of the logical relationships including all regulatory influences. The concept can be visualized as a street map. Individual streets, intersections, and sidewalks form an important part of the picture because they represent the basic connections between locations. However, the complete picture only emerges when we include traffic lights, street signs, and other regulatory mechanisms. Our goal is to understand traffic patterns and the forces that control them. Moreover, after a system-level understanding has been reached, it should be possible to predict the results of specific perturbations. One of the greatest challenges involves time-dependent monitoring of the changes that result from such perturbations. These measurements are often referred to as multidimensional— each dimension represents a particular concentration of a specific metabolite. A typical analysis involves many dimensions, many different metabolites, and a large number of time points. Only recently has it become feasible to collect and analyze the enormous amount of information generated by these experiments.

Gene-regulatory logic lies at the core of any biological systems problem. Several attempts are currently underway to construct databases containing large amounts of information about gene-regulatory and biochemical-pathway logic. Much of the data collected in these databases has been gleaned through microarray analysis. Although these experiments often reveal much about the coregulation of various genes, they lack detail about the underlying control mechanisms. Various methods have been proposed to automatically discover regulatory relationships within microarray data. Most of these calculations track the level of each species over time and use large numbers of comparisons to infer causality [1]. The process is both complex and cumbersome and cannot easily comprehend the effects of post-translational or post-transcriptional modifications. However, such analysis can form a springboard for hypothesis-driven experiments that ultimately reveal the required lower-level details.

Systems biology is still in its infancy, and millions of metabolic relationships remain to be discovered. Continued progress will require technical improvements that facilitate high-throughput accurate measurements of vanishingly small quantities of metabolites—often at the level of individual molecules. In addition, many of the molecular interactions that need to be measured occur in the femtosecond timescale. The required technological portfolio includes microfluidic handling devices, femtosecond laser spectroscopy equipment, and a variety of new sensors derived from the emerging world of nanotechnology. Moreover, the IT industry has only recently succeeded in delivering computers and storage devices that are capable of handling the large high-speed data streams implied by these experiments. As the technology matures, it will certainly become possible to use detailed models of metabolic regulation to provide new insights into the drug-discovery process. Signal-transduction cascades contain control points that may ultimately provide the best opportunities for regulatory control and drug intervention. Modeling these pathways has become a central theme in contemporary drug discovery because the models include information about systemic side effects. Ultimately, it might become possible to use this information to redirect malfunctioning cells while minimizing the side effects. Predictive modeling is likely to become an important component of the drug-approval process because it offers an *in silico* mechanism for proactively discovering potential dangers. Appropriate databases are already being constructed and will soon form the basis of the next generation of public biomedical infrastructure.

THE DELINEATION OF METABOLIC PATHWAYS

Surprisingly, biochemistry and molecular biology have not experienced parallel evolution. The discovery of the structure of DNA and elucidation of the amino acid code words preceded the invention of high-throughput gene sequencing technology by more than two decades. Moreover, the computer horsepower, storage, networking capabilities, and algorithms required for genome assembly were generally unavailable until the late 1990s. As a result, the first 50 years of biochemical research were focused almost entirely on small molecule biochemistry and the delineation of thousands of metabolic pathways.

The process used to unravel these pathways typically involved developing chemical assays and affinity-purification techniques that could be used to capture and purify large quantities of specific enzymes. Each pathway was traced, one reaction at a time, until all the enzyme reactions were well characterized, and the fate of each small molecule could be described. The work, which was both complex and time-consuming, ultimately resulted in a very complete metabolic picture of the cell. However, essentially all the purification techniques and enzyme assays used in these efforts shared certain flaws that ultimately resulted in fundamental misconceptions about cellular metabolic processes.

The first and most significant flaw is related to the disruptive action of the purification techniques on cellular ultrastructure. Gaining access to a cell's contents typically involves sonication, enzymatic digestion of the cell membrane, mechanical shearing, or some other type of physical disruption of the cell's structure. After the contents are free, various affinity techniques are used to serially purify and assay for specific enzymatic activity. Simply stated, the goal of most enzyme purification projects is to identify and characterize the purest substance possible that still exhibits a given metabolic activity. The process is repeated until each enzyme-substrate pair in a given pathway has been studied and the entire pathway is elucidated. The strategy makes sense and has withstood the test of time. Glycolysis, Kreb's cycle, oxidative phosphorylation, cholesterol biosynthesis, fatty acid metabolism, dozens of pathways for creating and degrading amino acids, carbohydrate biosynthesis and breakdown, and hundreds of other metabolic routes were all delineated using this strategy of large-scale purification [2].

As final verification of their results, researchers often adopted the custom of using *in vitro* experiments to reconstitute entire pathways in addition to individual enzyme-substrate reactions. The fact that these experiments appeared to accurately model *in vivo* processes gave rise to the view that cells are, with some important exceptions, tiny reaction vessels containing mixtures of enzymes and small biomolecules. Notable exceptions include such processes as oxidative phosphorylation, known to occur at large enzyme complexes located on the mitochondrial inner membrane; protein translation, a complex process involving many proteins and enzymes associated with ribosomes; steroid metabolism, known to occur on the surface of the smooth endoplasmic reticulum; protein glycosylation, a function of the golgi apparatus; and many other important intracellular processes. Further analysis soon revealed that hundreds of different structural proteins serve as the building blocks of these organelles, and that many of these are important members of large enzyme complexes anchored to these structures. The function of such proteins is diverse; some serve to anchor and orient large enzyme complexes in membranes, others behave as cofactors by forcing conformational changes in enzymes and increasing their binding affinity for a substrate, many undergo conformational changes upon binding to a ligand and thus transmit signals across a membrane, and others form the core structures mentioned earlier. Yet despite the recognition that various classes of proteins play key roles in metabolic processes, the majority of intracellular chemical processes were still viewed as test-tube-like reactions that freely occur when free-floating molecules collide with one another in the cytoplasm of a cell. This view makes perfect sense when one considers that these reactions work perfectly well in the free-floating environment of a test tube.

Early biochemists often made another critical mistake by operating under the assumption that reaction dynamics observed *in vitro* approximate those within the cell. Unfortunately this view of the relationship between large-volume solution chemistry and the reactions that occur within a cell is overly simplistic. Essentially all metabolic reactions take place in a matrix of proteins and enzymes—even those formerly thought of as purely solution-based. This view has evolved into a complex science—systems biology—which is based on the study of protein-protein interactions. Systems biologists use enormous compute power and large-scale databases to characterize and store the results of experiments designed to identify the sequence of protein-protein interactions associated with each metabolic pathway. Several early clues hinted at the structural dependencies of intracellular chemistry:

- Copurification of previously unknown proteins (thought to be contaminants) was traditionally a problem during large scale enzyme purification. Copurified proteins, often closely associated with the target enzyme, were very difficult to remove.
- Removal of a closely associated protein often caused loss of enzymatic activity. (Such enzymes were recognized as existing in complexes.) Over time, many such enzyme complexes were identified.
- Protein-protein, protein-nucleic acid, nucleic acid-nucleic acid, and protein-enzyme interactions have each been uncovered by researchers studying macromolecular synthesis. These new interactions seemed to hint that complex cellular processes often involve three-dimensional stabilization and nonenzymatic positional interactions.
- Chemical cross-inking experiments with membrane impermeant substances demonstrated that multi-enzyme complexes, such as those catalyzing the tricarboxylic acid

(TCA) cycle, are organized around the specific orientations of each enzyme component. Disrupting the structure often leads to loss of activity.

• Another level of structure was identified when certain enzyme complexes, such as the enzymes involved in oxidative phosphorylation—NADH-CoQ reductase (complex I), succinate-CoQ reductase (complex II), CoQ-cytochrome c reductase (complex III), and cytochrome c oxidase (complex IV)—were found to have very specific orientations with respect to each other. This orientation depends on the integrity of the inner mitochondrial membrane and involves dozens of structural and nonstructural proteins. The four complexes function most efficiently when the entire structure is left intact.

• In general, metabolic rates are much higher *in vivo* than they are *in vitro*. As long as the activity under investigation remained intact, however, researchers tended to avoid discussing special properties that might arise from more complex interactions that occur *in vivo*. Biochemistry was viewed as a sequence of discrete reactions rather than a mixture of complex systems.

• Early on it became apparent that thousands of proteins with unidentified functions were involved in metabolism. Only a small percentage of these appeared to have a purely structural role. Whole genome sequencing results combined with information about alternative transcript splicing and post-translational protein modification seemed to suggest the presence of millions of different proteins—many more than could realistically be considered building blocks of cellular structure.

Oxidative phosphorylation is an excellent example where early experiments revealed a variety of structural and chemical roles for a large number of small proteins. Figure 9-2 depicts the overall structure of the electron transport chain responsible for oxidative phosphorylation—the principal source of energy in animal cells. The chain includes four major enzyme complexes, of which three serve as transmembrane proton pumps. These pumps set up the energy gradient that drives ATP synthesis—the primary source of energy in animal cells. Each complex is capable of functioning well enough *in vitro* to enable the development of an appropriate assay. However, the complete system can only carry out its full set of oxidative functions while embedded in a membrane with all associated proteins. A systems view of oxidative phosphorylation would include all protein-protein (including enzyme-protein) and protein–small biomolecule interactions.

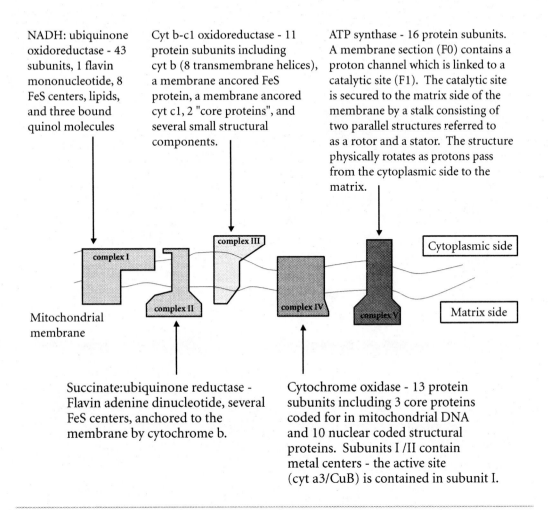

NADH: ubiquinone oxidoreductase - 43 subunits, 1 flavin mononucleotide, 8 FeS centers, lipids, and three bound quinol molecules

Cyt b-c1 oxidoreductase - 11 protein subunits including cyt b (8 transmembrane helices), a membrane ancored FeS protein, a membrane ancored cyt c1, 2 "core proteins", and several small structural components.

ATP synthase - 16 protein subunits. A membrane section (F0) contains a proton channel which is linked to a catalytic site (F1). The catalytic site is secured to the matrix side of the membrane by a stalk consisting of two parallel structures referred to as a rotor and a stator. The structure physically rotates as protons pass from the cytoplasmic side to the matrix.

Succinate:ubiquinone reductase - Flavin adenine dinucleotide, several FeS centers, anchored to the membrane by cytochrome b.

Cytochrome oxidase - 13 protein subunits including 3 core proteins coded for in mitochondrial DNA and 10 nuclear coded structural proteins. Subunits I /II contain metal centers - the active site (cyt a3/CuB) is contained in subunit I.

Figure 9-2 The eukaryotic electron transport chain involved in oxidative phosphorylation. Electrons pass through a series of respiratory enzyme complexes embedded in the inner mitochondrial membrane; the released energy is used to pump protons across the membrane. The resultant electrochemical gradient enables adenosine 5'-triphosphate (ATP) synthase to synthesize ATP from ADP and phosphate. (Energy is ultimately stored in the additional high-energy phosphate bond.) Each complex consists of several enzymatic subunits and a variety of associated proteins that serve either chemical or structural roles in the complex.

Protein-protein interactions are no longer viewed as a unique complexity of large membrane-bound complexes and signaling pathways. The current view places protein-protein interactions at the center of all metabolic processes. As a result, small molecule biochemistry is now thought of as a series of enzyme-substrate interactions that take place in a matrix of proteins, even when the reactions occur outside the context of a membrane or other cellular organelle. This new view has become the driving force behind systems biology which, in turn, seeks to make metabolic sense of gene-expression data.

In some sense, a protein-level view of metabolism can be thought of as more complex than a gene-level view because the protein-level view comprehends millions of entities and the gene-level view only thousands. Conversely, the gene-level view can be thought of as much more difficult to interpret because the data is far denser and more cryptic. An interesting analogy can be made by substituting automobiles for living organisms. Consider, for example, how difficult it would be to develop an understanding of the workings of a car by separately studying the plans for each part. Both living organism and car contain a large number of functioning components, and it is unlikely that a functional understanding of either could be obtained by systematically studying the design of individual components. Conversely, a low-level description of any system is invaluable when the goal is to understand the functioning of individual components. Automobiles and living creatures share another important design characteristic—they are composed of individual systems that interact in complex ways to define overall functionality. This buildup in complexity drives a requirement for descriptive information at every level—gene, transcript, protein, pathway, metabolic system, whole organism; nut/bolt/spring, assembly, major component (e.g., transmission, engine), system (e.g., drive train), entire car.

Reuse of basic building blocks is another interesting parallel, and a theme that runs through both the mechanical and biological worlds. Just as a bolt or fitting can have multiple functions in different parts of a mechanical system, individual proteins often exhibit multiple context-dependent functions in different cells or tissues.

Whether we are discussing cars or living creatures, a complete systems-level description can be achieved only by understanding the complex web of interactions between each of the individual subsystems—liver, lung, heart, brain, endocrine system; engine, transmission, suspension, frame, etc. Two important computational sciences have grown around the need to understand and predict the interactions of proteins: proteomics, and systems biology.

The first, proteomics, involves a mix of technologies bounded on one side by traditional protein chemistry and on the other by studies of the protein-level responses that a cell exhibits in response to changing environmental conditions. The second, systems biology, is an attempt to study the complex and subtle relationships between the millions of proteins that make up an organism. Systems experiments often involve perturbing a system at the mRNA level and measuring the complex downstream results through sequential purification of all pairs of interacting proteins. In some sense, proteomics is one of many tools used by the systems biologist.

Proteomics and systems biology are both computationally intensive and span a broad base of scientific disciplines. Generally speaking, the modeling of biological systems is a complex mathematical challenge that has recently become feasible because of rapid advances in information technology [3]. Protein structure prediction, for example, is closely associated with chemical and physical techniques such as x-ray crystallography, nuclear magnetic resonance, and mass spectrometry, in addition to its more computationally pure component—*in silico* structure prediction. Moreover, a variety of algorithmic approaches have proven equally powerful for predicting the folding of a protein. Some rely on structure databases or dictionaries of known folds; others take a more fundamental approach often referred to as *ab initio*, where physical principles are used to predict the pairwise interactions of individual atoms in the molecule. Structure prediction is another important example of the synergistic merger of two, once distant, disciplines—computer science and biochemistry.

The next section builds on our discussion of metabolic systems with a contemporary view of protein-protein interactions and metabolic pathways.

SYSTEMS BIOLOGY

Achieving a complete molecular-level picture of a biological system has always been an important goal of the molecular biology community. As is often the case in the modern scientific era, success is dependent on the convergence of several technical disciplines. Microarrays and other high-throughput transcriptional profiling technologies provide gene-expression information, nanoscale protein-identification techniques are used to monitor subtle metabolic changes, a new generation of algorithms for modeling large dynamic systems provide analytic and predictive capabilities, and high-performance computing platforms are used to build and test the models. Systems biology is a nearly perfect example of the convergence of information technology and biology.

A central theme of systems biology is the construction of protein-interaction maps. A complete map for a particular organism includes all possible protein-protein interactions and can be used to follow (or predict) any metabolic pathway. An important technology has evolved over the past decade for identifying interacting proteins. The strategy, commonly referred to as two-hybrid, depends on a sequence of straightforward genetic manipulations that lend themselves to execution in high-throughput environments. The technique depends on an important feature of many eukaryotic transcription activators—namely the presence of two distinct functional domains, one that directs binding to a promoter DNA sequence and one that activates transcription. In a two-hybrid experiment, the target protein is cloned into a "bait" vector. In this way, the gene encoding the bait protein is placed into a plasmid next to the gene encoding a DNA-binding domain (DBD) from a specific transcription factor (e.g., LexA), thus generating a DBD-bait fusion. Next, a second gene for a target protein (also referred to as the prey protein) is cloned in the same reading frame adjacent to an activation domain (AD) of a particular transcription factor. cDNA clones within the library that encode proteins capable of forming protein-protein interactions between bait and prey are identified by virtue of their ability to cause activation of the reporter gene. Activation of the reporter gene results from the physical joining of bait and prey, which brings a DBD into close proximity with a transcriptional AD to form a fully functional transcription factor. Plasmid DNA is recovered from cells expressing interacting proteins, and gene identities are determined by traditional DNA sequencing [4]. Figure 9-3 depicts the process.

Two-hybrid screening is often done in a colony array format where each colony expresses a specific pair of proteins. Because the particular protein pair expressed by each colony is defined by its position in the array, positive signals directly identify interacting proteins without the need for DNA sequencing. Most strategies involve the use of full-length open reading frames as opposed to fragments.

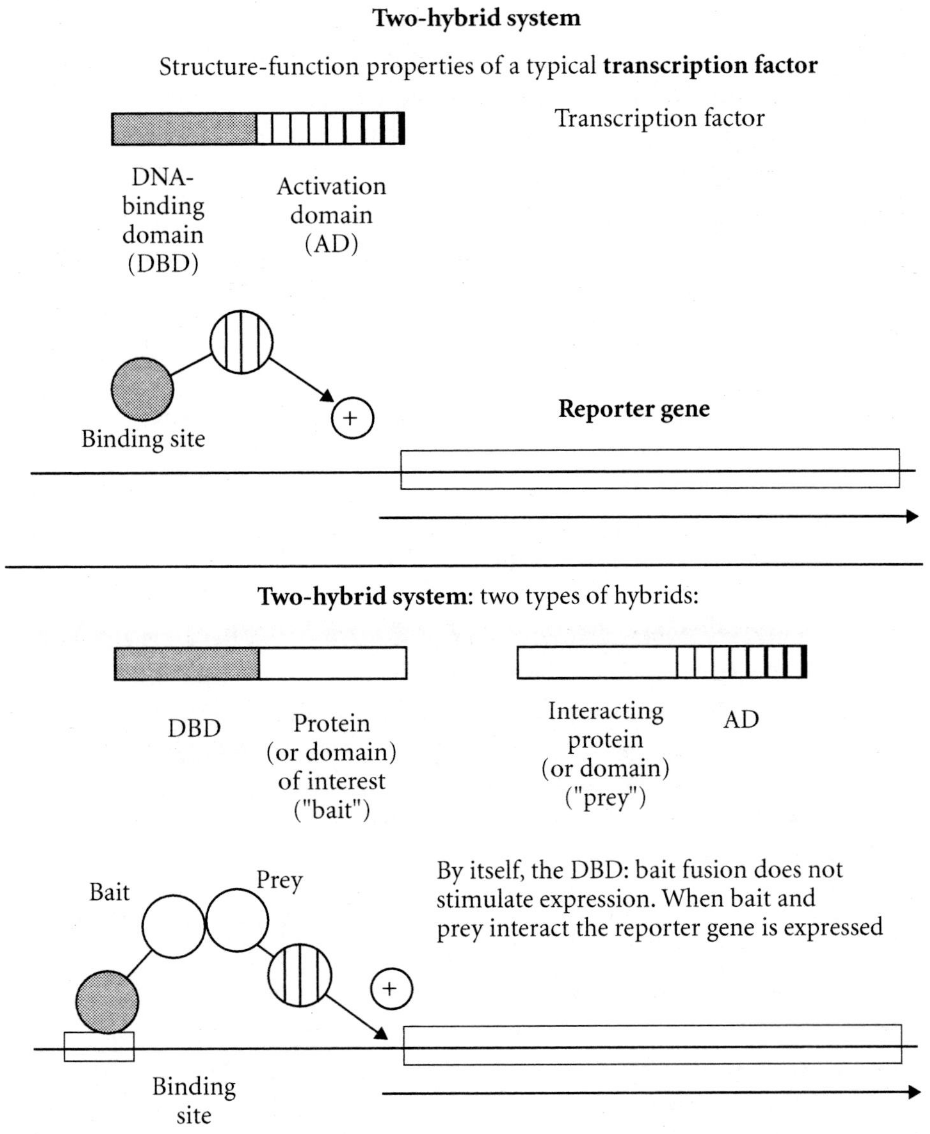

Two-hybrid system

Structure-function properties of a typical **transcription factor**

Transcription factor

DNA-binding domain (DBD)

Activation domain (AD)

Binding site

Reporter gene

Two-hybrid system: two types of hybrids:

DBD

Protein (or domain) of interest ("bait")

Interacting protein (or domain) ("prey")

AD

Bait

Prey

By itself, the DBD: bait fusion does not stimulate expression. When bait and prey interact the reporter gene is expressed

Binding site

Figure 9-3 Yeast two-hybrid system. When "bait" and "prey" proteins interact, they bring together a DNA-binding domain (DBD) and transcriptional activation domain (AD). The resultant complex triggers expression of a reporter gene.

Using a yeast two-hybrid system, Giot et al. recently produced a complete protein-interaction map of the *Drosophila melanogaster* genome. A total of 10,623 predicted transcripts were isolated and screened against cDNA libraries to produce a map containing 7,048 proteins and 20,405 interactions. Results were further refined using computational techniques that assign confidence ratings to two-hybrid interactions. The resultant high-confidence map contained 4,679 proteins and 4,780 interactions [5].

The process of developing high-confidence interaction maps is complicated by spurious interactions between proteins that may not have biological relevance. Various strategies for identifying the most relevant interactions have been proposed. Most approaches combine information about well-documented interactions with automated comparisons between interactions observed in different organisms. For example, the Drosophila map was produced, in part, using a neural network trained on positive examples whose yeast orthologs also had reported interactions; corresponding negative examples were based on Drosophila interactions whose yeast orthologs were separated by a distance of three or more protein-protein interaction links. (This distance was chosen because yeast proteins selected at random have a mean distance of 2.8 links.) Other predictors included the number of times each interaction was observed in either the bait/prey or prey/bait orientation, the number of interaction partners of each protein, the local clustering of the network, and the gene region (e.g., 5' untranslated region, 3' untranslated region, coding sequence, etc.). Furthermore, gene ontology annotations for pairs of interacting proteins were also a strong predictor; the confidence score for an interaction correlated strongly with the depth in the hierarchy at which the two proteins share an annotation. The correlation curve increased steeply for confidence scores above 0.5, suggesting a threshold for confirming biologically significant interactions.

Today the science of systems biology is focused on modeling the complete network of interactions that form the basis of cellular metabolism. However, the complete map contains little information about the dynamics of these interactions. A more complete picture would be represented by a series of protein-interaction maps organized into time slices, each slice based on the interactions occurring at a particular moment. Such a series of maps could be created only by combining information from many sources, including traditional assays of biological activity, two-hybrid experiments, gene sequences, and condition-specific mRNA-expression profiles. The development of a complete picture would also require analyzing the reaction kinetics of each step in each map at each time point. Systems biology is currently undergoing this transformation from static to dynamic views—a change that will dramatically accelerate the shift to information-based medicine.

The past few years have witnessed the launch of several publicly available protein-interaction databases designed to support the transition to a systems view. These databases often contain substantial metabolic and genomic information that complements the protein interaction data. Table 9-1 contains a representative list of some of the most

Table 9-1 Publicly Available Protein Interaction Databases

Database Name	URL	Information
Database of Interacting Proteins (DIP)	dip.doe.mbi.ucla.edu	Catalog of protein-protein interactions.
Biomolecular Interaction Network Database (BIND)	www.blueprint.org/bind/bind.php	An constantly expanding database of biomolecular interactions, pathways and protein complex information. Extensive set of tools to query, view, and submit records.
Munich Information Center for Protein Sequences (MIPS)	www.mips.biochem.mpg.de	Protein-interaction projects for several organisms, including extensive descriptions of experimental methods including basic statistical analysis, interpretation of MS-spectra, spot detection on 2DE gels, etc.
Danish Centre for Human Genome Research	www.proteomics.cancer.dk	Two-dimensional polyacrylamide gel electrophoresis analysis (PAGE) databases for functional genome analysis in health and disease. Protein files contain extensive links to other databases (MEDLINE, GenBank, Swiss-PROT, PIR, PDB, OMIM, UniGene, GeneCards, etc.). Procedures are illustrated with still images and videos. The site also features a gallery of two-dimensional gels of cells, tissues and fluids, as well as of two-dimensional gel immunoblots.

Table 9-1 *(continued)*

Database Name	URL	Information
GRID	biodata.mshri.on.ca/grid/servlet/Index	Species-specific protein interaction databases: Wormbase (C. elegans) FlyBase (Drosophila) SGD (Saccharomyces cerevisiae)
Proteome Bio Knowledge Library (Incyte Genomics)	www.incyte.com/control /researchproducts/insilico /proteome	Integrated information regarding protein function, localization, and interactions.
STRING	www.bork.embl-heidelberg.de/STRING/	Predicted functional associations among genes/proteins. Genes of similar function tend to have the same phylogenetic occurrence and are often fused into a single gene encoding a combined polypeptide. STRING integrates this information from as many genomes as possible to predict functional links between proteins. The database contains several hundred thousand genes from more than 100 species.

familiar sources of proteomic information currently available to anyone with a connection to the World Wide Web.

MODELING ORGAN SYSTEMS

Physiology can justifiably be defined as the functional interactions between various components of cells, organs, and organ systems. The information that describes these interactions is not present in the genome, expressed messages, or the individual proteins that these messages code for. It lies in the complex web of protein interactions that we have been discussing. Recent advances in computer technology and algorithms for kinetic modeling coupled with explosive growth in the volume of information about protein-protein interactions is paving the way for this sort of complex modeling. The transition we are discussing is the final step in the complexity buildup that forms the central theme of this book—gene to message to protein to metabolic system to whole organism.

The human heart is one of the most intensely studied organ systems. Models of the heart have become highly sophisticated; the most current are based on decades physio-logical experimentation, genetic and proteomic analysis, and mathematical modeling. Most recently, advances in expression-array profiling have facilitated an understanding of the variations in gene expression that modulate cardiac function. These variations are fundamental to an understanding of global phenomena such as changes in the electro-cardiogram. The link between physiological analysis and gene-expression profiling is beginning to yield an understanding of the mechanisms that regulate cardiac rhythm. For example, several different arrhythmias have been traced to specific gene mutations, and it is now possible to build mathematical models of these disorders after a specific gene-level alteration has been identified [6].

Surprisingly, many of the results obtained from such modeling display a counterintu-itive character. An excellent example involves modeling the biochemical processes that accompany ischemia. An example is the reconstruction of arrhythmias that result from delayed afterpolarizations arising as a result of intracellular calcium oscillations caused by excessive levels of intracellular sodium and calcium. These oscillations, which gener-ate an inward current carried by the sodium-calcium exchange system, lead to prema-ture excitation of the cell. The results of these studies have provided many physiological surprises with regard to the up and down regulation of sodium-calcium exchange in disease states involving cardiac ischemia. Consequently, mathematical models of trans-porter activity are beginning to play an important role in the development of drugs that treat arrhythmias.

SUMMARY

Modern biology is rapidly transforming itself into a quantitative science based on mathematical models constructed from enormous amounts of information contained in databases of gene, protein, and metabolic information. Most contemporary bioinformatic problems are comprised of a large number of discrete steps. Different algorithms, linked by their inputs and outputs, form the basis of the steps; they are connected by series of logical constructs—loops, conditionals, and branches. Taken together, the algorithms, connections, and flow logic make up a workflow that describes the underlying problem. Additionally, individual components of the workflow can often be executed in parallel. Such application execution almost always occurs in a clustered computing environment.

Vendors are beginning to offer tools that integrate and manage application workflows in compute clusters. Three major tasks must be addressed: resource management, data management, and application management.

The availability of large amounts of information about gene expression and protein interactions has facilitated the launch of a new science commonly referred to as systems biology. A variety of new biochemical techniques have contributed to the advance of this new science. One of the most important techniques is based on the identification of pairs of interacting proteins. The technique, which has come to be known as two-hybrid protein complex identification, has a central role in the development of large-scale protein-interaction maps. These maps have become the descriptors of metabolic systems. Several publicly available databases containing thousands of such maps are now available to anyone with an Internet connection.

The combination of protein-interaction maps, basic gene sequence information, gene-expression data, and knowledge about the functional roles of individual proteins has allowed the development of mathematical models that describe the behavior of large-scale systems such as the human heart. Such models are having a significant positive impact on the drug-discovery process and our overall understanding of the metabolic basis of health and disease.

ENDNOTES

1. Kitano, H. 2003. Systems biology: a brief overview. *Science* 295: 1662–1664.

2. Srere P. 2000. Macromolecular interactions: tracing the roots. *Trends in Biochemical Sciences* 25(*3*): 150–153.

3. Ideker T., Thorsson V., Ranish J., Christmas R., Buhler J., Eng J., Bumgarner R., Goodlett D., Aebersold R., Hood L. 2001. Integrated genomic and proteomic analysis of a systematically perturbed metabolic network. *Science* 292: 929–934.

4. Uetz, P. 2001. Two-hybrid arrays. *Current Opinion in Chemical Biology* 6: 57–62.

5. Giot L., et al. 2003. A protein interaction map of Drosophila melanogaster. *Science* 302: 1727–1736.

6. Noble D. 2003. Modeling the heart—from genes to cells to the whole organ. *Science* 295: 1678–1682.

Further Reading

BIOINFORMATICS

Baxevanis, A. D., and B. F. Ouellette. *Bioinformatics, Second Edition.* John Wiley and Sons, 2001

European Bioinformatics Institute Web site: http://www.ebi.ac.uk

Gene Ontology Consortium Web site: http://www.geneontology.org

Mount, D. W. *Bioinformatics.* Cold Spring Harbor Laboratory Press, 2001

National Center for Biotechnology Information Web site: http://www.ncbi.nlm.nih.gov

GENE STRUCTURE

Alberts, B., et al. *Molecular Biology of the Cell, Fourth Edition.* Garland Science, 2002

Lewin, B. *Genes VII.* Oxford university Press, 2002

Lodish, H. *Molecular Cell Biology, Fifth Edition.* W H Freeman & Co., 2003

SEQUENCE ANALYSIS

Fausett, L. V. *Fundamentals of Neural Networks.* Prentice Hall, 1994

IBM Computational Biology Web site: http://www.research.ibm.com/compsci/compbio/

Koski, T. *Hidden Markov Models of Bioinformatics.* Kluwer Academic Publishers, 2002

The SNP Consortium Web site: http://snp.cshl.org/

TRANSCRIPTION

Affymetrix Web site: http://www.affymetrix.com

Baldi P., et al. *DNA Microarrays and Gene Expression.* Cambridge University Press, 2002

Draghici, S. *Data Analysis Tools for DNA Microarrays.* Chapman & Hall, 2003

Grigorenko, E. *DNA Arrays.* CRC Press, 2002

Kamberova, G., and S. Shah. *DNA Array Image Analysis Nuts and Bolts.* DNA Press LLC, 2002

Kohane, I. S., et al. *Microarrays for an Integrative Genomics.* MIT Press, 2001

Lynx Therapeutics Web site: http://www.lynxgen.com

PROTEIN TRANSLATION AND PROTEIN STRUCTURE

Bourne, P., and H. Weissig. *Structural Bioinformatics.* John Wiley and Sons, 2003

Lesk, A. *Introduction to Protein Architecture.* Oxford University Press, 2001

Protein Data Bank Web site: http://www.rcsb.org/pdb

Protein Structure Prediction Center - Lawrence Livermore National Laboratory Web site: http://predictioncenter.llnl.gov

Swiss-PROT Web site: http://kr.expasy.org/sprot

INFORMATION-BASED MEDICINE

Buyya, R., and M. Baker. "GRID Computing." GRID 2000 First IEEE/ACM International Workshop, Bangalore, India, Dec. 2000 Proceedings. Springer-Verlag, 2001

Carter, J. *Electronic Medical Records.* American College of Physicians, 2001

Foster, I., and C. Kesselman, C. *The Grid: Blueprint for a New Computing Infrastructure.* Morgan Kaufmann, 1999

Source Precision Medicine Inc. Web site: http://www.sourcemedicine.com

NEW THEMES IN BIOINFORMATICS

The Institute for Systems Biology Web site: http://www.systemsbiology.net

Macdonald, P. N. *Two-Hybrid Systems: Methods and Protocols (Methods in Molecular Biology, Vol. 177).* Humana Press, 2001

Index

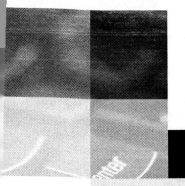